THE
HANDY
BOSTON
ANSWER
BOOK

About the Author

Samuel Willard Crompton is a native of Massachusetts who has visited about thirty of the fifty states. During a break from his literary endeavors he took a thirty-day train trip around the entire perimeter of the country, and he's never been the same since. Some of the highlights were the Four Mile Bridge at Astoria and Cut Bank, Montana. Crompton is the author or editor of many books, including *The Illustrated Atlas of Native American History* and Visible Ink's *The Handy Civil War Answer Book* and *The Handy Military History Answer Book*. He is a specialist in the French and Indian Wars and has served as a talking head for the Military Channel on its *First Command* program. Crompton teaches history at Holyoke Community College in Massachusetts, where he has seen his students move from the analog to digital ages. He resides in Hadley, Massachusetts.

Also from Visible Ink Press

The Handy African American History Answer Book
by Jessie Carnie Smith
ISBN: 978-1-57859-452-8

The Handy American History Answer Book
by David L. Hudson, Jr.
ISBN: 978-1-57859-471-9

The Handy Anatomy Answer Book,
2nd edition
by Patricia Barnes-Svarney and Thomas
E. Svarney
ISBN: 978-1-57859-542-6

The Handy Answer Book for Kids (and Parents), 2nd edition
by Gina Misiroglu
ISBN: 978-1-57859-219-7

The Handy Art History Answer Book
by Madelynn Dickerson
ISBN: 978-1-57859-417-7

The Handy Astronomy Answer Book,
3rd edition
by Charles Liu
ISBN: 978-1-57859-419-1

The Handy Bible Answer Book
by Jennifer Rebecca Prince
ISBN: 978-1-57859-478-8

The Handy Biology Answer Book,
2nd edition
by Patricia Barnes Svarney and Thomas
E. Svarney
ISBN: 978-1-57859-490-0

The Handy Boston Answer Book
by Samuel Willard Crompton
ISBN: 978-1-57859-593-8

The Handy California Answer Book
by Kevin S. Hile
ISBN: 978-1-57859-591-4

The Handy Chemistry Answer Book
by Ian C. Stewart and Justin P. Lamont
ISBN: 978-1-57859-374-3

The Handy Civil War Answer Book
by Samuel Willard Crompton
ISBN: 978-1-57859-476-4

The Handy Communication Answer Book
by Lauren Sergy
ISBN: 978-1-57859-587-7

The Handy Dinosaur Answer Book,
2nd edition
by Patricia Barnes-Svarney and Thomas
E. Svarney
ISBN: 978-1-57859-218-0

The Handy English Grammar Answer Book
by Christine A. Hult, Ph.D.
ISBN: 978-1-57859-520-4

The Handy Geography Answer Book,
3rd edition
by Paul A. Tucci
ISBN: 978-1-57859-576-1

The Handy Geology Answer Book
by Patricia Barnes-Svarney and Thomas
E. Svarney
ISBN: 978-1-57859-156-5

The Handy History Answer Book,
3rd edition
by David L. Hudson, Jr.
ISBN: 978-1-57859-372-9

The Handy Hockey Answer Book
by Stan Fischler
ISBN: 978-1-57859-513-6

The Handy Investing Answer Book
by Paul A. Tucci
ISBN: 978-1-57859-486-3

The Handy Islam Answer Book
by John Renard, Ph.D.
ISBN: 978-1-57859-510-5

The Handy Law Answer Book
by David L. Hudson, Jr.
ISBN: 978-1-57859-217-3

The Handy Math Answer Book,
2nd edition
by Patricia Barnes-Svarney and
Thomas E. Svarney
ISBN: 978-1-57859-373-6

The Handy Military History Answer Book
by Samuel Willard Crompton
ISBN: 978-1-57859-509-9

The Handy Mythology Answer Book,
by David A. Leeming, Ph.D.
ISBN: 978-1-57859-475-7

The Handy New York City Answer Book
by Chris Barsanti
IBSN: 978-1-57859-586-0

The Handy Nutrition Answer Book
by Patricia Barnes-Svarney and Thomas
E. Svarney
ISBN: 978-1-57859-484-9

The Handy Ocean Answer Book
by Patricia Barnes-Svarney and Thomas
E. Svarney
ISBN: 978-1-57859-063-6

The Handy Personal Finance Answer Book
by Paul A. Tucci
ISBN: 978-1-57859-322-4

The Handy Philosophy Answer Book
by Naomi Zack
ISBN: 978-1-57859-226-5

The Handy Physics Answer Book,
2nd edition
By Paul W. Zitzewitz, Ph.D.
ISBN: 978-1-57859-305-7

The Handy Politics Answer Book
by Gina Misiroglu
ISBN: 978-1-57859-139-8

The Handy Presidents Answer Book,
2nd edition
by David L. Hudson, Jr.
ISB N: 978-1-57859-317-0

The Handy Psychology Answer Book,
2nd edition
by Lisa J. Cohen, Ph.D.
ISBN: 978-1-57859-508-2

The Handy Religion Answer Book,
2nd edition
by John Renard, Ph.D.
ISBN: 978-1-57859-379-8

The Handy Science Answer Book,
4th edition
by The Carnegie Library of Pittsburgh
ISBN: 978-1-57859-321-7

The Handy State-by-State Answer Book
By Samuel Willard Crompton
ISBN: 978-1-57859-565-5

The Handy Supreme Court Answer Book
by David L. Hudson, Jr.
ISBN: 978-1-57859-196-1

The Handy Technology Answer Book
by Naomi Balaban and James Bobick
ISBN: 978-1-57859-563-1

The Handy Weather Answer Book,
2nd edition
by Kevin S. Hile
ISBN: 978-1-57859-221-0

Please visit the "Handy Answers" series website at www.handyanswers.com.

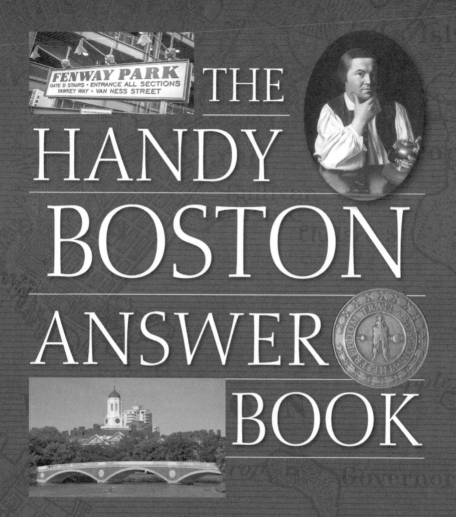

THE
HANDY
BOSTON
ANSWER
BOOK

Samual Willard Crompton

VISIBLE
INK
PRESS

Detroit

THE HANDY BOSTON ANSWER BOOK

Visible Ink Press®
43311 Joy Rd., #414
Canton, MI 48187–2075

Visible Ink Press is a registered trademark of Visible Ink Press LLC.

Most Visible Ink Press books are available at special quantity discounts when purchased in bulk by corporations, organizations, or groups. Customized printings, special imprints, messages, and excerpts can be produced to meet your needs. For more information, contact Special Markets Director, Visible Ink Press, www.visibleink.com or 734–667–3211.

Managing Editor: Kevin S. Hile
Art Director: Mary Claire Krzewinski
Typesetting: Marco DiVita
Proofreaders: Barbara Lyon and Aarti Stephens
Indexer: Larry Baker

Cover images: Shutterstock.

Library of Congress Cataloging–in–Publication Data

Names: Crompton, Samuel Willard, author.
Title: The handy Boston answer book / by Samuel Willard Crompton.
Description: Canton, MI : Visible Ink Press, 2016. | Series: Handy answers series | Includes bibliographical references and index.
Identifiers: LCCN 2016026089 (print) | LCCN 2016026303 (ebook) | ISBN 9781578595938 (tradepaper) | ISBN 9781578596188 (Kindle) | ISBN 9781578596171 (ePub) | ISBN 9781578596164 (uPDF)
Subjects: LCSH: Boston (Mass.)–Miscellanea.
Classification: LCC F73.3 .C94 2016 (print) | LCC F73.3 (ebook) | DDC 974.4/61–dc23
LC record available at https://lccn.loc.gov/2016026089

Printed in the United States of America

10 9 8 7 6 5 4 3 2 1

Dedication

This book is for my beloved Charlotte, who arrived in Boston many years ago, as the first step of her American pilgrimage.

Contents

Acknowledgments

This has been a labor of love, and all sorts of people have helped. I'd like to single out John S. Bowman, A. C. Doyle, Elise Bernier-Feeley, and all the people I grew up with in the 1970s, back when Boston was the city close-by, but which had all sorts of romance and allure for the outsider. Thanks also to Roger Jänecke and Kevin Hile, the people who keep Visible Ink cranking. On a material level, I need to thank the super little Honda Fit that carried me round the streets of Boston time and time again.

Photo Sources

Keith Allison: p. 222.

Joseph Barillari: p. 350.

Baseball Digest: p. 181.

Boston Public Library, Norman B. Leventhal Map Center: p. 28.

British Library: p. 155.

Andrew Campbell: p. 225.

Steven Carter: pp. 183, 215.

Casablanca Records: p. 299.

CBS Television: p. 291.

City of Boston Archives: pp. 128, 137.

Courtenay Guild: p. 285.

Sam Crompton: pp. 4, 10, 22, 31, 94, 105, 145, 241, 266, 313, 320, 321, 334, 347, 386.

R. Dikeman: p. 192.

Alain Edouard: p. 268.

Chris Evans: p. 186.

Googie man (Wikicommons): p. 200.

Henry Han: p. 338.

David Hay: p. 37.

Dirk Hillbrecht: p. 142.

Houghton Library at Harvard University: p. 102.

Internet Archive Book Images: p. 115.

Jaguar MENA (Wikicommons): p. 317.

Kafziel (Wikicommons): p. 195.

Fred Keenan: p. 214.

Library and Archives Canada: p. 109.

Library of Congress: pp. 13, 52, 116 177, 179, 252, 282.

Alan Light: p. 309.

Marathona (Wikicommons): p. 166.

Massachusetts Historical Society: p. 238.

Alec McNayr: p. 292.

National Archives and Records Administration: pp. 61, 67, 70, 255.

National Portrait Gallery, Washington, D.C.: pp. 30, 49.

New York Public Library: p. 43.

Dan4th Nicholas (Wikicommons): p. 232.

Jac de Niis: p. 162.

Hal O'Brien: p. 256.

Jack O'Connell, Sporting News Archives: p. 209.

Adanne Osefoh: p. 298.

Eckhard Pecher: p. 171.

Tim Pierce: p. 271.

Saboteur (Wikicommons): p. 228.

Perkins School for the Blind Archives: p. 99.

Shutterstock: pp. 3, 34, 84, 130, 217, 230, 235, 267, 275, 294, 297, 301, 303, 312, 314, 324, 327, 333, 352, 380.

Gage Skidmore: p. 260.

Aaron Tang: p. 172

Toasterb (Wikicommons): p. 197.

United Press International: p. 249.

U.S. Air Force: p. 221.

U.S. Department of Defense: p. 247.

U.S. Department of Justice: p. 263.

U.S. Department of State: p. 258.

U.S. Navy: p. 254.

U.S. Senate: p. 366.

Wellcome Trust: p. 348.

Public domain: pp. 5, 15, 17, 19, 21, 25, 39, 50, 55, 58, 63, 73, 77, 80, 82, 90, 93, 106, 118, 120, 122, 157, 160, 204, 206, 243, 276, 279, 286, 287, 341, 360, 368, 369, 372, 374, 381.

Timeline

Date	Event
1629	Puritans obtain a charter for settlement of the area from King Charles I
1630	Puritans settle on the peninsula the Indians call Shawmut
1631	Cambridge is settled as the "new town" in the region
1634	Boston settlers pool their funds and buy out Reverend William Blackstone
1637	Trial and banishment of Anne Hutchinson
1641	First Harvard Class graduates
1642	English Civil War begins
1649	Civil War ends with execution of King Charles I
1660	King Charles II restored to English throne
1661	Three regicides—men who signed King Charles I's death warrant—take shelter in Puritan New England
	Samuel Sewall arrives in Boston; his diary commences in 1672
1663	Reverend John Eliot publishes the Bible in the Algonquian language
1675	King Philip's War begins
	John Josselyn's account of Boston and New England published in London
1676	Metacom, also known as King Philip, is killed
1684	King Charles II revokes the Massachusetts Bay charter
1686	Sir Edmund Andros arrives as the first governor under the new royal regime
1688	William and Mary overthrow King James II
1689	Boston overthrows Sir Edmund Andros in bloodless coup
1690	Boston conquers Port Royal, Nova Scotia; fails to conquer Québec City
	Boston sees publication of first newspaper in North America

Date	Event
1691	Massachusetts receives a new provincial charter from William and Mary
	Sir William Phips is the first governor under the new charter
1692	Witch trials in Salem
1695	Recalled to England, Sir William Phips dies in London
1697	Hannah Dustin kills and scalps her Indian captors
	King William's War ends
	Generally believed to be the coldest winter of the seventeenth century
1700	Boston's population reaches roughly 7,000; that of Massachusetts is 60,000
1702	Queen Anne's War begins
1708	A list of Boston street names appears for the first time
1711	British fail to conquer Québec City
1713	Queen Anne's War comes to an end
1721	Boston suffers a terrible epidemic of smallpox
1722	First map of Boston streets (the so-called Burgis Map) is printed
1723	Benjamin Franklin runs from home, settles in Philadelphia
1739	Reverend George Whitefield comes to Boston for the first time
1740	Generally believed to be the coldest winter of the eighteenth century
1744	King George's War begins
1745	New Englanders capture Fortress Louisburg
1747	Knowles Riots in Boston
1748	Britain returns Louisburg to France
1754	George Washington starts the French and Indian War
1755	Boston suffers a powerful earthquake
1759	Québec City falls to the British
1760	Montréal falls to the British. King George II dies and is succeeded by his grandson
1763	French and Indian War ends with Peace of Paris
1765	George III and Parliament place the Stamp Act on American colonies
1766	Stamp Act revoked
1767	Townshend Acts places on American colonies
1768	First British troops arrive in Boston
1769	Tensions between troops and townspeople
1770	Boston Massacre takes place on March 5
	British soldiers are tried in November
1772	HMS *Gaspee* taken and burned in Rhode Island
1773	Parliament passes the Tea Act
	Bostonians carry out the Tea Party
1774	Parliament passes the Coercive Acts; General Gage comes to Boston

Date	Event
1775	Battles of Lexington and Concord on April 19
	Battle of Bunker Hill on June 17
	Washington takes command on July 3
	Benedict Arnold leaves for Canada on September 10
1776	Henry Knox brings cannon from Fort Ticonderoga to Cambridge
	Washington seizes Dorchester Heights, on March 5
	British evacuate Boston on March 17
1780	The Massachusetts state constitution is written and approved
1781	French fleet comes to Boston
1786	First bridge over the Charles River is completed
1789	John Adams of Quincy is elected the first vice president of the United States
1790	Population of Boston is 18,038
1796	John Adams is elected the second president of the United States
1798	USS *Constitution* is launched in Boston Harbor
1800	President John Adams fails of reelection and returns to Braintree
1806	First African American church founded on Joy Street near the State House
1812	Massachusetts Governor Caleb Strong opposes the War of 1812
	USS *Constitution* meets and defeats HMS *Guerriere*
1815	Boston cheers the end of the War of 1812
	Boston is attacked by the Gale of September 1815
1817	President James Monroe visits Boston, inaugurating the Era of Good Feelings
1821	Two dams are constructed, sectioning off much of what later became the "Back Bay"
1822	Boston incorporated as a city
1824	John Quincy Adams becomes the sixth president of the United States
1826	Lafayette comes to town for the dedication of the Bunker Hill Monument
	John Adams and his longtime rival, Thomas Jefferson, die on the same day, July 4
1828	John Quincy Adams fails to get reelected; he returns home to Braintree
1831	William Lloyd Garrison brings out the first issue of *The Liberator*
1834	The Ursuline convent in Charlestown is burned by a mob
1837	Ralph Waldo Emerson delivers "The American Scholar" speech at Harvard Commencement
1860	John Albion Andrews elected governor of Commonwealth of Massachusetts
1861	The Civil War finds John Albion Andrews as governor of Massachusetts
	Many Harvard men enlist in the Union Army
	M.I.T. receives its charter from the Massachusetts Great and General Court

Date	Event
1863	Two African American regiments are recruited in and around Boston
	The Massachusetts 54th Regiment makes a valiant attempt to capture Battery Wagner, South Carolina
1867	The Boston Conservatory of Music and the New England Conservatory are both formed
1869	Charles W. Eliot, son of Mayor Samuel A. Eliot, becomes president of Harvard
1870	The Peace Jubilee is held in Boston
1872	Boston experiences the worst of all its "Great Fires" with sixty-four acres of buildings destroyed
1874	*Gazetteer of the State of Massachusetts* lauds Boston's many accomplishments
1875	Report of the Bureau of Statistics of Labor presents a very different picture of life in Boston
1881	Boston Symphony Orchestra is formed
1885	The Boston Pops delivers its first performance
1886	Henry James novel *The Bostonians* is published in book form (it was previously a serial)
1897	The Boston Marathon is run for the first time
1900	Population of Boston is 560,892; population of United States is 76,212,168
1903	Boston Americans win the first World Series
1910	Charles W. Eliot steps down from Harvard presidency
1912	Fenway Park opens in April
1914	James Michael Curley is elected Mayor of Boston for the first time
1916	M.I.T. moves from quarters in Copley Square to the north bank of the Charles River
1917	John F. Kennedy born in Brookline
	World War I begins. 37,000 Bostonians serve during the conflict
1918	Red Sox win the World Series for the fifth time
1919	The Terrible Molasses Flood hits East Boston
	The Boston police strike makes news nationwide, bringing condemnation to the strikers and applause to Governor Calvin Coolidge
1920	The Red Sox trade Babe Ruth to the Yankees
1923	Massachusetts boy Calvin Coolidge becomes president of the United States
1924	The Boston Bruins are organized
1925	A non-Irishman is elected Mayor of Boston, the only such occurrence in the twentieth century
1928	The Boston Garden—home to the Bruins and later the Celtics—is completed
1930	Boston celebrates its tercentenary
	James Michael Curley becomes Mayor of Boston for the third time

Date	Event
1933	Numerous soup kitchens in operation in Boston
1944	Eldest of the four Kennedy boys dies in World War II
1945	John "The Elder" Kelley wins the Boston Marathon for the second time
1946	John F. Kennedy elected to the U.S. Congress
	Red Sox win pennant but lose World Series
	Boston Celtics are formed as part of the American Basketball Association
1950	Population of Boston is 790,863; population of United States is 151,325,798
	Arnold "Red" Auerbach comes to Boston to manage the Boston Celtics
1956	Bill Russell comes to Boston to enter the Celtics organization
1957	John "The Younger" Kelly wins the Boston Marathon, becoming the first American to do so since 1945
1957	Boston Celtics win their first NBA championship
1959	Boston Patriots admitted as eighth and last team of the American Football League
	Bill Russell and Wilt Chamberlain face off for the first time
1960	John F. Kennedy wins Democratic nomination and defeats Richard M. Nixon in the general election
	Ted Williams takes his last at-bat in Fenway Park
1962	President Kennedy shows a firm hand during the Cuban Missile Crisis
1963	President Kennedy assassinated in Dallas
1964	The fifty-two-story Prudential Building is completed
	Celtics owner Walter Brown dies
1967	The "Impossible Dream" year of the Red Sox
	Amby Burfoot becomes first American to win Boston Marathon since
1968	New York Senator Robert Kennedy assassinated in Los Angeles
1969	Student protests at M.I.T. force the administration to close one of the most important laboratories for U.S. Armed Services research
1970	*Love Story* is released to wide screen
	Boston Bruins win the Stanley Cup
1971	Foxboro Stadium, home of the New England Patriots, is completed
1974	Federal Judge Arthur Garrity rules that Boston schools must integrate
1975	Red Sox win pennant but lose World Series to Cincinnati Reds
	Bill Rodgers wins the Boston Marathon with a time of 2:09:28
1976	Boston and eastern Massachusetts experience tourist revival with Bicentennial Year
	Shocking photograph of racial anger appears in papers around the nation
	Rock group Boston has groundbreaking success with album of the same name
	The John Hancock Tower is completed

Date	Event
1978	Boston endures the Blizzard of '78
	Red Sox lose heart-breaking, one-game playoff to Yankees
	Celtics great John Havlicek retires
	Federal Reserve Building in East Boston is completed
	The Paper Chase, a very popular television program, debuts on CBS
1979	John F. Kennedy Library is opened at Columbia Point
	Larry Bird comes to Boston for the first time to sign with the Celtics
1980	Ted Kennedy runs for Democratic nomination, losing to incumbent Jimmy Carter
	Bill Rodgers wins the Boston Marathon for the fourth time, tying Gerard Cote in second place of all-time winners
	Cheating scandal taints the Boston Marathon when Rosie Ruiz "wins" in record time
1982	*Cheers* appears on TV for first time
1982–83	Boston experiences frigid winter
1985	*Spencer for Hire* debuts on CBS
1986	New England Patriots reach the Super Bowl but are thrashed by Chicago Bears
	Red Sox come close to victory in World Series, but are foiled by New York Mets
	Boston Celtics have an outstanding year, culminating in another NBA championship
1988	Governor Michael Dukakis wins Democratic nomination but loses the general election to Republican George H.W. Bush
1992	Sail Boston brings the Tall Ships to Boston Harbor
	Construction of the new Boston Garden begins
1993	The last episode of *Cheers* airs in May
1995	The last games are played in the (old) Boston Garden
1996	*Infinite Jest*, a novel based on life in Brighton, is published
1997	New England Patriots reach Super Bowl but are bested by Green Bay Packers
	The old Boston Garden is demolished
	Good Will Hunting appears on the big screen to first-rate reviews
1998	USS *Constitution* celebrates her 200th birthday
1999	Bill Russell's number is retired by the Boston Celtics
2000	Sail Boston brings back the Tall Ships
2002	New England Patriots win Super Bowl XXXVI
2004	New England Patriots win Super Bowl XXXVIII
	Massachusetts Senator John F. Kerry wins Democratic nomination but loses the general election to Republican George W. Bush
2005	New England Patriots win Super Bowl XXXVIX

Date	Event
2008	Boston Celtics win their seventeenth NBA championship, the first since 1986
2012	Former Governor Mitt Romney wins the Republican nomination but loses the general election to Democrat Barrack Obama
2013	Boston Marathon is spoiled by the detonation of two bombs by terrorists
	Red Sox win the World Series, after having placed last in baseball in 2012
2014	Boston Marathon sees 35,000 runners, and the new slogan, "Boston Strong"
	American wins Boston Marathon for first time since 1980s
2015	New England Patriots win Super Bowl XLI, making it a total of four for the dynasty
	Boston experiences its coldest winter, and greatest amount of snow, in decades
2016	Boston Magazine publishes list of 100 Greatest Bostonians of all Time

Introduction

Boston is a city of many moods. Strolling across Longfellow Bridge in May is not the same as huddling for cover on that same bridge in February. Many cities have varying weather patterns, but few have so distinct a personality as Boston. To put it bluntly, Boston is not your father or your mother's city. It belongs to your grandparents.

Like a marvelous grandmother, Boston shows you the charms of the area. Holding your hand in hers, the grandmother escorts you along the Freedom Trail, perhaps the single most exciting and intriguing piece of history tourism ever developed. The grand old lady puts salt water taffy in your mouth, and takes you to the Public Garden for a ride on the famous swan boats. And then, to top it off, she allows you to stroll the Esplanade, and perhaps invites you to hear the Boston Pops perform. But as you head for home, you remember: I have a grandfather, too!

Like a grumpy grandfather, one who has seen too many winters, Boston acts like the personification of Saturn, the Roman God of the passage of time. Your grandfather can chuckle, but he growls as well, and he wants you to know the seamy, as well as the sensational, part of life. With you trailing behind, your grandfather walks down the old and tired streets of Boston, pointing out where the Boston Strangler was found, and where the riots over busing began. He never tires of pointing to the discrepancy between rich and poor, saying that when the world comes to an end everyone will have to account for their actions. Walks with grandfather are not the same as those with grandmother. But on one thing Grandmother and Grandfather concur: The Red Sox are the greatest team the nation has ever seen.

She is a lady of many moods, the great city of Boston. Though men have often served as her leaders, there has never been any doubt about her identification as feminine. Very likely it stems from the fact that the Charles and Mystic Rivers rush right past her on their way to the great bay from which Massachusetts gains its name. And, like any *grande dame*, she has her eccentricities and peculiarities. Even the casual visitor knows strolling on Longfellow Bridge in May is one experience, and that taking one's life in one's hands in December is entirely another.

The Puritans named her, but the Native Americans were the first to drink from her waters; in fact, the name "Shawmut" means "place of the beautiful spring." Even in Puritan times—less grim than we sometimes suppose—Boston was known for her ale and wine. A festive spirit managed to conceal itself behind the ramparts of religious perfectionism. And, over time, that desire to be the best altered its course, moving from the religious to the political sphere. The Revolutionary leaders—men like James Otis and Samuel Adams—were no less persuaded of their righteousness than their Puritan great-grandparents.

The Revolutionary generation saw the town sink to a very low ebb, but the architectural genius of Charles Bulfinch brought Boston to new heights; just a generation later, people began calling Boston the "Athens of America." The genius of the founding Puritans could still be seen as late as 1880, but it was equaled by their arrogance, as proper Bostonians refused to yield ground to the Irish and Italian newcomers, who, of course, have been followed by the Poles, Lithuanians, African Americans, and others. If there's one great lesson to learn from the ethnic conflict it is that Boston belongs to no special group: she is always at the beck and call of those willing to serve her.

Can the story of Boston be told without research in her libraries? Of course not, and equally one can ask if it is possible for Boston to be known without an understanding of the Red Sox and New England Patriots. Even the most diehard sports fan will admit that the crowds are fundamentally different: the thousands who pour into Fenway on a July afternoon are not the same as those who crowd the Garden on a Saturday night. Boston has a thousand dimensions, but she has only four great obsessions: education, sports, architectural beauty, and the pursuit of personal perfection. Whether the last of these is demonstrated in research at the Massachusetts Historical Society, skulling on the Charles, or making the best masonry chimney is entirely up to the individual.

One can, of course, go the comparative route and ask where Boston stands compared to its many rivals. And though such competitions are necessarily self-limited, we can participate and say that Boston—at her best—is the very best place in the United States for a college-aged person. No other city offers so many opportunities and venues, ranging from the purely academic to the social and cultural. There was a time, perhaps as recent as the 1950s, when critics declared Boston was a great place to go to school, and not a bad one for one's retirement, but not good for any age in between. If this was once true, it certainly is not so today. The theatre, opera, and Boston Pops are almost unrivaled, and the discriminating middle-aged person can find plenty of fun. The urban renewal that changed Boston in the 1960s brought about far more condos and developments than anyone imagined, and there's plenty of room for those with deep pockets.

This, of course, brings up one of the great complaints about Boston: no one can afford to live there and no outsider can find a parking place. If it is true today, it was true in Civil War Boston, as well, except that the competition was for horses and stalls back then, rather than parking for cars. The truth was, and remains, that Boston opens her arms to those who love her unreservedly.

And so we come to the greatest of all questions concerning modern Boston. Is it the city of John Winthrop, of Paul Revere, or of John Kennedy? Does the ethos of Sam Adams prevail, or is this the land of the countercultural 1960s? The answer can never be final, but the best way to approximate it is to take a three-mile stroll from the Old North End to Fenway Park (watching out for the automobiles!) One passes the brownstones of the high-browed intellectuals, and the apartments of the newcomers. One sees the signs for the latest political election, and observes the many faithful entering the famous churches. And somewhere along that three-mile route, he or she realizes that Boston belongs to those who live in the moment and give it their all. This is the land of Robert Lowell and Isabella Stuart Gardener, but also of Blondie, the rock group Boston, and the latest Red Sox game.

Will Boston continue to thrive? Her future has always been precariously balanced on New England granite and sliding clay: she has never enjoyed the easy greatness of Manhattan or San Francisco. But the challenge to make something has inspired each generation, right since the time of the Winthrop Fleet. One can bet against Boston, but does so at his or her own peril.

And so, meander the streets that began as Puritan cow paths. Admire the granite statues on Boston Common, as well as the cloth ones in Chinatown. Walk Longfellow Bridge and photograph Zakim Bridge (from a safe distance). And remember that Boston is a treasure, a difficult lady at times, but one that is well worth your time.

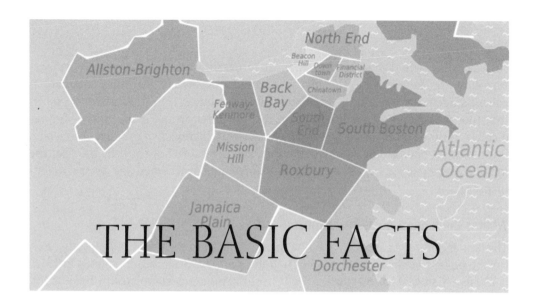

THE BASIC FACTS

What is Boston in the simplest and most direct terms?

Boston is an incorporated city with a charter dating to 1822. It is also the capital of the Commonwealth of Massachusetts.

Where is Boston located?

Boston is located in the eastern United States in the state of Massachusetts. At 42.5 degrees north latitude and 71 degrees west longitude, it is close to the halfway point between the North Pole and the Equator. If one were able to draw a straight line from Boston, right across the North Atlantic, one would end up in northern Spain.

How many people live in Boston?

According to the U.S. Census of 2010, there were 617,594 residents of Boston.

What is Boston's elevation?

Most of Boston is at around 130 feet above sea level. This means the city usually has a temperate climate. However, the Boston area experiences a rather steady air movement of about 11.6 miles per hour, making it one of the windiest cities in the United States. One feels this especially in December and January, when "wind tunnels" are felt, especially in the area around Kenmore Square.

What is Boston's weather like?

Longtime residents will answer that Boston has a complete map of the four seasons, meaning its weather varies from fairly warm temperatures to extreme cold. Spring is usually the best of all times for Bostonians with gentle but pervading sunshine, and warm breezes: perhaps it is not a coincidence that opening day of the Red Sox season is

1

such a favorite with the crowds. Summer can be overly warm, and many Bostonians escape either to Maine or Cape Cod on the weekend. Autumn is filled with excitement as college students arrive, and the beauty of the season builds right to Christmastime, as the students head home for break. Then comes winter, which is thoroughly unpredictable. Boston sometimes enjoys mild winters with plenty of warm rain; then again, it can also get pounded by cold temperatures and several feet of snow, as was the case in the record-breaking winter of 2015. But before long, April comes, and the cycle commences again.

What is the highest point in Boston?

The land is quite level and low, and one therefore looks to the major buildings to identify the highest landmarks in Boston. The John Hancock Building, completed in 1976, is 790 feet high, and has 62 stories. The Prudential Building, completed in 1964, is 750 feet, and contains 52 stories.

What are Boston's geographic characteristics?

Boston lies at the extreme north-central corner of the famous bay from which Massachusetts gains its name. The original Boston—the location Puritans arrived at in 1630—was a peninsula, about 850 square acres in size. Today, the city of Boston is much larger, but one still finds evidence of its Puritan and Yankee past in the crowded streets, the frequent dead-ends, and the occasional cobblestone.

Boston lies on the south side of the Charles River, which rises in the little town of Hopkinton and runs to join with the Mystic River: together, the two streams enter Massachusetts Bay, which eventually yields to the North Atlantic Ocean. Boston is best observed from air and today this is possible through helicopter tours and other activities. For example, at the Prudential Building, best known as the "Pru," one can take an elevator to the fifty-second floor and gaze at the marvel that is the city of Boston.

How many islands are there in Boston Harbor and the Massachusetts Bay?

More than twenty, almost all of which have played some part in the history of the city. Deer Island, for example, is where Native Americans were imprisoned during King Philip's War. Little Brewster Island is the site of Boston Light, the nation's oldest surviving lighthouse. Georges Island is where many soldiers—from colonial conflicts right down to the Civil War—were quartered. And Hog Island has practically disappeared: it has been taken over by Logan Airport.

What are the best places to visit in Boston?

There are at least a half-dozen. Anyone interested in exploring Boston and Cambridge's educational history will do best in Harvard Square, while someone more interested in sports will enjoy visiting Boston Garden and Fenway Park. Admirers of landscape architecture might want to visit Brookline's numerous parks, but the one place that lays the strongest

There are over twenty islands in Boston Harbor, including Georges Island on which tourists will find Fort Warren, a military installation from the days of the American Civil War.

claim to all Bostonians—and to the vast majority of visitors—is the Boston Common. In all the United States, there is nothing quite like this fifty-acre piece of common land.

As early as the 1640s, sections of downtown Boston were spliced together to create "The Common," an area where everyone could bring their horses, ponies, cows, and chickens. The idea of a "common" dates to the Middle Ages, when every European town had one. The Puritans who arrived in 1630 were conscious of the need for common space, and their early sectioning of the town has lasted to the present day. Of course one can compare the Boston Common to New York's Central Park. The big difference, however, is that Central Park was never used in such a functional way.

What is the best way to enjoy the Charles River?

The great stream called the Charles River is a magnificent sight. Coursing past downtown Boston on one side and Cambridge on the other, the Charles River is the reason the Puritans first settled in the region: they needed a fast-moving stream of fresh water from which to draw their supplies. To the best of our knowledge none of the Puritans— not even the redoubtable Governor John Winthrop—ever suspected that high-rise buildings would be built in Boston or that the city would be home to 630,000 folk.

But to the main question: the best way to enjoy the Charles is to stroll along the many sidewalks along its banks. Being Americans, Bostonians have naturally upped the ante, and one sometimes gets run over by people on bicycles or rollerblades, but the essence of the joy remains. There's nothing like a stroll along the Charles and a crossing of Longfellow Bridge, named for the famous poet of that name.

3

Taking advantage of an evening stroll along the Charles River is one of the benefits of living in the city.

How many tourists come to Boston each year?

If we include the many thousands of parents that bring their eighteen-year-olds to attend college in the fall, Boston may see as many as five million visitors per year. Logan Airport receives many thousands of people each day: many of these, to be sure, are "repeat" customers. The tourists come from every conceivable direction and in addition to Logan, they arrive by bus, train, and even taxicab; and many of them arrive by automobile. Traveling to Boston via car is considered the most complicated because of Boston and Cambridge's narrow streets.

Is Cambridge fully independent of Boston? And how about Dorchester, Brookline, and other municipalities?

Cambridge is truly its own place, and sometimes it seems like its own world. This was especially the case during the 1960s, when a handful of Harvard professors led the way in the use of LSD. But most of the other towns that surround Boston have long since been incorporated into the great municipality. When one speaks of "Boston's Finest," one does not mean the police or just the 630,000 people of Boston, but also those residing in the twenty-two surrounding neighborhoods.

To be sure, there are places in and around Boston that seem independent of the great city. For example, East Boston used to be the home of many shipyards, and Dorchester often seems to possess a mind of its own. But when one looks out from the Skywalk Observatory of the Prudential Building, one realizes that all these areas are many pieces of one grand puzzle, which add up to the modern-day miracle that is the city of Boston.

Given its remarkable history, why is Boston not the largest and greatest of all American cities?

That's the question that has bedeviled Bostonians for more than two centuries. Up through about the year 1800, it seemed that Boston would be number one in culture, education, population, and industrial strength. But in the two decades that followed, Philadelphia and New York powered their way right past Boston, and the number of American cities that exceed it in size has only grown since that year. One should not feel sorry for Boston, however; of all American cities, it is the one that combines historic legacy with higher education and public culture to the greatest possible extent.

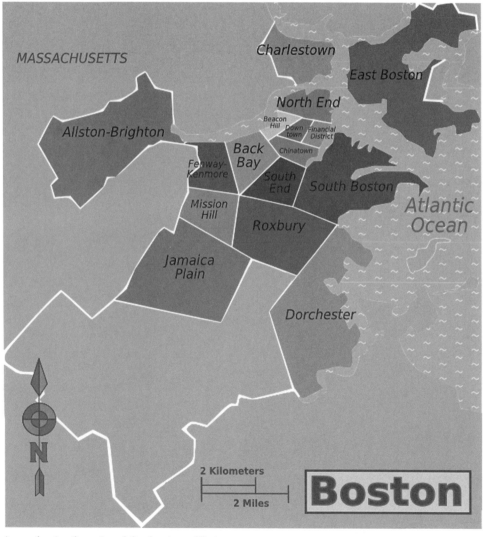

A map showing the various defined regions of Boston.

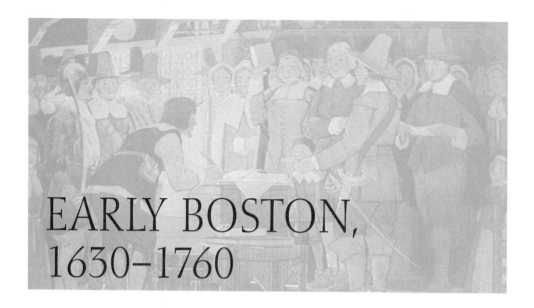

EARLY BOSTON, 1630–1760

What does "Puritan" mean?

In the original sense—the one employed in the seventeenth century—Puritan meant "one who purifies." The term derived from the ongoing conflict between the Church of England (Anglican) and a group of religious minorities. The minority group most important to the city of Boston, and to us today, are the Puritans. These people—who were classified as religious extremists by many of their countrymen in England—wanted to purify the Church of England, to rid it of anything that even remotely resembled Roman Catholicism. Over time, however, the Puritans became known for other qualities. Not only were they keen on religious purity, but they tended to be excellent merchants and tradesmen. A century later, the stereotype of the fierce New England Puritan evolved into that of the grasping New England Yankee, meaning a man who would not be parted from his money.

Why did the Puritans come to New England?

It is difficult for us to comprehend what would persuade people to leave the relative safety of Old England for the great dangers of the open sea, and New England. It may be useful to read the words of Edward Johnson, the author of the first printed history of New England, who wrote about the subject in his 1654 work *Wonder-Working Providence of Sions Savior in New England*.

> When England began to decline in religion like luke-warm Laodicea, and instead of purging out Popery, a farther compliance was sought not only in vain idolatrous ceremonies, but also in profaning the Sabbath, and by proclamation throughout their parish churches, exasperating lewd and profane persons to celebrate a Sabbath like the heathen to Venus, Bacchus, and Ceres.

It was in times such as these—the 1620s—that many Puritans in the motherland began to search their hearts, and wonder whether they should immigrate to America.

The same author expressed it thus:

Oh yes! Oh yes! Oh yes! All you the people of Christ that are here oppressed, imprisoned and scurrilously derided, gather yourselves together, your wives and little ones, and…be shipped for his service in the Western World.

How did the Puritans know about the land soon to be called New England?

Their knowledge came from the maps and charts of a handful of sailors, the most important of whom was Captain John Smith (1580–1631). Smith is better known as one of the founders of the Jamestown colony in Virginia, but after Jamestown was established, Smith made a series of voyages to New England, which, he declared, possessed even greater commercial possibilities than the southern colonies.

One often hears of the Pilgrims and the *Mayflower* that brought the first group of English settlers in 1620. Why are the Puritans ships less known?

Quite likely this is because there were so many of them. The Pilgrims could only afford one ship in 1620 and modern day tourists who visit the *Mayflower II*, a replica of the original ship, realize just how cramped conditions were for the original Pilgrims. The Puritans, who sailed a decade later, were much better supplied. They had perhaps a dozen ships, and none of them acquired the lasting name recognition of the *Mayflower*.

The Puritans that sailed in 1630 also had a big advantage over the Pilgrims of 1620: the latter group possessed a charter, endorsed by King Charles I, allowing them to settle. The charter of 1629 granted sweeping powers to the settlers, allowing them a broad measure of what we would call self-government. To be sure, neither King Charles I nor his son King Charles II saw it that way, and the granting of that charter led to many conflicts between Old and New England.

What was so special about Boston to the Puritans who arrived in 1630?

The landscape was pleasant, and it reminded them of aspects of life back home in Old England. The key thing, though, was Boston's superb geographic location. Located at the inner corner of the great bay from which Massachusetts gains its name, Boston was a peninsula of about 840 square acres, connected to the mainland at Roxbury. This means Boston was ideally situated for trade, both from inland areas and from the Atlantic Ocean.

How and when did the first Puritan settlers arrive?

In the spring of 1630, the so-called Winthrop Fleet—named for Governor John Winthrop—departed England. The fifteen or so vessels carried nearly 1,200 settlers, making this the largest English attempt yet to settle in New England. Arriving at Salem, which had been established in 1627, the Winthrop Fleet then moved on to what is now Charlestown, just on the other side of the Charles River from Boston's North End. In late August of 1630, a few dozen settlers crossed the Charles for the first time. They came in search of blueberries and strawberries, but the single most important item on their agenda was fresh water.

The Puritans were in luck. The Native American name for Boston was *Shawmut*, meaning place of the beautiful spring. Historians continue—right to this day—to dispute the precise location of the spring that produced such fine fresh water, but it was, quite likely, on the northwest side of what is now Beacon Hill. Speaking of "the Hill," one should note that the Puritans briefly called the place TriMountain—in honor of its three hills—before renaming it Boston in honor of the town in Lincolnshire from which many of them came.

What did Boston look like to the first settlers, those that arrived in 1630?

The peninsula that the Native Americans called Shawmut was about three-fifths the size of today's downtown Boston. Shawmut resembled a five-leaf clover, jutting out from the mainland at what is now Roxbury. To the Puritans who first arrived in 1630 Shawmut seemed an oddly shaped place, and perhaps ungainly too, but it had the great advantage of possessing excellent fresh water. In fact, Shawmut means "place of the beautiful spring."

What those first Puritan explorers, and settlers, found was a peninsula tucked into the farthest corner of what we now call the Massachusetts Bay, the geographic formation from which Massachusetts gains its name. They knew their ships would be safe in the anchorage—at least ninety percent of the time—and yet they were still positioned in a way that maximized their contact with the open sea. It made sense for the Puritans to settle Boston, which they first named TriMountain.

How did Beacon Hill gain prominence?

A long time passed before Beacon Hill became the fashionable part of town, or the site of the Massachusetts State House. When the Puritans arrived in September 1630 they called the area TriMountain because it had three protruding hills, which, over time, were named Fort Hill, Copp's Hill, and Beacon Hill. Beacon Hill was named after the wooden beacon erected there in order to warn against attack. An iron pot at the top of this beacon was always ready to be spilled and light a fire, warning people about an attack with a flame that could be seen for miles around. Interestingly enough, the beacon was never used.

For perhaps the first week, the settlers called the area TriMountain, and it seemed that this might become the name, but when they wrote their first documents, the Pu-

Does the name TriMountain live on in any part of Boston?

It does indeed. Tremont Street, which runs right through the most packed and exciting part of the city today, is named after the original TriMountain.

ritans renamed it Boston in honor of the town in Lincolnshire from which many of them hailed. Boston, England, is itself believed to be a corruption of the words St. Botolph's Town, and there is a St. Botolph's Club in Boston today.

Do we have any idea what early Puritan settlers looked like?

Puritans were not great visual artists, and most of our representations of them therefore come from nineteenth-century artists, who attempted to depict their ancestors. The image of "The Puritan" also comes to us from the prose writings of authors such as Nathaniel Hawthorne and the poet Henry Wadsworth Longfellow. We have no reason to doubt the basic veracity of these descriptions. The Puritans, as well as their Pilgrim cousins in Plymouth, favored stiff hats and dark clothing. Whether their faces were as grim and hard-set as the sculptors suggest is difficult to say. One thing is for certain. These early Puritans—who became the first Bostonians—believed in hard work and rising in the world. Quite likely, they would applaud if they could see what Boston looks like in our time.

Is there any truth to the story of Ann Pollard?

We think so. Decades after the first landing of the Puritans on the north side of the Shawmut peninsula, old Ann Pollard told her grandchildren and great-grandchildren of how she stepped out of the first boat and gingerly came ashore. She recounted the event with great pride and enthusiasm, declaring that she had foraged for strawberries and blueberries all day, and with some success. She was nine or ten in 1630, and she lived

This bronze plaque on Boston Common celebrates the landing of the first Puritan settlers in 1630. Ann Pollard is shown at center right.

to the remarkable age of 105. A painting of her, executed in her old age, hangs today in the Massachusetts Historical Society on Boylston Street. And Pollard's story naturally begs another question: What were the Puritan women like?

If the Puritan men are shadowy figures, available to us mostly through poetry and old wives' tales, then the Puritan women are even less accessible. We do know that they came in numbers roughly equal to the men, and that the Puritans were great believers in large families: the population of "Shawmut-Boston" began growing right away. Families of eight, nine, or ten children were not unusual, and the large number of offspring testifies to the idea that the Puritans expected to lose many of their children to disease. Fortunately, this proved not to be the case.

Why was Boston—and New England in general—so much healthier than the Middle and Southern colonies?

The terrible New England winters—which continue to strike us with great force today—form a large part of the answer. The cold and freeze that sometimes comes in the last week of November and often lasts till the second week of April means that many types of insects that carry disease don't survive. Beyond this, New Englanders developed a stronger medical tradition than their Southern counterparts. As a result, a larger percentage of the population of youngsters survived, and New England's population expanded much more rapidly than it did in most of the southern colonies. One can, perhaps, push the point too far, but it's worth noting that Boston—in modern times—has become the location of more fine hospitals than any other city of comparable size.

What happened to the Native Americans who lived on the peninsula which they called Shawmut?

Though no one will claim that the Puritans were "nice" or "kind" to the Native Americans, it has to be said that there was no violent takeover or expulsion of the Indians. When the Puritan settlers arrived in September 1630 they found only one person living on Shawmut. He was the Reverend William Blackstone—for whom the Blackstone River is named—and he lived a solitary existence on the peninsula. It is quite possible there were Native Americans on the peninsula in earlier times, but also quite certain that none were living there in 1630.

THE FIRST GOVERNMENT

Did the Puritans of Boston establish a democracy, a theocracy, or an oligarchy?

This is one of the great and controversial questions with no definitive answer. Some historians argue that the Puritans quickly established a theocracy, a system in which the ministers or priests ruled. Others contend that Boston was really an oligarchy, a system

11

in which the wealthy—merchants especially—dominated. Still others examine the same set of data and conclude that Boston was more democratic than almost any other town among the early American colonies.

The best answer is that the Puritans believed in a system of hierarchy: they were *not* democrats. It made perfect sense to them that their rulers would come from the better educated and wealthier men, and it does not seem to have occurred to any of them that women might one day gain the right to vote. Because the Puritans were ardent church-goers, ministers naturally played an important role. But the Puritans were early believers in separation between church and state. Magistrates—meaning secular officials elected by the people—were just as important as ministers.

What was the name and shape of the early government in Boston?

By 1634 the Boston Puritans had established the Great and General Court of the Colony of Massachusetts Bay, and with only a few alterations, this remains the expression used to describe the Massachusetts legislature of today. The Great and General Court was composed of a governor—elected by the freeholders (part-time legislators)—a governor's council (chosen by the governor), and a House of Representatives. The Puritans placed all three together in a figurative sense and called it the Great and General Court.

For a handful of years, Boston was the only town in the colony, but as other areas were established (Newtown was the first) it became necessary to differentiate the government of the town of Boston from that of the colony. Boston held its first town meetings in the 1640s, and the New England form of town meeting was thereby born: a day in May was usually the time when the freeholders met to discuss and vote on articles brought before them by the town selectmen. To the best of our knowledge, Boston and Massachusetts politics were rather fractious, right from the beginning.

Did one have a sense in the 1630s that the Massachusetts Puritans might one day break away from Old England?

Yes. The English officials that came to examine Boston—and they were few in number—remarked on the independent quality of the Bostonians and their country cousins. In 1676 the governor of Massachusetts commented to an English customs inspector that the laws of Old England were bounded by the Four Seas—meaning the English Channel, the North Sea, the Irish Sea, and the North Atlantic—and did not apply to the American colonies. Even if inspector Edward Randolph exaggerated it a bit in the telling, there is little doubt that the Puritans regarded themselves as a people set apart with a great destiny. This idea is also reflected in the words of John Winthrop's famous sermon in which he described the mission of the colonists as follows: "we shall be as a city on a hill."

Did the early Bostonians have any trouble earning a living?

Cash—in the sense of copper and silver coins—was rarely used and the early settlers worried much more about getting in their supply of cord wood for the winter (this was

The *Mayflower Compact,* signed aboard the ship of that name, established the pattern for Pilgrim and Puritan self-government.

difficult because the trees of Shawmut peninsula disappeared very quickly). But over the next four decades, Bostonians discovered more need for cash, and in 1653 mint master John Hull made the first "Pine Tree Shillings." A truly New England currency, these shillings provoked much concern among British officials, who claimed that the Bostonians wanted to be independent in all but name.

Earning a living in early Boston usually meant doing something connected with the waterfront. Bostonians built docks and wharves at an incredible rate, and their ships commenced a trade with the West Indies (Caribbean) by the 1650s.

Blessing of the Bay was the first ship built in Boston; it was followed by dozens of others. Boston also provided a number of truly expert sailing masters, who made all sorts of transatlantic voyages. It's hard to pick out just one, but Master John Balston, a second-generation Bostonian, turns up in the records time and again. His family were natives of England's West Country, and they may have navigated the shores of Devon and Cornwall long before coming to America. All we can say for certain is that Balston made the trip from Boston to London, and from Boston to Plymouth, England, a great number of times.

How did outsiders view Boston and its new merchant community?

One of the best descriptions of mid-seventeenth-century Boston comes from the pen of John Josselyn, an Englishman who traveled to the colonies twice and wrote an extensive commentary on his travels.

13

The town hath two hills of equal height on the front part thereof next the sea, the one well fortified on the superficies with some artillery mounted, commanding any ship as she sails into the harbor.... The houses are for the most part raised on the sea-banks and wharfed out with great industry and cost, many of them standing upon piles, close together on each side the streets as in London.... The town is rich and very populous, much frequented by strangers, here is the dwelling of their governour. On the North-west and North-east two constant fairs are kept for daily traffic.

Proc. Mass Historical Society, Vol III, 3rd Series, Cambridge, 1833, p. 319

BOSTON TURNS INTO MASSACHUSETTS

Did the Puritans conquer the wilderness as well?

Not as readily and never with so certain a conviction of their ultimate victory. The Bostonians were not urban folk in the modern-day sense of the word, but they were definitely townspeople, accustomed to long-settled areas. Within a decade of arriving in Boston they established Cambridge and Newtown, as well as Roxbury and Watertown, but they did not immediately move to the far countryside. During its first century, Boston had many inhabitants who never went west of Concord and some that never even ventured out of the town itself.

Speaking of Cambridge, when was Harvard College established?

In 1636 the first scholars were set up at Harvard and the first graduating class came in 1641 (there were nine in that class). The college was made possible by the will of John Harvard, who left his books and much of his money for the establishment of the same. Very few people suspected, however, that Harvard would become so venerable, or so rich for that matter.

The early Bostonians were great believers in education, but they meant schooling for young males, not girls. Some Boston females managed to acquire an education, but it was almost always thanks to a male benefactor, who acted on his own, rather than from a societal impulse. This does not mean early Boston was especially male-chauvinist; rather, it implies that Boston was much like other parts of the English-speaking world at the time.

How important was John Winthrop to the establishment of Boston?

It's likely that the place would have been settled without John Winthrop (1588–1649), but it never would have taken on so definite and Puritan a character. Winthrop was a rather elegant English gentleman who defied many of the Puritan stereotypes, but as governor (he was elected a total of nine times) he promoted the belief that Boston was a "proper" place where proper gentleman and ladies were to live their lives under the su-

pervision of the magistrates and ministers. And when someone stepped out of line—as they inevitably did—Winthrop was among the foremost in establishing law and order.

In 1637 Governor Winthrop presided over the special court trial of Mistress Anne Hutchinson, who had the temerity to hold discussion groups in her home on Sunday afternoons. Found guilty of religious heresy, Anne Hutchinson was banished from Boston and the entire colony. She and her family moved to Pelham, Long Island, where all but one of them were killed in a massacre by local Indians in 1643. Hutchinson Parkway is named in her honor.

A wealthy attorney, John Winthrop served as Massachusetts' governor on numerous occasions.

One often hears of other religious rebels. Why does the name Mary Dyer ring a bell?

Like Mistress Anne Hutchinson, Mary Dyer was a Puritan who crossed the great Atlantic and settled in Boston, only to yearn for even greater freedom. Joining the Society of Friends—also known as the Quakers—Mary Dyer was banished from Boston. She moved to Rhode Island, but returned to Boston on several occasions, always to preach about the value and virtue of the Quaker faith. Once the Puritan authorities were so angry that a noose was placed round her neck before she was let go. Incredibly, she returned the following year (1660) and was hanged on Boston Common. There is a monument in her honor at the Massachusetts State House.

Were the Bostonians always so tough on those that disagreed with them?

Most of the time. Puritan Bostonians had a self-righteousness that is difficult to describe in our more secular and permissive world. They believed their mission was to establish a "city on a hill," in the immortal words of Governor John Winthrop. This meant there could be no back-sliding, no doubts, and no doubters. At the same time, however, it's important to note that these religious conformists were becoming extremely successful merchants and tradesmen: Boston prospered even while its ministers spoke of the virtues of cleaving only to God.

Is the cod fish really as important to Boston and Massachusetts as one sometimes hears?

Today, the cod fishing trade is but a shadow of earlier times. In the seventeenth and eighteenth centuries, however, it was the very livelihood of Boston and the other coastal towns. Boston captains sailed up to Newfoundland, fished off the Grand Banks, and then carried their catch of cod fish all the way to Portugal, France, and Spain to sell. These Catholic nations had a built-in market of customers, eager for fish, which did not violate the Roman Catholic Church's prohibition against the eating of meat on days of religious observation.

What makes the Puritans of Boston different from the Pilgrims of Plymouth?

In terms of religion, both groups were quite similar. The people we call the Puritans termed themselves Nonconformists, meaning they did not conform to the laws and regulations of the Church of England. The Pilgrims called themselves Separatists, meaning they were separate from the Church of England. But in terms of economic and social status, the two groups were rather different.

The Pilgrims were a smaller group, and they tended to come from the middle and working classes with a strong emphasis on the latter. To them it was entirely sufficient to establish a small colony on the edge of what some called the "howling wilderness." The Puritans, by contrast, tended to come from middle- and upper-class families, with the emphasis on the latter. Immensely ambitious, they wanted to establish a godly commonwealth in America, and to appear as a "city upon a hill" (to use the famous words of Governor John Winthrop).

Did the Pilgrims and Puritans know each other well?

They did. Governor William Bradford of Plymouth was a frequent visitor to Boston, and Massachusetts governors, from John Winthrop onward, were quite familiar with Plymouth. In neither case did the close affiliation lead to great affection, however. The Plymouth Pilgrims were eager to keep their distance and political independence, and they managed to retain both until 1691, when a new royal charter brought both Boston and Plymouth in as part of the new Province of Massachusetts Bay. Toward the end of his long life, Plymouth Governor William Bradford penned these lines:

> O Boston, though thou now art grown
> To be a great and wealthy town,
> Yet I have seen thee a void place
> Shrubs and brushes covering thy face;
> No houses then in thee there were,
> Nor such as gold and silk did wear.

How did Boston get on its feet, economically speaking?

It took less than a decade for this to transpire. The Bostonians were extremely ambitious, and they first turned to the soil, hoping to find some bumper crop (such as what tobacco was in Virginia) that might allow them to become wealthy. The squash, pumpkins, and corn that grew so readily were all beneficial to the Puritan diet, but none of these fetched much money, so Bostonians turned to the humble cod fish instead.

Boston ships sailed to the Grand Banks off Newfounsulad, where they caught immense numbers of cod fish. Bringing the cod ashore to salt and dry it, the Bostonians then shipped the fish to European nations such as France, Portugal, and Spain. These Roman Catholic countries provided an excellent market because the Catholic Church prohibited the eating of meat on many days of the religious calendar. In 1783 an image of the "sacred cod" was placed above the Speaker's chair in the Massachusetts House of Representatives, showing how important cod was to the making of Boston, and Massachusetts.

Given that they had a sturdy religious foundation, and a growing economic one, what else did the Bostonians need?

To their mind, they needed elbow room. Shawmut Peninsula had grown thickly settled, and the Bostonians expanded outward in the 1630s and 1640s, establishing places such as Cambridge, Newton, and Watertown. Some of them went much further afield, however; one group from Newton went all the way to northern Connecticut, to establish the first towns of that neighboring colony.

The Bostonians also desired religious uniformity. In 1637 Anne Hutchinson (1591–1643) was banished from the Massachusetts Bay Colony after she dared to hold religious discussion groups in her home (to the leading Puritans, this was both heretical and seditious). In 1660 Mary Dyer (c. 1611–1660) was hanged on Boston Common after she dared to preach the Quaker faith one too many times. Statues dedicated to both women now stand near the Massachusetts State House.

How far and wide did the Bostonians conduct their trade?

No one knows precisely why the early Bostonians were so fearless; all we can say is that they traveled the Atlantic Ocean as if it were their backyard. Boston skippers went as far south as Barbados, as far north as Newfoundland, and were very familiar with the trip to the motherland. This does not mean the voyages were danger-free (far from it), but that the Bostonians showed a great disdain for any sort of fear. It's difficult to say who holds the all-time record for Atlantic crossings, but Master John Balston (1648–1705) may be close: he seems to have made the round-trip voyage at least twice a year, for a generation and more.

An illustration of Anne Hutchinson on trial for holding religious discussion groups in her home.

Though none of these early Bostonians knew the Pacific, some of them did venture to the Indian Ocean, and quite a few of them turned pirate. Captain William Kidd was not a native Bostonian, but he was arrested in that town and sent to Old England for trial.

Was there anything that these early Bostonians feared?

One is hard-pressed to give an answer. The forests, which were thick over New England in the seventeenth century, seemed to hold more terrors for them than the open sea, but there are remarkable stories of Bostonians who escaped from Indian captivity and made their way home. It may seem a little trite to say that the early Puritans feared witches and wizards, but the time period of the Salem witch trials is evidence of the fear felt by the ministers and magistrates of the colony.

What were relations with the motherland like?

The Pilgrims and Puritans both left (some say fled) Old England because of a lack of religious freedom. Once in New England, both groups showed surprisingly little tolerance for any other religious faiths. But Pilgrims and Puritans both remained suspect where the English motherland was concerned, and few of them were sad when King Charles I lost the Civil War (1642–1651) to Parliament. After Charles I was beheaded in 1649, England became a commonwealth for a decade, under the rule of Oliver Cromwell, but the monarchy was restored in the person of King Charles II in 1660.

The Boston Puritans were not thrilled by the reestablishment of the monarchy, and they did their best to evade, and sometimes even flout the Navigation Laws passed by Parliament. During the 1670s, Bostonians faced their first tormentor from overseas; Edward Randolph was King Charles II's customs collector. During that decade, the Bostonians had other concerns, however, the foremost of them being King Philip's War, which commenced in 1675.

INDIAN WARS

One hears of the Pequot War, but it is not always clear if Boston was involved?

The Pequot War (1637–1638) was one of the earliest and among the most savage of all wars between the Indians and white settlers. In 1636 relations between the Pequot tribe and the settlers of southern Connecticut worsened, and in 1637 the conflict turned into a full-fledged war. The tiny colony of Connecticut carried out most of the actions, but Bostonians were among the officers that led the colonial soldiers.

The climactic end to the war came in present-day Mystic, Connecticut, where an Indian fort was surrounded and set aflame. The Puritans killed nearly seven hundred Indians that day. Few of the Bostonians, or Connecticut men, expressed any sadness or regret: to them, the Pequot were a savage people that hindered the growth and development of

The Pequot War pitted indigenous people against white settlers from 1637 to 1638. The Narragansett and Mohegan tribes allied themselves with the settlers to defeat the Pequot.

Puritan New England. Historians note today with some irony that the Pequot finally obtained a measure of revenge when their casino was established in Ledyard, Connecticut.

What was King Philip's War? Was Philip an Englishman or a Native American?

The grandson of Chief Massasoit, who welcomed the Pilgrims in 1620, King Philip was as Native American as they come. His English name was given him by the Pilgrims and Puritans, who employed it in disdain. They did not realize that Philip had already decided they were his mortal enemies, or that he would fight them to the death.

In June 1675 Philip led the warriors of several southern New England tribes against the Pilgrims and the Puritans. For almost fourteen months, he and his men terrorized the Massachusetts Bay Colony, taking and destroying more than a dozen towns. Boston was not attacked, partly because its inhabitants fortified The Neck, the sandy, windswept isthmus connecting the peninsula to the mainland.

What happened to King Philip?

Realizing he could conquer neither Boston nor Plymouth, Philip headed west, and conducted a very successful hit-and-run campaign in the Connecticut River valley. The town of Northfield was wiped out, and the towns of Deerfield, Northampton, and Hadley were

19

Where was "The Neck" in relation to the modern city of Boston?

If one stands right where the Leonard P. Zakim Bridge connects Boston with Charlestown and then walks south for three-quarters of a mile, he or she will stumble right upon where The Neck once was. It was in the South End, very close to the public gardens tended by many of the locals today. Bicyclists now fly along the broad streets that exist where The Neck once connected Boston to the mainland.

endangered. But the Bostonians had drawn a bead on King Philip, and their revenge came in the late winter of 1676. Three hundred troopers from Boston traveled west to attack the Indians in present-day Turners Falls, named for Captain Jonathan Turner. The Indians were nearly wiped out.

Philip escaped this disaster and continued his raids for a few months, but he was eventually run to earth in Rhode Island. After Philip was killed, his head was severed from his body and placed atop the stockade of Plymouth as a warning to other Indians.

Was there any way the Indians and Puritans could live together in peace?

Almost none. The English mindset, especially where real estate and private property were concerned, was too different from the more permissive Native American one. As a result, Puritans and Native Americans were almost fated to misunderstand and mistrust each other. One of the few exceptions to the general rule was Reverend John Eliot, who translated the Bible into Algonquian, and who established several villages of "Praying Indians" in the western suburbs of what is now the modern city of Boston.

Did Boston's economic and commercial growth continue to expand?

Until about the year 1670, Boston and Massachusetts expanded with great vigor. Boston fell into an economic recession by 1675, however, and this lasted for nearly a decade. Fewer ships called at the Puritan town, and it was more difficult for the shipmasters, as well as the sailors and rope makers, to earn a living. Of course there were some exceptions to the general rule, and it is in the 1670s and 1680s that we make our first acquaintance with that man-about-town, Samuel Sewall.

I know the name Samuel Sewall and believe there is some connection with the Salem witch trials. Was he a Bostonian?

Born in England, Samuel Sewall (1652–1730) crossed the ocean with his family at the age of ten, and he never looked back. Not only did he inherit land and houses from his parents, but he married Hannah Hull, daughter of the Massachusetts Bay Colony mintmaster. The legend that Sewall received his wife's weight in gold as her dowry can be laid to rest, but there is no doubt he benefitted from the marriage, emotionally, materially, and otherwise. What makes Sam Sewall so special, from our point of view, is that he left an extensive diary that chronicles both the public life of the colony and his personal inner life, including accounts of many of his dreams.

For example, on January 1, 1686, Sewall recorded a dream in which he witnessed Jesus Christ in the time of his ministry come to live at Boston and choose to dwell at the house of John Hull, Sewall's father-in-law. Sewall's powerful religiosity comes through in this account, and in many other parts of the diary, but he also emerges as a very human and likeable person, not at all the strict definition of the Puritan as we often imagine. The reader comes to empathize with Sewall on many levels, not least because he lost nearly three-quarters of his numerous children

Samuel Sewall was a popular judge who presided over the witch trials in Salem, a role for which he later apologized.

to disease. As a result of his prominent position as a Boston merchant, Sewall served as a judge during the Salem Witch Trials. A few years later, he issued a statement of remorse, apologizing for his involvement in the trials, the only judge to do so.

What insight does Sam Sewall provide regarding Harvard College?

Founded in 1636, Harvard College started out small, but it had big goals from the very beginning. There were lean years, as when only four scholars graduated in 1673, but there were also more successful ones, such as 1690, when nearly twenty-five obtained their degrees. Though he lived in Boston, Sewall attended almost every Harvard College commencement, and from his diary we know the weather conditions, especially because he took a barge from downtown Boston to Cambridge. Beyond the weather, though, we learn that the Latin disputations were the highlight of the ceremonies, and that plenty of beer was consumed in the late afternoon (Sewall was no teetotaler).

Where are some early Puritan cemeteries?

There are at least four major grave sites, but the most prominent is Copp's Hill Cemetery in the extreme northern part of the Old North End. Located three hundred yards north of the Old North Church and Paul Revere Square, Copp's Hill has the tomb of the Mather family.

What was the state of Harvard College toward the end of the seventeenth century?

Harvard was already *the* place to study and, in terms of higher education, it had no rival until the College of William and Mary was established in 1693. The records of the graduating classes suggest that Boston and Cambridge already had a well-established hierarchy with the names of certain families dominating both the college and the local towns. In 1699, for example, there was a Dummer, a Belcher, a Bulkley, and a Quincy (they were numbers one through four, at the top of the social standings).

LOSS OF THE CHARTER

How important was the charter of 1629 issued by King Charles I?

To Bostonians, and their country cousins, the charter of 1629 was the single most important document of the time, perhaps even the century. Signed by King Charles I, the charter was granted to the "governor and company of the Massachusetts Bay," an expression that outlived the document itself. Because King Charles did not anticipate the rapid growth of Boston or Massachusetts, he granted a rather liberal charter, which practically allowed for self-government, just so long as the laws of the Great and General Court did not conflict with those of the English motherland. To Bostonians, the charter of 1629 was the fount of their liberties.

The Old North Church of Paul Revere fame, seen from the narrow confines of Hull Street in the Old North End.

Bostonians tended to assume that the charter would always remain in existence, that they would remain forever protected from the laws and regulations of the motherland. But in the early 1680s, one sign after another pointed in the opposite direction. King Charles II—best known as the Merry Monarch—had indeed been indulgent toward Boston and New England, but the tone of his government changed over time. In 1683 Boston was served with a summons, either to submit to the king's mercy, legally speaking, or to send attorneys to defend her in London law courts.

How did Bostonians respond to the summons issued by King Charles II?

To the best of our knowledge, Bostonians were more willing to submit than were their country cousins. Men from the towns

That the Old North Church was prominent in the Revolution of 1775 is well known. What about its role in the 1680s?

Reverend Increase Mather was pastor of the Old North Church (he was simultaneously president of Harvard College). In 1688 Reverend Mather snuck out of town in disguise to escape the watchful eye of the English customs agent, Edward Randolph. Upon arriving in London, Mather importuned the king and queen to grant a new charter to Massachusetts. Upon his return in 1692, Reverend Mather was hailed as the foremost defender of Boston's liberties.

of the hinterland proved keener to resist royal authority. Perhaps Bostonians were more conscious of the threat that might be posed by the Royal Navy.

What does Sam Sewall tell us about the charter controversy?

To Sewall and other devout Puritans, loss of the Massachusetts Bay charter was akin to spiritual death. In 1684 lawyers of King Charles II revoked the charter, and in 1686, King James II sent a new royal governor, armed with a powerful commission to reshape Boston, Massachusetts, and, indeed, all of New England.

Sir Edmund Andros came ashore on December 21, 1686, bringing with him roughly sixty British soldiers (these were the first redcoats seen in Boston). Sewall was in front of the Town House (right about where Faneuil Hall stands today) when the new commission was read aloud, and it seemed to him that Massachusetts Bay was in its death throes. Over the next twelve months, Sir Edmund Andros abrogated many of the liberties of the people of Massachusetts, and even questioned the land titles of many of the early Puritans. Sam Sewall, who owned part of Hog Island (where Logan Airport stands today) had good reason for concern.

Was there any hope? Was there any hero who could perhaps change the situation?

Sam Sewall hoped that Sir William Phips (1651–1695) would be that man. Born on the coast of Maine, Phips came to Boston in his twenties, and rose in a spectacular fashion. In 1687, he found the wreck of a Spanish treasure galleon, and after bringing up thirty tons of silver, he sailed to London where he was knighted by a grateful King James II. If there was anyone with the special combination of brains and brawn to restore the Massachusetts charter, it was Sir William.

Events moved faster than anyone anticipated, however. In November 1688, William and Mary, the Prince and Princess of Orange, crossed the English Channel from Holland and ejected her father, King James II, from the throne of England. When Bostonians learned that Old England had carried out its so-called Glorious Revolution, they resolved to accomplish something similar. The stage was set for Boston's first revolution.

23

What was the Boston Revolt of 1689?

Whether one calls it a revolt or a coup, it took about nine hours. On April 18, 1689, Bostonians rose against the governor, Sir Edmund Andros. They knew that his sponsor, King James II, had been removed from the British throne, and it seemed a good bet that the new monarchs, King William and Queen Mary, would approve their action. Even so, it required some nerve to challenge the royal governor, who was backed by about one hundred redcoats and the HMS *Rose,* a frigate in Boston Harbor.

Amazingly, the entire episode transpired without the loss of a single life. Captain John George, the frigate commander, was arrested while ashore, and the HMS *Rose* yielded without a fight. Sir Edmund Andros hung on at Fort Hill—one of the three original hills of Shawmut Peninsula—till mid-afternoon; then he, too, surrendered. All of his counselors were in custody by the end of the day. Boston—and Massachusetts—proudly sent word to England that they had overthrown Sir Edmund and asked for re-confirmation of their old political charter.

How did William and Mary feel about Bostonians taking matters into their own hands in this fashion?

The king and queen never went on record. They left it to their high judges and coun-selors to sort out the matter. In the end, Sir Edmund and all his people were exonerated of the many charges against them, but none of them ever returned to Massachusetts in any positions of authority. Boston, and the Bay colony, had to wait while the king and queen made up their minds about the charter issue.

In the year that followed the revolution—or the one-day coup, as some call it—Bostonians were eager, even anxious, to demonstrate their loyalty to William and Mary. When they learned that England and Holland had gone to war with France, Bostonians decided to prove their loyalty by undertaking a military campaign in William and Mary's honor. In May 1690, about seven hundred Boston militia—led by Sir William Phips—captured French Port Royal in present-day Nova Scotia. Emboldened by their success, the Bostonians planned an even greater effort, hoping to conquer Québec City.

One often hears of Nantasket, but it seldom appears on the maps. How close is it to Boston?

As the crow flies, Nantasket is less than a dozen miles from downtown Boston, but the curve, or arc of the land means it is twice that distance by land. One has to travel south into Dorchester, make a hard "left" or turn to the east to arrive at Nantasket Beach, which is almost four miles long. Nantasket is a quiet place today, but in the late nineteenth century it was the place to go swim, and scores of thousands of Bostonians went there on muggy days.

Nova Scotia is one thing, but the City of Québec is quite another. What on earth convinced the Bostonians they could pull off so grand a feat?

One has to remember that the Bostonians had never been shy. They viewed themselves as the "city on a hill," there to show the rest of the world how to conduct itself. So in the summer of 1690 Boston collected thirty-two ships of various shapes and sizes and placed 2,200 men aboard. Sir William Phips commanded this, the greatest enterprise New England ever attempted, and the ships sailed from Nantasket on August 9, 1690.

When was the first American newspaper printed?

Publick Occurrences issued its first edition on September 25, 1690, while the soldiers were off in Canada. Printed by Benjamin Harris, the four-page newspaper was the first attempt ever made in North America. The opening words tell us something about the times, hinting at the idea that the political quarrels of our own time are nothing new: "That something may be done towards the curing, or at least the charming of that spirit of lying, which prevails among us." The Puritan authorities did not like some of the language employed, however, and they stopped Harris from ever printing a second edition. Boston had to wait until 1704 to see its first continuing newspaper, the *Boston Gazette*.

What happened to the Bostonian expedition to Canada?

Around November 20, 1690, Sir William Phips (1651–1695) returned. The expedition had come close to success, almost within a hairsbreadth, but as the saying goes, close only counts in horseshoes and hand grenades. The Bostonians failed to conquer Québec City, and perhaps five hundred men were lost, from battle wounds and disease (smallpox struck especially hard on the return voyage). Four of the thirty-two vessels were lost. The Massachusetts General Court hurriedly printed paper currency, the first seen in North America, to pay the costs of the expedition.

Many people blamed Phips, but he did not seem downcast or dismayed. He quickly left Boston for London, where he somehow, almost miraculously, persuaded King William and Queen Mary that this expedition was but the first, and that with help from England, Boston would eventually succeed in conquering Canada. Equally amazing is that William and Mary named Phips royal governor. The king and

Sir William Phips was the first governor of the Province of Massachusetts Bay, serving from 1692 to 1694.

queen did not restore the old charter—that of 1629. Instead, they drew up a new one, the Charter of 1691, under which Massachusetts was governed as a royal province rather than a semi-independent colony.

Phips seems like a one-of-a-kind fellow, a continual winner. Did he ever fall from grace?

He did indeed. When he and Reverend Increase Mather—leader of the very influential family of pastors and Harvard presidents—returned to Boston in 1692, they found the province in an uproar over the Salem Witch incidents. Phips was confounded by the accusations of witchcraft, and he left most of the decisions to a special court appointed to handle the matter. Sam Sewall was one of the judges that heard the cases, and in the end, sentenced twenty men and women to death.

Phips did not receive all the blame for the witchcraft outbreak, but he earned demerits for his high-handed manner. Phips ignored the Great and General Court, and he even got into two known fracases in downtown Boston. Once he used his cane to thump a royal official. It came as little surprise when William and Mary summoned him to London to defend against charges of misconduct. Phips sailed to London, apparently confident he would meet and beat the charges, but he died of a bad fever shortly after arriving in the English capital.

War, failure, expeditions, witchcraft … this sounds like a truly crazy time. Did Bostonians recognize it as such?

They did. Phips was an embarrassment to the more dignified Puritan leaders, and no one could sort out or explain the witchcraft episode (people continue to attempt to do so today). The war with French Canada did not go well, and numerous Massachusetts residents were captured and taken north, to be held for ransom. To top it all off, many Bostonians were displeased with the Charter of 1691, which, they asserted, did not provide them with the liberties they had previously enjoyed.

Could things get any worse? That is a natural question that emerges from this period. And the one way in which matters did get worse was the weather. The 1690s saw some of the coldest, most ferocious winters in all of Boston history. Many believe 1697 was the worst. Through this decade, which Reverend Cotton Mather labeled the "dolorous decade," the economic recession continued. It was with little sadness that Bostonians witnessed the end of the seventeenth century, and Sam Sewall penned their sentiments in some of the most memorable words:

Once more! Our God, vouchsafe to shine

Tame thou the rigor of our clime.

Make haste with thy impartial light

And terminate this long dark night.

Did the beginning of the eighteenth century improve anything for Boston?

It did, but the improvements came rather slowly. One of the first and most noticeable changes came in 1705, when the streets received official names for the first time. From the famous map of Boston, drawn in 1722, we see that King Street, Province Street, and Long Wharf all have their proper names, and that the peninsula has taken on a more organized appearance. By then, Boston had a population of between eight and nine thousand folk.

Trade, too, made a strong comeback early in the eighteenth century. The foundation for quite a few fortunes was laid, with Bostonians trading lumber, horses, and mules (three of the favorite exports) for sugar, molasses, and rum. Of course, it's important to say that slaves were also part of the bargain.

Do we know the street names of early Boston?

We know some of them, but a good number went unnamed (at least to our knowledge) until early in the eighteenth century. Tremont Street, which comes from "Trimountain," for the three hills of Boston, was named as early as the 1630s, and King Street just a bit later. But we turn to the record book of Benjamin Franklin, the uncle of the famous printer, philosopher, and scientist, to obtain more knowledge. Around 1706, Franklin made a long list of the names that had been approved by the town's selectmen. Among them were names that we might expect, such as Sun Street and Long Wharf, but also less-known names like Bridle Lane, Cow Path, and so forth, were given to various streets. These names lasted until the time of the American Revolution, when most were renamed in honor of heroes of that conflict.

One often hears about African Americans in the later, or subsequent, history of Boston. But how many of them lived in the early town?

Far more than we used to think. The town fathers were skilled at writing blacks out of the record, and referring to them, politely, as "servants" rather than slaves. A lot of research has been done in recent decades, however, and we believe blacks represented at least ten percent, perhaps as much as fifteen percent, of the total population of Boston. Of these people, less than three dozen were free (they show up in the records). The great majority were household slaves, owned by ministers, merchants, and magistrates.

How often do the African Americans of Boston show up in the newspapers?

Boston did not have its first permanent newspaper until 1704, but the town had many "broadsides," or broadsheets, released to the public. One of the most telling, where African Americans are concerned, was the "Rules for the Society of Negroes," printed in 1693. The document begins as follows:

"We the miserable children of Adam and of Noah, thankfully admiring and accepting the free-grace of God that offers to save us from our miseries, by the Lord Jesus Christ, freely resolve with his help, to become the servants of that Glorious Lord. And

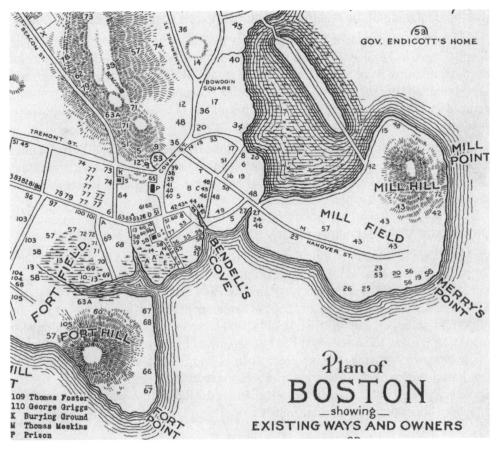

A detail of a 1635 map of Boston.

that we may be assisted in the service of our Heavenly Master, we now join together in a society, wherein the following rules are to be observed." The rules suggest that control of the African American population may have been as important to the (presumably) white organizers as any religious impulse.

How can a place that is so proud of its antislavery past reconcile the fact that plenty of slaves once lived there?

That is one of the toughest questions for any Bostonian. The city, in the mid-nineteenth century, would do many fine things for the cause of abolition, but the Puritan town, in the early eighteenth century, floated partly on the labor of black slaves. Bostonians are proud, and they are quick to point out that the first anti-slavery pamphlet was printed by one of their own. Once more, Sam Sewall plays a leading role.

When he watched the court trial of Adam, a black slave of John Saffin, Sewall was moved to pen *The Selling of Joseph*, a pamphlet printed in Boston in 1700. Sewall did not come right out and say that slavery was evil, but he called for greater racial understanding and he certainly pointed in the direction of eventual emancipation.

How can one person—Sam Sewall—be involved in so many aspects of the life of one town?

Anyone that studies Sam Sewall's life story comes away amazed by the variety of his activities. He was a member of the governor's council, a judge at the Salem Witch Trials, a confidante of Governor Simon Bradstreet, a very successful man of business, a good husband, and father to fifteen children, many of whom did not make it to adulthood. A close examination of Sewall's life suggests that Boston—with its eight or nine thousand people—may have been precisely the right size for someone like Sewall, who came to know most of the townspeople by sight and name. He was the first of the great Boston diarists, and though many others would later come, none of them would know the place as intimately as he did.

Was Boston involved in any more military campaigns against French Canada?

It was inevitable that Boston would play a leading role in Queen Anne's War, which began in 1702. Soon after learning that war was declared between England and France, Bostonians learned that the little town of Deerfield in western Massachusetts was conquered and sacked, and that more than one hundred people were taken to Canada as captives. Governor Joseph Dudley played a major role in ransoming many of these captives, who were returned to Boston by ship. Upon arriving safely at Boston, Deerfield pastor Reverend John Williams gave an inspired sermon that later became the title of his bestselling book, *The Redeemed Captive, Returning to Zion*. Captivity narratives became one of the most popular of all publications in eighteenth-century Boston. Beyond this, however, Boston also became involved in a major attempt to conquer Québec City.

We sometimes hear of the Four American Kings and wonder who they were. Did they come to Boston?

In 1710 four Native American sachems—three of them Mohawk and one Mahican— came first to Boston and then to London, where they appeared before Queen Anne. These Indians went to ask the English queen to help in the reduction of Canada, which, they claimed, would benefit everyone involved. The immediate connection between the four sachems and Boston has to do with the military campaign of 1711, but it's also possible—though not proven—that the popularity of the four "American Kings" was linked to the eventual use of Mohawk clothing at the Boston Tea Party.

Duly impressed by the chiefs, Queen Anne sent a major British task force, which arrived in Boston Harbor in July 1711. Admiral Sir Hovenden Walker already had five British regiments, but he took on nearly one thousand Massachusetts militiamen, and the entire fleet sailed for Canada. Seven of the ships came to grief on the shoals near the

Queen Anne was the monarch of Great Britain and Ireland at the time of the War of the Spanish Succession, which was sometimes referred to as Queen Anne's War.

entrance of the St. Lawrence River, and nearly seven hundred men were drowned. Rather than continue, Admiral Walker called it quits. He sailed to England, where the final tragedy occurred when his flagship blew up in Portsmouth Harbor, shortly after arrival. Bostonians long remembered the disastrous summer of 1711, and it lowered their opinion of the British military.

What were conditions like as Queen Anne's War came to an end?

In 1712 Bostonians learned that the second of the so-called French and Indian Wars was over, and that England had gained title to Nova Scotia and Newfoundland. Bostonians, and their country cousins, did not see any immediate profit, or improvement in their lives, however, and there was some sourness in British-American relations. Queen Anne was, at least, a native-born English queen, and when she was succeeded by her German—and German-speaking—brother, King George I, many colonists wrote off the English motherland (at least privately).

Boston had plenty of issues and concerns of its own. In 1721 the town was visited by its third major epidemic of smallpox, and this one was much worse than the previous. More than a thousand Bostonians died of the disease, and many others picked up and left town, never to return. It was during this, the great smallpox epidemic of 1721, that Boston implemented its first attempts to control disease.

Is Boylston Street named for Dr. Boylston?

There have been so many Boylstons in the history of Boston that it is difficult to say, but one can argue that Boylston Street should be named for Dr. Zabdiel Boylston, who undertook the first inoculations for smallpox. In 1722, Boylston joined forces with Reverend Cotton Mather. Together, they attempted to persuade Bostonians of all social classes to receive inoculation, which meant inserting some of the pus into a section of the forearm or shoulder. For his pains, Cotton Mather received a handmade bomb, or grenade, thrown through his window. The inoculations were a remarkable success, however; only one-fifth as many people who had the inoculation contracted smallpox, and those that did had a much greater chance of survival. Bostonians of this period were deeply conservative, and it took another two generations for inoculation to become the rule rather than the exception.

How did the Bostonians get around?

They used nearly all the devices and means we associate with that period: on foot, on horseback in carriages and wagons. Boats of all shapes and sizes were perhaps the most important means of transport, however. It was easier to cross the Charles River by long-boat and then walk to Harvard College than to go around. And the first stable bridge across the Charles River had not been built. We see, therefore, the interesting career of Reverend Increase Mather. He was pastor of Boston's Old North Church—in the North End—but he was also president of Harvard College. In his contract, it was written that a ferry should be continually at his disposal so he would not have to go on horseback.

Did the early Bostonians enjoy life?

They certainly did. The work hours of a summer and spring day were long by our standards, but almost everyone relaxed a bit in winter, working shorter hours, and spending more leisure time indoors. From Samuel Sewall's diary we learn that many upper-class Bostonians enjoyed beer and ale, and the chances are that their working-class contemporaries did the same. One holiday that the Bostonians did not celebrate was Christmas. Believing it a Popish invention, they chose to treat December 25 as any other day in the calendar. And while we are on the subject of the Pope, it's worth discussing what Pope's Day meant to the Bostonians.

The English celebrated November 5 as Guy Fawkes Day, the celebration of a failed Catholic attempt to blow up the Houses of Parliament. Bostonians celebrated it as Pope's Day, meaning one long extravagant festival to ridicule the Pope and Roman Catholi-

An Italian religious house in the Old North End.

cism. On a typical Pope's Day, the gangs of the Old North End and Old South End met each other in mock combat, while gunpowder was exploded in the streets. The Pope was often carried about in effigy. Of course, these celebrations sometimes went too far, and in 1764 one gang member was killed.

Where was the young Benjamin Franklin in all of this?

Born in Boston in 1706, Franklin was the youngest son of an Englishman who crossed the Atlantic in 1683. The Franklin family was a large one, and young Benjamin ended up an apprentice to his elder brother James, who was editor and printer of the *New-England Courant*. By the age of fourteen, Ben Franklin was expert at employing ink on the printing press, and he contributed a number of essays of his own—under the pen name of "Silence Dogood." The elder brother beat the younger one on many occasions, and in 1723, Ben Franklin skipped town, heading first to New York and then Philadelphia. The rest, as they say, is history.

One can, of course, ask the poignant question: How could Boston have lost the most talented of its sons, a boy who later became the most famous man of his era? The same question will later be posed in regard to Babe Ruth. How could Boston have traded that outsized talent to the New York Yankees, and thereby ensure its own defeat in numerous baseball seasons? The answer is that Bostonians do not always treat their own very kindly, and they sometimes expel those that would render them the best service.

What did Franklin have to say about Harvard College?

We believe he had mixed feelings where Harvard was concerned. Before the age of eleven, he'd hoped to attend Harvard one day: this hope was dashed when his father apprenticed him, first to the candle-making trade, and then to his brother the printer. As "Silence Dogood" (the pen name he used for essays he wrote for the *Boston Gazette*), Franklin

What is the earliest writing from Ben Franklin's hand?

To the best of our knowledge, it is a charming, if trite, section of poetry on the topic of Edward Teach, the pirate known as Blackbeard.

Will you hear of a bloody battle,
Lately fought upon the seas,
It will make your ears to rattle,
And your admiration cease;
Have you heard of Teach the Rover,
And his knavery upon the Main;
How of gold he was a lover,
How he loved all ill got gain.

heaped scorn on the pomposity of those that believed Harvard would turn a common person into a scholar. Franklin wrote:

> At length I entered upon a spacious plain in the midst of which was erected a large and stately edifice: It was to this that a great company of youths from all parts of the country were going: so stepping in among the crowd, I passed on with them, and presently arrived at the gate. The passage was kept by two sturdy porters named Riches and Poverty, and the latter obstinately refused to give entrance to any who had not first gained the favor of the former; so that I observed, many who came even to the very gate, were obliged to travel back as ignorant as they came, for want of this necessary qualification.

Did Franklin talk about his youthful days in Boston?

Yes, and his comments are a fascinating mixture of nostalgia and disdain. He modeled his own early career on that of Reverend Cotton Mather, the industrious Bostonian who penned roughly 450 books, pamphlets, and placards during his amazing career. Franklin admired many aspects of Puritan Boston, but he never regretted the move to Philadelphia; on the contrary, he believed it necessary to break from one's roots in order to achieve one's full potential.

How much do we know about the streets of Boston in the early eighteenth century?

Thanks to the famous "Bonner Map," made by Captain John Bonner in 1722, we have a rather good idea of the streets, the cow paths, and even the docks and wharves. We know, for example, that Orange Street, named for Prince William of Orange, was the longest street in town, running all the way from The Neck to the downtown area. Boston Common was larger in the early eighteenth century than it is today: it sprawled over the northwest side of town. The North Mill Dam ran from the Old North End to what is now Beacon Street: the Mill Pond was later filled in, adding to the size of the downtown. King Street, which had some of the most fashionable houses, ran straight from downtown to Long Wharf, which easily dwarfed the other thirty wharves of the town. The Old North End was the most densely populated section of town with Salem, North, and Ship Streets dominating the whole (their twenty-first-century descendants do the same today).

Boats, ships, and pleasure vessels are shown on the Bonner Map, indicating that Boston was the most nautical of all the towns in colonial North America. Boston was still in first place in terms of maritime activity, but it would soon lose this role, coming in third, behind New York and Philadelphia. But when one examines the Bonner Map, he or she almost inevitably sighs for what once was: a tight-knit town in which almost everyone was known and recognized, and where people got around quite well without cars, taxis, or subways.

Does the Burgis Map show us the same things as the famous Bonner Map?

No. The Burgis Map was executed about the same time, but it shows primarily the harbor and merchant fleet, rather than the town itself. One clue to the map's importance lies in its title, however: "A North East View of the Great Town of Boston." The artist clearly wishes us to think of Boston as London in the New World, and the types of boats that are sketched, while not unrealistic, make Boston Harbor seem rather like the River Thames in downtown London.

What about Boston Light? When did it come into being?

Constructed in 1716, Boston Light was the first permanent beacon in any of the original Thirteen Colonies. Three years later, a cannon was placed near the lighthouse so the keeper could warn vessels in a fog. The first known illustration of Boston Light was executed in 1723: the portrait shows a ten-gun sloop passing between the viewer and the lighthouse, which looks to be around fifty feet high. Situated on Little Brewster Island, Boston Light served its

Boston Light in Boston Harbor is the oldest lighthouse in the United States.

purpose very well until the American Revolution, when it was burned twice (once by each side!). When the new stone edifice was erected in 1784, it was meant to be permanent and though Boston Light is not manned today, radar continues to warn sailors of the many dangers involved in entering Boston Harbor.

Was there any movement to incorporate Boston as a city?

We sometimes call eighteenth-century Boston a city, but that's because we don't take the terminology of the time seriously. In truth, Boston was a town, and was run by a town meeting style of government, the same which had been established in the 1630s. Just to demonstrate that Bostonians were conflicted on the subject, a pamphlet circulated in Boston in the year 1714. Entitled "A Dialogue between a Boston Man and a Country Man," this pamphlet was one of a kind.

The Boston Man—as he is identified throughout the pamphlet—speaks against the idea of incorporation, saying that the town and its people will be inundated by new costs and charges. He concludes his argument by declaring that the "ancient rights, and undoubted property of our voting at town meetings" will be taken away. The Country Man—as he is identified—replies that any negative aspects will be overshadowed by the streamlined efficiency that will take place. The Country Man even speaks words on the subject of immigration (perhaps the first ones to enter the American record). "They will be able by this to regulate your town better than now it is, and to take notice who comes into the town; and to let in or keep out who they please."

SCIENCE AND RELIGION

We know that the Puritans were a deeply religious people. How did they feel about science?

Generally speaking, the early Bostonians were deeply practical, and they therefore embraced the aspects of science that seemed likely to help them. There were occasions when they cut off their noses to spite their faces, however.

Bostonians feared two things more than anything else: death from fire and death from drowning. The town endured roughly six "great fires" between its founding and the 1750s. But in the 1720s, Boston experienced another great fear, and this one came from the appearance of smallpox. Dr. Zabdiel Boylston attempted to inoculate the population, and his methods clearly showed great efficacy, but many Bostonians rejected inoculation as a newfangled and dangerous business. Reverend Cotton Mather, who supported Dr. Boylston, spoke out loudly and often: as a result, someone threw a handmade bomb, or grenade, through his window!

What did the occasional English visitors think of Boston and its people?

John Josselyn and John Dunton penned the most noteworthy descriptions of Boston. Both men marveled at the industry of Bostonians and poked fun at the hidebound customs of the Puritans. To be sure, it is unfair to compare Boston with a population of 12,000, to London, which had 750,000. But it's true that Boston sometimes had a deeply conservative appearance, meaning that its people did not believe in change.

John Dunton commented that Bostonians liked their beer and ale so much that the taverns were the most important places in town. He did not write very much about Harvard College, but had he spent time in Cambridge, Dunton would have witnessed the rise of a truly fine college, one that combined the best of the new and old styles of learning. Harvard commencement was held on the first Sunday in July in those days, and it usually was a festive event with everyone that was anyone in Boston taking a boat across the Charles for the occasion.

How did Boston fare during the long peace that came after 1713?

Queen Anne's War ended in a draw with England and France stepping back from what had been a truly fratricidal conflict. Massachusetts, indeed most of New England, benefited from the end of the war, but Boston went into a financial funk from which it took decades to recover. It's difficult to nail down the precise reason, but the appearance of Manhattan and Philadelphia as trade rivals had something to do with it. Boston skippers still took horses, mules, and lumber to the Caribbean, and returned with sugar, molasses, and slaves, but the profits were smaller than in the past.

35

Speaking of slavery, how many slaves lived in eighteenth-century Boston?

Far more than we might think. Slavery was never a big business in Boston, but the upper-class families nearly all had at least one slave to cook and clean. Even at this early stage of the game, Bostonians had highly developed sensibilities, and they referred to these African Americans as *servants*, rather than slaves. There is no doubt as to their real status, however.

Blacks also appear in the public records. "Jeremy the Negro," as he was labeled in the town reports, may have been the first African American appointed to a position of public trust. For several consecutive years, he was chosen as one of the four official chimney sweeps for the town. Jeremy was a free person, and there may have been a few dozen such in Boston in the 1720s. They were far outnumbered by those that were slaves, however.

How did Bostonians feel about King George I and King George II?

The Hanoverian Dynasty was a German family that came to London in 1714. King George I spoke almost no English, and when his son became King George II in 1727, little improvement was seen. The English, back home, treated the new Hanoverians with a mixture of fondness and contempt, but the Bostonians had little sense of there being any difference. To them, the king or queen was a distant figure at best. One of the few occasions on which this changed was when the king, Parliament, or both attempted to regulate the colonies in terms of taxes and trade.

The Molasses Act of 1733 was one of the first attempts by the motherland to collect revenue from the colonies. Bostonians were strongly affected by this because sugar and molasses formed an important part of their trade. But during the short reign of King George I, and the relatively long reign of George II, Bostonians did their best to avoid and evade taxes rather than show any outright defiance.

What influence did the motherland have on religion in Boston and Massachusetts?

Up to about the year 1730, Bostonians and their country cousins did not care a whit about what the motherland did or did not do in terms of religion. But the Puritan influence, which carried Boston such a long and powerful distance, began to wane in the third decade of the eighteenth century. Many reverend pastors confessed that attendance was slack, and that they sometimes felt as if they were skating on ice, as far as relationships with their parishioners were concerned.

The big change came in the early 1740s. First there was a religious revival in western Massachusetts. Reverend Jonathan Edwards of Northampton, which is located in the Connecticut River valley, witnessed and testified to an extraordinary new spirit among his parishioners. This, often called the first Great Awakening in American religion, reached Boston in due time. But the more dramatic, and powerful, event was the appearance of the Reverend George Whitefield (1714–1770), who made his first visit to Boston in the autumn of 1740.

Why was an outsider such as Reverend George Whitefield given such importance?

He had sensational talent as a preacher. Most Puritan—perhaps Yankee is now the more appropriate term—ministers preached to congregations of two to three hundred people. Reverend Whitefield, by contrast, reveled in preaching out of doors and to truly large crowds. We believe there were ten thousand people at his first outdoor sermon in Boston, and that he may even have attracted a larger crowd in Philadelphia. Without really trying to accomplish it, Whitefield became the first intercolonial uniting force of the eighteenth century. The colonies were by now full of Quakers, Baptists, Scots-Irish, and German settlers. One of the few uniting experiences—enjoyed by people from all social and religious groups—was that of listening to Whitefield preach on the overwhelming *mercy* of God.

This was a relatively new message for Bostonians, more accustomed to hearing of God's overwhelming power and his righteousness. Whitefield struck the right chord, however, and when he returned to England after nearly a year of preaching, America was not the same. A leavening had taken place, and the old-line Boston Puritans never again had the power and influence of an earlier time.

How strange that an outsider could have such influence! Did Whitefield return?

He did. Whitefield and Jonathan Edwards, between them, had ignited a transatlantic phenomenon. Whitefield returned to the colonies six times over the next thirty years, and when he made his last voyage, he was buried in Newburyport, forty miles north of Boston.

Do we have any idea of how long-lasting Whitefield's influence was?

We feel confident in saying that he influenced a majority of all American colonists between 1740 and 1770, and that hundreds of thousands of colonists met him in person. The extent of his influence can be seen in his relationship with Benjamin Franklin, who by 1740 was one of the lead-

The Reverend George Whitefield, who happened to be cross-eyed, was a noted minister who was instrumental in spreading the Great Awakening in New England.

ing men of Philadelphia. Franklin was a self-acknowledged skeptic in matters of religion, but he was deeply impressed by Whitefield.

How did Boston fare during the 1740s, which some people called the era of Whitefield?

Economically, Boston faced difficult times. The population rose to about 14,000, but plateaued there, and saw no visible increase for some time thereafter. Competition from other coastal towns inside and outside of New England, cut into the profits of the Boston merchants. One of the outstanding changes of the decade was seen in the creation of Faneuil Hall, still known today as one of the most popular and attractive of all places in Boston.

Andrew Faneuil was the son of a Huguenot merchant who escaped France during a period of religious persecution and settled in Boston. Andrew built a large establishment close to Long Wharf, and when his financial situation called for retrenchment, he asked the town to take Faneuil Hall as a free gift. Bostonians are known for prickly, even suspicious behavior; even so, it was astounding that the special Town Meeting approved the gift by the narrow margin of seven votes! One wonders if the subsequent public history of Boston might have been different if the voters had rejected the measure.

Did the rise of George Whitefield come at about the same time (1740s) as that of the House of Hancock?

Thomas Hancock was a very successful merchant who raised himself by his bootstraps to become the richest man in town (he profited mightily from the trade in food stuffs and military stores during King George's War). Not having any son to leave the business to, Hancock eventually adopted his nephew, John Hancock, and the family firm was on its way to prosperity and fame.

How did King George's War affect Boston?

One might think the Bostonians would be blasé where war was concerned, but this turned out to be false. When the news arrived that King George II of England had exchanged declarations of war with King Louis XV of France, Massachusetts was eager to strike a blow on behalf of the Hanoverian monarchy. Two birds could be felled by the same stone, some merchants argued because the fortified town of Louisbourg, on Cape Breton Island, competed with Boston in the lumber and cod fish trade. Governor William Shirley was already popular with the people of Massachusetts, but he went one step further by recommending a naval expedition to subdue Louisbourg. On previous occasions, Boston had supplied most of the men and materiel, but this time the entire Province of Massachusetts—which then included Maine—came forward. Farmers and fishermen from all parts of the province volunteered, and numerous merchants offered their ships to the flotilla.

In March 1745, more than one hundred vessels sailed from Boston, carrying more than four thousand men and a great deal of military supplies. The Yankee fleet rendezvoused with a British naval squadron, commanded by Admiral Sir Peter Warren off the coast of Nova Scotia, and the combined Anglo-American force sailed on to assault Louisbourg.

The year 1745 seems early in the life of Boston and Massachusetts to launch such an ambitious undertaking as the assault on Louisbourg. Were there any foul-ups?

There were quite a few, in fact. Not only did certain men and officers refuse to serve under those from other towns and counties, but there was quite a deal of competition between the sailors of the British men-of-war and the American transport ships. Even so, the force landed in May, at the cost of only a few men wounded. The French knew that Americans were coming, but their preparations were, if anything, even more delayed.

How long did it take to subdue Louisbourg?

The siege ran for just about forty days, during which the French garrison resisted stubbornly. The Anglo-American force had too much firepower, however, and when the Yankee soldiers captured the so-called Grand Battery and turned its guns against the fortress, Louisbourg was doomed. On June 17, 1745, the French garrison hauled down its flag, which was replaced by the Union Jack. The extremely audacious expedition had succeeded.

Town after town, up and down the eastern coast of North America, celebrated as the good news arrived. One newspaper after another ran special extras, singing the praises of Governor Shirley and Major-General William Pepperrell (both men were soon knighted as a result of their efforts). Two sour notes were sounded, however. First, the British Royal Navy men took a hefty share of the prize money, and second, many Mas-

A c. 1747 painting of the siege of Louisbourg in 1745. Boston forces aided the English to capture the French garrison. Interestingly, it would not be that many years before the Americans and French were allies.

sachusetts men died from smallpox while guarding the captured fort over the next two years. Many Yankees had a bitter taste in their mouth, especially when Louisbourg was returned to France under the Treaty of Aix-la-Chapelle in 1748.

Did the capture of Louisbourg better Boston's economic prospects, at least?

Even this failed to materialize. Louisbourg was out of economic action for several years, but Boston did not see any corresponding rise in its own wealth. Many Massachusetts men declared the entire Louisbourg enterprise a debacle, and they vowed to have nothing further to do with any military events that included the British. Then too, Boston saw several riots against British press gangs in the autumn of 1747. All told, the 1740s were a decade that witnessed Boston growing further apart from the English motherland.

FORESHADOWING
THE REVOLUTION

Most of us know Boston either as "The Cradle of Liberty" or "The Athens of America." Where did the phrase "Cradle of Violence" come from?

Historian Russell Bourne issued his book *Cradle of Violence* in 2006, and discussions of early maritime history have been better informed ever since. Bourne saw it as his job to free the Boston waterfront mobs from the negative impression most people had of them; he successfully argued that the Boston waterfront mobs were, in fact, vital to the winning of American independence. In his book, Bourne presented his first case, about the Knowles Riots of 1747, to readers who had never heard the story before.

Who was Commodore Knowles and why were there riots in 1747?

In 1747 Commodore John Knowles commanded the British vessels in and around Boston. Many of these ships had been involved in the Louisbourg expedition of 1745, and bad feelings lingered, especially between the Royal Navy sailors and the people of the Old North End. In November 1747, Knowles learned that thirty of his men had deserted, and, furious that they found shelter in Boston, he sent press gangs right into the heart of the town. The press gangs succeeded initially—they brought back forty-six men to replace the thirty that were lost—but they also evoked the anger of the Boston mob. Perhaps three hundred men participated in the initial resistance, but they were joined by perhaps two thousand others. Governor Shirley had to take refuge on Castle Island.

Not surprisingly, Commodore Knowles threatened to bombard the town, and there is no doubt he would have singled out the North End for special punishment. Governor Shirley was able to dissuade him, and Knowles sailed away a few weeks later, but lingering fears and suspicions developed. Was the Boston mob truly this unruly? Why was the civil authority unable to deal with the situation?

Was there any way to differentiate a native Bostonian—in around the year 1750—from a recent arrival?

True Bostonians claimed they could tell the difference in a heartbeat (some of their descendants make that claim today). The native Bostonian tended to be cool on first acquaintance, but if he or she became a friend, it was usually as a friend for life. The average Bostonian tended to be more concerned with nautical matters than with agricultural ones, and to be keen on learning everything possible about what transpired in other parts of the Atlantic world.

Where was Benjamin Franklin during the 1750s?

Franklin was by now the leading citizen of Quaker Philadelphia, and he had long since shaken the dust of Boston from his boots. Franklin was farsighted enough, however, to see that the calendar change might be followed by other innovations, and he was one of the first of all colonial Americans to propose a colonial congress. Franklin's proposal, known as the Albany Plan of Union, was debated at Albany in the summer of 1754, but was not brought to a vote.

How did Bostonians feel about some type of intercolonial government by the 1750s?

Two generations earlier, they would almost certainly have welcomed one. But by 1754, Boston was the third-largest town on the East Coast, behind New York and Philadel-

How and why did Boston change from the Julian to the Gregorian calendar?

By 1750, the various English towns up and down the East Coast were in closer touch than ever before. England wished to standardize its relations with the American colonies and to ensure better regulation of what happened in America. One measure adopted as a means towards that end was the change from the Julian to the Gregorian calendar.

The Gregorian calendar had been used in France, Spain, and other European nations since 1582, but the Protestant nations, and their colonies, rejected it as a Popish innovation. In September 1752, Great Britain and her American colonies finally moved from the Julian to the Gregorian calendar. The difference between the two calendars was only eleven minutes per year, but when this was multiplied by the thousand-odd years since the Julian calendar was adopted, it was found necessary to "drop" eleven days from the Protestant calendar. September 3, 1752, was followed by September 14, and many people—on both sides of the Atlantic—protested, saying that they wanted their eleven days back.

phia, and it no longer seemed certain that Boston would be the number-one political leader in such a union. Bostonians, therefore, were less keen on the idea of an inter-colonial government at this time than in the past. Then too, the crisis that brought such considerations to the fore soon resulted in the French and Indian War, the fourth and last of these colonial conflicts.

THE GREAT WAR FOR EMPIRE

How many names are there for these various colonial wars?

There are a great many. King William's War (1689–1697) was known in Europe as the War of the League of Augsburg. Queen Anne's War (1702–1713) was called the War of the Spanish Succession. And the French and Indian War (1754–1763; the Great War for Empire is, perhaps, a better name) was called the Seven Years' War by Europeans.

How did the French and Indian War—the fourth and final colonial war—begin?

The French had repeatedly entered the Ohio River valley, showing a desire to dominate what was then the heartland of the colonized areas of North America. In 1754 George Washington—then all of twenty-two years—led a group of Virginia militia into western Pennsylvania to eject the French. The Pennsylvania Quakers were pacifists, and Virginia claimed the right to dispute the area with the French. In May 1754, Washington fought and won the first skirmish of the French and Indian War; but in July of that year he was cut off and forced to surrender to the French. Washington was soon paroled, and his deeds had the effect of bringing on the final stage of the great colonial conflict.

Did Bostonians know the name of Washington?

In 1753 almost no one outside George Washington's family circle knew the name. By the end of 1754, most newspaper readers throughout the Atlantic world knew the name of Washington. Not only was the skirmish and Washington's surrender reported, but the text of his surrender, at Fort Necessity, was reprinted in many newspapers on both sides of the Atlantic. Bostonians did not realize that this was but the first time they would hear of this man, whose actions would play so large a part in their efforts in the winning of independence and the building of the nation.

In 1755 King George II's government sent two British regiments under General Edward Braddock. The troops landed in Maryland and proceeded by slow stages to western Pennsylvania. Braddock took on George Washington as an aide-de-camp, but did not listen to the young man's advice where wilderness warfare was concerned. On July 8, 1755, the French and their Indian allies ambushed Braddock and his men on the banks of the Monongahela River, just shy of present-day Pittsburgh. Braddock's defeat was a colossal failure for the British military in North America; for the next three years, many frontier towns, from New England to the Carolinas, were endangered.

How were Bostonians involved in General Edward Braddock's defeat by the French in 1755?

In the summer of 1755, even before Braddock's defeat became common knowledge, a New England force helped capture French Fort Beauséjour in present-day Nova Scotia. The Anglo-American conquest led to the expulsion of many Acadian settlers of Nova Scotia, some of whom ended up in Louisiana and became known as "Cajuns." Boston was also involved in the sending of troops to attack Fort Crown Point in upstate New York and Fort Niagara, hard by the falls of that name. The really big event of that year was the earthquake, however.

BURIAL OF BRADDOCK.

An illustration depicts the British preparing to bury General Edward Braddock, who died fighting the French in the Ohio Valley.

Was there an earthquake in Boston in the 1700s?

At 4:15 A.M. on November 18, 1755, Bostonians were awakened first by a rumbling and then by a series of terrific shakes. Centered off Cape Ann, the quake of 1755 lasted only four minutes, but during that time roughly 1,500 chimneys in Boston collapsed. Almost no one was killed because the good Yankees of Boston were just beginning to stir when the quake occurred. The following two months were a time of accusation investigation, and popular discourse, as everyone who was anyone attempted to put his spin on the matter.

Several old-time Puritan ministers claimed that God was angry at New England. A handful of others asserted that the quake stemmed from a combination of divine and natural causes. And a small number of leading men—including Professor John Winthrop IV—declared it a truly natural event. To them it was obvious that God could bring about an earthquake any time he desired, but that the rules of the natural world made sense on a logical level. The really big surprise came when Bostonians learned that Lisbon, the capital of Portugal, had been swamped by a terrible earthquake, followed by a tsunami, on November 1, 1755.

How was Voltaire connected to the 1755 earthquake in Lisbon, Portugal?

Nearly 40,000 Portuguese died on November 1, 1755, leading many European scientists and philosophers to question previously held beliefs. Voltaire, for example, abandoned the "feel-good" philosophy of the philosopher Gottfried Wilhelm Leibniz, who claimed that we live in the best of all possible worlds. Voltaire felt strongly enough about the tragedy that he wrote *Candide*, a novel, to demonstrate his displeasure with those that asserted all was well.

For Americans in general, and Bostonians in particular, the Lisbon quake appeared to be validation of what Leibniz had proposed. Boston had seen a great quake, but no one was killed. Lisbon saw an even greater one in which many thousands lost their lives. Surely, it meant that the Almighty had a special interest in the preservation of Boston and, indeed, America.

How did the French and Indian War proceed?

The defeat in western Pennsylvania was balanced by an Anglo-American victory at the Battle of Lake George in September 1755. Anyone who examined the map of North America could see that the French held a major advantage in terms of holding "interior lines." It was, and is, much easier to traverse the St. Lawrence River and the Great Lakes than to concentrate troops from the original Thirteen Colonies. At the same time, however, the Anglo-American colonists possessed an enormous advantage in terms of population and the size of their military. There were perhaps two million people in the thirteen colonies, compared to less than 80,000 in Canada and Nova Scotia.

France did reasonably well in the first two years of the war. The Marquis de Montcalm (1712–1759) arrived as the new military commander in 1756; he proceeded to capture Fort Oswego, and then Fort William Henry, at the southern end of Lake George. In the immediate aftermath of the fall of Fort William Henry, there was concern, even in Boston, that the French and Indians would run amok over the entire New England frontier. When Montcalm and his army withdrew to Canada, calm returned, and this time it was the icy calm that comes before the final resolution. New Englanders in general, and Bostonians in particular, were determined that Canada must fall.

Could the American colonists ever have conquered French Canada on their own?

It was possible but not likely. The colonists had a vastly greater population, and plenty of arms and ammunition, but they lacked unity. It was up to Old England, therefore, to apply the final pressure and bring about the final victories. In 1758 General Jeffrey Amherst—after whom Amherst College is named—captured Fortress Louisbourg on Cape Breton Island. Bostonians, naturally, pointed out this would have been unnecessary if the motherland had simply left Louisbourg in their possession. The following year, 1759, General Amherst captured Fort Ticonderoga and then Crown Point, as he took control of the Lake Champlain Valley. Meanwhile, British General James Wolfe sailed up the St. Lawrence River to besiege Québec.

Again Bostonians pointed out that their own plans had been much simpler. If the daring adventure of Sir William Phips had succeeded in 1690, there would now be no need to attack Québec City. But the British did their job with consummate thoroughness. After a siege of three months, General Wolfe brought his men to the Plains of Abraham, on the western side of the city. The climactic battle lasted only fifteen minutes, but it endured that England would capture Québec, and eventually possess all of Canada. General Wolfe died during the battle; the Marquis de Montcalm died of his wounds several days later.

How did Bostonians receive the news of Québec's fall?

They could not have been more exuberant. Only one last campaign was required, and when it ended with the capture of Montréal in September 1760, the French and Indian War was well and truly over.

One sermon after another, delivered from the pulpits of Boston churches, proclaimed the end of the war and freedom from fear. For almost three generations, Bostonians and their country cousins had lived in fear of French invasion, Indian attack, or some combination of the two.

Are there any testimonials as to how Bostonians felt at the reduction of French Canada?

Many exist in the form of sermons and broadsides (large printed sheets that circulated as "extras"). One of the best-known is entitled simply "Canada Subjected—A New Song."

The Savages lay down their arms.
The French do cease to raise alarms.
Now Canada is fallen down
Before the troops of GEORGE's crown.

When did the transition from one monarch to another take place?

King George II died suddenly in October 1760, and the British throne immediately passed to his twenty-two-year-old grandson, King George III. At the time of his accession, George III was popular, both in England and the colonies, not least because he spoke English as his first language.

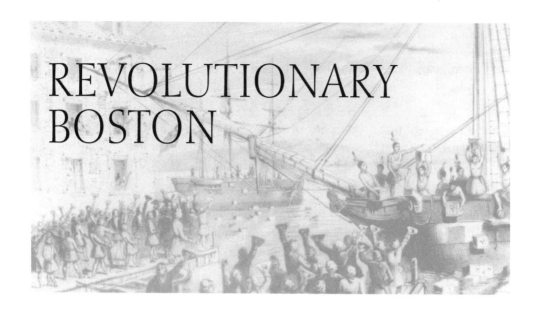

REVOLUTIONARY BOSTON

What does "Yankee" mean?

The derivation of this word is uncertain. Some historians believe that the word was given to the colonists by the Native Americans, some of whom used "Yen-geez" to describe someone who did not speak very much. Others assert that Yankee is a word developed in New England, and its appearance indicated a difference between the Bostonians of around 1770 and those from a century earlier. What can be said with confidence is that the word Yankee has come to mean a New Englander who is tight with his money.

Later, during the Civil War, Yankee became a derogatory term, meaning a Northerner who came south to disturb and disrupt the lives of the Confederates. Sometime during the nineteenth century, Yankee also became the term used by many foreigners, English men and women especially, to describe the Americans as a whole.

What did Boston look like in or around the year 1770?

The topography and landscape were much the same as a century earlier, but the town was beginning to acquire a look of sophistication. In the decade prior to the American Revolution, Boston was divided between a small upper class of perhaps ten percent, and a struggling working class of perhaps fifty percent. In between these two were all sorts of middle-class folk, few of whom enjoyed much economic security. For that upper ten percent, however, life was fine indeed.

Coaches had appeared in Boston as early as 1720, but the really sumptuous ones—those that echoed of wealth and status—came in the 1760s. The two-story house continued to be the staple, but one could imagine the time when the three-story mansion would come into its own. Upper-class Bostonians could be identified (by their poorer counterparts) half a mile away based on their dress, manner, and attitude. But one of the most telling commentaries was the extent to which the person partook of tea.

47

One often hears of the Boston Tea Party. Is it true that most Bostonians were tea drinkers?

For the lower class it's difficult to say because few of them left diaries. For the upper class, it's apparent that the drinking of tea was one of the signs of a sophisticated and cultured person. Tea and the vessels in which it was served appear in many portraits and paintings from the period. And while we're on the subject of painting and tea, it's impossible to refrain from saying something about John Singleton Copley.

Was Copley the genius that his friends and neighbors believed him to be?

Copley—after whom one of the most important squares in Boston is named—was an American painter of undeniable genius. His great skill lay in depicting the wealthy and well-to-do of Boston, and he achieved this with great flair. From Copley's pencil, and then ink, we see the Bostonians of the 1760s and 1770s. The men tend to be handsome with just a touch of rural ruggedness; the ladies seem more at ease and urbane. Copley had special skill in the painting of faces, and we therefore know what a good many of the prominent Bostonians looked like.

Thomas Hutchinson—the unfortunate last Loyalist governor of Massachusetts—was tall and thin with a youthful arrogance that evolved over time into a sad resignation. Samuel Adams, perhaps the best-known Bostonian of that remarkable time, comes across as strong, uncompromising, and perhaps too heavy-handed. Of all the many portraits Copley painted, his of Paul Revere may be the most remarkable. Revere comes to us as the serene, hard-working artisan, a person who knows he has done his best, and is willing to leave the rest to Providence. But perhaps the most important of all the Copley portraits—for our purpose—is the one of his own extended family.

Did John Copley become a patriot? Or was he a Loyalist?

One senses that Copley didn't really want to make the choice: that he could have remained on the fence a very long time. But this was not true of the family he married into: the Clarkes were among the most notorious of Boston Loyalists. Copley's portrait of the Clarke family shows a clan intensely devoted to family, duty, and the British crown. With Richard Clarke at center, these people are *Anglo*-Americans with the emphasis on the first half of the word: not for them the revolutionary antics that will follow.

Upper-class Bostonians such as those Copley painted tended to love their town, but they wanted it to remain part of the British Empire. When forced to make the choice, most of them reluctantly departed Boston.

Did Copley discriminate between those that turned out to be prominent revolutionaries and others who became ardent Loyalists?

He did not. Copley departed Boston shortly before the Revolution began, and, thanks to his in-law connection with a major merchant family, he was largely Loyalist in sentiment. In portrait painting, however, Copley seemed as interested in the patriots as the king's loyal friends. Perhaps the two most memorable of his many portraits are those of Paul Revere and John Adams.

Paul Revere appears to us as the successful craftsman, he who has already made good, and whose good-hearted approach to life calls to much that is good within the viewer. Sam Adams comes across as a trifle stern, but his obvious sincerity and intentionality make up for this.

Speaking of Paul Revere, was he not an artist himself?

Revere was a silversmith, a family man, a dispatch rider, and an engraver of no small skill. His engraving of the British troops

The artist John Singleton Copley painted many prominent Bostonians in the 1760s and 1770s. This is a self portrait.

landing in Boston in October 1768 brought him to the attention of many colonists; his engraving of the Boston Massacre made him famous.

Do we have any specific information about Boston's population from the 1770s?

Thanks to a handful of Boston newspapers, we surely do. We know, for example, that between January 1, 1772, and January 1, 1773, there were a total of 595 burials in Boston: 533 whites and 62 blacks. We know that the number of people baptized in the various churches came to 485 for the same period, suggesting that Boston required immigration for its overall population to increase. Moving to the succeeding year, the record states that there were 458 white burials and 59 blacks (for a total of 517) in the year 1773, and that only 393 persons were baptized during that period. We can also state unequivocally that black slavery continued to be a fact of life in pre-revolutionary Boston. The *Boston Gazette* carried this advertisement on February 28, 1774:

> WANTED: A Negro man of an unexceptional character, warranted, for such an one a good price will be given, brought up in a country town, and understands a little of house business will be preferred.

KING GEORGE III AND HIS COLONISTS

History tells us that King George III is responsible for many of the problems between Old England and American colonists. What was he like?

When he ascended the British throne in October 1760, George III was twenty-two years old. He succeeded not his father, who had died, but his grandfather, King George II.

49

Both to his English subjects at home and the American colonists, George III seemed a big improvement on his grandfather. The "Georges," as Bostonians sometimes call them, were a German family who inherited the English throne after the death of Queen Anne in 1714. King George I spoke virtually no English, and George II spoke it haltingly. George III, by contrast, was English born and bred, and he was sometimes so well liked in England that his subjects called him "Farmer George," referring to his love of the land and agriculture. George III had one bad trait, however: he was determined to make the crown more powerful, both in Old England and America. And he had an innate stubbornness that pushed him to move ahead even when he should, by reason, have slowed down.

King George III reigned over Britain during the American Revolution. He was popular in England, but reviled in America.

Did Bostonians and Americans recognize that they were in for a difficult time with George III?

They did not. The succession of George III brought a wave of congratulations and applause from the American colonists. Boston, however, encountered difficulty long before running into any problems with the monarch. In February 1761, the town was hit by another of the "Great Fires" which bedeviled its existence. This fire was so extensive that commerce, as well as individuals, suffered for years to come.

Bostonians had dealt with financial difficulty for so long that it seemed perpetual. Not only had commerce fallen off with fewer ships visiting than in previous decades, but the collection of town taxes was significantly in arrears. Some people blamed the lax tax collectors, one of whom was Samuel Adams.

One normally has the impression of Boston being quite powerful. Could Boston not leverage its position as capital of the Massachusetts colony?

In earlier times that was possible. By 1760, however, the towns of central and western Massachusetts had gained leverage of their own. Though Boston was the capital, the Great and General Court was largely controlled by men from the inland towns. They might sympathize with Boston's economic woes, but they could not and would not rescue it.

If the American Revolution had not taken place, might Boston's plight have been even worse?

Yes, indeed. It's quite possible that the town would have languished for decades.

THE STAMP ACT

How and when did George III act where taxes were concerned?

The American colonists had long paid various kinds of customs duties, but they had never experienced *direct* taxes from Great Britain. Even the loudest of revolutionary orators, such as Sam Adams and Patrick Henry, admitted that customs duties were lawful because the colonists imported goods from the motherland. But to the notion that England could tax them directly, the Americans nearly always responded with a firm negative.

The first significant test of American resolve came in 1762, when Parliament issued a new version of the Sugar, or Molasses, Act. The colonists did not feel any need to turn out against the king's officials in part because they were so few in number. But Bostonian James Otis, who was a native of Barnstable, argued long and hard against the Sugar Act and the Writs of Assistance, which were designed to make it easier for royal officials to search colonists' homes. In 1765, Bostonians learned that Parliament passed and King George assented to the Stamp Act (England already had one of its own). Under this act, colonists had to purchase special paper that carried the king's stamp for use in all official letters, correspondence, and so forth. Newspapers, and even playing cards had to bear the king's stamp.

Why was Boston in the forefront of the opposition?

Boston had long been a place of dissent. The original Puritan settlers came to Boston to get away from the king and his established church. Economic factors contributed as well. New York, Philadelphia, and Charleston were all doing reasonably well in the 1760s, while Boston suffered from unemployment inflation, and a host of uncollected property taxes. The economic plight of the town led many people who might otherwise have been quiet to refuse the brand-new Stamp Act.

How rich was John Hancock?

He owned a mansion on Beacon Hill, and for many years his was the only mansion there. Hancock owned a bevy of ships that carried out trade all over the Atlantic world. It's difficult to measure his wealth against modern-day wealthy Americans; suffice to say that his personal income was probably as large as the treasury of the town of Boston!

51

Precisely when the "Sons of Liberty" were formed, or who drew up the first list of members is difficult to say, but there is little doubt that Sam Adams, Paul Revere, James Otis, and James Warren became the leaders of this semi-official group. John Hancock, known for his wealth and social grace, later became an important member, but in the early years he was distrusted, as being too darned rich for a group that intended to resist taxes.

How effective were the Sons of Liberty?

One can only marvel at what they were able to accomplish. Up to the year 1765, Boston was a reasonably law-abiding town, and one which showed a good deal of respect toward British leadership. By the end of 1765, Boston was on the verge of a genuine political revolution, and at least nine-tenths of the reason for that change was the Sons of Liberty.

One can accuse the Sons of bullying, and there is much truth to the accusation. One can accuse them of inflaming passions at a time when calmness and moderation were called for, but this was one thing they would not do. In the entire history of eighteenth-century America, one looks in vain for a political group as well organized and successful as the Sons of Liberty.

Did British officials expect the furor that arose following the passage of the Stamp Act?

They did not have a clue. For one thing, there were very few of them. The official collector of the stamps was Peter Oliver, a native-born Bostonian. For another, the British

A 1903 postcard commemorating the burning of the Stamp Act declaration by Bostonians.

I often thought that the "Liberty Tree" was symbolic rather than actual. Am I mistaken?

Half and half. There was indeed a large elm tree on The Neck, the narrow isthmus that connected Boston to the mainland, at Roxbury. That is where the Sons of Liberty often gathered. Over time, however, the "Liberty Tree" became a symbol that was appropriated by other groups, and eventually it was enshrined in American poetry and literature.

were quite accustomed to paying taxes, and it both infuriated and amazed them that the Bostonians would not do so.

During the mid-summer of 1765, resistance in Boston grew to such a point that no one wanted even to try to carry out King George's new law. And in August some of the Sons of Liberty brought Peter Oliver to what they called the Liberty Tree on The Neck and made him swear, over and over again, that he would never attempt to collect Stamp Act taxes. They made him drink to the health of the Sons of Liberty, and it was obvious they would tar and feather him if he refused.

How inflamed did the situation become?

Ten days after forcing Peter Oliver to give up his office, the Sons of Liberty attacked the mansion of Lieutenant-Governor Thomas Hutchinson. It seems odd the way the Sons of Liberty persecuted one of their neighbors (Hutchinson was born and raised in town), but Hutchinson's elegant demeanor and arrogant attitude epitomized, for many of them, the worst qualities of the British aristocrat. Hutchinson got out of the house in time, but the Bostonians torched it; along with many valuable possessions, Hutchinson lost the manuscript for what might have been an enlivening history of early Boston.

By the end of 1765, no supporter of George III or the Stamp Act dared show his face. The mob, which is what the Sons of Liberty were on their bad days, practically ran the town. Not until the spring of 1766 did Bostonians learn that George III and Parliament had rescinded the Stamp Act.

Was Boston really strong enough to resist the Stamp Act all on its own?

Not quite. Boston showed the most powerful resistance of all the American towns, but other coastal towns demonstrated outrage of their own. Americans up and down the coast even sent delegates to the Stamp Act Congress, held in Manhattan. So while Boston was in the forefront, plenty of other American colonists were ready to resist.

Learning of this, George III and the leaders of the House of Commons decided to revoke the Stamp Act. On the same day this was done, however, Parliament also passed the Declaratory Act, which asserted that the king and Parliament had the right to legislate

53

for the American colonies "in all cases whatsoever." Bostonians chose to ignore the quiet threat in those words: they simply rejoiced over the Stamp Act's repeal.

THE DECLATORY ACTS

Given that the Stamp Act had failed, could England and America go back to previous relations?

They should have done so. Mutual self-interest was involved. Much of England's trade derived from the colonies. But in 1767, Charles Townshend (sometimes called "Champagne Charlie") persuaded George III to create a new set of taxes for the colonies. Known as the Townshend Acts, these regulations imposed taxes on paper, paint, glass, lead, and tea.

None of these taxes were terrible on their own: it was the combination of five that infuriated many colonists. The tax on painter's colors and the one on glass caused the most hardship, but the tax on tea created the most dissatisfaction. The American colonists were, by 1767, primarily a nation of tea drinkers.

How much was the tax on tea?

It was three pence per pound of tea, and this was enough to discourage quite a few Bostonians from purchasing the bundles of leaves that produced the wholesome beverage. Bostonians were again in the forefront, but other towns and colonists followed in establishing a policy of non-importation of the five taxed goods. Some Americans went even further, boycotting all British goods. And the results were soon felt in London, where merchants complained bitterly about the unpatriotic American colonists.

How do we know so much about the temper of this time (1768)?

Naturally we don't wish to rely on the words of the patriots in and around Boston. We turn, therefore, to the diary and letters of Ann Hulton. Presumably she was in her thir-

How do we know so much about the consumption habits of Bostonians in the 1700s?

Plenty of records of financial transactions exist, but the paintings of John Singleton Copley, for whom Copley Square is named, provide our best glimpse of upper-class Bostonians from the 1760s. Copley painted dozens of portraits, many of individuals but others of whole families. Through his eyes and his exquisite skill with the painter's brush, we see the Bostonians of the 1760: well-clad, healthy and strong, but above all elegant and self-possessed.

ties when she came to Boston in 1768, as the unmarried sister of Henry Hulton, the brand-new customs inspector for the port of Boston.

Whether her brother prepared her or not, Ann Hulton soon found herself in a situation quite unlike any she'd seen in the British motherland. Just three weeks after arriving in Boston, Ann Hulton penned a letter to a friend in London. "Dear Madam," she began. "I presume it will be agreeable to you to hear that my brother's family had a good voyage of 5 weeks & arrived all well at Boston the 5th instant [the fifth of June, 1768]. You will be surprised to hear how we were obliged to fly from the place in six days after & take refuge aboard the *Romney*, man of war lying in Boston Harbor."

How could the Bostonians eject the king's lawful inspector?

That was precisely the question that Ann Hulton marveled over. In the letter to her London correspondent, she explained that the Boston crowds—or mobs—were not the same as in Old England.

> Mrs. Burch, at whose house I was, had frequently been alarmed with the Sons of Liberty surrounding her house with the most hideous howlings as the Indians.... The occasion soon happened, when my sister & I accompanied her at 10 o'clock to a neighbor's house, not apprehending much danger, but we soon found that the mobs here are very different from those in Old England where a few lights placed in the windows will pacify ... here they act from principle & under countenance, no person daring or willing to suppress their outrages.

Even in the twenty-first century, we can detect from a distance the sneer in Ann Hulton's tone as she uses those words "from principle & under countenance." The simple answer is that the Bostonians believed any measures were proper to employ when resisting the new customs laws.

What did Governor Bernard say to Ann Hulton?

In the summer of 1768, Ann Hulton and her relatives—all of whom were connected with the odious taxes—fled Boston for the relative safety of The Castle, on present-day Castle Island. They and their friends were drinking tea one afternoon when Governor Sir Francis Bernard (1712–1779) arrived. Joining the party, the governor declared that another year like the previous two (1767 and 1768) and the British Empire would be at an end.

From our modern-day perspective, this sounds extreme, as if Governor Bernard did

Sir Francis Bernard, 1st Baronet, was the British governor of New Jersey (1758–1760) and then, from 1760 to 1769, of Massachusetts.

not see all the Americans that were still loyal to the crown. But he was on the ground, as we say today, and the chances are that he really felt that the British Empire—in America, at least—was coming to an end. The proof is that he summoned the first British regiments to Boston. They arrived on October 1, 1768.

What did the Massachusetts legislature say to King George III?

In January 1768, the Massachusetts House of Representatives sent a humble address to King George III. Some of the language is overdone, and even flighty, but there are sections in which the Bostonians' case is laid out extremely well.

> It is with the deepest concern that your humble suppliants would represent to your Majesty that your Parliament, the rectitude of whose intentions is never to be questioned, has thought proper to pass diverse acts imposing taxes on your Majesty's subjects in America with the sole and express purpose of raising a revenue. If your Majesty's subjects here shall be deprived of the honor and privilege of voluntarily contributing their aid to your Majesty.... If these Acts of Parliament shall remain in force ... your people must then regret their unhappy fate in having only the name left of free subjects.

In all this time, had there been no real British regular troops stationed in Boston?

Correct. George III and his ministers believed, until 1768, that the disturbances in America were essentially civil in nature: that they could be contained by just a handful of officials. Governor Bernard's dispatches convinced them otherwise, and the first British redcoats arrived in October 1768. Paul Revere, who doubled as a silversmith and an engraver, made a fine illustration of the soldiers coming ashore, complete with horses and artillery. Lacking barracks, most of the soldiers pitched tents on Boston Common.

How did Bostonians respond to the arrival of British troops?

One way to answer this is to quote from the *Boston Evening Post*. On October 3, 1768, the paper editorialized: "We now behold the Representatives' Chamber, Court-House, and Faneuil-Hall, those seats of freedom and justice occupied with troops, and guards placed at the doors, the Common covered with tents, and alive with soldiers; marching and countermarching to relieve the guards, in short, the town is now a perfect garrison." Two months later, on Christmas Day, the same paper commented "One great objection to the quartering of troops in the body of a town, is the danger the inhabitants will be in of having their morals debauched. The ear being accustomed to oaths and imprecations, will be the less shocked at the profanity, and the frequent spectacles of drunkenness."

Did the townspeople adjust to having troops in their midst?

One thousand soldiers came at first, but their number was increased and by the summer of 1769 there were four thousand British soldiers in town, about one for every four civilians. Not only did this make the narrow peninsula crowded, but there were inevitable tensions between troops and townspeople. The Bostonians took a "good cop, bad cop" approach, meaning that they were very accommodating at certain times, and absolutely maddening at others. The British soldiers were not well paid by King George, and many were pleased to take up odd jobs working for the townspeople. The rope walks, which turned out the vital necessaries for ships, were a popular place of work.

THE BOSTON MASSACRE

Do we know everything about the Boston Massacre?

We don't. Even though hundreds of pages of testimony were included in the official record, and even though there were dozens of anecdotal reports, some parts of the Boston Massacre remain somewhat obscure. Why did the terrible occasion take place on this particular night, for example, and not earlier? Why didn't someone in authority ascertain the danger, and do something to put out the flame of discontent?

What we can say is that no one planned the Massacre. Neither the British soldiers who emptied their muskets in the direction of the crowd, or even the most aggressive member of that crowd, really believed it would turn into the first bloodshed of the American Revolution. British soldiers and Bostonians had conflicted many times previous, but no group of British soldiers had ever opened fire on a crowd.

Is it surprising that tensions grew between Bostonians and the British soldiers in the winter of 1769–1770?

Not at all. Firewood was very costly (all the trees in the local area had long since been cut down), and both townspeople and soldiers found it difficult to stay warm. That winter was no worse than average, but that meant plenty of ice and snow. And when a crowd of Bostonians came to the door of the Customs House on March 5, 1770, they were looking for trouble.

Two weeks earlier there had been a nasty scuffle outside the home of a firm Loyalist. Rushing upstairs, he seized a pistol and discharged it, killing a nine-year-old boy. Some historians consider Christopher Seider the first casualty of the American Revolution. Nearly two thousand people attended his funeral, and Bostonians were tense beyond the usual degree when February turned to March. On the evening of March 5, a group of perhaps forty Bostonians came to the Customs House, and harassed the one British soldier standing guard outside the door.

How did the discontent turn into the Boston Massacre?

Private Hugh White stood his ground for some time, using his bayonet to keep the Boston crowd at bay. Bostonians hurled snowballs, and then ice balls at him. White ran

The Bloody Massacre perpetrated in King-Street Boston on March 5th 1770 by a party of the 29th Regt.

Unhappy Boston! see thy Sons deplore,
Thy hallow'd Walks besmear'd with guiltless Gore.
While faithless P—n and his savage Bands,
With murd'rous Rancour stretch their bloody Hands;
Like fierce Barbarians grinning o'er their Prey,
Approve the Carnage, and enjoy the Day.

If scalding drops from Rage from Anguish Wrung
If speechless Sorrows lab'ring for a Tongue,
Or if a weeping World can ought appease
The plaintive Ghosts of Victims such as these;
The Patriot's copious Tears for each are shed,
A glorious Tribute which embalms the Dead.

But know, Fate summons to that awful Goal,
Where Justice strips the Murd'rer of his Soul:
Should venal C—ts the scandal of the Land,
Snatch the relentless Villain from her Hand,
Keen Execrations on this Plate inscrib'd,
Shall reach a Judge who never can be brib'd

Engrav'd Printed & Sold by Paul Revere Boston

Copy Right Secured.

The unhappy Sufferers were Messrs Saml Gray, Saml Maverick, Jams Caldwell, Crispus Attucks & Patk Carr
Killed. Six wounded; two of them (Christr Monk & John Clark) Mortally

An engraving by Paul Revere depicting the Boston Massacre is, admittedly, somewhat sensationalized for effect.

inside the Customs House and rang the one large bell, which summoned seven other soldiers and Captain Thomas Preston. Eight British soldiers stood with their muskets in front of a crowd of Bostonians that grew to over two hundred.

To this day no one really knows if Captain Preston shouted "fire!" or "hold your fire!" And in a sense it doesn't matter. The situation had grown to an uncontrollable level, and violence was just about a certainty. Whatever words their captain employed, the soldiers let loose with a blaze of musket fire, and when the smoke cleared, five Bostonians lay dead or dying in the snow.

Was the Boston Massacre the moment when the American Revolution became inevitable?

It was pretty darned close. This is when British soldiers first fired on American civilians. Both sides were shocked, and appalled, but it demonstrates how high tensions had become. And, as most soldiers today will say, once blood-letting begins, it is difficult to stop.

Who were the five people killed by British soldiers in Boston during March 1770, and how do we know so much about them?

They were Samuel Gray, Samuel Maverick, James Caldwell, Patrick Carr, and Crispus Attucks. Of the five, Attucks is the best known. His name appears in all sorts of descriptions and depictions. He was a mulatto of Native American and African American descent.

We know so much about these men and the night of the Boston Massacre because of the engraving Paul Revere made just three weeks later. Revere's engraving contains numerous exaggerations and inaccuracies (he makes the Boston mob seem like only two dozen in number) but his vision of the event is what was seen by tens of thousands of colonists, up and down the East Coast. We also know a good deal about the British soldiers involved, and this thanks to their trial in Boston in the autumn of 1770.

Were there two separate trials related to the Boston Massacre?

Yes. Captain Preston had a six-day trial that resulted in his acquittal. The seven British soldiers were tried later. Six of them were found not guilty, and two others were found guilty of manslaughter. Privates Hugh Montgomery and Matthew Kilroy were found guilty of manslaughter, and sentenced to be branded on the thumb as punishment. Lieutenant-Governor Thomas Hutchinson had already arranged in advance, for anyone found guilty to receive a royal pardon, but this did not prevent the two soldiers from being burned on their left thumbs.

It seems as if Boston could have gone up in flames in 1770. Why did this not happen?

For once in their long lives, Sam Adams and Thomas Hutchinson saw things the same way. The two detested one another, but they worked together to prevent the Boston Massacre from becoming much worse. Within a matter of days, the two British regiments were taken out of the city and quartered on islands in Boston Harbor. Hutchinson and Sam Adams persuaded their relative constituencies to keep things quiet for the summer, and when the results of the Boston Massacre trials were announced, Bostonians seemed ready to let bygones be bygones.

How long was it relatively quiet before violence erupted again?

There were about two years of calm between 1771 and 1772 while Rhode Island took the lead in asserting patriot rights. When HMS *Gaspee*, a British revenue vessel, ran aground in Narragansett Bay, it was men from Providence that rowed out to attack, capture, and then burn her. King George III and his ministers were angry, but their officials could find no one to testify against the men of Providence, and the crime against the flag and His Majesty's government went unpunished.

Were Bostonians ready to relinquish the role they had so long played?

They seemed willing to do so. But in the summer of 1773, Bostonians and other Americans learned of a new parliamentary act, legislation designed to save the East India Tea Company from bankruptcy. King George III and his ministers had miscalculated again.

To save the East India Company, Parliament passed special legislation allowing the company to market its tea directly to the American colonists without it first arriving in London. This helped the company, and, the ministers argued, it helped the colonists who would receive their tea much more cheaply than before. But at the last minute, Frederick Lord North, the new British prime minister, slapped a special three pence tax per pound of tea. Lord North was warned by the Loyal Opposition in the House of Commons that the Americans would not overlook his action. He chose to take the risk.

Was George III particularly ill-served by the members of his government?

A peculiar combination of self-delusion and foolishness does seem to have descended on Lord North and his advisers. They knew the Americans had resisted the Stamp Act and the Townshend Acts, yet they went ahead and ruined the good results that attended the passage of the Tea Act.

For once, Boston was not in the vanguard. Bostonians declared their dislike of the Tea Act, but it was the people of Philadelphia that shouted most loudly. Perhaps eight thousand people crowded in and around the Philadelphia State House in 1773 to protest the three-penny tax. And there was no doubt that the tax would be resisted. Boston did not seem likely to cause the most trouble, but, as so often, the Sons of Liberty became the most aggressive fighters for American liberty.

Did Bostonians realize the consequence of defying the king and Parliament?

They did not. They had successfully stopped the Stamp Act, and they thought they would get away with it again. When three ships arrived, carrying tea, Boston did not seize or impound the ships; rather, the Sons of Liberty placed a volunteer guard on the wharf, declaring that none of the tea would come ashore. Thomas Hutchinson, who had been promoted to full governor, was at his wits' end. He believed he had to stand for royal authority on this occasion, and he therefore denied every effort the three ship captains made to head home for England.

The ship captains were in a very bad place. They would be blamed if the tea was not landed; on the other hand, they would be attacked if they made the attempt. Each time they applied for a special pass to depart Boston, Governor Hutchinson refused.

On the afternoon of December 16, 1773, Sam Adams presided over a special town meeting of the citizens of Boston. Many arguments were heard, and Adams acted more impartially than was his usual style. As evening approached, a messenger arrived to say that Governor Hutchinson had denied the final request. The tea ships could not depart Boston, he said. Adams and his fellows knew that a special twenty-day deadline was about to expire, and that the British Royal Navy would soon be able to seize the tea, and, presumably, land it in town. Adams closed the meeting with memorable words: "This meeting can do nothing more to save this country," he declared.

When did the Tea Party—or the Destruction of the Tea—take place?

Immediately. Just minutes after Adams uttered those words, war whoops were heard, and scores of men—most of them dressed as Mohawk Indians—were seen on the street, headed for Griffin's Wharf. Arriving at the wharf, the 150-odd men boarded the three ships. No violence was offered to the sailors, but the chests of tea were brought to the main deck, broken open with hatchets, and the contents unceremoniously heaved into Boston Harbor. One aspect which is often overlooked is that the tide was low that evening, and that the tea settled on to the wharf area, stinking up the surroundings!

Within ninety minutes, the "Destruction of the Tea," as the Bostonians called it, was complete. Three hundred and forty-two chests of tea had been heaved over the side

One of the most famous acts of defiance before the actual revolution was the Boston Tea Party of 1773, when colonists dressed as Indians boarded three British ships and dumped their cargoes into the harbor.

61

of the ships, and the "Mohawks" went home, presumably to celebrate. British Admiral Sir John Montagu happened to stay ashore that evening, and he called out that the Bostonians had had their fun, but they would soon have to pay the piper. He was right.

Do we have any first-hand accounts of the Boston Tea Party?

Our best account comes from the mouth of George Robert Twelves Hewes (1742–1840). Decades after the event, and just shortly before his own death, Hewes related his experience to not one but two biographers, and his stories provide our best understanding of the Tea Party.

"When we arrived at the wharf," Hewes wrote, "there were three of our number who assumed an authority to direct our operations, to which we readily submitted. They divided us into three parties, for the purpose of boarding the three ships which contained the tea at the same time." None of the sailors aboard the tea ships offered any resistance, and the Americans quickly went about their work, which sounds as if it all was accomplished within an hour and a half.

Did Bostonians really think they would get away with it?

They did. Bostonians were appalled in the spring of 1774, to learn that King George III and Parliament had slapped a series of new acts upon them. These laws were not about taxes; they were much more important than that. The Massachusetts Government Act formally closed Boston as the seat of royal government, removing it to Salem. The Boston Port Act closed the port until the tea was paid for. And the Quartering Act asserted that Bostonians would have to house troops in their homes until further notice. King George III and his ministers called these the Coercive Acts, but Bostonians soon labeled them the Intolerable Acts. The latter title is the one that stuck.

King George III's resolution was admirable, but he chose the wrong man for the job. Lieutenant General Thomas Gage was a seasoned military officer who knew the colonies well, but he was a fainthearted man, not the right person to enforce a tough series of acts. Gage's wife was an American, a beauty from Philadelphia, and she may have persuaded her husband to go even more gently on her countrymen.

Was anyone ever tried, or even remotely punished, for actions at the Boston Tea Party?

No one was punished for their actions at the Boston Tea Party. Like the destruction of HMS *Gaspee* the year before, the Destruction of the Tea was a flagrant violation of British law, but no one could be found to testify. Too, the actors were cleverly disguised in their Indian clothing. The last surviving member of the Tea Party died around the year 1845.

AN AFRICAN AMERICAN VOICE

How did Phillis Wheatley become so well-known in pre-Revolutionary Boston?

Born in Senegal, Phillis Wheatley (1753–1784) was captured, enslaved, and brought to Boston around the year 1762. The name of the ship that brought her was *Phillis,* and the name of the family that purchased her was Wheatley. Her story was unremarkable to this point; many African Americans came to Boston as slaves. Something different emerged during her first decade in America, however: Phillis Wheatley had the same level of education as a typical upper-class white girl of her time.

John and Susannah Wheatley were very fond of their slave girl, and they raised her up to be something of a prodigy. There may have been some black poets prior to Phillis, but none of them are known. Phillis, by contrast, became known as early as 1770, when she wrote an elegy in honor of Reverend George Whitefield. As she entered her twenties, Phillis extended her literary skills even further, and her first selection of poems were published first in London, and then in Boston (in 1773 and 1774).

Was Phillis Wheatley as talented as her many admirers like to claim?

Her poetry has, over the last two centuries, been both acclaimed and despised. Many literary scholars characterize her something of a copycat, declaring that almost any well-educated girl of the time could have turned out those lines. What these scholars ignore is the depth of feeling that emerges from Phillis's poems. Here was a person who saw almost the worst life had to offer, and through the kindness of her mistress, as well as her own considerable great efforts, she rose above the situation.

Phillis Wheatley and her mistress returned to Boston from London in 1774. Susannah Wheatley died soon thereafter, and Phillis was freed. She remained close to the Wheatley family, and, during the Siege of Boston, she became known for the poem she wrote in honor of General George Washington.

What was the life expectancy of Bostonians, and other residents of Massachusetts, during the eighteenth century?

Most of us know the large variety of illnesses and incapacities that struck almost without warning: they included smallpox,

A 1773 engraving of Phillis Wheatley.

diphtheria, and tuberculosis. Occasionally the record reflects something quite different, a testimony to good health and long life. An obituary ran in the *Boston Gazette* on November 21, 1774.

> Died at Danvers, Mr. Thomas Nelson in the 104th year of his age. He was born at Norwich in England, June 1671 in the reign of King Charles the II. At the [Glorious] Revolution he was an apprentice to a weaver in that city when he enlisted as a soldier under King William, to go over to Ireland, to drive out James II. He served also in Queen Anne's Wars; was a sailor in the fleet under Sir Cloudesley Shovell at the siege and taking of Barcelona, and was in the expedition to Canada, 1711, at which time he settled in Danvers, and till within this year or two, was able to walk miles. He had but one eye, and his hair white like the driven snow, but retained his reason and walked remarkably erect—*At length the weary wheels of life stood still.*

THE BRITISH OCCUPATION

When did General Gage arrive?

Thomas Gage (1719–1787) came to Boston in May 1774, and the official trade stoppage began immediately. Even if a Boston skipper was lucky enough to evade port authorities, he would run into British ships of war anchored in the bay. For once, the British had the right combination of will power and military strength. They did not count on the reaction of the other colonies, however.

Until June 1774, Boston was essentially on its own, a town that had in some ways gone rogue. But that month, the leaders of most of the other colonies decided to help Boston in its time of need. Food and clothing were dispatched from other colonial towns, and though the Royal Navy blocked the harbor, General Gage did not prevent these articles from crossing The Neck. As a result, the people of Boston would make it through the winter of 1774–1775.

How important was Massachusetts to the establishment of the First Continental Congress?

Boston's plight was the future plight of all the colonies, or so the argument ran. Twelve out of the thirteen colonies (Georgia refrained) sent delegates to the First Continental Congress, which convened in Philadelphia at the beginning of September 1774. The mood was troubled but also electric.

John Hancock, Sam Adams, and John Adams were all present at the Congress. They helped shape the pamphlets and essays that came out of the meetings in Philadelphia. Most delegates to the Continental Congress still considered themselves Englishmen, and subjects of King George III, but they were also in the process of becoming Americans. Their letters and memorials to the king and his ministers were not exactly defiant, but neither were they conciliatory. And while the First Continental Congress met, Boston went through another alarm, which suggested outright war was not very far off.

What was the Powder Alarm?

In September 1774, General Gage, who was also governor and commander-in-chief of Massachusetts, sent a strong detachment of soldiers to seize the powder magazine in Cambridge, Massachusetts, just across the Charles River. Though the powder had already been moved, and was out of reach, the mere movement of these men into the countryside caused general alarm. Within forty-eight hours, thousands of Massachusetts militiamen had gathered at Cambridge and Medford and were ready to take violent action against the British. When people calmed down and the rumors were dispelled, the militia went home, but General Gage could scarcely believe what had happened. He began to fortify The Neck at once to make sure no one could cross into Boston without his permission.

News of the Powder Alarm reached the Continental Congress at the same time that Massachusetts passed the Suffolk Resolves, named in honor of the towns of Suffolk County. While the Resolves did not call for outright rebellion, they stopped only just short of it.

What was life in Boston like during the winter of 1774–1775?

It was not an especially hard winter as far as the weather was concerned, but quite a few Bostonians—from the working class, especially—suffered from a lack of fuel. Upper-class Bostonians fared better, but some were already packing their bags, hoping to get out of town in the spring. And Bostonians of all social ranks disliked and mistrusted the British soldiers who were now in the neighborhood of four thousand strong.

General Gage, meanwhile, wrote London asking that his troop strength be increased to twenty thousand. Nothing short of this would enable him to control the situation in Massachusetts, he declared. And though Gage did not say so explicitly, it was increasingly apparent that other towns and colonies were almost ready to back Massachusetts. The First Continental Congress broke up in the autumn of 1774, but its delegates agreed to reconvene on May 10, 1775.

Was there even a remote possibility that armed conflict could be avoided?

By the early spring of 1775, the odds were nine in favor and only one against. Everyone in Boston knew it was likely that the British would move into the countryside; everyone in the countryside realized that Boston was the key to the strategic situation. General Gage was not eager for the confrontation, but his latest orders, direct from King George, left no room for discretion. Massachusetts was in a state of rebellion, the king wrote, and Gage must move to confiscate gunpowder from the rebels.

Was King George still in his right mind?

Moviegoers may remember the inspired performance of Nigel Hawthorne, who portrayed the aged king in *The Madness of King George*. In fact, George III was still in full possession of his senses in 1775, but his innate stubbornness had become even worse. Knowing that the king suffered from porphyria, a rare disease that results from the accumulation of porphyrins in the system, allows the modern-day observer to have more sympathy for this man known as the monarch who lost the American colonies.

APRIL 19, 1775

What was the weather like on April 19, 1775?

The third week of April 1775 had notably mild weather, lending buoyancy to the spirits of many of the locals. General Gage put the finishing touches to his plans that week, and by mid-afternoon of April 18, Bostonians could see that something was up. Paul Revere, who had become the number-one dispatch rider for the Sons of Liberty, rowed across the Charles River at sunset. He had an arrangement with the sexton of the Old North Church. If the British marched out of Boston via The Neck, he was to hang one lamp in the belfry: two if they went by boat, across the Charles. Revere did not use the precise words "one if by land, two if by sea": these are the invention of the poet Longfellow, who wrote about Paul Revere's ride eighty-five years after the fact (see below).

When did the British make their move?

By 11 P.M. over one thousand British soldiers were moving off Boston Common and into boats: they soon landed at Phips Farm in Cambridge. Paul Revere, seeing the signal lamps from the Old North Church, got on his horse and began to ride. Contrary to popular belief, he did not shout "The British are coming!" but rather "The regulars are out!"

Revere could not be sure of the British destination, but their landing at Cambridge suggested they were on the way to Lexington. He galloped in that direction, warning everyone he could. The British, meanwhile, lined up in ranks and began the long night march that brought them to Lexington Green by 7 A.M.

Why does Revere always get the lion's share of the credit?

He really does deserve it. His ride brought out hundreds of men, who, by alerting their fellows, turned out thousands of others in the next twenty-four hours. But it is true that Revere is always more hailed than William Dawes, who went by way of The Neck, and Dr. Samuel Prescott, who continued on to Concord.

Another reason has to do with the power of poetry. Henry Wadsworth Longfellow (1807–1882), inspired and influenced by the events of the Revolutionary War, wrote poems about the Battle of Lexington and other major events. Some of his best-known

This circa 1937 engraving depicts Paul Revere's famous ride to warn the colonists about the invading British.

words are the ones that open his poem about Paul Revere (perhaps he had a harder time finding rhymes for Prescott or Dawes). "Paul Revere's Ride," first published in 1860 in *The Atlantic Monthly,* begins:

> Listen my children and you shall hear
> Of the Midnight Ride of Paul Revere,
> On the eighteenth of April in Seventy-five;
> Hardly a man is now alive
> Who remembers that famous day and year.

How did the British do on their march?

Lieutenant-Colonel Francis Smith led the nine-hundred-odd British from Phips Farm. All night the British marched, and dawn found them on the eastern edge of Lexington. Proceeding to the town green, Smith and his men found about seventy American militiamen drawn up, ready to defend the area. Tradition has it that Captain John Parker told his men, "Don't fire unless fired upon, but if they mean to have a war, let it begin here."

As they approached the green, the British split into two groups. One group marched past the patriot defenders, while the other headed straight to confront them. Major John Pitcairn, commander of the marines, rode out in front of the British lines to shout, "Lay down your arms! Disperse, ye rebels, disperse I tell you!"

How did the fighting commence?

No one knows who fired that first shot, or even from which direction it came. All we know is that one musket was fired, and that the British and Americans immediately let loose a blaze of gunfire. A solid two minutes later, as the smoke cleared, it became evident that the British had won this, the first skirmish of the Revolutionary War. Eight Americans lay dead or dying, and several others were wounded. Captain Parker and his surviving men had escaped the green. The British had two men wounded.

Major Pitcairn and Colonel Smith conferred, and agreed it was time to move on to Concord. After shouting several cheers, the British moved out, heading west.

> ## So that was it? This was the Battle of Lexington?
>
> It was a very small affair in the annals of military history, but in terms of national identity and eventual independence, Lexington was hugely important. The battle is reenacted on Patriots Day, a legal holiday in Massachusetts.

Were there any Bostonians in the battles at Lexington and Concord?

Very few. The people of Boston were living under what amounted to martial law. It was nearly impossible to pass The Neck without permission. Bostonians were primarily observers of the events of April 19, 1775.

When did the British get to Concord?

The British arrived in Concord by 10 A.M. on April 19, 1775. The weather was fine, and both Colonel Smith and Major Pitcairn felt pleased with how things had developed. They confiscated a good amount of gunpowder at Concord, but found that a second part of their mission, which was to arrest Sam Adams and John Hancock, was not possible. Both men had already escaped the area. Tradition has it that Adams, hearing the guns at Lexington from a distance, turned to Hancock to observe that it was a beautiful day. Hancock replied that it was. Adams pressed his point, saying it was a great day in the history of America.

What the British did not realize was how many American militiamen were now converging on them. Thousands of men had been alerted, and, true to their nickname as "Minutemen," they were hastening to Concord. By 11 A.M., there were more than one thousand militiamen on the west side of the narrow bridge that spanned the Concord River. Seeing a pall of smoke, and fearing the British had set fire to the town, these men began to move on that bridge.

Could the British have held the North Bridge?

Only if their entire force had been present. Most British soldiers were in the town of Concord, however, and not on hand to fight for the bridge. A sharp skirmish ensued with about equal casualties on the two sides, but it was the British that gave way. By noon, the Americans had the bridge, and Colonel Smith decided it best to turn his men for home. He had already sent word to Boston, asking for reinforcements.

What was the retreat like?

The British, naturally, did not describe it as a retreat. To them it was an orderly withdrawal, conducted after having achieved virtually all their goals. What they did not realize is they had stirred up a hornets' nest. On their way back to Boston, the British were attacked, time and again, by groups of Americans who fought in a very disorganized fashion. The British were accustomed to opponents who fired and moved in orderly ranks, and who played by the "rules" of civilized warfare. The American militia, by contrast, fought in ways similar to the American Indians, from whom they had learned much over the previous century.

Around the time they reached Lexington, the British were met by Hugh, Lord Percy, and nearly 1,200 British soldiers. These reinforcements came in the nick of time: lacking them, Smith's detachment might have been wiped out. And even with Lord Percy, the British still had a devil of a time on their way back: the Americans kept coming. Just as the sun went down, the British reached the Charlestown peninsula, where they found safety under the guns from the fleet. By then they had suffered 273 men killed, wounded, or missing. American losses were about one-third of that number.

Is it safe to say that Lexington and Concord were American victories?

Lexington was a minor loss, but it led to the victory at the North Bridge. By the time the sun rose on April 20, 1775, there was little doubt that the Americans had done extremely well. Thanks to Paul Revere and other riders, the Americans had been warned. Thanks to the alacrity of their response, the Americans prevailed over the British on the first day of the Revolutionary War.

When did the Siege of Boston begin?

As early as April 20, 1775, there were thousands of Americans in a ring around Boston, but it took a week or so before they were organized into regiments and companies that took up their respective tasks. By about the first of May, the siege began in earnest.

Roughly twenty thousand American militiamen, most of them from within one hundred miles of Boston, arrived to take up the siege, but it was by no means certain how many of them would remain. In the early days of the siege, there was not even a general commander. Most of the New England men voted their own lieutenant and captains, and good discipline did not prevail. About the only thing the men agreed on was that General Artemas Ward of Shrewsbury, who was a veteran of the French and Indian War, would be the commanding general.

How did the Bostonians themselves respond to the situation?

Some Bostonians liked being under the protection of British rule, but many did not. Hundreds of them promptly asked permission to depart, and General Gage made a bargain, under which people who turned in all their weapons (for which they received an official receipt) were allowed to leave. More than one thousand muskets, hundreds of blunderbusses, pistols, and bayonets were surrendered by those that were eager to get out of town.

What kind of shape were the British in, at this early stage of the siege?

They were truly shocked by the American performance on April 19, 1775, but with each week that passed, the British became more confident that it was a one-time affair: that

69

the Americans would not be as successful in the future. General Thomas Gage was still in overall command, but he knew three major-generals were on their way to act as his closest subordinates. Anyone that met General Gage in May 1775 was impressed with how resigned he was to the situation. Gage had never been keen about shedding American blood; he now worried that it was British blood that would flow. During May, Gage remained on the defensive, allowing the Americans to take up positions in Cambridge, Watertown, and Roxbury. All that remained to the British was the peninsula itself, the place the Indians had once called Shawmut.

The same cannot be said of the British naval commander, Admiral Thomas Graves. Almost immediately following the Battles of Lexington and Concord, the admiral asked General Gage to allow him to bombard Charlestown and the surrounding area, to be certain the Americans could not take up position on the heights to the north of Boston. General Gage refused, but Admiral Graves remained the most aggressive of the British leaders, eager to attack the Americans.

Why were whaleboats so important in the Siege of Boston?

Whaleboats were already one of the most innovative American contributions to the maritime world. The first ones were built late in the seventeenth century, and by 1775, the state of building was so advanced that the Americans, using whaleboats, outsailed their British opponents in Boston Harbor. It was the use of whaleboats that allowed the patriots to (twice!) attack Boston Light, on Little Brewster Island.

This illustration shows American soldiers, led by Henry Knox, transporting artillery to Cambridge, where it will be used in the final segment of the Siege of Boston.

What was the build-up to the Battle of Bunker Hill?

In the early days of June 1775, both the British and Americans cast their eyes on the Charlestown peninsula. If the Americans could take and hold it, they could bombard Boston. Likewise, if the British could take the heights, they could control all the northern approaches to Boston. But neither side wished to tip its hand, and the action waited till the third week of the month.

In the meantime, HMS *Cerberus* arrived, carrying three major-generals to Boston. General Sir William Howe was senior of the three; General Sir Henry Clinton the middle; and General John Burgoyne was the junior of the three. All three men thought themselves superior to General Gage in terms of ambition and aggressive spirit, but he remained their commanding officer for the next three months. Burgoyne was especially loud among the three, declaring that they had arrived in time to carve out more "elbow room."

BUNKER HILL AND BREED'S HILL

One usually hears of Bunker Hill, but sometimes of Breed's Hill, as well. Are they connected?

The Charlestown peninsula was pretty much where the Anglo history of Boston had commenced in 1630. This is where the Puritans first landed. In 1775 Charlestown looked a good deal as it had in 1630 with one major difference, a pretty town of about four hundred houses now existed on the southwest corner of the peninsula. Battle of Bunker Hill is actually a misnomer because nine-tenths of the fighting occurred on Breed's Hill. Bunker Hill was about half a mile up the peninsula, heading toward the mainland, while Breed's Hill was much closer to the mouth of the Charles River.

Learning that the British would soon move against these heights, the various American commanders took action of their own. On the night of June 16–17, 1775, almost two thousand men, under the command of General Israel Putnam, moved from Cambridge onto the Charlestown peninsula. Their original intent was to dig in and fortify the crown of Bunker Hill. During that night, however, the lead units of the American force realized that Breed's Hill afforded an even better view of Boston, and that cannon placed on its crest would have a devastating effect. Leaving a small rear guard to hold Bunker Hill, the main forces moved on to Breed's Hill instead.

What did General Gage and his three major-generals see the following morning?

On June 17, 1775, the four British generals awoke to find that the rebels, as they called them, were atop Breed's Hill in force and were digging in. Somehow, the American movement passed unnoticed during the night, but at 8 A.M., the HMS *Lively* began firing cannon shot at the earthworks atop the hill. The Americans were there, and it was plain to the British that they must be dislodged.

General Gage was never one to move quickly, but even he saw this was do-or-die. Give the Americans just forty-eight hours, and they would have cannon atop Breed's Hill, and the town would be at their mercy. Gage gave command of the enterprise to General Sir William Howe. The middle son of a family that provided three notable eighteenth-century British leaders, General Howe was not only experienced, he was a specialist in the development and use of light infantry. This meant he was skilled in the deployment of fast troops, the kind needed to seize the heights on the Charlestown peninsula.

Why wasn't Breed's Hill reinforced?

In retrospect it seems criminal that this was not done. Generals William Prescott and Israel Putnam sent numerous messages to the leadership at Cambridge, but no one really seemed in command that morning. Only General Joseph Warren, who was better known as a physician and an inspired member of the Sons of Liberty, was on hand in Cambridge. Despairing of rousing a true reinforcement, Warren simply seized a musket and declared he was headed for the heights. Friends attempted to dissuade him, but Warren declared he could not allow those men to fight, knowing that he was not at risk.

There were disagreements, too, between General Israel Putnam and General William Prescott. Both men were veterans of the French and Indian War, but they did not get along. One of the few things on which they agreed was their surprise when Colonel Seth Pomeroy arrived. He had commanded the American artillery at the Siege of Louisbourg (1745), and he had led Massachusetts men at the Battle of Lake George (1755). Now, thirty years after Louisbourg's fall, Pomeroy hastened to Charlestown and got there just before the action commenced. Tradition has it that Prescott greeted him with: "Pomeroy, you here? Why, a musket ball would waken you from the grave!"

Didn't the Americans realize the British would attack?

Both sides underestimated the other. The Americans did not anticipate the British would move rapidly, and the British did not understand that the Americans had already achieved great things, throwing up earthworks overnight.

The Americans were reinforced, and they had more than one thousand men on the peninsula, but they could send no more because British cannon, aboard the Royal Navy ships, controlled access to the peninsula.

How tough was it to climb the steep slope of Breed's Hill?

Anyone who ascends the hill today can testify as to its steepness. The British, though, were carrying equipment that was in excess of forty ponds. Given that June 17 was the warmest day of the season to that point, the British performed some heavy labors.

How quickly did the British move into action?

By 2 P.M. more than two thousand British troops were on the Charlestown peninsula. At this time, Admiral Graves gave the order to fire on the town itself, and within one hour, roughly four hundred homes were burned. For many patriots, the burning of Charlestown was the bitterest part of the Battle of Bunker Hill.

The British battery on Copp's Hill was already hurling cannon balls at the position; so were British ships in the harbor. American General William Prescott delighted in acting as if the cannonballs made no difference: he marched up and down the parapet, almost taunting the British to hit him.

When did the British make their move?

At around 2:30 P.M., General Howe ordered his men to the attack, and in typical style he went right with them. One British column came up the east side of the peninsula to confront the New Hampshire men of General John Stark; a second column was near the town, and the third, heaviest concentration of British went straight up, aiming for the crown of Breed's Hill.

When did the Americans open fire?

Tradition has it that General Prescott told his men not to fire till they could see the whites of the eyes of their opponents, but most research suggests it was a bit closer than

An undated illustration shows General Israel Putnam rallying his men for the final defense during the Battle of Bunker Hill.

that, perhaps in the neighborhood of forty yards. The Americans poured accurate fire from all three defensive positions, but their deadliest aim was concentrated in the center. Taking special pains to pick off the British officers, the Americans poured one musket volley after another, and the British reeled.

No one has ever been able to make a firm declaration of how many British fell in those first few minutes, but it may have been four hundred men in all. Whole regiments withstood American fire for minutes and then turned to run. To do otherwise was simply suicide.

Having been repulsed in this manner, why did General Howe try a second time?

He had no choice. His honor, reputation, and the success of the British army in America depended on his actions at that moment. To give up the fight for Bunker Hill with the eyes of the Americans and the civilians of Boston upon him, was simply unthinkable.

Half an hour later, General Howe and his men came back for the second assault. The Americans were perilously short of gunpowder, but they poured forth a second blast of smoke and flame that devastated the British lines to an even greater degree. If four hundred men were killed and wounded in the first assault, it's possible that five hundred went down in the second. For perhaps two minutes, General Howe stood completely alone: his close officers and even his orderly had fallen. Amazingly, he went unscathed.

Having failed twice, how on earth did General Howe persuade his men to make a third attempt?

This was not as difficult as we imagine. The British were maddened by the loss of so many of their fellows, and the loss propelled them to get atop Breed's Hill and chase the Americans out. Shouts of "victory or death" were heard in the British ranks. And at 3:30 P.M., General Howe led his men in the third and final assault.

Both of the Americans wings began to cave in, but the crisis was at the center point, at the crown of Breed's Hill. The Americans were nearly out of gunpowder, and though they felled quite a few more of their opponents, the British were soon atop the earthen parapet, where some furious fighting ensued. In this hand-to-hand conflict, the British lost Major John Pitcairn, while the Americans mourned the loss of Major-General Joseph Warren, the physician-turned-patriot/legislator.

What was the final stage, or the net result, of the battles at Breed's Hill and Bunker Hill?

Chased from Breed's Hill and then Bunker Hill, the patriots escaped the Charlestown peninsula. The British gained the high ground and would hold it for months to come, but they did so at a terrible price. General Howe had 1,054 men killed, wounded, or missing that afternoon, and he had precious little to show for it. The Americans suffered between 400 and 450 men killed, wounded, or missing.

Given these terrible casualty figures, who really won the Battle of Bunker Hill?

Neither side won. The Americans made an excellent stand and proved their worth as military men, but they did not succeed in the objective of driving the British from Boston. The British displayed their valor to the tenth degree, but lost so many good men that it was some time before they were willing to sally forth again. And the single greatest casualty of the Battle of Bunker Hill may have been General Howe's confidence. Though he would rise to become commander-in-chief, and though he would win several important battles, Howe never again risked so much on a direct attack against entrenched Americans.

Was there any follow-up to the Battle of Bunker Hill?

No. Both sides lay low for weeks. The most important action was not in the field, but in the parade ground in Cambridge. On July 2, 1775, Virginia native George Washington arrived. Designated as commander-in-chief of the new Continental Army, he took command of the men in and around Cambridge on July 3.

How did the town of Boston fare during the summer of 1775?

Boston was at a very low ebb. The civilian population fell to around five thousand, and very few of those who remained had good, or even decent, morale. Their greatest fear was that the Americans would launch a full-scale attack, and that the town would burn, much as Charlestown already had.

What was the situation in the American camp(s)?

It was a curious combination. Many of the men showed good, lively spirit, and were eager to come to grips with the British, but there were others that displayed a sluggish spirit. Many New England men resented that a Virginian was their commander-in-chief, especially one that had such firm, even rigid, ideas about military discipline.

George Washington was not, at this stage of his career, the ideal commander-in-chief. Everyone recognized his physical presence and aura of command, but the second of these characteristics caused problems. Coming from Virginia, where his word was law to his slaves, Washington was not adept at managing the men of the Continental Army. One of the few areas of success for him in those first months had to do with Canada. In September 1775, Washington sent Colonel Benedict Arnold, who later famously turned traitor, north to Maine as part of a two-pronged offensive. The effort to conquer British Canada and turn it into the fourteenth colony came close to success, but Québec itself was not captured.

What did George Washington plan during the autumn of 1775?

Though he came across as dignified and very much in control, Washington was deeply concerned that most of his men would not re-enlist at the beginning of 1776. He therefore drew up a number of plans, all of them notable for audacity. In October 1775, he proposed—first to his major generals and then to three delegates from the Continental Congress—that the army attack Boston once ice had formed on the Charles River (of course he could not be certain how thick and deep the ice would be). The plan was so daring that the delegates refused to pass judgment, saying they needed to ask the entire Continental Congress. The major-generals of the army—Charles Lee, Artemas Ward, and Israel Putnam—were deeply ambivalent about the plan: they believed the American militia much better at defense than offense.

What Washington did not realize was the extent to which the British occupiers were also dismayed and demoralized. The morale of the average British soldier in Boston plummeted during the autumn of 1775, largely because they had no plan or visible goal. Life for the occupiers turned into a dismal search for food and firewood with the latter being the greater concern.

Would there have been a terrible bloodbath if Washington's plan had been put into action?

Very likely, yes. Washington overestimated the quality and temper of his men where an offensive operation was concerned. Then too, he did not realize the terrible conditions under which many of the British occupiers lived. They would have fought to the death, and even if Washington had prevailed, the cost would have been too high.

A DIFFERENT SOLUTION

When did Henry Knox become recognized for his talents?

The owner of a Boston bookstore in Cornhill Square, twenty-five-year-old Henry Knox owed all his military knowledge to the books that passed through his hands. Knox was also one of the largest and heaviest men in Washington's army: at a time when people were smaller than now, Knox weighed roughly three hundred pounds. His cherubic face made many people underestimate him, but Washington saw the energy and strength. In November 1775, he sent Knox to upstate New York with the intention of bringing back cannon, for use in the siege.

Fort Ticonderoga, near the southern end of Lake Champlain, had been important in the French and Indian War. American forces seized it in May 1775. No one put two and two together until Knox arrived late in November, bringing men more skilled at moving and transporting heavy equipment than in actual battle. In December, Knox departed Ticonderoga with over 100 pieces of heavy artillery, including mortars.

How thin did the American lines become during the winter of 1775–1776?

At its maximum extent, the American army numbered almost twenty thousand, but by Christmastime of 1775, it was about half that many. George Washington came close to despair; the one thing that gave him some hope was the knowledge that the British had very low morale. When the Americans probed the British lines, especially at Lechmere Point, the British made no attempt to engage.

Knowing that Henry Knox was on the way with heavy artillery, Washington planned a desperate action to take Boston in one fell swoop. Knowing there would be heavy casualties, and that the town might be destroyed, Washington consulted his major generals, who gave conflicting opinions. The Americans certainly were more conscious than the British that the icing over of Boston Harbor could alter the situation.

A circa 1784 portrait of Henry Knox by artist Charles Willson Peale.

How did Knox's arrival change the situation?

In January 1776, Knox and his men brought a "noble train of artillery," as he expressed it, to Cambridge. The Americans were still low on gunpowder, but they at least had the means to threaten the British defenders of Boston. Late in February 1776, Washington and his senior officers formed a plan to seize and fortify Dorchester Heights, on the southern side of the town.

In retrospect it is somewhat amazing that neither side had yet made a move on Dorchester. Washington planned the action for the evening of March 4; he did so intentionally, expecting that the big battle would be fought the next day, which was the sixth anniversary of the Boston Massacre.

How did the action proceed?

Three thousand American militiamen moved into action on the evening of March 4, 1776. Having already put together combined platforms—called fascines—they moved on to Dorchester Heights, and when morning came they gave the impression of having thrown up immense earthworks.

General Howe was astounded when he first surveyed Dorchester Heights from his spyglass. His first response, however, was to mobilize his front-line troops, and observers recalled that he had previously threatened to attack, regardless of the cost. The Americans atop Dorchester Heights saw the British gathering on Long Wharf, making preparations to move to Castle Island before making the grand assault. Washington hastened to the Heights, where he shouted that this was the fifth of March, an excellent day on which to fight the British!

How big and nasty would that battle have been?

It's possible that the battle would have been three times as bloody as that of Bunker Hill, if only because so many more men were involved. The British moved too slowly to take advantage of the early afternoon tide, however, and when they settled in for the evening, the Americans breathed a big sigh of relief. The weather had the final say. A major storm, which some people called a hurricane, blew over Boston on the night of March 5–6. Many buildings were damaged, and when morning came it was apparent that it would be too difficult to mobilize the British attack force (two medium-sized ships had been wrecked in the storm).

Two days later, a British envoy approached the American lines to declare that General Howe would not set the town afire so long as Washington's cannons did not open fire from Dorchester Heights. Tense days followed in which neither side made a military move, and the British worked furiously to pack their belongings.

How did the Bostonians view the situation?

Our best clue comes from the journal of Timothy Newell, one of the town selectmen. He commented that

> … the inhabitants in the utmost distress, through fear of the town being destroyed by the soldiers, a party of New York carpenters with axes going through the town breaking open houses &. Soldiers and sailors plundering of houses, shops, and warehouses—Sugar and salt & thrown into the river, which was greatly covered with hogsheads, barrels of flour, house furniture, carts, trucks, &c—One person suffered four thousand pounds sterling, by his shipping being cut to pieces.

> MHS *Proceedings,* Vol. 1, 4th series, 1852, p. 274

How difficult was it for Howe to extricate his followers?

Not only did Howe have more than ten thousand soldiers, he was also besieged by Loyalists, asking him to take them away. Howe did his best, and in the end nearly 1,500 Loyalists embarked with his troops. Tensions continued, and when the British departed, on March 17, 1775, the Americans could scarcely believe their eyes. This happened to be Saint Patrick's Day, which had been celebrated by Boston's Irish Protestants for almost fifty years, and in the years that followed, it came to be known as Evacuation Day.

What did Boston look like to the entering Americans?

The town was a disaster. Grass had grown on some of the streets, and many of the churches were in poor repair. The British had used the Old South Meeting House as the site of a riding academy!

How narrow was Boston's escape?

If General Howe had assaulted Dorchester Heights, there would have been an intense, pitched battle. At the same time, however, General Washington had four thousand men near Charlestown, and they were ready to come across and attack the north side of Boston. The casualty list might have been huge, and the town of Boston might have been utterly destroyed. Some of the townspeople recognized this fact, and they composed a laudatory address to Washington, thanking him that their town was spared.

Did Washington remain in Boston in order to savor his success?

He remained for fewer than three weeks. By mid-April, Washington and a considerable percentage of the Continental Army had departed for southern Connecticut and New York City. Washington correctly anticipated that the British would ignore Boston in future campaigns, and that the struggle would be for New York and the middle colonies.

Once the Continental Army had departed, Boston had the tough task of picking up the pieces. Not only had thousands of townspeople departed, but hundreds of others had sailed with the British. Many people wished the Loyalists good riddance, but this ignored the fact that they were some of the wealthiest and most productive people in town. Years passed before Boston was able to regain what it had lost in a commercial sense.

What impression did Washington take as he left Boston in 1776?

Washington never liked the New Englanders very much, and the feeling was mutual. One of the few exceptions was Washington's admiration for the black poetess, Phillis Wheatley. In the winter of 1776, he wrote to her, thanking her for her flattering lines of poetry, and inviting her to visit him any time she was in Cambridge.

Were there any subsequent battles in the Boston area?

Nothing that even approaches the dignity of a skirmish. Boston and eastern Massachusetts formed the center of the war effort for both sides during the first calendar year of the Revolutionary War. By mid-1776, the theater of war had altered, however, and it never came back to the Bay Area. Bostonians remained conscious of what they had attempted and accomplished, however. They had a number of leaders, including John Hancock and Sam Adams, that remained prominent for the duration of the war.

How did Harvard College fare during the Revolutionary War?

The Harvard Class of 1775 saw forty graduates, and 1776 witnessed the graduation of roughly thirty-five. From there it was downhill, however, with only twenty-six graduates in 1779. Not until 1787—four years after the Revolution ended—did Harvard see as many young men graduate as in the banner year of 1775. The leadership of Harvard was quite distinguished during this period, however.

Why did a major French war fleet visit Boston in 1778?

In March 1778, the government of King Louis XVI signed two treaties—one of commerce and the other of military alliance—with the young United States. A major war fleet, led by Admiral Charles-Hector, Count d'Estaing, visited Boston in the late summer of 1778. D'Estaing received great courtesy from John Hancock and the leading Bostonians, but workaday Bostonians, especially those on the docks, remembered the time when France had been the enemy. There was a brawl and at least two French sailors were killed. Then, when another squadron of French ships arrived in 1782, a fine French warship, *Le Magnifique*, was wrecked on a sandbar in Boston Harbor.

How large a role did Boston play in the creation of the Massachusetts state constitution?

Legal scholars concur that the Massachusetts state constitution is the oldest operating constitution, not just in the United States, but in the entire world. Bostonians

The Count d'Estaing came to Boston in 1778 to offer France's support of the American cause via a fleet of warships.

did not play an overly large role in the writing of the document, but when the work was finished, Boston had become the town in North America most closely associated with human rights and the dignity of mankind (one cannot yet use the word humankind). The opening article says much about the document, and the political spirit that prevailed in Massachusetts in and around the year 1780.

"All men are born free and equal, and have certain natural, essential, and unalienable rights; among which may be reckoned the right of enjoying and defending their lives and liberties; that of acquiring, possessing, and protecting property; in fine, that of seeking and obtaining their safety and happiness." Was this as revolutionary as the Declaration of Independence, written four years earlier? The words are somewhat different, but the spirit is fundamentally the same.

What did visitors have to say about Boston in the 1780s?

Samuel Breck was a native Bostonian who spent several years abroad. He returned home in the summer of 1787, at the very time when the new federal Constitution was being debated in Philadelphia. Breck did not comment on that document, or the political nature of the times because he was much more interested in the actions of the people. Years abroad had made him more sober and restrained, he found, and the Bostonians—especially the younger sort—seemed to revel in all sorts of entertainments.

"Thither we went," Breck wrote, "a good deal tipsy, making a zigzag course over the bridge, and ascending the hill by a steep and narrow street.... I was sober; most of our party were otherwise, and by their noise and insolence in passing a tailor's house raised the choler of the whole shopboard, who swore they would cuff and trim us, and send us home with a stitch in our sides." The ensuing altercation led to a court action, and many of the young gentlemen had to pay fines. Breck went on to relate, however, that most of the young men in the frolic later became "magistrates, legislators, fathers, and venerable square-toes of the community."

What did foreign observers have to say about Boston in the 1780s?

Frenchmen formed the largest number and percentage of foreign visitors, and their comments tended to be positive. They remarked on the cleanliness of the streets and the attractiveness of the young women. These French observers were quite aware that their nation had once been the enemy during the French and Indian wars, and they remarked that the intense Puritan style of religion had yielded to a much gentler form of Congregationalism.

FROM REVOLUTION
TO NATIONALISM

How did Boston shed its revolutionary garb (and attitudes)?

It happened very subtly, but once the process commenced it could not be reversed. As late as 1779, or thereabouts, Boston remained the quintessential revolutionary town, the place that birthed the Sons of Liberty and the Tea Party, and which weathered the terrible siege of 1775–1776. Bostonians became more conservative during the 1780s, however. When Shays' Rebellion began in western Massachusetts, Boston contributed many of the troops and officers that marched to quell the rebels. And by the time George Washington was selected as the nation's first president in 1789, Boston had become as conservative as any town on the East Coast.

When was Boston first connected to the mainland by bridge?

For slightly more than 150 years, the only way in to Boston was by The Neck, which stretched from Roxbury to the Shawmut Peninsula. Of course there were numerous boats, and even boat services that could convey passengers, but it was desirable to have another means, and in 1785 the Charles River Bridge Company was incorporated. The first pier was laid in June 1785, and the final one in May 1786. The new bridge, which was 1,503 feet long, was opened for traffic on June 17, 1786, the anniversary of the Battle of Bunker Hill. The Charles River Bridge was considered a marvel, and it soon passed from private property to being held by the Commonwealth of Massachusetts.

The West Boston Bridge, generally known as Cambridge Bridge, was opened in November 1793, just seven months after the first pier was laid. The wooden part of the bridge was 3,438 feet in length and was supported by no fewer than 180 piers.

How did Boston and its residents look in and around the year 1789?

Our best answer comes from a news sheet that was printed shortly after the arrival of President George Washington. Boston turned out an enormous parade in honor of the nation's first president with the order of floats and marchers listed.

The town selectmen came first, followed by the overseers of the poor, the town treasurer, and the town clerk. Then came a long list of workingmen, listed by occupation. There were bakers, blacksmiths, block-builders, boat-builders, cabinet- and chairmakers, clock- and watchmakers, glaziers and plumbers, goldsmiths and jewelers, and so forth.

The Frenchman Jacques Pierre Brissot wrote favorably in his journal about the character of the Bostonians he met while in America.

Who were some of the most perceptive foreign observers of Boston?

Jacques Pierre Brissot (1754–1793) came in 1788 and positively enthused about almost everything he observed. The Bostonians he describes in his journal are calm to the point of being grave, level-headed, and serene. They show neither the wild passions of the Parisians (he wrote this one year before the French Revolution) nor the haughtiness of the English. Boston society is so calm and orderly, Brissot wrote, that a young girl will trust herself to the promise of a beau, and he either will be good to his word, or be shamed all the way out of town.

Brissot also wrote extensively about the drive toward commerce and trade. Boston had recently sent its first two ships to Canton, opening trade with China, and he accurately forecast that this would continue to grow. Brissot attributed most of the success and prosperity he saw to a republican spirit. Unlike the English, who continued to work for imperialism, and unlike the French, who lived under a despotic regime, the Americans were truly free, and that freedom bore them many fruits.

What did Brissot say about the condition of rich and poor in Boston?

Here are his words on that subject:

> I saw none of those livid ragged wretches that one sees in Europe, who, soliciting our compassion at the foot of the altar, seem to bear witness against Providence, against our inhumanity, and against the chaos of our society. Sermon, prayer, ritual—everything had the same simplicity.

Brissot also commented that the religious intolerance that had previously marked Boston (such as in the persecution of the Quakers in the seventeenth century) had disappeared, leaving tolerance the most notable quality.

When did Boston celebrate the first American circumnavigation of the globe?

Bostonians had been crack sailors right from the beginning. By the time of Captain Kidd (the 1690s), they had reached the Indian Ocean. No Bostonian—indeed, no American—went all the way round the globe until 1790, however. This was the year Captain Robert Gray returned home, after having sailed to the Pacific Northwest, China, and all the way home.

Bostonians were thrilled by Captain Gray's accomplishment, and a flourishing trade sprang up between Boston and China. Silk, tea, and porcelain were among the most desirable Chinese commodities.

What was Boston like in 1790, the year of the first federal census?

Not surprisingly, Boston listed its most prominent citizens first. John Hancock, Samuel Adams, James Bowdoin, and John Scollay came first on the list of heads of families. The Hancock family was listed as having two free white males, three free white females, and seven people under the category of "all other free persons" (presumably these were servants). Once one passes the illustrious town leaders, the census document becomes even more fascinating. The great majority of names continued to be of Anglo descent, but the Irish were making inroads. Then too, there was the occasional oddity, such as a house that did not have a "named" head of household, but was listed simply as "Negroes and Mulattoes," with a total of thirteen people under one roof.

The overall population of Boston was around 18,038 in 1790, a considerable increase from 1780, when it was estimated there were no more than 10,000 people in town. Prosperity, however, had not returned to Boston. Both the 1780s and 1790s were decades of economic depression and downright discouragement for many of the common folk. The trouble was that few of them had any place to go. Bostonians had not yet developed the habit of moving to Manhattan or any other American town. Boston remained *the* place to be, so far as most of them were concerned.

END OF THE EIGHTEENTH CENTURY

How did Bostonians respond to George Washington becoming the first president of the United States?

They were thrilled. When he commanded the Continental Army during the Siege of Boston, Washington had earned some critics, including those that declared he did not understand the nature, or temper of the New Englanders. This attitude ended with the

83

passage of the Constitution and the establishment of the new nation, however, and by 1789, Washington was as close as America came to having a national hero.

One often learns that France, under Louis XVI, helped the Americans in their revolution. How is it possible that America soon went to war with France?

It's an indication of the confused, and confusing, politics of the time. During the 1780s, Bostonians, and the majority of their countrymen, felt very affectionate toward France, which had done so much to help them achieve independence. But sentiments changed soon after the death of King Louis XVI, who went to the guillotine in January 1793.

The new leaders of revolutionary France anticipated that the United States would assist them in their struggle against Great Britain, but George Washington, who was then serving as the first president of the United States, instead issued a careful declaration of neutrality. Infuriated, the French revolutionary forces—those at sea, most especially—did their best to attack American property. Between 1795 and 1797, many American merchant vessels were seized by the French. As a result, the United States began building its first official navy, and Boston, not surprisingly, played an important role.

How did the USS *Constitution* come to be built at Boston?

It was agreed that six frigates would be launched, and that each of the major East Coast towns would be the building site for one. The frigate built in Boston Harbor was named

The USS *Constitution*, the oldest commissioned warship in the world, was built in Boston, and she is docked there to this day.

USS *Constitution* in honor of the document which had knitted the original Thirteen States together. *Constitution* was launched in May 1797, and she soon played an outstanding role in the development of the United States Navy.

As the eighteenth century neared its end, was there any sense that Boston's best days were over?

Yes, indeed. Numerous letters, diaries, and even letters to the editor testify to the sense that the action was now on the western frontier in territories such as Ohio and Indiana, rather than on the eastern seaboard. Bostonians feared this might prove to be the truth, but they were quick to point out that their town had weathered change before.

What few people realized was the cultural importance that Boston had acquired, and which it was about to employ. New York had more ships, and Philadelphia saw more goods pass through on a daily basis, but no other American town had so many newspapers and educated persons as Boston. Then too, few people anticipated the way Boston would become the conscience of the nation, so far as the eradication of slavery was concerned.

THE PHYSICAL SCENE

What did Boston look like in the final years of the eighteenth century?

The town was on its way, however slowly, to becoming a city. The material elegance that was seen thirty years earlier, when John Singleton Copley painted his portraits, was not yet in evidence, but Boston was doing reasonably well. The economic depression of the 1780s and early 1790s was beginning to fade, and some merchants predicted that the best of times still lay ahead.

Topographically, the town still looked fairly similar to what it had looked like a generation earlier, but the townspeople were beginning to complain about the lack of space. Boston had to expand, they declared, or else it would perish. No one had yet projected the idea of cutting down Beacon Hill, or Fort Hill, to provide landfill for the expansion of the town, but the coming century would see those developments.

Were there any particularly apt descriptions of the town, as opposed to the people?

In 1794 an anonymous observer penned this description of the maritime section of town.

> There are eighty wharves and quays, chiefly on the east side of town. Of these the most distinguished is Boston pier or the Long Wharf, which extends from the bottom of State street, one thousand seven hundred and forty-three feet into the harbor. The breadth is one hundred and four feet.... Boston pier has a long range of handsome warehouses erected on the north side of it built of wood. These and the wharf are private property, and have a number of proprietors.

85

Boston was clearly a town of capitalist interests, and it would be a long time before the government—town or state—would have much say in the commerce of the town.

What did the people of Boston look like as the eighteenth century came to an end?

Perhaps the best answer comes from the watercolors of Gilbert Stuart, the foremost American portrait painter at the end of the century. One can tell almost at a glance that Stuart was not John Singleton Copley. The former made the Bostonians look even more dignified and stately than they were; the latter portrayed them with a heavy dose of realism. Stuart's portraits of John Adams and Abigail Smith Adams show the ravages of age on a proud couple who have weathered the great, even incredible, changes of their times.

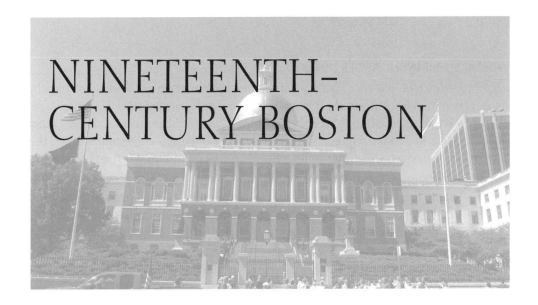

NINETEENTH-CENTURY BOSTON

Where does the expression "The Hub" come from?

To the best of our knowledge it was coined by Oliver Wendell Holmes, Sr., M.D. (1809–1894), one of the truly quintessential Bostonians. It's difficult to know whether he used the expression ironically or in earnest, but he spoke to the sentiment—so common in nineteenth-century Boston—that the City on the Hill or the City on the Bay was the "hub" of the universe.

In more recent times, the expression has been used, or adapted, to describe the top of the Prudential Building in downtown Boston. At fifty-two stories, the Pru—as it is often called—is the second highest point in Boston, and the restaurant on its top floor is known as "Top of the Hub." Regardless of whether one uses the expression in the nineteenth-century context or the modern one, "The Hub" refers to the narrow and provincial belief that Boston is the fount of all, the center of all good things. And to be fair, there are times when this seems very nearly true.

What was Boston like at the turn of the nineteenth century?

The population, surprisingly, had not yet hit forty thousand, and Boston still had the feel of a large town rather than a small city. And this was reflected in the fact that Boston was not incorporated as a municipality until 1822.

Trade, whether with other American cities or overseas, had faded in the late-eighteenth century, and the town did not experience real prosperity as the new century dawned. On the other hand, Boston was unquestionably the leader of New England, and it now drew more of its strength—economic and otherwise—from the hinterland. In terms of architecture, Boston still looked a good deal like the place that had weathered the American Revolution, but the beautiful new churches, such as those designed by Charles Bulfinch, gave Boston a Federalist look, one which it would maintain for the next forty years.

What is meant by "Bulfinch's Boston"?

Charles Bulfinch (1763–1844) had one of the most celebrated and dramatic of all public careers in nineteenth-century Boston. Born during the late colonial period, he traveled abroad after graduating from Harvard College, and on his return he showed signs of becoming a first-rate architect. Though he encountered some difficulties along the way, including some tough times in his personal finances, Bulfinch rose to become the designer of early nineteenth-century Boston.

First came the Hollis Street Church. Down came its colonial-era structure, and what rose in its place definitely belonged to the Federal style, albeit with a European flair. From there, Bulfinch moved on to numerous other churches and public buildings.

Was there a recognizable community of African Americans?

Yes. During the late colonial period, there were perhaps 1,500 blacks in Boston, the great majority of them slaves. They were emancipated shortly after the Revolution, and they now formed the nucleus of what became, and would remain, the African American community of Boston. One of the first signs of their success came in 1806, when the African Meeting House, on Joy Street, just a few hundred yards from the Massachusetts State House, was completed. Until 1898, it remained the single most important sign of African American presence in Boston.

Was there any discussion of how the slaves might eventually be freed?

Very little. A century had passed since the publication of Samuel Sewall's *The Selling of Joseph* (1700), but the average white Bostonian believed it might be the fate of the South-

---

Was Boston a multiethnic place in 1800?

Not at all. To be sure, there were small enclaves of Irish, and perhaps some Germans, but they were the five percent minority, which had no influence on the elections, governance, or economy of the town. At least ninety percent of the town leaders were still of Puritan-Yankee stock and many of them imagined it might remain this way for all time. They did not foresee the waves of immigration that would commence in the 1840s.

Carriages and wagons dominated the streets by day, and walkers ran the town at night. There was little, if any, sign of the Industrial Revolution, which was also in its birth throes. The mills, primarily located in Waltham and Woburn, were beginning to turn out more cotton and woolens, and one could imagine a time when Boston would become an industrial leader. But this knowledge was available only to the upper class, those men and women that were in the know. The hard-working laborer, and the sailor who was idled because of the slack trade, knew almost nothing of this future.

ern blacks to languish in slavery for a century or even more. If any group was willing to do something to bring about black freedom, it was the Society of Friends, but the Quakers were less influential in Boston in 1800 than they had been a half-century earlier.

What products would enable Boston to keep up with the times, and to allow for a modicum of economic success?

The most obvious one was granite, and it came primarily from New Hampshire. Boston merchants delighted in arranging the cutting and transportation of granite, which became the building staple for most of the great nineteenth-century American monuments. The Bunker Hill Monument, for example, was first envisioned in 1825, but it did not come fully into reality until 1843. The big surprise, however, was the marketability of ice.

MISCELLANY

Are there any handful of words that can describe early nineteenth-century Boston?

It's important, right up front, to say that "elegant" is not among those words. Boston had the potential for elegance, but in and around the year 1800 it had a faded, antiquarian look that dated back to the town just before the Siege of Boston.

"Ambitious," "excited," and even "dramatic" are words that can be employed in a description of Boston at this time. The people of the town (it did not officially become a city until the year 1822) were very conscious of being where the American Revolution began, and they were proud of their contribution to the effort that culminated in establishing the nation. But if Boston were to be anything more than a "looking glass" or "history box," it needed to generate new wealth. The sources that had made numerous colonial era Bostonians wealthy—the trade in silk and tea, as well as in lumber and molasses—would no longer cut it. Proper Bostonians—the expression had already appeared—looked for new sources of trade and income.

Was there any thought of making the slave trade part of this search?

Not a bit. Bostonians had not led the way in the banning of the slave trade (which was accomplished by Congress in 1808), but they did rejoice in the end of slavery in most of the Northern states. Critics of that time and of our own could doubtless declare that Bostonians were not doing enough to bring slavery to an end, but the small, feeble beginnings of the abolition movement could indeed be seen, and they were most concentrated in New England. No, if Bostonians needed new sources of wealth, they would find them in cod, oil, and of all things, ice!

Cod fish had long been an important commodity. Did this remain the case?

The trade in cod fish remained one of the most important sources of income up and down the New England coast, with Boston itself receiving a smaller market share with each passing decade. But the search for the humble cod led some Bostonians to think of other humble products, and none could be more ubiquitous than ice.

The New England winters of the early nineteenth century were often severe, with 1844 ranking high on the list. The reason this is important is that some New Englanders, principally Frederic Tudor of Boston, began to cut, section, and then sell ice.

This seems impossible. How could ice be an important item for sale?

Today, the average person makes his or her own ice in record time, and with remarkable convenience. This was not the case in the nineteenth century. And people living in tropical climates wanted—and needed —ice to a far greater degree. In 1806 Frederic Tudor (1783–1864) made financial

Businessman Frederic Tudor made history by being the first to ship ice out of Boston as a commodity.

history by sending the first shipment of ice from Boston: the ship reached Martinique. Tudor was the youngest son of a family in which most of the boys went to Harvard College, but he was much more interested in commerce than education. That first shipment of ice (the ice came from Fresh Pond in Cambridge) encouraged Tudor, and he spent years experimenting, tinkering with the notion.

Over time, Tudor found that wrapping the ice in sawdust was the key to preserving it during long shipping voyages. The War of 1812 nearly ruined his business, but he was back at it during the 1820s, and by the end of that decade he was selling ice as far off as New Orleans and Havana. The farther south his ships sailed, the more money he made. Tudor had another run of bad luck during the 1840s, but by 1855 he was known as the "Ice King." His ships carried cargoes of ice all the way to British-controlled India, where army officers popularized the idea of "mixed" drinks, meaning liquor mixed with ice.

Could such a humble product as ice really make a financial difference to Boston?

No one anticipated it. But Massachusetts ice, like New Hampshire granite, became one of the great surprise commodities of the mid-nineteenth century. People like Frederic Tudor became wealthy, but entire sections of Boston, notably the sailors on the waterfront, also did better as the result of his actions. Maritime success seemed certain for Boston, with trade and commerce following right behind. No one expected the negative downturn that came as a result of the Embargo Act, however.

THE WAR OF 1812

What role did Boston and Massachusetts play in the lead-up to the War of 1812?

In 1807 President Thomas Jefferson announced the Embargo Act, which forbade trade with Britain. England supplied nearly seventy-five percent of Boston's maritime trade, and the town and state suffered severely during two years of embargo. When Jefferson left office, the Embargo Act was allowed to expire, but Boston soon found itself front and center during the War of 1812.

When Congress declared war in June 1812, neither Massachusetts nor the nation was ready for the conflict. Historians debate at length as to James Madison's reasons, but the basic fact is that the people of Boston, and Massachusetts, were largely opposed to the conflict. Governor Caleb Strong promised that Massachusetts militia would not be used out of state, and for a time it even seemed possible that the New England states might secede from the Union.

What altered the situation, at least to some degree?

In September 1812, just three months after war was declared, Captain Isaac Hull piloted USS *Constitution* past Nantasket Beach and up into Boston Harbor. The news he brought was electrifying. *Constitution* had met and utterly defeated HMS *Guerriere*, a British frigate of similar size and strength. *Guerriere* was so badly damaged she had to be sunk, but Hull brought the incredible news of his victory, and 250 British prisoners.

Constitution had been built in Boston in 1797, and she now had a new nickname, "Old Ironsides" (British cannon balls had been seen bouncing off her sides). Bostonians took *Constitution* as their single most important war symbol, and long after the War of 1812 ended, she remained in Boston as the nucleus of the northeast squadron of the U.S. Navy. Bostonians still were not thrilled about the war, but they accepted it had some brighter aspects.

Was Boston ever placed under siege during the War of 1812?

The danger existed, but the British Royal Navy never followed through. Bostonians were thrilled by *Constitution*'s victory in 1812, and downcast when USS *Chesapeake* was defeated and captured by the British in 1813. Generally speaking, however, the damage done to Boston in the War of 1812 was almost entirely composed of what did not happen, meaning that trade came to a virtual standstill.

When Boston learned of the peace treaty, and war's end in February 1815, the town put on one of the largest celebrations seen on the whole East Coast. It was not that Bostonians loved the British, or Old England, but they knew which side of bread received the butter from overseas trade.

What was the single biggest weather event in the early nineteenth century?

Boston knew so many storms and blizzards that they are treated as relatively normal events in the records. This is not the case with the infamous Boston gale of September 1815, however.

On Saturday, September 23, all seemed normal till 11 A.M., when a sudden wind came from the southwest. At noon the wind direction changed to the southeast. Most of the damage was caused in about three hours' time. Many churches lost their steeples, and the chimneys of numerous homes were damaged. One building was entirely blown down, and then consumed by fire (this was the old wooden-glass house in Essex Street). Observers and those that came to calculate the damage asserted that the loss of so many trees on Boston Common was the worst damage of all. Many of the trees that are so well-loved today were planted in the aftermath of the great gale.

When did Boston the town finally become the City of Boston?

On March 4, 1822, the people of Boston accepted the formal charter that turned their hometown into the City of Boston with a mayor and city council. Gone was the town meeting form of government that had dominated since early colonial times. The charter showed that Boston had a population of 46,226 in 1822.

The difference between town and city government had been debated many times with the arguments for the former generally prevailing until 1822. Many Bostonians feared they would be overwhelmed by a variety of new taxes. This did not happen in the 1820s, or even 1830s, but by the 1850s, the taxpayers would be presented with many new headaches, especially as new sanitation laws required the construction of all sorts of new tunnels and dams.

BOSTON AS SEEN BY LAFAYETTE

Who was the most famous of all foreign visitors to Boston during the 1800s?

It was actually a close tie with the Marquis de Lafayette (1757–1834) arriving in 1825, and Charles Dickens (1812–1870) and his wife coming in 1841. The sixty-seven-year-old Lafayette came to the United States in 1824, and he concluded his extended tour at Boston in June 1825. Partly through good luck, Lafayette arrived in the city just in time for the dedication of the memorial to the Battle of Bunker Hill: he was on hand to lay a wreath on the bottom of the granite structure. Lafayette commented that of all the places he saw, Boston had changed the least. The city and its people seemed like the continuation to their Revolutionary-era grandparents.

Bostonians loved to hear this, but if Lafayette had arrived even five years later he doubtless would have said something else. When the marquis came to town in 1825, one could still find all sorts of evidence of the Revolutionary era, but it was being dismantled, day by day. Paul Revere had died in 1818, and the Revolutionary clothing he made so famous, including the tricorn hat, was going out of style.

How much different was Boston in 1841, the year of Dickens' arrival?

No foreign visitor—not even Lafayette—was ever so eagerly anticipated as Charles Dickens, who visited Boston in the winter of 1841. Dickens' first novels were just as successful in the United States as in Europe, and Bostonians were thrilled to have their first look at the literary titan, who was redefining the very status of authorship. Sadly, Dickens was not as pleased with what he saw.

Gilbert du Motier, the Marquis de Lafayette, traveled extensively in the United States, including Boston, recording his impressions in his writings.

Dickens' comments were not specific to Boston; it was Americans in general that he found lacking. The author who did so well connecting to the poor of London's slums looked down his nose on the American cities and towns, declaring it would take them decades to catch up with Old England. American manners, he found appalling (this, it should be added, was common to many visitors from overseas).

Was Dickens fair to Boston—and the United States?

No. Dickens did not make a true comparison between his own nation, which had plenty of income inequality as well as coarse manners, and the young republic. And when his opinions were published in *American Notes*, many Bostonians who had initially welcomed Dickens declared they were pleased to see the back of him.

One thing Dickens did get right was his estimation about the difference of opinion in the United States where slavery was concerned. Britain had banned the slave trade as early as 1806, while America still participated to a lesser degree. Bostonians in Dickens' opinion, did not do enough to ensure that slavery would one day come to an end.

TURNING WATER INTO DRY LAND

Where does the expression "Back Bay" come from?

Much of what is now Boston's most fashionable, prestigious, and expensive real estate once lay under brackish water. The Shawmut peninsula, which the Puritans came to in

1630, was shaped like a five-leaf clover with the upper left section in what is now the Back Bay. This area was composed of tidal flats, which flooded with each high tide, twice a day. The Puritans made no headway in changing or layering this area: nor did they need to. Not until Boston reached the crowded level of 100,000-plus inhabitants did it become necessary to change the topography of the city. And even then, there were plenty of skeptics.

When was the first topographical change made?

In the years immediately following the War of 1812, Boston—indeed much of America—buzzed with a confidence concerning the future. More capital was available than in any previous era, and Boston's town leaders (Boston became a city in 1822) exerted their influence to change

Late afternoon sunlight illuminates a section of the Back Bay in a recent photo.

the landscape. In 1821, two major dams were built on and near the Charles River in order to deflect the flow of water from a large section of the five-leaf clover (as early Boston is so often described). Both dams were finished in 1821, and they heralded a major success in changing water into dry land, but there were, inevitably, side effects. Over the next thirty years, the Back Bay became terribly polluted because the rising tide could no longer reach into the area to clean it. Boston's population, meanwhile, soared, and it was evident that something had to be done.

Who came up with the idea of sawing down Boston's two major hills?

The idea actually had been debated for almost a generation, but it was the political leaders of the 1850s that brought about the change. Primitive steam shovels were used to reduce Fort Hill, on the southeast side of town, from about 120 feet to roughly 40 feet. Tremendous amounts of steam energy and human labor were required to move that earth the 1.5 miles to the Back Bay. Meanwhile, the first reduction of Beacon Hill was attempted. This seemed like the perfect place from which to obtain the earth because it was right on Back Bay. Numerous well-connected Bostonians protested, however, and Beacon Hill was never reduced by more than thirty feet in height.

THE CAUSE OF HUMANKIND

Was Boston not the center of the abolition movement?

It became so. But as late as 1840, one could level plenty of criticism at Bostonians regarding the condition of blacks in the area. Their city was the cradle of liberty, where the American Revolution began, but the blacks of Boston lived in relative squalor.

The first African American church in Boston was completed on Joy Street in 1806, but blacks were not made to feel welcome in the city. Another generation was required for some of them to win social acceptance, and another generation after that for most Bostonians to see them as equals. What mobilized the sentiments of white Bostonians was not the positive qualities of African Americans, but the negative ones of Southern whites. And the writings of William Lloyd Garrison played an important role in bringing about the change.

Who was Garrison and how did he become so important?

William Lloyd Garrison (1805–1879) remains one of the most controversial of all Boston heroes. In his time, he was either praised or condemned by his fellow whites: they saw him either as a heroic, even Christ-like figure, or as the worst type of rabble rouser.

Born in Newburyport, Garrison knew something of difficulty and failure. His father abandoned the family, and Garrison, the middle child, had to work from an early age. His first ventures into journalism all ended in failure, and it was not until he published the first issue of *The Liberator*, on January 1, 1831, that he knew the taste of success. His famous words "I am in earnest—I will not equivocate—I will not excuse—I will not retreat a single inch—and I will be heard." were a clarion call to the early abolitionists.

Was Garrison a Bostonian down deep?

He was. It is no happenstance that he made his mark in journalism, or that he yearned for approval from many of the public figures that he sometimes condemned. In the abolitionist cause, however, Garrison found something larger than self-interest: he endured much suffering along the road to success. A Boston mob once dragged him round the streets at the end of a rope, and his life was threatened on many occasions.

How did Bostonians respond to Garrison's truculent manner?

For the most part they loathed him. To proper Bostonians, Garrison represented the worst type of firebrand, one who might help bring about a war with the South, yet who did not praise the North for what it had done so far.

Did any other town or city in the nation rival Boston as a cultural center?

Not yet. New York City was coming on strong, and within a generation it would establish its first publishing houses and theaters. In 1825, however, Boston remained pre-

For whom is a trust fund intended?

Essentially invented in Boston, the trust fund was designed as a way of keeping wealth in the family. A wealthy ship owner sometimes entrusted all his money to a local bank with the trust officers of the bank establishing a portfolio of stocks and bonds for his descendants. The practice eventually spread to other cities and localities, and there are many "trust-fund persons" in the United States today, people who do not have to work for a living. Trust funds have always had their critics. Right from the beginning, it was pointed out that young men and women who do not have to earn a living may be less productive, over the course of their lives, than those who do.

eminent. Perhaps 50 percent of all the books published in the United States originated from Boston, and the town had no rival where poetry, music, and drama were concerned.

Conscious of their position as the arbiters of national culture, Bostonians were eager to affect an upper-class attitude which was later described as the life of the "Boston Brahmins." The expression has its beginnings in India, where the Brahmins have long been the super-intellectual of the various castes, and the image of the Boston Brahmin, who lives in a brownstone on Beacon Hill, and spends Monday at the theater, Tuesday at the social club, and Thursday at a concert first appeared during the 1830s and 1840s. At the same time, the notion of the "trust-fund" Bostonian was born.

THE TORCH PASSES

When did Manhattan surpass Boston in terms of population and economic power?

Greater New York City already had more inhabitants than Boston by the early 1800s, but the decade of the 1830s witnessed the transfer of financial leadership to Manhattan. Boston merchants still made good money, and the city employed more people than ever, but Boston could not compete with the number of immigrants, or the amount of goods that were created. A major reason is the Erie Canal, which, when completed in 1825, brought the agricultural goods of the Midwest right to New York City's door.

To be sure, all Bostonians were not willing to take second-place to New York City. And it is not a coincidence that as Boston's relative financial power diminished, she continued to assert broad cultural and educational leadership. Harvard College was alive and well in the 1830s, but the most dynamic scenes of learning were neither in Boston nor Cambridge, but in Concord, eighteen miles to the northwest.

Is Concord, then, more than the scene of the second battle of the Revolutionary War?

It is. During the 1830s and 1840s, a group of artists, poets, and writers of prose gathered in Concord. Virtually all of them had strong ties to Boston, but they preferred to live in the country, and it helped that they dwelled practically within sight of Concord Bridge, evoking memories of the battles of April 19, 1775.

Ralph Waldo Emerson (1803–1882) never claimed to be leader of the group, but his great success as a writer and speaker kept him at the forefront. Henry David Thoreau (1817–1862) never wished to be known as anything other than a quiet mystic, but his voluminous writings made him one of the best-known Americans of the 1840s and 1850s. And Amos Bronson Alcott (1799–1888) was seldom ambitious for himself (or his family), but the establishment of the communal farm "Fruitlands" made him a minor celebrity. What all these men, and quite a few other men and women, had in common was the loosely held belief in Transcendentalism.

Can anyone really explain, much less define, Transcendentalism?

Not well. It was—and is—too mystical a path to be delineated with precision. Men and women like Emerson, Thoreau, Alcott, and others believed that rationalism had grown to such a point that the world needed more wonder and spontaneity. To them, the hyper-busyness of Boston, and the commercial orientation of many Bostonians, was little short of obscene. Life, they asserted, is too grand and various an adventure to be contained in financial ledgers and pursuit of the divine is too exciting and important to be left only to the ministers and priests.

Emerson came from a long line of ministers and preachers. Soon after graduating from Harvard College, he abandoned the ministry, however, to become a free thinker. Thoreau had few of Emerson's advantages; one point on which they agreed, however, was the need for "self-reliance." Expressed in Emerson's essay of that same name, the concept came to mean much more than earning one's daily bread. To Emerson, Thoreau, and others, Americans needed more self-reliance in cultural and religious matters most especially. (Also see the "Prominent Bostonians" chapter).

How many Americans from other parts of the nation were influenced by the Transcendental Movement?

The closer one lived to Concord and Boston, the more likely one was to be affected by the movement. But the Transcendental thinkers proved their worth. More college students have read Emerson's "Essay on Self-Reliance" and Thoreau's *Walden* than any comparable collection of prose from any other part of the country. Not everyone agreed with the transcendental thinkers, but it was difficult to ignore them.

THE IRISH

Is there still conflict and contention between Yankees and "The Irish"?

As of this writing in 2015, conflict between the two groups is at the lowest ebb. But when the Irish first arrived in the 1840s, their entrance to the scene prompted a conflict that lasted for generations. Nothing could be snootier than a Boston Yankee, the Irish immigrants declared, and no one could be dirtier or more uncouth than a "Paddy," said the original Bostonians.

Had there not been some Irish immigrants to the United States already?

Yes, but their numbers had always been small. Until about 1845, the year of the Potato Famine in Ireland, there were only a few thousand Irish in Boston, and they had long since learned to conceal the aspects that made them distinct. The Famine, which lasted three solid years, changed that.

Irish immigrants started arriving in large numbers, settling in the Old North End, which once had been the very bastion of Yankee respectability. This was the part of town where Paul Revere had lived, and where his famous ride began following the lighting of two beacons in the belfry of the Old North Church. By about 1850, however, the Old North End was primarily inhabited by recent arrivals from Ireland, the great majority of whom did not speak English.

Were there not any schools at which the Irish could learn English?

Schools were few, and they catered almost exclusively to those who spoke English as their first language. The Irish did not make matters easier, however; many of the older generation refused to learn English, and they cast scorn on those that did make the attempt. Boston only became a city in the year 1822, and it seemed, for the next twenty-five years, as if it would maintain its traditional appearance. But the census of 1850 revealed that there were 35,000 Irish in Boston (out of a total population of 136,000) and this number only grew in the decades that followed.

How did the Boston Brahmins—if that is the right phrase—keep the Irish at bay?

They used any number of stratagems to accomplish this. Some Boston shops posted big bold signs with the letters "NINA" on the top. The abbreviation stood for "No Irish Need Apply." Membership in the various social clubs was almost exclusively Yankee for the next two generations, and the Irish and Yankees seldom met in the streets. Their neighborhoods became carved by invisible lines of separation, meaning that old-time Bostonians did not mix with the newcomers. If the crisis over slavery and secession had not arisen in the 1850s, it is likely that the separation, and real segregation, of the Irish would have lasted even longer.

BOSTON AREA HUMANITARIANS

Would the humanitarians—or the "humane influence"—have been so successful without the Civil War?

It's a great question. Both the desire to free the black slaves and the desire to help the blind, the insane, and the helpless arose from a new social consciousness that came to maturity in the 1850s. Very likely, there were just as many blind, indigent, and insane people prior to the great reform era, and the belief that these people *could* be helped was a huge part of beginning the process. The humanitarian impulse merged with the abolition movement during the Civil War, and the great struggle on the battlefield allowed the reforms to be pushed to high levels.

Who was Samuel Gridley Howe?

Born in Boston, Samuel Gridley Howe (1801–1876) was one of the most important of Boston's numerous social reformers. As a young man, he attended Harvard Medical School, but he soon left home to participate in the Greek Revolution, which stirred the hearts of many Bostonians. On returning to the United States, Howe hit upon the notion of organizing an asylum for the blind in Boston. Until that time, the blind were practically prisoners in their homes and completely dependent on the good will of relatives. After another trip to Europe, Howe began teaching a few children at his father's house in Boston. This was the small beginning that led to the formation of the Perkins School for the Blind.

Howe's efforts on behalf of blind Bostonians generated a genuine social movement, but it was not until later in the nineteenth century that it came to full fruition. When blind and deaf Helen Keller came north to live in Massachusetts, she generated intense interest among Bostonians, and the movement Howe had begun burst into full flower.

Who was Samuel Gridley Howe's wife, and why is she important to Boston's story?

Julia Ward Howe (1819–1910) was born in New York City, but upon her marriage to Samuel Gridley Howe she became a Bostonian. In 1861, upon hearing Union sol-

Samuel Gridley Howe (shown with Laura Bridgman, who was under his care) made great reforms in helping the blind.

99

diers sing "John Brown's Body," she penned "Battle Hymn of the Republic." One can quibble as to which is the better or more popular song, but the power and strength of both cannot be denied. With her pen and that alone, Julia Ward Howe gave additional strength to the cause of the Union.

Who was Dorothea Dix?

Born in Maine, which was then part of Massachusetts, Dorothea Dix (1802–1887) was one of the most tireless social reformers of nineteenth-century America. Following a lonely, painful childhood, Dix opened a school for girls in Boston. As a teacher, she was excellent, but significant stretches of ill health limited her effectiveness. When she visited the East Cambridge jail in 1841 to teach a Sunday school class, Dix was horrified by the conditions of the prisoners. Discovering that there was no separation between those that were incarcerated for crime and those deemed criminally insane, she singlehandedly commenced a reform movement.

Dix revealed what she had found to the Massachusetts state legislature in 1843. Though a long road lay ahead, she eventually helped to pioneer the building of special hospitals for mental patients. Widely acclaimed in later life, she traveled far, and even met the Pope.

COMING OF THE CIVIL WAR

How did Boston become the center for abolitionists?

Many people pointed to the discrepancy between Boston rhetoric and Boston's reality. Here was the place where American independence began, yet the city seemed to do nothing for the freedom of African Americans. This began to change in the 1850s.

Bostonians were not thrilled when William Lloyd Garrison—the nation's preeminent abolitionist—published harsh words in *The Liberator* in 1831. A Boston mob attacked Garrison some days later, declaring that he was inciting racial tensions. Over the next two decades, though, Bostonians rethought their beliefs. And, as it turned out, the Compromise of 1850 was instrumental in changing their minds.

What did the Compromise of 1850 have to do with Boston?

Three-fourths of the provisions of the Compromise of 1850, a series of laws related to slavery and new territories, had nothing to do with the City on the Bay. But the new, enhanced, fugitive slave law required sheriffs and constables to assist Southern slaveholders in regaining their "property." Many Bostonians hailed the Compromise when it was first written into law, but they soon regretted their stance.

In May 1854, escaped slave Anthony Burns was apprehended on the streets of Boston. Handed over to the city jail, he spent a few days there, and, if circumstances had been normal, he would shortly have been returned to his owner in Maryland. These were not normal times, however.

How many Bostonians turned out in support of Anthony Burns?

In the first few days it was a few hundred Bostonians. Within two weeks, the number swelled to over three thousand people, many of whom had regular work that they ignored in order to stand guard outside the Boston jail. Much like the Sons of Liberty, who refused to allow the tea to be unloaded in 1773, the Boston crowd refused to allow Anthony Burns to be brought to the ship and returned to slavery.

Unfortunately, the noble stance of the protesters was marred when an ill-designed attempt to break into the jail (and free Burns) ended in the death of a policeman. Public sympathy was very much with the protestors to this point: after the murder, public sentiment moved in favor of Burns' being returned. Even so, two regiments of federal soldiers, as well as many Boston militia, were needed to escort Burns from the jail and on to the ship which carried him back to slavery in Maryland. And even then the siege was not over. Burns' owner found that a slave who had tasted freedom was not that good a worker, so he put him up for sale. A group of Boston abolitionists raised the money to purchase Burns' freedom, and it was anticipated he would stay in Boston for the rest of his days. Not so. Burns did not like Boston very much, and he soon moved to Canada.

What connection did John Brown have to Boston?

John Brown (1800–1859) was born in Connecticut and raised there and in Ohio. He was much more of a midwesterner than an East Coast person, but when he looked for moral support and people to back his audacious and sometimes outrageous enterprises, Brown turned to two places: Boston and Concord. He appealed to the conscience of the Boston merchants and to the sentiments of the Concord Transcendentalists. In neither case was he very successful.

In October 1859, John Brown seized the federal armory at Harpers Ferry, Virginia (now part of West Virginia) in an attempt to start an armed slave revolt. Despite a

---

Was any other city in the nation as much of a "test market" for the coming of the Civil War?

Not even close. In moral terms, Boston was the staging ground for the verbal battles between abolitionists and those that wanted to get along with the South. In material terms, Boston was the only city ready to apply economic pressure on the South (Manhattan proved singularly unwilling to do so). As the Civil War approached, Boston only became more important, as the place where the abolitionists raised their voices the loudest.

promising start, his venture was doomed to failure, and Brown was captured, tried, and executed. His noble stance during the trial won him many new adherents, however, and even some of the Concord Transcendentalists admitted they may have misjudged Brown.

What role did Boston play in the months leading directly to the Civil War?

There are those who claim there would have been no Civil War without the rise of Abraham Lincoln, and others who assert that the New England Yankees—those of Boston especially—played the most important role. A strange phenomenon took place in many Northern and Eastern cities in the autumn of 1860, and Boston was no exception. The "Wide Awakes," as they called themselves, were middle-class white men who believed the victory of the Republican Party in the national election was absolutely vital to the survival of the nation. Holding massive rallies on Boston Common—with each of the several thousand men holding a candle to the darkness—the Wide Awakes were dead-set and in earnest.

How did Boston respond when the Civil War came?

Like most Northerners, Bostonians were both jubilant and surprised. Right up to when the first guns were fired at Fort Sumter, most Bostonians believed war would not come, that their Southern cousins would not be so foolish as to provoke the great colossus that was the North. But the moment the news came, Boston was in the forefront because of the actions and attitude of Massachusetts Governor John A. Andrews (1818–1867).

Elected governor in the same month that Abraham Lincoln won the White House, Andrews was Lincoln's strongest supporter among the governors of the Northern states. When Lincoln put out a call for 75,000 volunteers, to quell what he called the "insurrection," Massachusetts was first in line, and had more men ready to take the field than any other state. Not only did this win the Bay State credit where the nation was concerned, but Massachusetts men were among the first to die in the Civil War.

How would Massachusetts men—as opposed to New Yorkers or Pennsylvanians—be first in the line of fire?

Two Massachusetts regiments were raised before the war began, and when the call for volunteers was sent, they departed Boston

John A. Andrews was governor of Massachusetts from 1861 to 1866 and a staunch supporter of President Abraham Lincoln.

by train, headed for Washington, D.C. Their trip was uneventful until they reached Baltimore, and it was in the act of changing railroad cars (and lines) that the men of the Massachusetts 61st were attacked by a Baltimore mob. Three Massachusetts men were killed; several others were wounded; and the Civil War saw its first blood.

Not surprisingly, Boston and the Bay State continued to play a leading role in the first year of the war. There were more Massachusetts men, on a proportional basis, at the Battle of Bull Run than there were from Pennsylvania, for example. But in 1862, when the bloodletting reached an entirely new level, the Massachusetts contribution faded somewhat, meaning that New York, Pennsylvania, Ohio, and Illinois—all of which possessed greater reserves of manpower—played a larger role. It was left to Massachusetts to demonstrate a whole new type of moral leadership, however.

AFRICAN AMERICAN SOLDIERS FROM BOSTON

Why is the Massachusetts 54th Regiment so well-known?

Much of this is thanks to the movie *Glory*. Released to the wide screen in 1989, *Glory* is one of the best of all Civil War films. Starring Matthew Broderick and Morgan Freeman, the movie depicts the raising and first combat of the Massachusetts 54th, which led the way in attempting to capture Battery Wagner, on the coast of South Carolina. While the film takes an occasional liberty, it is largely faithful to the true story, and highlights the heroic contribution made by black soldiers.

Then too, millions of visitors to Boston have seen the magnificent granite monument to the men of the Massachusetts 54th. The monument stands on the very top of Boston Common, directly across the street from the Massachusetts State House. It's difficult to miss the monument, especially when one sees the school buses parked nearby.

Was the Massachusetts 54th entirely from Boston?

No. The regiment was raised in neighboring Readville, and there were quite a few blacks who came from other Massachusetts cities and towns. Boston furnished the majority of the soldiers, however, and the city—which had already earned praise for its action in the Civil War—now became known as the city in which the abolitionists spoke the loudest, and the city which raised the only regiments of African American troops.

How painful was the baptism of fire of the Massachusetts 54th?

The soldiers were all African American; the officers were all white. Lieutenant-Colonel Robert Gould Shaw led his men in a gallant but impossible task, the attempt to capture Battery Wagner, on the south side of Charleston Harbor. As the film *Glory* accurately depicts, the Confederate defenders waited until the attack was too far launched for the

103

Northern men to turn back, and then blasted them with cannon and rifle fire. The Confederates displayed an extraordinary animosity toward the African American soldiers, sometimes killing prisoners the moment they were taken. But the failed attempt in July 1863 convinced many Northern leaders that blacks could fight just as well as whites. The Massachusetts 54th and 55th regiments fought throughout the rest of the war, and the Massachusetts 5th, a black cavalry regiment, was also raised. Other states recruited black soldiers into their ranks, but no other state allowed African Americans to play such an important role in the great contest.

BOSTON'S TRIUMPH AND THE GOLDEN YEARS

How did Bostonians greet the end of the Civil War?

They were thrilled, of course. The long struggle seemed to validate many, if not all, of Boston's goals. Four million men, women, and children were now freed, and Bostonians congratulated themselves on having played a major part in their release. What was not evident, however, was a desire to integrate African Americans into the regular life of white Boston.

How did Boston fare during the end of the war?

Boston thrived. The city was more prosperous, on a pound-for-pound basis in 1865 than in 1840 or even 1820. Boston could not catch Manhattan as the great commercial city of the East Coast: that race had already been run and lost. Boston could, and did, make a major comeback in the 1870s, however. She was the city of the fine arts, and she continued to market the goods of most of New England.

Why is the final part of the nineteenth century considered a "golden era" for Boston?

One has to work hard to count all the reasons. Boston was the center of major inventions with Alexander Graham Bell bringing out the world's first telephone. The Massachusetts Bell company was founded on the basis of his invention. Boston was the center for all sorts of artistic and cultural activities, and it possessed more charitable, philanthropic, and educational centers than any other metropolis. Before Bostonians could completely revel in these advances, however, they had to survive the terrible fire of 1872.

Do we know what Boston looked like prior to the Great Boston Fire of 1872?

The airplane was not yet invented, but there were skillful and imaginative artists who drew panoramas of the major American cities. One such panorama of Boston was released in 1871, and we can therefore see what the City on the Bay looked like.

The Massachusetts State House has been in continuous use since 1789.

Industrial activity plays a major part in the drawing: smoke belches from factories in East Boston and East Cambridge. The Charles looks narrower than before, and this is the result of landfill, which had been ongoing for decades. Boston Common stands out nicely with the golden dome of the Massachusetts State House gleaming in the foreground. Boston looks like a truly dynamic city. The big surprise is how quickly the city disappears once one looks to the north and west. Harvard exists in the panorama of 1871, but it looks rather small, and once one passes Watertown and Brighton, the countryside emerges.

When did Boston's Great Fire occur?

It came in the autumn of 1872, just a year after the Great Fire of Chicago.

How did the Great Boston Fire of 1872 get started?

Seldom has any urban conflagration been studied and examined so thoroughly. The fire, which began in the early evening of November 9, 1872, started in an elevator in the rear of the basement of the building known as 83 and 85 Summer Street. The first alarm was sounded at 7:24 P.M., and thanks to windy conditions the fire spread much more rapidly than anyone anticipated. The Great Chicago Fire was only one year in the past—September 1871—but the Boston fire was nearly as shockingly destructive as it moved from one street to another.

The faulty construction of the elevator, which, like most, had only a wood-covered sheathing, was blamed. Had the elevator possessed even a handful of self-closing hatch-   **105** ways, Boston might have been spared one of its worst disasters. Instead, however, the fire spread from Summer to Otis Street. This was the point at which the Boston Fire Department might have succeeded in putting out the flames, if only it had possessed enough horses.

What was wrong with the Boston Fire Department's horses?

They existed in plentiful number, but most of them had contracted a distemper just a few weeks earlier, which rendered them useless during the crisis. Boston had only six main fire engines, but they were of first-rate quality, and had they reached the flames in time, the great disaster might have been prevented. Instead, the fire only grew for the first few hours. Not until noon of the following day was it contained, and Bostonians could then go about the ghoulish business of totaling the losses.

On a human level, the Great Fire was not a terrible disaster: only a few people perished. On a material level, it was an enormous disaster: 65 acres of apartment buildings, churches, and department stores were destroyed. Photographs taken the day after the fire show enormous devastation.

What was the impact of the Great Boston Fire of 1872?

Over thirty people died in the Great Boston Fire of 1872, and the downtown business area was virtually destroyed. The Massachusetts State House emerged untouched, and most of the major churches escaped destruction, meaning that the casualties were primarily to business establishments.

One thing that the Great Chicago Fire, the previous year, had already demonstrated was the remarkable strength of the American city. Just as Chicago came back even

This lithograph shows what Franklin Street in Boston looked like before and immediately after the 1872 fire.

stronger from the Great Fire of 1871, so did Boston from the calamity of 1872. Within five years, nearly all the business establishments were rebuilt, and Boston's downtown was stronger than ever.

THE NEW TRINITY CHURCH

How many churches were consumed by the flames in 1872?

Perhaps two dozen were destroyed, but the one that was by far the most grieved was Trinity Church. Located in the Old South End, Trinity Church was much loved by its congregants, who looked around for a different location. Before long, they decided on the east side of Copley Square.

Today, Copley Square is one of the most popular and recognizable parts of Boston. In the 1870s, however, it had a rather run-down look, and was known only for the fact it was named for John Singleton Copley, the great eighteenth-century portrait painter. One thing the architects and builders of Trinity Church soon realized was that special care was necessary. Nearly all of Copley Square is landfill, from the early to mid-nineteenth century.

What did they do to secure the foundations of Trinity Church?

Piles were driven into the landfill, and connections were made with the salty, briny muck below. This was the great age of construction, and the builders of Trinity Church employed much that had been learned from the building of lighthouses. Even so, it was risky, and months of experiments were required before the foundations of Trinity Church could be constructed.

Who was the architect of Trinity Church?

Henry Hobson Richardson (1838–1886) was not a native of Boston (he hailed from New Orleans), but he contributed a great deal to the development of the city in the late nineteenth century. Perhaps the most gifted and one of the most prolific architects of his time, Richardson intended Trinity Church to be a celebration of the best of the medieval style, executed in a modernist format. It took five years, but when Trinity Church opened its doors on February 9, 1877, virtually all the viewers were astonished. The darkness that Trinity shows on the outside is nearly matched by light within, and the murals—executed by John La Farge—are little short of a miracle. Bostonians still marvel at Trinity Church today, and they are often rewarded with a spectacular sight: the reflection of old Trinity Church from the glass panes of the John Hancock Tower. The two make an unforgettable sight.

BOSTON IN 1874

Why choose 1874, or any other particular year?

Bostonians are very conscious of dates and chronology, and as the national Centennial approached, they outdid themselves in promoting the virtues of their fair city. Eighteen-seventy-four is conveniently placed, two years after the Great Fire of 1872, and two years prior to the Centennial. This is how a group of authors viewed Boston in 1874.

"Boston, the metropolis of New England," they wrote, "embraces five distinct sections—Boston proper, or Old Boston, a peninsula extending from the mainland northeasterly, about two miles in length by one in breadth; East Boston, formerly known as Noodle's Island; South Boston; Roxbury, or the Boston Highlands; and Dorchester. The city is, to a large extent, surrounded with rivers, creeks, bays, and inlets, and hence remarkably irregular in its outline."

Did Bostonians of that time understand the history of how the narrow peninsula had been changed?

They did. The editors of the *Massachusetts Almanac of 1874* waxed about how so much water had been converted to dry land. They saved special mention for the many means of transportation that existed in the city.

"By these radiating lines of railway, their various branches and connections, the city has immediate communication with every section of the country; and, by the interchange of merchandise passing over them, its wealth and prosperity have been of late, surprisingly augmented." The facts spoke well for themselves. Boston saw 3,161 ships from foreign ports deposit papers at the Customs House in 1873, as well as 1,344 from the American coastal trade, for a total of 4,931 ships. Seventy-three ocean steam vessels arrived from Liverpool that year.

Did this particular publication say anything about the Irish of Boston?

The reader can gain the impression that there *were* no Irish in the city. The many statements of praise by the editors made no reference to the fact that Boston was a divided city.

Where does one look to gain a view of the less fortunate residents of Boston?

This is found in the *Report of the Bureau of Statistics of Labor*, issued in 1875. The editors paint the picture of two different families, one headed by a skilled laborer and the other by a day laborer. The latter is more important for our consideration.

> Laborer on Wharf … Earnings of Labor $221, Earnings of Wife $110, Total $331. Family numbers five, parents and three children from two to ten years of age. Live in three rooms in a tenement block with miserable surroundings. The apartments are poorly furnished and inconvenient. Family ill-dressed. The mother goes out washing and the father worked but very little last year; would

have starved if they had not received assistance; most of their clothing was given to them. The fuel used by this family is picked from the streets by the children.

One could certainly find similar descriptions of the poor in other American cities, but Boston, which had been settled for so long, was held to a higher standard. One who looked under the surface was often appalled by the level of poverty.

How important is Alexander Graham Bell to the identity of modern Boston?

His name is not invoked as frequently as in the past, but for more than a century after his invention of the telephone, Bell (1847–1922) was considered a Boston inventor; many other people attempted to capitalize on his success. Briefly put, he was not a Bostonian by birth (Edinburgh, Scotland) or education (Edinburgh and London), but he became thoroughly identified with the city and its commercial success.

Born in Edinburgh, Scotland, in 1847, Bell came from a talented family that specialized in the science of elocution. Both his father and uncle greatly admired the United States, and when the Bell family crossed the ocean they settled first in Ontario, Canada. Alexander Graham Bell soon moved to Boston where he taught at the School for the Deaf and Dumb. Perhaps it was from his early studies—then again it may have primarily been a spontaneous development—that Bell became fascinated with the notion of a speaking instrument, which could carry the voice over long distances.

How long did it take Bell to invent, and then patent, the telephone?

The actual work moved along much more rapidly than we might think: roughly three years passed between Bell's first drawings on the subject and his first practicable telephone. He was assisted by the promotion that came from the Centennial Exposition in Philadelphia in 1876, and by 1878 he had an instrument that could transmit sound over perhaps one hundred feet. Boston soon became known as the city for telephone innovation, and the company Bell founded eventually became known as "Ma Bell," the Massachusetts Telephone Company.

How rapidly did the telephone spread from Boston to the suburbs?

Just about everyone wanted a phone in those days, and the instrument itself was

Inventor Alexander Graham Bell was long associated with Boston, though he was from Scotland, originally.

not that hard to manufacture. The telephone wires themselves were quite a different matter.

In the first ten years of telephone development, everyone in Boston and its suburbs needed a separate wire running to every house to which they wished to speak. As a result, downtown Boston began to resemble a disaster zone with wires here, there, and everywhere. Only after the terrible blizzard that struck Manhattan in 1888 did the telephone companies discover the wisdom of installing telephone wires underground, and of having switching stations so that no one needed a separate wire for every house he wished to call.

When did Boston become the center for industrial development in the Northeast?

It had been in the forefront for decades—the cotton mills along the Woburn River attest to that—but the 1870s and 1880s were the decades when Boston become the leader in terms of industrial patents and innovations. Boston inventors tended to specialize in very practical instruments, such as steam boilers, compasses, and industrial clocks, but they moved into other areas, always excelling in the movement toward time pressure and efficiency.

Perhaps it was the Yankee heritage that made the nineteenth-century inventors so time conscious; in any event, they turned out more instruments for keeping time and measuring productivity that the city became the leader in all such mechanisms.

ETHNIC WARS

Is "war" really an appropriate word to describe the tensions in late-nineteenth-century Boston?

It's true that violence was pretty well restricted. But the animosity between old Yankees and new Irish and Italians could hardly be overstated. The Yankees believed Boston was "their" city, and that the newcomers pulled down the elegance and beauty of the city. The Irish, Italians, and others declared that this was "their" city because their labor did so much to build it, and they resented the arrogance of the Yankees. Of course there were some exceptions, areas in which newcomers and old timers got along. But on the streets of Boston one found a type of urban segregation that was appalling: Irish stuck to their part of the city, meaning the Old North End and South Boston, and Yankees kept to the other. Downtown Boston looked as thoroughly Yankee as ever, but one only had to stroll one mile to find the congested neighborhoods of Irish Boston, and it sometimes seemed as if the two peoples came from different worlds.

How bad was it for the Irish in the beginning?

Mention has already been made of signs that read "NINA" meaning "No Irish need apply."
Had the Yankees been able to maintain this type of economic discrimination, things

would have been even worse. But the Yankees who controlled most of the money in Greater Boston found it necessary to employ the Irish—the women, especially—both as domestic laborers and in the new department stores. This was the first foot in the door, and the Irish immigrants took full advantage of the fact. By about 1880, most domestic servants in Boston were Irish, and the Irish neighborhoods were beginning to improve in appearance.

Irish men had it worse than their wives. Irish men were virtually shut out of every means of employment, and the stereotype of the lazy Irishman who stayed at home while his wife worked spread throughout Boston. The turning point for the Irish male was when he—and his neighborhood fellows—gained their first spots in the Boston fire and police departments. In the 1880s, one found only a few of these Irishmen, but they began hiring their kin, and by about 1900, the Irish made up nearly half of the fire and police forces.

How deep were the religious differences between the Irish and Yankees?

When the Irish first showed up in the 1840s the religious divide ran very deep. Puritan and Yankee Bostonians had for generations celebrated "Pope's Day" (November 5) with anti-Catholic slogans, and even a ritual burning of the Pope in effigy. The Irish that migrated to Boston in the decades prior to the Civil War encountered deep religious and ethnic prejudice. But by the end of the nineteenth century, the emphasis had changed from religion to finance. One could tell an Irishman, many Yankees declared, by the stench of his clothes and breath. Economic differences loomed as large as religious ones.

Did Boston ever become a true physical battleground between Irish and Yankee?

It came close a number of times, but there were just enough level-headed people on both sides to keep matters under control. In the 1880s and 1890s, ethnic rivalry was so strong that one could almost smell it, but it seldom broke into open violence. Even so, Boston was, quite likely, the most segregated city in the northeastern United States.

Who were the most prominent Bostonians at the end of the nineteenth century?

The list was very long, filled with men and women who had achieved great things a generation earlier, and with the names of others who were on the cusp of great achievement. Near the top of almost everyone's list was Oliver Wendell Holmes Sr., the medical doctor and humanist who did so much to make Boston "The Hub" where intellectual matters were concerned. He was followed by Harvard president Charles W. Eliot, under whose leadership the university across the Charles River had become truly world famous. They were followed by a bevy of other leading Bostonians.

Did Boston also have its share of rebels?

It certainly did. In the landmark *Brahmins & Bullyboys: G. Frank Radway's Boston Album*, the author shows the divided city that Boston was at the turn of the century. Pleasure and wealth co-existed along with poverty and depravity, and the city was on the edge of being radicalized. Labor unions were not strong yet, but they were winning favor from a larger percentage of the population. One could anticipate the class struggle that lay ahead.

THE MODERN METROPOLIS

How did Protestant and Yankee Boston become the multiethnic metropolis of today?

It happened slowly, beginning with the Irish migration of the 1840s. Most of us know that the Irish became Boston's number-one minority group, and they remained so for decades. But the Italians came in great numbers toward the end of the nineteenth century, and they were followed by many other groups. The largest "burst" of ethnic migration was seen in the decades that followed the Vietnam War. First came Vietnamese and Cambodians; they were followed by Chinese and Japanese; and today there are sections of Boston which look almost as Asian as European.

What was Boston like in and around the year 1900?

Boston had seen better times. The city population had fallen to 450,000, putting it further down the list of all American cities. Industry and manufacturing continued to move at a good clip, but here, too, Boston had slipped when compared with its competition. The steel mills around Philadelphia had propelled that city well past Boston in overall wealth, and Manhattan produced far more goods and services than the City on the Bay. Despite the depressing statistics, however, Boston was beginning to show signs of new life.

The single most dramatic improvement was the arrival of the subway, Boston's—and the world's—first. When ground near Boston Common was torn up in the mid-1890s, critics had a field day, asserting that this would ruin the aesthetics of the city, but when the first subway connection was made, and when passengers emerged at the Common without having to dare the streets, most people applauded.

What were the sights and sounds of Boston in 1900?

Like most American cities, Boston was poised half-way between the era of the horse and that of the automobile. Horses were seen everywhere in Boston, and the smell of their manure gave the streets a noxious perfume, but this, too, was the case almost everywhere. The sights and sounds mostly had to do with hawkers selling their wares, and with the bells and whistles of streetcars. Boston was a decidedly noisy place in 1900.

What the casual tourist saw depended very much on which section of the city he or she visited. Anyone who came to the West End and the fashionable Back Bay was impressed by row after row of brownstone buildings, most of which housed the doctors, lawyers, writers, and, of course, the ones who were so lucky they did not even need to work. The Back Bay was only about fifty years old in 1900, and it showed little of the wear and tear that was visible in other sections of the city.

Was there a typical, or stereotypical, Boston family of the year 1900?

What follows is anecdotal, rather than statistical. Numbers are important, but they seldom tell the full story. Whether the Boston family was Irish, Italian, or Yankee, it tended to be close-knit with fierce allegiance both expected and delivered. On those occasions when someone did not fit the mold, or refused to conform, he or she could expect to be ostracized. The typical Boston family was composed of two parents, four children, and perhaps two aunts, uncles, or grandparents. In many cases, the extended family members lived in the same house.

The Boston family of 1900 was a hard-working one: there was no place for slackers. The father was definitely the breadwinner, but his wage was supplemented by the part-time income earned by the mother, and the children often had jobs of one sort or another by the age of twelve.

How were the Irish and Italians doing in and around the year 1900?

The Irish had come a long way, but they were eager to make up for lost time. The first Irish mayor of Boston was elected in the 1880s, and by 1896, the Irish had pretty much taken over City Hall. Rather few Irish had yet reached the professional class, which was almost entirely occupied by Yankees, but the police and fire departments were roughly half Irish by this time. One could envision a future in which the Irish would be the masters of Boston, but that day had not yet arrived.

The Italians, by contrast, were just getting by. They had nearly replaced the Irish in the Old North End, and they found much work along the waterfront, but the Italians were blocked from nearly all the better-paying jobs. There was no love lost between the Irish and Italians: the neighborhood lines were sharply drawn.

What was the most noticeable part of Boston in 1905?

The first airplanes were in the process of being invented, but no one had yet commenced the art of aerial photography. One has to rely, therefore, on the imagination of the artists from the ground, and they sometimes did a very good job indeed. A drawing executed in 1905 shows a busy, hustling city in which the docks and wharves play the largest role. Shipping was still the lifeblood of Boston in 1905.

As soon as one departs the central city, the suburbs and neighborhoods beckon, and they were much filled in even from a generation before. Streetcar and subway lines now laced many parts of the western city, and workers in the suburbs could get to their jobs more rapidly than before. One of the less attractive aspects of life in Boston in 1905 was the air pollution. Hundreds of factories—many of them in East Boston and Cambridgeport—belched fumes all day, and the city often lay under a cloud of smog.

A street scene of Boston photographed in 1905.

Did Bostonians have much sense about the wider world in 1905?

Not yet. It's true that many ships paid call at Boston each year, and that the upper class went on long vacations, sometimes to Europe. But in the era prior to television—and even radio—Boston had an insularity that is difficult for us today to imagine. Plenty of Bostonians did travel, but many others seldom ventured out of the city, and some hardly ever left their neighborhoods.

Was Boston a "man's" town or a "woman's" city in 1905?

Again, the answer depends on which social class is referenced. Among the Brahmin elite, the grandmother of the clan often was the real mistress, and she made certain that the daughters of the family fared as well as the sons. But in the rough working-class neighborhoods, life was difficult for girls and women. No one will ever be able to put names and statistics to the many domestic tragedies of the early twentieth century (in part because there were so many!). But from the anecdotal record, we are confident that alcoholism was more prevalent than in our world today, and that many families lived right on the edge of poverty.

Boston had not yet experienced the "great clean-up" that would soon come to the cities of America. The Progressive Era had commenced by 1905, but its effects were not yet seen. Over the next two decades, much would change in terms of sidewalks, street lights, and other amenities that would help make Boston a friendlier town, to men and women alike.

Who was the mayor of Boston in 1906?

One of the most colorful, and successful of all Boston Irish politicians was John Francis Fitzgerald (1863–1950). Born in East Boston in 1863, Fitzgerald was the son of Irish immigrants, and his early family life witnessed many of the tragedies that accompany immigrant stories. Through hard work, and some good breaks, he became one of the first Boston Irish to graduate from Harvard University, and by the 1890s he was in politics.

Affable, charming, and blessed with a melodious voice, Fitzgerald was first elected mayor of Boston in 1905. His administration was not marked by any great advances, but neither was it marred by corruption. What made a big difference and won people to him was Fitzgerald's personal style. He had the common touch to the ninth degree. When he ran for re-election, he became known as "Honey Fitz" because of how he spontaneously broke into song, especially when he sang "Sweet Adeline."

John F. "Honey Fitz" Fitzgerald was a colorful Irish politician who was a popular Boston mayor and also a U.S. congressman.

Did the Yankee community have any politician capable of equaling "Honey Fitz"?

No, and it never would. Once the Boston Irish took over the wards, which happened in the 1880s, they worked their way up to city council. Once they won the mayor's office in the 1890s, they held on to it for decades. There may have been some masterful politicians hiding beneath the carpets in Yankee Boston, but something about the social mores of that ethnic group made it nearly impossible for them to emerge. The Irish had come to City Hall to stay.

Was there any big building program in the first decade of the twentieth century?

The success of Victorian Boston, its architecture most especially, meant that there was no compelling need to alter the look of the city. The downtown area was fashionable, and the suburbs were models of efficiency. As far as the North End and East Boston went, most Boston voters did not wish to spend money on them. As a result, public architecture lagged during the first decade of the new century. Anyone who wished to see something impressive was told to go look at the great buildings erected in the 1880s, Trinity Church most especially.

The department stores were another matter. No expense was spared where they were concerned. Some of the biggest of the stores had already been built, but those that were established between 1900 and 1910 were marvels for the time. In this area alone could Boston compete with Manhattan.

At a time well before air conditioning how did Bostonians get relief from the heat?

They went to two beaches. Nantasket Beach stretches for almost four miles along the Atlantic, and is the last "port" of call as one departs the Massachusetts Bay. Revere Beach is three miles north of downtown Boston. Virtually everyone in Boston went to these beaches when possible during the summer months, and they sometimes displayed a charming vista of early twentieth century life at its best. Nantasket and Revere Beaches were perhaps the only two places in Greater Boston where the social and ethnic distinctions were relaxed: Irish, Italians, and Yankees all needed to enjoy the fresh air coming in from the great ocean.

A giant Ferris wheel was later erected at Nantasket, and the place became Boston's equivalent to New York's Coney Island: the place where entertainment ruled supreme. When one visits Nantasket Beach today, he or she is struck by how the fair or carnival-like atmosphere has disappeared: condominiums, rather than merry-go-rounds, line the coast today.

How important had sports become to the average Bostonian?

The first decade of the twentieth century was a breakthrough period for sports. The Boston Marathon attracted more observers every year, and the Boston Americans, soon to be renamed the Boston Red Sox, were enormous crowd-pleasers. Fenway Park, which was completed in 1912, was another of the places in which social and ethnic distinctions counted for less than usual. Yankees, Irish, Italians, and others rubbed shoulders in the brand-new ballpark.

Was fire still as great a danger as before?

Fire had been the greatest source of death and destruction for generations, but by 1910 the danger had been seriously curtailed. The Boston Fire Department was considered one of the best of the time, and the Boston fire stations became models that were copied by other major cities. The one time of the year that Bostonians really feared fire was in February and March, when homeowners turned up the furnace—usually supplied with coal—or overstoked the fireplace. There may have been as many home fires as ever with the major difference being that the fire department could keep them under control.

Did Boston and its people know that the world they knew was about to change?

No, and the same can be said for the people of most of the United States. In the spring of 1914, the human and material improvements of the preceding twenty years seemed to indicate that life was good and getting better. Very few people realized that events in Europe were about to overturn the apple cart for almost everyone.

WORLD WAR I

Was Boston connected to the big events of the summer of 1914?

For once the answer was a flat "No." Boston played no significant role in the build-up to war, and its people were largely mystified as to why anyone would wish to risk the peace that had brought so many good things. When Bostonians read the newspapers of July and August 1914, they realized that something very big was in the works, but they hoped, and perhaps prayed that it would not affect them.

Britain, France, Russia, and Belgium faced off against Imperial Germany and the Austro-Hungarian Empire in the summer of 1914. Had Boston been the recipient of recent immigrants, the city people would have been more concerned, and interested. But the recent arrivals from Eastern Europe—those that really cared about places such as Bosnia, Herzegovina, and so forth—had mostly settled in New York City.

Who was the mayor of Boston when World War I began?

James Michael Curley (1874–1958) won the first of four unprecedented terms as mayor of Boston in 1914. Easing out John F. Fitzgerald ("Honey Fitz"), Curley became mayor at a time when Boston needed strong leadership, and this he provided.

In 1914, there were numerous "war bosses" in the United States with municipal politics often dictating the pace of state elections, but nowhere was this more evident than in Boston. Honey Fitz had been an excellent politician, able to bridge the gap between the Irish, Italian, and Yankee communities. James Michael Curley was something else: a quintessential Irish politician who looked after his own.

Was Mayor Curley, or the Boston population, concerned about the shadows cast by World War I?

Most Americans believed they would do well to stay out of the troubles of Old Europe, and most were confident that President Woodrow Wilson would enable them to do so. Bostonians knew, however, that if the nation did go to war, they would be called upon to make extra sacrifices: this was because their port would play so important a role.

In 1915 and 1916, Bostonians, like most of their countrymen, watched the

James Michael Curley was mayor of Boston duing World War I and would go on to serve four terms in office.

European scene with concern, but continued to hope they'd manage to remain aloof. Only when Imperial Germany resumed submarine warfare in February 1917 did it become apparent that the United States would enter the conflict. Bostonians had few, if any, radios in 1917; they read the newspapers avidly, and when they learned that Congress had declared war, they girded themselves for what would be a great contest.

How did the Boston Irish feel about entering a war that would quite likely benefit Old England?

They were not pleased at all. Many Boston Irish expressed distrust of the British as allies, and some pointed to the bloody suppression of the "Easter Rebellion" in Ireland as a prime example. Mayor Curley was not enthusiastic at first, but he soon became a convert. Germany and her allies must be defeated, he declared.

How large was Boston's effort in World War I?

World War I brought more ships, sailors, and soldiers to Boston than the city had ever seen previously. Boston Harbor was one of the linchpins of the American merchant marines during World War I. The factories in East Boston and Cambridge seemed to belch fire constantly, as the city was placed on a war footing. Of course, all of this was secondary to the simple fact that so many of Boston's sons went off to the battlefield. Though no one predicted it at the time, World War I provided a small example of how Yankees, Irish, and Italians could work together toward a common goal.

Boston reached the ultimate of its exertions during the summer of 1918. Hundreds of thousands of men passed through the city on their way to France. The shipyards and factories strained under the effort, and it is truly questionable whether Boston could have kept up under the strain. Mercifully, the war ended on November 11, 1918.

AFTERMATH OF THE GREAT WAR

In what way was the aftermath worse than the war itself?

Imperial Germany was a mighty adversary, and Bostonians breathed easier when the war ended. But in the same month that the armistice went into effect, Bostonians and their country cousins found something even more deadly pressing in on them: the flu.

The Influenza Epidemic of 1918–1919 claimed a total of roughly 630,000 American lives, far more than the war itself. Boston and the inland city of Worcester were hardhit because so many returning American infantrymen were routed through Fort Devens in north-central Massachusetts. The young men got off their ships either in Boston or Portsmouth, New Hampshire, and they brought the contagion with them.

The 1919 Molasses Flood killed twenty people and took weeks to clean up.

How many Bostonians died in the Influenza Epidemic?

Thousands of people got sick, and perhaps as many as 5,000 died. But there was a wartime boom as workers were needed to staff the factories, which resulted in Boston coming out of World War II with a significantly increased population. In 1920, Boston had 748,060 residents, marking a growth of nearly fifty percent since the turn of the century.

What was the Molasses Flood?

It sounds comical to the ear, but the Great Molasses Flood of January 1919 was one of the worst disasters to strike Boston in the twentieth century. The Purity Distilling Company had long owned and maintained a huge building, designed for the holding of 2.3 million pounds of molasses. Molasses was no longer in great commercial demand.

In normal circumstances, the molasses vat did just fine, but when Boston experienced abnormally warm weather on January 16, 1919, the vat practically melted. Out came the molasses in a flood the like of which had never before been seen. Twenty people were killed and another fifty were injured. The cleanup of the streets—those of the North End especially—took more than two weeks. The Boston Molasses Flood was never repeated, but it remains a signpost for urban planners today.

POSTWAR CONSERVATISM

Is it true that Boston become more conservative in the wake of World War I?

The city on the bay has long been regarded as one of the most liberal of American cities, but there are exceptions to the general rule. The United States as a whole underwent a conservative backlash in the years following World War I. The major event that demonstrated the new trend was the Boston police strike of 1920.

The Boston police had not had a pay increase for several years, and in March 1920, they went out on strike. Massachusetts Governor Calvin Coolidge ordered the men back to work, and they refused, even when looting began in downtown Boston. The governor called in the National Guard, and issued a famous statement, "There is no right to strike against the public safety by anybody, anywhere, anytime." Not one of the policemen that went out on strike was ever hired again, and the new police force was largely composed of young men returning from the war.

Who was Charles Ponzi?

Born in Italy, Charles Ponzi (1882–1949) came to Boston for the first time in 1903. He lived for a while in Canada, but returned to Boston, where in 1920, he promoted a fantastic financial scheme that has ever since borne his name ("Ponzi scheme"). Ponzi pledged to deliver a 50 percent profit in 45 days and to double his investor's money in 90 days. His clever scheme—never fully explicated to the investors—was to purchase discounted postal reply coupons in other countries, and then redeem them at face value in the United States. The actual plan was not illegal: the means of persuading investors was.

Ponzi established an office in downtown Boston and became the number-one holder of certificates from Hanover Trust Bank. When state, and then federal, officials investigated his activities, the pyramid scheme collapsed, wiping out $20 million in wealth. The Hanover Trust and five other banks collapsed. Ponzi's actions not only alerted an entire generation of investors to clever swindler, but he also caused a backlash against Italians in Boston.

How important was the trial of Sacco and Vanzetti?

For those who believe the American system of justice is nearly perfect, the Sacco and Vanzetti trials demonstrate the truth of their belief. For those that believe American justice is excellent in conception, but often poor in performance, the Sacco and Vanzetti trials are the strongest evidence of proof. So it was during the 1920s: so it remains today.

Nicola Sacco (1891–1927) and Bartolomeo Vanzetti (1888–1927) were Italian-Americans who emigrated to America in 1907. They were working-class men, who earned their daily bread from a number of different occupations. Both became thorough radicals, even anarchists, during the 1910s, a decade which witnessed radicalization in many different spheres of American life. In the rush to round up and deport undesirables, both the local and Massachusetts state police committed errors. Sacco and Vanzetti were rad-

Nicola Sacco (left) and Bartolomeo Vanzetti.

icals (of this there was no doubt): whether they committed the crimes of killing two people during a robbery is questionable.

How long did it take before Sacco and Vanzetti were executed?

Sacco was tried first in Plymouth, Massachusetts, in the summer of 1920. Most scholars believe that his trial was a travesty. Sacco and Vanzetti were tried jointly in the late spring and early summer of 1921. The same judge presided. A guilty verdict was rendered on July 12, 1921, setting off an intense, six-year struggle on the part of many Bostonians to save Sacco and Vanzetti.

Most fair-minded observers commented on the noble deportment of Sacco and Vanzetti during their trial(s). These men seemed quite capable of actions against a state or government, but they seemed highly unlikely murderers. The Sacco-Vanzetti case(s) attracted attention from all parts of the United States—indeed, many other parts of the world. A large, unlikely alliance was formed between anarchists, liberals, and college professors, who were united only in their belief that the justice system had failed in fairness. Six years of attempts, and no fewer than eight motions for a new trial, all failed to persuade the judge. Sacco and Vanzetti were electrocuted in Charlestown State Prison on August 23, 1927.

How quickly, or slowly, did the Great Depression come to Boston?

It came with surprising speed. The reason is that the Boston economy had been weak throughout the 1920s, and the great stock market crash of October and November 1929 merely piled on to what was already a bad situation. To be sure, it didn't always look as if Boston was in trouble. The city on the Charles handled a staggering 54 percent of all New England wholesale trade, and over 3,400 industrial concerns employed nearly 49,000 people in 1929. But, just beneath the surface, Boston's over-dependence on three forms of income took their toll.

Boston had not been a fishing capital for three generations, but it was still a great mercantile port, one of the best on the East Coast. Returns from the waterfront diminished during the 1920s, however, and when the Great Depression arrived, trade was practically at a standstill. The other two consistent producers of income—shoe and woolen manufacturing—had both been stretched to the breaking point. There was no capital for the establishment of new firms, and the old ones began laying people off in great numbers.

Were the effects of the Great Depression visible immediately?

No. As Boston prepared to celebrate the 300th anniversary of its founding, all sorts of photographs, including some from the air, were taken, all in order to show off what the city had to offer. The best of the aerial views was used as the frontispiece to *Fifty Years of Boston: A Memorial Volume,* and from that photograph, we learn much about the city in 1930.

First, Boston was a low-lying city in 1930. Unlike Manhattan, which had gone through an immense architectural transformation, Boston had not a single skyscraper, or anything even resembling one. The aerial photograph reveals that the highest buildings in Boston were the octagonal-shaped Custom House, the Merchant's Exchange Building, and perhaps two to three churches. The taller buildings were almost entirely concentrated in the Financial District, trending to the South End. The Boston Common figured even more strongly in this photograph than in ones taken decades later: it gave the Boston of 1930 an appearance that suggested some rural tranquility. And finally, the wonderful brownstones along Beacon Hill and Commonwealth Avenue were considerably lower than the ones we know today. Nothing in the photograph suggests that Boston was about to undergo ten years of financial hardship; at the same time, nothing suggests that the city could break the cloister-like grip of its nineteenth-century past.

What were the three hundredth anniversary proceedings like?

As one might expect, they had a strongly Puritan and Yankee tone, meaning that even the most ebullient Bostonian was still expected to keep his love for the city at a respectfully low level. Bostonians have seldom been very good at blowing their own horn: it helped, therefore that they had an outsider to help in 1930. Her name was Helen Keller, and she was one of the most admired women in America.

Didn't Helen Keller come from the South?

She did, indeed, but she and her teacher Annie Sullivan had come north. Over more than three decades, Helen Keller examined the city and its people, and she pulled out all the stops in her congratulations to the place on its three hundredth birthday.

"I have countless times pleaded the cause of the handicapped and the unfortunate in Boston," Helen Keller wrote, "and the city has never failed to hold up my hands. It has ever been in Boston's creed to render life safer and happier for the coming generation. In 1903 the Massachusetts association for promoting the interests of the adult blind was formed.... Out of the campaign in Boston has sprung the National Committee for the Prevention of Blindness and the American Foundation for the Blind."

Did Helen Keller speak on topics other than blindness?

She did. For Boston's three hundredth anniversary, she chose to extol the qualities of a number of leading Bostonians, most of whom were connected with higher education. Perhaps her most fulsome praise was reserved for Professor Josiah Royce.

[He] throbbed and vibrated with knowledge. His imagination gave the Absolute a kind of reality. I think he made the dullest of his class sense the immensity of the universe and the infinity of thought.

Is there a qualitative way to describe the difference between the Boston of 1930 and the one we experience today?

The city of Boston and its suburbs lacked the excitement that we associate with Boston in our time. Of course there were exciting aspects, including the moving in of roughly 100,000 college students each September, but the overall look and feel of the city were rather dreary. There was almost none of the play of light on buildings, such as we experience in our time. And when we contrast the photograph of 1930 with ones from our own time, we quickly see that the big difference has been caused by the erection of larger, taller buildings. There's nothing quite like the play of light on metal and glass, such as what one experiences looking at the John Hancock Building, for example.

THE 1930s

How did James Michael Curley respond to the Great Depression?

On January 6, 1930, James Michael Curley was sworn in as mayor of Boston for the fourth time. Curley was as battle-tested as any city leader could be, but the 1930s brought pressures that neither he nor the twenty-two members of the city council could remedy. The first and most obvious was the number of people that were hungry, cold, or both.

Though Mayor Curley steadfastly denied it, Boston had soup kitchens, quite a few of them. They are known to us from photographs of that time, but the anecdotal record is also fleshed out by numerous letters. As Franklin D. Roosevelt headed toward the American presidency, for example, he received letters from numerous Bostonians, most of them male and nearly all of them out of work. One such Bostonian claimed he had not eaten for two days, and that he'd spent the previous night in a paid shelter, which cost him all of ten cents.

Did anyone actually starve in Boston during the Great Depression?

The Boston hospitals underreported the number of cases of malnutrition during the Depression, and some people may have simply given up and died, long before their time. In terms of raw food, there was usually enough to eat, but it was a rare Boston family that did not experience privation during the 1930s. Much as would happen during the 1980s—another decade that saw much hardship in Boston—people died more frequently from accidents, such as stepping into traffic, than from actual starvation.

Could things have been even worse?

To be sure. Boston was in the same boat as Chicago, New York, and Philadelphia, but it had a hinterland that was not far off where plenty of fresh fruit and vegetables were available. The chances are that the entire city would have been placed on an emergency basis.

Did Mayor Curley do much to combat the Great Depression?

Like President Franklin D. Roosevelt, Mayor Curley believed in public works projects rather than charity or government handouts: Curley mobilized the youth of Boston for a number of such plans. On one occasion, simply in order to boost morale, he ordered and then led the burial of "General D. Pression," a skeleton-like effigy that Curley tossed dirt upon. Only slowly, as the decade advanced, did Curley agree to fund larger direct handouts, and the number of Boston families on poor relief soared between 1930 and 1935.

Do we know whether Boston's upper class took it on the chin?

Generally speaking, the answer is yes. The stock market crash of 1929 brought many proud Boston families low, and quite a few had to liquidate everything. What the upperclass Bostonian possessed, in comparison to his working class counterpart, was the likelihood that, whether in the city or the countryside, relatives would take him in. There was no mass exodus from the city. Boston hunkered down during the Great Depression.

How did Harvard fare during the Great Depression?

The university on the northern side of the Charles River did rather well. Not only did thousands of families nationwide still hope that their sons would go to Harvard, but the institution benefitted from its close association with President Roosevelt and the New Deal. Dozens of Harvard professors were recruited to Washington, D.C., where they served as advisors to President Roosevelt on all manner of issues. The only other institution of higher education to do as well during the Great Depression was Columbia University, which likewise sent many of its brightest and best thinkers to Washington.

Did any new buildings get built during the Great Depression?

Very few. The building projects that Mayor Curley sponsored tended to be of a very practical nature with roads and bridges coming first. Very little capital existed for the development of new office buildings, and some critics claimed that any such development was a complete waste of time, as no one could be certain when new officer workers would be needed.

How did Boston fare relative to other great American cities?

Boston was only the seventh-most populous city of the nation in 1930, but its manufacturing came in at number three. The hit to Boston was more severe than that experienced by Chicago or New York, and of all the great American cities, Boston and Baltimore seemed the most vulnerable. They would follow parallel tracks in the decades that followed, each attempting to beef up and revitalize its ports and its manufacturing base.

How important was Boston on the national stage during the 1930s?

It never quite made it. For a brief time it seemed that a political alliance between Mayor Curley and President Roosevelt would lift Boston to new prominence; as this hope faded, so did Boston's importance on the national stage. On the whole, Americans were much more conscious of the difficulties Chicago, Philadelphia, and San Francisco faced than those endured by Bostonians.

Did the new medium of radio make any difference to Bostonians of the 1930s?

It did. Radio, which spread throughout the nation in the second half of the 1920s, knitted the nation together more effectively than any previous technology. Bostonians got their news much more rapidly than before, but an even greater improvement was registered by their suburban cousins. The man or woman of Braintree, Dorchester, Melrose, or Arlington received weather reports much more rapidly than before, and the commuter could plan, or alter, his day accordingly.

WORLD WAR II

How did Boston fare during World War II?

It was the last hurrah for the Port of Boston. Other cities, notably Manhattan and Portland, Maine, exceeded Boston in overall ship traffic, but vast numbers of U.S. soldiers spent time in Boston either before or after their time in service. One can argue that Boston was the most visited and popular port on the East Coast.

Enormous amounts of materiel were transferred in and out of Boston. The city's tradesmen enjoyed a last hurrah, packaging all sorts of goods for the Allied war effort. Generally speaking, however, Bostonians did not deceive themselves; they knew that this wartime prosperity could not, and would not, last.

How quickly did the wartime prosperity recede?

One felt the difference by January 1946. Boston had exceeded its financial strength during World War II, and one could see it in the run-down shape of the major buildings. Harvard and MIT remained as popular as ever with thousands of students applying each year, but the City of Boston was in marked decline. And though popular affection for James Michael Curley remained strong, most Bostonians realized he was not the right person to carry them through the postwar era.

Throughout his long and colorful career, Curley played up the differences between Irish and Yankee Bostonians. Certainly he did not invent the animosity that existed, but he made it worse. And by 1946, it was evident that although the Irish controlled City Hall, the Yankees continued to dominate the Financial District. As a result, they could deny funds for public projects.

Did James Michael Curley enjoy a "Last Hurrah"?

The expression comes from the novel *The Last Hurrah* by Edwin O'Connor, written in 1956, soon after Curley retired. But it applies not only to Curley, but to two generations of Boston Irish politicians who dominated the scene, and in many ways, made things better for their ethnic group. What became painfully evident after 1946 is that the era of ethnic politics was dying. The Irish had caught up to the Yankees in many respects; the Italians had never been as strident in their demands. And if Boston continued to practice ethnic warfare, the city would not make it in the mid-twentieth century.

What was Boston like in or around the year 1950?

Boston had a decayed look and feel in 1950, the result of decades of strife between the Yankee bluebloods and the Boston Irish. The latter had gained control of city politics in 1894 and never relinquished it, but the former were able to dictate where capital investment was concentrated. One of the few ways that the Boston Brahmins could punish the Irish politicians was to deny them money for public projects: as a result, Boston looked like a city from the early 1920s.

If one had to place a bet on which city would thrive in 1950, he or she would almost certainly have chosen Cambridge rather than Boston: the city on the north side of the Charles River was doing well as a result of Harvard's position in the educational sector. The Massachusetts Institute of Technology (MIT) was also doing quite well.

Was there a reasonable stereotype, or composite, of the typical Bostonian of 1950?

The 1950s were, quite likely, the last decade in which a composite could be created: after 1960, the population would vary to a much greater degree. In or around 1950, the typical, or average, Bostonian was Irish or Italian, and the grandson or granddaughter of immigrants. This composite person was in his late thirties, lived in a two-decker house, and earned in the neighborhood of $12,000 per year. That was sufficient to pay the rent, or mortgage, and it may have sufficed for the purchase of a second-hand car, but there was no room for vacations in the family budget. The family might occasionally get to Cape Cod, usually to room with relatives. And as for higher education, everyone in the family understood that scholarships were a necessity. The typical Boston family felt even more pressure than before, thanks to the

John B. Hynes was mayor of Boston from 1950 to 1960.

rising income experienced in the local suburbs. Wellesley, Natick, and Newton were good examples of a rising tide that would drain wealth away from the central city.

How was City Hall different from in previous decades?

James Michael Curley had already earned his place as the most successful of all Boston politicians, but his long run had ended. In 1950 John B. Hynes (1897–1970) was mayor, and though he, like Curley, was Irish, Hynes had a much more cosmopolitan approach. Hynes was able to attract more capital investment than Curley, and the expression "urban renewal" was first heard during his tenure as mayor.

How was life on the street different from in the past?

It had never been easy to be on the streets of Boston: nature accounted for a lot of the difficulty. But in and around the year 1950, there was a grimy quality to the buildings and streets that had never been seen before: much of this can be attributed to lead in gasoline. Of course there were compensations, aspects which made life on the streets seem cozier than one might think. In the numerous Boston neighborhoods, people knew each other, up and down the street, and violent crime, while not unknown, seldom went unpunished.

The biggest concern was that the city would lose population in the decades to come. Fortunately, there were enough young urban planners graduating from first-class schools, and enough money was available on the federal level to bring about a major change in the life of the city.

128

URBAN RENEWAL–PHASE ONE

What happened to Scollay Square?

During World War II, Scollay Square earned the reputation of being the seamiest part of town, where prostitutes and peep shows abounded. This made the square the favorite of servicemen, whether they were in town for a short or long spell. Under Mayor John B. Hynes, plans were laid for the destruction of Scollay Square, which was architecturally dated as well as aesthetically challenged. Buildings began coming down in 1951, and by 1953 the destruction was complete. The question, of course, was what would rise from the ruins, and the planners did not disappoint.

When did Logan Airport become one of the great transit centers on the East Coast?

Logan was a very small place until about 1945. The proof comes from aerial photographs, which show regular passengers able to bring their autos to within a hundred feet of the terminal (and there was only one terminal in those days). The soldiers and sailors that brought their dollars to Boston during World War II mostly arrived by ship or by train; not until the late 1960s did Logan became a major place of arrival and departure. Once that trend commenced, however, Logan never looked back. Boston became *the* departure city for New Englanders heading to Western Europe, and it later entered the Caribbean and Floridian tourist routes. The only trouble was that Logan Airport kept running out of room to expand. Today, the airport encompasses all of what once was Noodle's Island, and a fair section of Hog Island as well.

What was the so-called Central Artery?

To those who remember, the Central Artery was the single biggest mistake made in the planning and reconstruction of the city of Boston. In the mid-1950s, it was decided by the planners at City Hall to build a new highway, dozens of feet above the level of the main city, and drive it straight through the eastern sections of the city. This would allow commuters from the north to enter Boston more rapidly, and permit people leaving town for the Cape, for the weekend, to exit in an easier fashion.

All was set for success. The construction companies made a lot of money (no one knows just how much), and in the first few months, the Central Artery proved its worth. Those that traveled from Salem, Gloucester, Newburyport, and so forth had easier trips in to the city. But those same commuters found the drive home more difficult than ever. The reason is that the Central Artery caused large traffic jams within the central city, meaning it took longer to get out on that big highway.

How about the aesthetics of the matter? How did the Central Artery look?

It was, almost from opening day, a complete disaster in an aesthetic sense. The plan was for the elevated highway to free the central city from some of the noise and pollution caused by the cars. Some of this actually was accomplished, but the eyesore that re-

129

Logan Airport opened in 1923, but it didn't become a major aiport until the 1960s.

sulted led most Bostonians to lament that the "world's biggest parking lot" (as they called it) had ever been built.

The worst aspect of the Central Artery was that it effectively cut off the Old North End from the central part of the city. Tourists found it just too difficult, and nerve-wracking, to find their way through the underpass, and the sheer noise turned them off. Tourism, which had long been a mainstay of the economy of the North End, fell off sharply in the 1960s. Not until the Bicentennial of 1976 and the attendant interest in all things Revolutionary and Colonial did the tourists begin to return.

Where was urban renewal contested the most?

The Old South End of Boston, which should not to be confused with "Southie" or South Boston, was both historic, filled with churches and buildings from the early nineteenth century, and ethnic, meaning it had more African Americans and Caribbean Islanders than any other section of the city. As the Prudential Tower rose to its impressive height of 770 feet, more and more tourists complained that the South End was an eyesore, that it blighted communication between the fashionable downtown and outlying areas. As a result, City Hall—this time led by Mayor John F. Collins—began demolishing buildings and relocating residents.

Why does every major construction project in Boston seem to last for so long?

Some people claim it's the last remaining evidence of when Boston was a "ward" town, dominated by its political bosses. Some photographs appear to bear this out, showing one man using a shovel and nine others standing by. It has to be admitted that Boston projects take longer than those of other cities, and that the cost overruns can be pretty dramatic. But in the case of the South End, the time involved was not as controversial as the number of people who had to be relocated. About seven hundred buildings were demolished, and an equal number of people lost their housing.

Bitterness over the changes in the South End lasted for decades. Lawyers demonstrated that the people who were relocated came from the poorest part of the city and pressed for damages. Almost none were paid. City Hall got its way and Boston did look better when the new South End emerged. But the acrimony lasted a very long time.

THE 1960s

Why did San Francisco, rather than Boston, become known as the "city of love"?

For a brief time, Boston was as well positioned as San Francisco to lead the youth movement of the 1960s. Quite a few Harvard professors dropped acid, and many college and university students dropped out of the "rat race," as they called it, for good. But 1964 was the turning point. The Free Speech Movement started at the University of California at Berkeley, not at Harvard or MIT, and the rush to the West Coast was on.

Hippies could be found on Boston Common, and one could discover small communes located within twenty miles of the city. Boston's great historic legacy worked

Where do we get that wonderful expression, "I love that dirty water.... Boston you're my town!"

The Standells, a California rock group, coined the words in 1965. "Dirty Water" is about the contradictions of Boston, the place where American liberty was born but where no one could swim in the water. Perhaps it is appropriate that the Standells were from California, a state that led the way in environmental rules and regulations, while Boston and Massachusetts lagged far behind. But the words are so marvelous that Bostonians soon adopted them as a badge of honor, and they are now played at the end of sports contests in which Boston is victorious.

Yeah, down by the river
Down by the banks of the river Charles (aw that's what's happenin' baby)
That's where you'll find me
Along with lovers, muggers, and thieves (aw, but they're cool people)
Well I love that dirty water
Boston, you're my town (you're the number-one place).

131

against it becoming the icon of the Sixties, however. For every young college student eager to thwart the Establishment, there were two others eager to visit the Paul Revere House, and to dream of the glory that would come to them one day. Boston and Massachusetts sent an outsized number of people to the Peace Corps, and they accomplished much good overseas, but the city on the Charles never was able to compete with "Baghdad by the Bay" for leadership in the counter-cultural movement.

What did Boston look like as the 1960s came to an end?

The city was much improved in a visual sense, the major exception being the Central Artery. The downtown had become fashionable, and the suburbs were thriving. One still found a lot of dirty, grimy areas in the neighborhoods, and quite a few young folk that claimed they loved the dirt and grime. City Hall was not yet ready to initiate a second round of urban renewal. The real winner, from the 1960s, was Cambridge, however.

Perhaps because it did not descend to the level of "free speech and free love" that San Francisco did, Cambridge came out of the 1960s with an enhanced reputation. Applications at all the big colleges and universities increased in the 1970s, and it seemed that every hip and adventurous young person wished to go to Harvard or MIT. The only drawback was that one could no longer swim in the Charles River: the pollution had become too great.

THE KENNEDY INFLUENCE

How important was 1960 in the history of Boston and, indeed, of Massachusetts?

It can hardly be exaggerated. Massachusetts had seen three previous presidents—John Adams, John Quincy Adams, and Calvin Coolidge—but John F. Kennedy had more personality and charisma than all three of them rolled into one. Never as intellectual as his biographers have insisted, Kennedy had a quick mind, and he understood Boston politics as well as any man since James Michael Curley. Kennedy might well have become mayor of Boston had his father not aimed higher, and in 1960, Kennedy announced his candidacy for the Democratic presidential nomination. At the time, he was all of forty-three.

Kennedy won the primaries, and then he challenged Republican Richard M. Nixon, the sitting vice-president, for the nation's highest office. In different circumstances, Nixon would have prevailed, but the campaign of 1960 featured the first presidential debates, and in these Kennedy was the clear winner. Much of it had to do with style rather than substance: Kennedy was the "made for television" candidate. Very few voters realized that the handsome, urbane Kennedy, who seemed the embodiment of physical fitness, actually lived in acute physical pain, and that he needed frequent visits to doctors.

How much did President Kennedy do for his home city and state?

After winning the election by a narrow, razor-thin margin over Richard M. Nixon, John F. Kennedy moved to the White House, where he proved to be the most dynamic occupant in many years. One thing Kennedy did not do was favor his home city. Boston received only a moderate infusion of federal funds during his presidency. Massachusetts as a whole benefitted considerably, however, and no place benefitted so much as the city of Cambridge.

Like Franklin D. Roosevelt, John F. Kennedy drew an inordinate number of policymakers and top advisers from Harvard University. As a result, Cambridge loomed even larger in the state and national landscape than before, and one can argue that what was good for the city on the north side of the Charles was equally good for Boston.

THE 1970s

What kind of place was Boston in the early 1970s?

Some people wrote Boston off, saying it was a has-been, and others hoped and prayed that better times were coming. The city budget was not in terrible shape (tax receipts had risen) but the town had a multilayered personality. Roxbury, which had the largest African American population, was practically off-limits so far as many whites were concerned. The downtown showcased large department stores, but the Combat Zone (the adult entertainment district) became the number-one place after 7 P.M. The theater district was barely holding its own, as many well-heeled patrons continued to move out to the suburbs. The best that Boston could offer was generally seen in the early- to mid-afternoon Boston restaurants were relatively cheap on a pound-for-pound basis, and thousands of school children poured in to town on each balmy spring day. The drivers of those school buses knew beyond the shadow of a doubt, however, that they needed to embark the children and be out of the city before 4 P.M., when the traffic jams began.

Was there a typical Bostonian in and around the year 1975?

There was not. The African American population had risen considerably, and young people were taking over the music scene. But if one looked for the new generation of those in their thirties, they could be found. These were Irish or Italian, but they were also black or Cuban or Haitian. The two-deckered homes in which they had grown up were mostly gone, replaced by split-level homes and mini apartment buildings. Rents had risen, though not astronomically, and the typical Boston family of four could still make its way through the daily grind.

The father was very much the leader of the family. He headed off to work early, and earned his bread in one of the building trades. The two school-aged children were not as respectful as he might like, and they admired the youth scene too much. But the single biggest change, by the year 1975, was that the woman of the house also went to work.

Was there a previous time when the typical Boston woman did *not* work?

Until the early 1970s, about three-fifths of the women of Boston did not sally out to earn a wage or salary. They worked of course, meaning they kept the family and home to-   133

Suburban wives did just as much work as their inner-city counterparts, but there tended to be more fun and recreation along the way. By 1975, the Boston suburbs had exploded to house a population of nearly 1.5 million, and all sorts of amenities were provided to keep the suburbanites happy. The big department stores, such as Filene's and Jordan Marsh, commenced operations in downtown Boston, but they soon had stores in the suburbs. As a result, the family station wagon tended to be rather full of children as well as with toys. Everyone had their hands full.

gether, and as the old expression has it, "woman's work is never done." But rising financial pressures, as well as the desire for personal liberation, led many thousands of middle-aged Boston women into the work force in the 1970s. They found plenty to do.

Women became nurses and laboratory clerks: they also worked as stenographers and laundresses. None entered the Boston police or fire departments; that was still two decades away. But the Boston scene was notably different in the mid-1970s, and the major difference was that women were much more visible. One can argue that all the work did not lead to very much "liberation." The female of the household now worked thirty-plus hours while feeding the children and doing the shopping, and sometimes she had to pack the station wagon so everyone could get to the Cape for the weekend. Along with the drudgery came a very important paycheck, however, and it helped the self-esteem of the Boston woman, while it allowed the family to contemplate a move to the suburbs.

PRIDE AND SHAME

Why was the Bicentennial so big in Boston?

One could just as well ask why it was so big nationwide? And the answer is rather simple. The United States underwent several traumas during the 1960s, not least of them being the Vietnam War. As the two hundredth birthday of the nation approached, Americans from all parts of the nation got ready to celebrate. The nation had come through one of the worst times of its history, and the future looked a good deal better than the recent past.

Boston had a double reason for celebration. Not only did the city look better than it had for decades, but it, too, was emerging from the multiple traumas of the 1960s. And Boston contained, on its streets, more remnants of the Revolutionary era than any other city (Philadelphia being the only competitor that came close). As a result, Boston got ready to celebrate the Bicentennial in a major way.

What was best: the fireworks or the music?

One had to be there to make a choice, but it really was the combination that made the Bicentennial so memorable. For years, the Boston Pops had been a major draw, but the young people had regarded it as passé. This changed with the Bicentennial celebrations in July 1976. Thousands of people flocked to the Esplanade to hear the Boston Pops perform, and the venerable musical organization gained a legion of new followers.

Boston was not visited by a parade of Tall Ships in 1976: that waited until 1992. But there were enough waterfront festivities to bring Boston's nautical past to mind, and this image added to the celebrations. And of course it didn't hurt that rock 'n' roll also contributed to the festive feeling of the summer of 1976.

How did one small band such as Boston become such an incredible sensation?

The five members of the band Boston asked themselves the same question. Their debut album, *Boston,* was released on August 8, 1976, and in one of the lead songs, the group tried to explain their sudden success.

> Well, we were just another band out of Boston
> On the road to try to make ends meet
> Playin' all the bars, sleeping in our cars,
> And we practiced right on out in the street.

Boston had seen plenty of bands before, but none with this kind of star power. The debut album eventually sold seventeen million copies worldwide. Boston and Cambridge had lagged behind San Francisco and Oakland for a decade and a half, but the phenomenal success of *Boston* reversed that for a matter of years.

What was the downside of life in Boston in the mid-1970s?

Boston had known many ups and downs during its history, and most people would argue that it has had more of the former than the latter. One of the truly shameful episodes of Boston history, however, has to do with busing, and the endless controversies that followed a judicial decree.

How "cool" was Boston in the late 1970s where popular music was concerned?

For the space of five years, Boston became the hippest place of the entire music industry. The Rathskeller, better known as "The Rat," became the center-point for *avant-garde* bands, notably Blondie and the Ramones. The music success fed off itself with groups as utterly different as the Boston Pops and Boston contributing to each other's success.

In June 1974, U.S. Judge Wendell Arthur Garrity issued his 150-page ruling that the school system of Boston was fundamentally segregated, if not precisely by race, then certainly by income. Garrity's methodical outline showed that roughly eighty percent of the school districts of Boston were segregated. As a result, busing was to commence that very year with the children of well-heeled families being bused to low-income African American communities, and the same in reverse. Seldom, if ever, has a single judicial ruling caused so much contention.

One often hears of "Southie" and the determination of its residents. Did other communities resist busing?

Virtually no community or neighborhood of Greater Boston welcomed the ruling. For almost everyone involved, busing meant longer hours, greater headaches, and more concerns. Even so, it was appalling to many people around the nation to see the city that spawned the American Revolution turn into a place where bigotry and segregation were—even for a short time—the order of the day.

South Boston was especially virulent in its protest, perhaps because it was so tight-knit a community. Many residents had been there for four generations, and some could recall the times when their grandparents and great-grandparents had been shut out of employment in Boston. Southie residents were dead-set against busing, which seemed to them to be the second part of a vicious cycle of discrimination. Southie residents had a legitimate gripe in that they—not the prosperous members of other communities—had been singled out. What they lacked was the voice of calm and reason.

Could the busing controversy have been avoided?

No. Once Judge Garrity issued his ruling, it was a foregone conclusion that there would be bitterness and heartbreak in Greater Boston. What no one anticipated was the sheer ugliness of the situation.

Southie residents drew the most attention—nearly all of it negative—because of the manner in which they resisted busing. The annual St. Patrick's Day parade, usually a source of great pride, turned into an ugly display of racism.

Dorchester and other neighborhoods had their difficulties, but there is no doubt that Southies contributed the worst voices to the busing controversy. Of course, one can suggest that other communities, such as Brookline and Newton, might have done the same if so many of their youngsters had been compelled to go to different schools.

Was there ever a time when Greater Boston seemed ready to melt down over busing?

Yes. Between 1975 and 1978, many white families pulled their children out of the school system altogether, sending them to private, usually religious schools. The tax base was threatened, and Greater Boston saw the worst publicity it had ever witnessed. The great irony was that Boston was simultaneously undergoing a revival of tourism, based on the Bicentennial Year of 1976.

Can anyone identify the single moment or incident when busing showed its ugliest face?

Thanks to modern photography, the moment was captured on film. On April 5, 1976, perhaps two hundred South Boston High School students—all of them white—went to Government Center to protest busing. This was not unusual: they had done so a number of times before. But as late winter turned to early spring, the mood of the protestors became uglier, and at around 10 A.M. on that particular day came the single worst display by a Boston crowd. Some called it the Second Boston Massacre.

A black attorney happened to walk by the protestors, and he paused for perhaps thirty seconds to view the scene. Perhaps he would have escaped the beating if he had walked straight on: then again, no one can say for certain. What we do know is that the crowd turned its attention on him, and as one person held him, several others took swings with their fists. This was nasty enough, but the real centerpiece, the crowning disgrace, was when one of the protestors, a seventeen-year-old, seized an American flag and directed the lower part of the staff directly at the black man. As chance would have it, the black attorney was not skewered, but his injuries were serious.

How did Bostonians react to the photograph?

The great majority—even those that opposed busing—were appalled. Here in the Cradle of Liberty, was a young white person attempting to stab a middle-aged black man

South Boston High School became a salient example of the busing issue in 1976, when students there protested having blacks sent to their school.

with the American flag. The photograph, which was reprinted in virtually all the national newspapers and magazines, won the Pulitzer Prize for photography in 1976.

The Boston newspapers expressed the shame of many, but the national newspapers took it straight to the City on the Hill. How on earth could this happen in Boston, many people asked? Bostonians had no answer, and the pride that surrounded the national Bicentennial was blunted in the Boston area.

Did this particular photograph indeed say a thousand words?

It certainly did, and most of the words were unfavorable to the people of Greater Boston. In one important respect, however, the photograph "lied." Only on lengthy examination of the photograph was it revealed that the white man was not using the end of the flag to stab the black one, that he rather was waving the flag furiously. Of course this does not diminish the impact of the photograph; rather, it helps us to understand the moment better. The full story did not come out until 2008 with the publication of *The Soiling of Old Glory: The Story of a Photograph that Shocked America*.

Could things have been even worse during the Boston busing crisis?

We ask this question on many occasions, but perhaps the most appropriate parallel is the Boston Massacre of March 5, 1770. On that occasion, things could have been much worse, and the same is perhaps true of the events of April 5, 1976. Anger continued, but it did not intensify. Cool heads prevailed in the summer of 1976, just as they had in the winter of 1770.

How and when did the situation turn around for the Boston busing controversy?

This one is difficult to answer with precision. As late as 1979, it seemed that the busing controversy would never go away. But a handful of events, and trends, conspired to take people's attention away from busing, and once this happened, they intentionally chose never to look in that direction again.

BLIZZARD TO BLIZZARD

What was so different about the Blizzard of '78?

To people in central and western Massachusetts, the storm that came in February 1978 was not unusual. To them, it seemed only a little worse than normal. But to Bostonians, the Blizzard of '78 was a sensational event, one remembered decades after the fact.

The snowfall went on for more than a hundred hours, during which sections of Boston got as much as three feet of the white stuff. Even for rural communities, this would have been difficult, but for a major city with as many winding streets and one-ways as Boston, it was truly a catastrophe. Plenty of ice found its way into the mixture, making matters even worse. To be honest, Bostonians coped rather well. Hundreds of vehicles were abandoned, and many people took to skiing their way to work, but good humor prevailed for the most part. Though few people realized it at the time, the Blizzard of '78 pushed away the last vestiges of Boston as a ward city, dominated by small-time politicians. It was obvious that the old ward system could never have handled an event such as this, and that the big-time city government that commenced in the 1930s was essential.

Why do we seldom, if ever, hear of the blizzards of 1982 and 1983?

Because Boston learned how to deal with the severe weather. Contracts were made with companies that delivered snow removal on a big-time basis. Bostonians learned how to bundle up for the severe cold, and to enjoy life while doing so.

It is difficult at the time of this writing in 2015, to realize just how cold Boston was in 1981, 1982, and 1983. The climate change that we refer to as "global warming" had not yet kicked in, and in the early 1980s, Americans—not only Bostonians!—were much more frightened of the cold than the heat. Perhaps the biggest surprise came on April 6, 1982. Bostonians and their suburban relatives were enjoying a fine spring when a sudden winter storm occurred and smacked everyone with a last dose of winter. But the good news was that Bostonians coped rather well.

What was the other significant phenomenon of early 1980s Boston?

No one expected them: the yuppies.

In the early 1980s, well-heeled young couples began heading to the inner-city neighborhoods. This phenomenon of the young urban professional was nationwide, but a handful of East Coast cities with Boston and New York in the lead, showcased the movement. What the young urban professionals discovered was that suburban property had become so expensive that inner-city buildings began to look like deals, even steals. Boston saw more than its share of the yuppies, who flocked to the inner city and neighborhoods. They tended to be newly minted lawyers, doctors, and administrators, and

Did many homeless people perish during the 1980s?

The true and full statistics will never be known. Perhaps there were a few hundred people who actually froze to death in Greater Boston while attempting to warm themselves over grates. But the number that suffered appallingly bad conditions runs well into the tens of thousands, and the shame that Americans experience over poverty meant that most of them never related the full story. What can be said without a shred of doubt, is that the American city—Boston included—was being remade yet again in the early and mid-1980.

they delighted in buying up dilapidated real estate for a hundred thousand dollars or so, and turning it into a gold mine.

Was there any downside to the energy of the early 1980s?

Not that anyone could see. Plenty of people remained in the suburbs, but the infusion of young people to the inner city meant a bigger tax base, and more energy in the downtown sector. The theater district, for example, went on a roll by the mid-1980s.

Yes, the inner-city neighborhoods witnessed increased poverty. Many people who had previously been able to afford apartments could no longer do so, and homelessness increased at a dramatic rate. Given that the winters of the early and mid-1980s were colder than normal, Boston and New York, as well as Chicago and Detroit, became centers of a national conversation about homelessness.

THE SHOCKING CHARLES STUART CASE

Who was Charles Stuart?

Born in 1959, Charles Stuart was a prime example of the yuppie movement. In 1989 he held a mid-level executive position at a Boston furrier. His wife, Carol, was a tax attorney. The couple, who were expecting their first child, appeared to have it all: looks, money, and a stunningly bright future. But during the evening of October 23, 1989, they were allegedly shot at by a black man who invaded their automobile. Mrs. Stuart died at the hospital hours later, and Charles Stuart had a nasty gunshot wound to his stomach.

When examined by the police, Charles Stuart described a black gunman who could fit all sorts of profiles and stereotypes in Greater Boston. A manhunt followed with a number of suspects being brought in. A strong case developed against one of them, and Charles Stuart, recovering in the hospital, was seen as a hero, or at least a man deprived of all the good things of life. And then the bottom fell out.

Who blew the whistle on the crime?

Charles' brother, Matthew Stuart, came to the police on January 3, 1990, to confess that he had played a part in Carol's murder, and that life insurance money was the motive. Charles Stuart committed suicide one day later, and Matthew Stuart was later convicted of obstruction of justice.

Can a person really be so low as to kill his spouse in order to gain life insurance money?

This is the question that came up, time and again, during the winter of 1990. As the case against the prime suspect collapsed, attention went back to Charles Stuart. He took his own life in January 1990 insuring that the whole truth would never be known. If all that is suspected is indeed true, then Charles Stuart represents one of the worst police cases of Boston history: a despicable person who would sacrifice his wife and unborn child in order to turn a profit, and one who would cast aspersions on the African American community. Of course, it is unfair to turn the whole case on to the hands of the yuppie community, but even the word became disreputable.

TALL SHIPS AND TALL BUILDINGS

How long had it been since Boston hailed its nautical heritage?

The docks and wharves which once had moved millions of tons of goods were mostly idle in the early 1990s. Other than the Old North End and the Charlestown Navy Yard, Boston seemed only faintly aware that it had once been one of the great centers of East Coast commerce. When it was announced that "Sail Boston" would bring dozens of Tall Ships to Boston, the populace was energized and excited. Even so, the sheer size of the crowds was extraordinary.

In July 1992, the Tall Ships, including coast guard vessels and training vessels, came to Boston. Perhaps two million people came to Boston during the two-week period, making Sail Boston the number-one tourist success of Boston in the twentieth century. Tourists hired motor boats to carry them past the long line of frigates, schooners, and so forth. Boston enjoyed one of its best summers ever.

When did Boston gain one of the most dramatic skylines to be found in the United States?

Assuredly it was not during the 1920s and 1930s. Those were the decades when Manhattan surged past all rivals to become the city of skyscrapers. And Boston languished for a long time. But with the completion of the Federal Reserve Building in 1978 Boston was on its way, and the Financial District showed the greatest improvement. When one stands in East Boston today, gazing back at the district, he or she is amazed at the difference a few decades can make.

THE BIG DIG

How bad were traffic conditions in Boston around the year 1990?

They were so bad it is difficult to describe. The Central Artery, completed thirty-one years earlier, had become a true nightmare with 150,000 vehicles a day, and traffic jams that went on all through the afternoon. Traffic fatalities on the Central Artery were four times higher than on other, similar stretches of highway, and Bostonians had long since declared they could not stand the monstrosity, which created shadows in the central part of the city, and seemed to make just about everything uglier. When Massachusetts

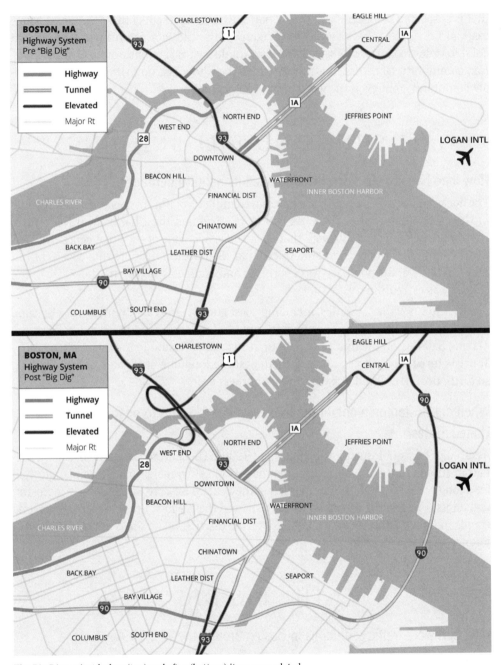

The Big Dig project before (top) and after (bottom) it was completed.

transportation officials declared that the Central Artery would be removed, one could hear the cheers from all over Boston. Inevitably, however, those cheers were followed by questions. What would replace the eyesore?

The answer, as expressed by Governor Michael Dukakis (1933–) and his advisors, was that the Central Artery would be completely dismantled, and two new bridges built over the Charles River, connecting the North End of Boston with East Cambridge. So far so good, many people said. But the second and third parts of the answer sounded wildly implausible. A brand new tunnel would be constructed so that traffic would now pass underground, and an entirely new tunnel would go under Boston Harbor, connecting South Boston. If the Central Artery was a disaster, what was the remedy?

Almost everyone had an opinion, but the informed reply came from the brain of Fred Salvucci, secretary of transportation under Governor Michael S. Dukakis. Salvucci brought an engineer and architect's passion, but there was something personal at work: his grandmother's house had been taken by the state in an action of eminent domain a generation earlier. Determined to prevent future use of eminent domain, Salvucci envisioned a Boston where the Central Artery was dropped underground, and where magnificent new bridges speeded traffic on its way. All this could be accomplished, he assured, but the price was high, and the city would be disrupted.

Had Boston learned anything from its mistakes in the South and West Ends?

It had to. If Boston had carried out the Big Dig in an arbitrary fashion, the project would never have been finished: it would have been blocked by lawsuits. As it is, first the Dukakis administration, and then the administration of William Weld, hired community spokespersons, who held numerous meetings, always seeking to ease to situation for the locals. After long discussions, it was agreed that work would not be done at night, and that construction sites would be kept clean.

Did anyone say that all this was impossible that it couldn't be accomplished?

Nearly everyone recognized that the technical skill existed to construct these tunnels, albeit at tremendous expense. But no one really believed this enormous project could be accomplished in seven years, as the engineers claimed, and the greatest concern was over how the city would operate while the work was in progress. In his secretary of transportation, Governor Dukakis had a first-rate advocate. Fred Salvucci was an Italian-American whose grandmother's house had been taken by the Commonwealth of Massachusetts by eminent domain, thirty years earlier. She had received a check for one dollar in return for her home that was taken.

Salvucci was the right person to "sell" this project to the general public. He knew the hardships it might impose upon people, and he pledged all the support of the governor's office to minimize them. As a result, there were hearings with people in the different neighborhoods, and strong measures taken to minimize environmental impact. What no one realized in 1990, was that the biggest claims of outrage would not come from Bostonians, but from *outside* the city.

143

How did the opening months of the Big Dig go?

Dismantling the Central Artery was an enormous undertaking that lasted nearly three years. Of course, the building of the new, underground tunnel commenced at almost the same time, and significant progress was made, but Boston traffic became even worse in 1992 and 1993, leading to many complaints. Significantly, the larger number of these came from outsiders, people who landed at Logan Airport, and had a difficult time getting into the city, much less any of the suburbs. Outside criticism also mounted during election years that featured important Massachusetts political contests: the most significant of these were 1992, when Senator Paul Tsongas (1941–1997) made a brief bid for the Democratic nomination, and 1994, when millionaire Mitt Romney challenged Ted Kennedy for his longtime seat in the U.S. Senate. Charges of cronyism were widespread, but they were not as effective, or as on the mark as those that charged the Big Dig was growing too expensive, day by day.

Was there ever a time when the Big Dig might have been abandoned?

It was not possible. Once the elevated highway known as the Central Artery was taken down (at great cost thanks to the hazardous material), there simply had to be the new solution: there was no turning back. Perhaps the knowledge of this allowed certain contractors and politicians to ratchet the bill up even more than would otherwise have been the case: about the only thing no one could argue was that the Big Dig was hideously expensive. What was anticipated as a $3 to $4 billion dollar job turned into a $7 to $8 billion project, and then into a $10 to $11 billion boondoggle. The taxpayers, especially those in Central and Western Massachusetts, were outraged.

Was there a saving grace, something that made the whole thing worthwhile?

In the first five years of the project, no one could see any saving grace. It seemed that Boston had, once again, succumbed to the worst aspects of cronyism and self-indulgence, where the politicians' pockets were concerned. But when the beautiful new bridge began rising over the Charles River, people took notice.

Known today as the Leonard P. Zakim Bunker Hill Bridge, this white giant is a thing of beauty. Its shape is intended to hearken to the sailing days of Boston, and it resem-

---

How did the Big Dig survive the change from Democratic to Republican administrations?

Many Republican politicians inveighed against the Big Dig, calling it the worst sort of old-style Massachusetts politics. Once in office, however, Republican governors and secretaries of transportation found themselves chained to the Big Dig just as firmly as their Democratic predecessors. There was no way to disentangle the city and its politics from the massive reconstruction.

bles, in some respects, the Bunker Hill Monument, half a mile in the distance. Controversy continued to swirl, right down to who the bridge should be named for, but Leonard P. Zakim (1953–1999), longtime leader of Boston's Anti-Defamation League, won out.

How can one bridge make such a difference?

Ask any San Franciscan about the Golden Gate. Ask any Londoner about Tower Bridge. There one finds the answer: a beautiful bridge brings pleasure to the eye, and lifts the spirits. To Bostonians and outsiders alike, the Leonard P. Zakim Bridge has become one of the permanent symbols of Boston. Almost any time that the network news interviews prominent Bostonians—usually on political matters—the Zakim Bridge is used as the background.

The Zakim Bridge rose slowly, allowing Bostonians to see the full difference between the old that was passing away and the new that was still in process. Towering over the last remnant of the Central Artery, the Zakim Bridge looked like an image for the twenty-first century, while the Artery harkened back to some of the worst architectural designs of the twentieth.

As the Zakim Bridge rose, where else did Bostonians look for inspiration?

The Ted Williams Tunnel, intended to connect South Boston to Logan Airport, was a project equally as daunting as the building of the Zakim Bridge. The major difference is that the Zakim was there for everyone to see, while much of the work that went into the Williams Tunnel was hidden from view.

Early on, the designers decided that the Tunnel must be sturdy enough to defy any intrusion of water, and to prevent any opportunity for complaint by the critics. Instead of building the Williams Tunnel in the old-fashioned way, blowing out air and water on a constant basis, the builders constructed the tunnel in twelve pre-made sections, and then "dropped" them into Boston Harbor to begin the tremendous job of fitting.

It all sounds so dangerous! Was anyone killed?

Not a single worker died in the process of construction. Some may have sustained injuries that were hushed up, and the general public will never know. But there is little doubt that the construction of the Ted Williams Tunnel was a work of genius. Enormous catamaran boats were brought in to lay the concrete tunnel sections just so, and GPS and laser-guidance allowed the workers to come within one inch of anticipated position.

Created by the infamously expensive Big Dig, the Zakim Bridge is a marvel of twenty-first-century engineering.

145

Of course there was still the trouble of connecting the two "ends" of the gigantic tunnel to the mainland. This required the building of the largest coffer dam ever seen in North America, 80 feet high and 280 feet in circumference. All the water was pumped out, allowing the workers to go to their tasks with welding, drilling, and masonry. Bostonians, of course, could not see the work that was being done, but many were proud of the early results.

How loud did the critics become?

By 2001 critics of the Big Dig were legion. One heard them on Boston radio, but also on national television. Everyone, it seemed, had a Big Dig story to tell, and they often concurred in the matter of shameless exploitation by the politicians and contractors. It's worth noting, however, that Bostonians never gathered in large numbers to protest the work. Fred Salvucci's neighborhood hearings had been very effective, and the majority of Bostonians believed the Big Dig would be justified in the course of time. Only on one occasion did it really seem that the roof might cave in, and this was in response to some small amounts of water getting in to the Ted Williams Tunnel. Traffic was stopped for a few days; an investigation was launched; but almost everyone in a position of responsibility realized that there was no way to go but forward. The tunnel, and the Big Dig, must be completed.

When was the Big Dig complete?

In 2005, years behind schedule and billions of dollars further down the road than anticipated, Massachusetts officials declared the Big Dig to be complete. Taxpayers breathed a major sigh of relief, even though the bonds which had been issued would still need to be paid. And for about three years, there was much less talk of the Big Dig.

The revelation came in 2010, when the Rose Kennedy Greenway was substantially complete. Done with much less fanfare and with far fewer critics, the Greenway was intended to complete the so-called Emerald Necklace chain of parks constructed by Frederick Law Olmsted a century and a quarter earlier. The Greenway was stunning in its results, but it required the Big Dig to make it fully visible.

How different was Boston in the year 2015 from what it had been in 1995?

One has to struggle to count all the ways. There are sections of the central city that look much as they did a generation earlier, but the eastern and northeastern parts of the city look radically different. Instead of a noisy and congested elevated highway, traffic simply disappears for half a mile, and then emerges from a tunnel to view the glorious Zakim Bridge. Instead of allowing three hours to thread one's way through traffic on the way to Logan Airport, the commuter from the Massachusetts Turnpike scurries in with barely a twenty-minute movement. And the easternmost part of the inner city has become a thing of beauty, dotted and ringed by green with all sorts of small parks and large venues. There's nothing quite like the new Boston, the section created by the Big Dig and the Kennedy Greenway.

Are there still any critics of the Big Dig?

Some of its foes and opponents will never be convinced. They regard the Big Dig as the premier example of how not to change a city and its traffic. To Bostonians, however, the proof is in the pudding. The easternmost part of the city—which had been the poorest section since the 1840s—has been remade into one of the great centerpieces of Boston. Fine new restaurants compete with old established ones in the North End, and the traffic moves briskly along Atlantic Avenue on the way to the New England Aquarium. If they were called upon to rate the project on a scale of one to ten, many Bostonians would reply that it was only a "five" in terms of conception and a "seven" in terms of schedule, but that what it delivered ranks somewhere between a nine and a ten.

Does anyone anticipate another enormous construction job, one in the near future?

Architects and city planners are never idle: they are always turning over the possibilities. One hoped-for change is to alleviate the enormous congestion that now plagues the westernmost part of the city. The Mass Turnpike and Route 128 bring in so much traffic that the backups and delays are becoming legendary. Perhaps it is not likely, but certainly it is possible that there will be another massive Big Dig, and this time the shovels will alter the angle of the highways that ring Boston.

TURN OF THE CENTURY

What was the typical Boston household like in or around the year 2000?

It was substantially different from that of 1950 or 1900. The single largest difference was the reduction of household size. Less than ten percent of Boston households were composed of one person in 1950; by 2000 this had increased to well over twenty percent. Of course, the statistic was sometimes misleading. The city had so many apartment-style houses that one landlord living downstairs counted as "one" person, living alone, and the three that lived upstairs, each in their separate rooms, all counted as "one" for a total of four.

The second largest difference had to do with length of commutes. To be sure, some Bostonians still lived, as their grandparents had within walking distance of work. The majority, however, embarked on daily commutes that took them to all different parts of the city, and sometimes beyond. As late as 1950, it was a rare Bostonian that worked out of town; by 2000, there may have been five percent of the total who did so. They drove, or took the train to office buildings out on Route 128, and returned home well after dark. But even with all the people taking subways, buses, and trains, the sheer

147

number of commuting vehicles continued to rise. The typical Boston household in 1900 had zero autos (they had barely been invented), those from 1950 possessed one to two, and by 2000 there were plenty of households with a total of three.

Did the Bostonians of 2000 enjoy life more than their great-grandparents— those that lived in the city in 1900?

Here the answer becomes qualitative, rather than quantitative. In sheer number of days spent on vacation, and in the ability to zip away to Cape Cod or the coast of Maine, the average Bostonian from 2000 was much better off than his or her great-grandparents. But in terms of actual leisure time—meaning hours when no labor of any sort was required—the typical Bostonian may have worked longer, if not harder, than his ancestors.

Where did the people of Boston work in the 2000s?

Much like their 1950s counterparts, the Bostonians of 2000 worked in health care, education, transportation, and communication. The city's many hospitals employed the greatest number of people; the many colleges and universities came in second. The biggest difference was in the tools that these workers used during their hours of employment: they used fast communication devices that seemed to ensure everyone could know everything necessary at the moment of first meeting (of course this often proved not to be the case).

Because the Big Dig was still underway in 2000, the number of people employed in construction soared to new levels, but this number dipped after about the year 2005. And many of the jobs that had provided well-being for a generation or two were entirely gone: it was rare to find employment at manufacturing giants such as Gillette, for example.

What did Bostonians in the 2000s do for entertainment?

In this area, twenty-first century Bostonians suffered from what can only be called an embarrassment of riches. If one had the time and money, he or she could hear a first-class classical recital on Monday, followed by an indie rock band performance on Tuesday, and a poetry recital on Wednesday. Depending on the time of year, this could be followed by a Red Sox game on Thursday, or a Patriots game on Sunday. Very few Bostonians suffered from a lack of entertainment options, though it could be said they had to juggle their schedules to attend.

ETHNIC REALITIES

How much better (gentler and easier) are ethnic relations in twenty-first century Boston?

When one examines the early twenty-first century record and compares it to the previous 100 to 150 years, the difference is startling, almost amazing. By the year 2015,

Boston ceased to have strong geographic ethnic divisions. To be sure, Chinatown remained, and there were more African Americans in Roxbury than in other neighborhoods, but Boston was more integrated than any other major northeastern city.

The same could not be said of the suburbs: they tended to be heavily white. Even there, however, one found penetration by different ethnic and racial groups with Asian families leading the way.

THE BOSTON MARATHON

How did the Boston Marathon become so steeped in tradition?

Bostonians and New Englanders are suckers for tradition, meaning that they venerate the past. It has always been beneficial to the Marathon that it is run on Patriot's Day, which in Massachusetts falls on the nineteenth of April, the anniversary of Paul Revere's ride. That has changed more recently, however (see sidebar on page 152).

How did some of the traditions get started?

Let's take the matter of who gets to fire the starting gun. Ever since 1905, this honor has been accorded to a member of the Brown family of Hopkinton. One Brown played a big role in establishing the Boston Marathon in the first place; his son was owner of the Boston Celtics; and the family continues to carry on. It's rare to hear the runners complain about these traditions, however: most of them are fully supportive of them.

THE BEGINNINGS

How did marathons become part of modern-world sport?

Oddly enough, the ancient Greeks, who excelled in track and field, were not marathoners. Ancient Olympics featured numerous running contests, but all of them concentrated on speed and explosive energy, rather than endurance.. But when the first Olympics of modern times was held in Athens in 1896 the marathon was conceived. It was developed as a twenty-four-mile race, which is the distance between downtown Athens and the beach at Marathon, the place where the Athenians smashed the Persian invaders in 490 B.C.E.

Fewer than twenty men competed in 1896 (no one even thought of the possibility that women might one day do so). The winner was Spyridon Louis, who came over the 151

Why is the Boston Marathon always run on the third Monday of April?

When the event was first organized in 1897, the Boston Athletic Association wanted to make a strong tie to Paul Revere and his famous Midnight Ride. For many years, the Boston Marathon was always run on the nineteenth of April, rain or shine. But in the early twentieth century, as the event gained larger crowds, it became awkward to run the race on a Tuesday, Wednesday, Thursday, or Friday, and it was agreed that henceforth the Marathon would always be run on the third Monday in April. This means that it often, but not always, coincides with the anniversary celebrations at Lexington and Concord.

finish line with a time of 2:58:50. The modern marathon was thus born, even though its length was not quite the same as what we know today.

How did Boston get in on this new act?

A number of Americans went to the 1896 Olympics in Athens, and a group of young Bostonians proved especially keen on the idea of long-distance running. All of them belonged to the Boston Athletic Association (BAA). Upon returning home, these young men looked for a venue to hold an American marathon, and they were keen on the idea of linking this long-distance run to the long-distance *ride* of Paul Revere, back in 1775.

The intention was to hold the first Boston Marathon on April 19, 1897, and to have the run mimic Paul Revere's ride in some way. The more the BAA organizers examined the situation, however, the more difficult a precise emulation proved to be. There was simply too much traffic in Charlestown and Cambridge for a race of any size to be run. Additionally, the organizers decided it was better to have the runners commence in the suburbs and finish in downtown Boston, rather than the other way around. Many preparations were necessary, and the organizers barely managed to put things in place for April 19, 1897.

How many men ran in the first Boston Marathon?

Only eighteen were there when the starting gun was fired: the idea of long-distance running had not yet caught on. And the race began in the little town of Ashland—not Hopkinton!—because it was almost precisely twenty-four miles from downtown Boston.

The first Boston Marathon was won by John J. McDermott of New York with a time of 2:55:10. Bostonians were sad, but not downcast that no hometown boy was even in the top four. What really struck the observers, however, was the vigor necessary to undertake this feat. Eighteen men started the race; only ten finished. And in 1898, the year of the Spanish–American War, an outsider won again. This time it was Ronald J. Mac-Donald of Canada, who came in with a finish time of 2:42:00.

What can account for such a major difference in finishing time between 1897 and 1898?

Finishing times were more fluid in the first decade of the Boston Marathon than ever since, meaning that they fluctuated to a greater degree than is true today. In our time, the early twenty-first century, the difference of fifteen or twenty seconds can mean a great deal. In the early Boston Marathons, finishing times fluctuated much more than today because the runners were not as acclimated to road conditions (they also ran with what we would consider sub-par footwear.)

Who were the first "outsiders" to win Boston?

In 1899 virtually all the finishers—and there were only eleven—were Americans. The very next year, however, Canada came to steal the show. John Caffery of Hamilton, Ontario, won the race with a time of 2:39:44, and the second and third place finishers also were Canadians. This was an exceptionally good year for the Marathon in that twenty-nine men started, twenty-six of whom finished the race. No animosity between Americans and Canadians emerged: everyone seemed happy just to know that the Boston Marathon had entered the new century, and that it continued to draw a good crowd. John Caffrey repeated with another victory in 1901.

What kind of sports equipment did these early marathoners wear?

Compared to the equipment of our modern time, they lived and ran as if in the Dark Ages. The tee-shirts were much longer, and the shorts sometimes extended below the knees, but the biggest difference was in the shoes. There were no athletic sneakers, and these men really ran in shoes. Not only did they endure greater physical hardships than the runners of today, but these men earned no prize money. There was no Marathon purse, and endorsements, such as they were, did not come until the 1930s.

Speaking of physical endurance, the runners of the early Marathons sometimes went through very tough conditions. The chill or wind of an April day is well-known to the people of Boston and Massachusetts, but it can sometimes also be surprisingly warm. The 1909 Marathon was known simply as "The Inferno." A warm southeasterly air flow brought Boston temperatures up to 83.4 degrees that day, and as the runners progressed, they experienced both heat and stale air. Henri Renaud of Nashua, New Hampshire, was an ironworker, accustomed to handling heat. He won the race with a time of 2:55:36 the slowest finishing time of that decade.

Did the outsiders keep coming and winning?

They did. Harvard graduate Dick Grant was the local favorite, but he came in seventh in 1898 and second in 1899. Any thoughts that the new century would mark "his" moment were disabused by the arrival of more Canadians.

John Caffery of Ontario won in 1900 with a time of 2:39:44 and he repeated his win in 1901 with 2:29.33, marking an improvement of slightly more than ten minutes. A New Yorker won in 1903, and by 1904, the first year a local man won the Marathon, Dick Grant's time had come and gone. John Lorden of Cambridgeport was the first Bostonian to win the Boston Marathon, and he was upended the succeeding year by yet another New Yorker. By then, the field had increased to as many as sixty men running each year, and the number of spectators had positively swelled: there may have been half a million people along the twenty-four miles between Ashland and Copley Square. Even so, there was a decidedly calm feeling to the Boston Marathon in these years: it was usually one lone runner that approached the finish line with one policeman on a motorcycle accompanying him.

Did the weather just keep on cooperating, meaning that the race was always run?

The Boston Athletic Association made plain from the very beginning that the Marathon would always be run, rain or shine (this has remained true for every Marathon to date). And in the first decade, the weather cooperated in that it was neither too warm nor too cold, meaning that it was predictable weather for the Boston area: cloudy and damp with an occasional peak of sunshine. All that changed in the Marathon of 1909, which is known simply as "The Inferno."

Boston weather is both predictable and changeable, meaning that its position near the Atlantic allows for sudden squalls to change the weather. No one anticipated the incredible heat of April 19, 1909, however. At spots along the route, it was only 84 degrees Farenheit, but at others, thanks to gusts of warm wind, it may have been closer to 93 degrees. None of the runners were prepared for this blast of heat: virtually all of them suffered. Henri Renaud of Nashua, New Hampshire, was an ironworker, and daily work in the heat enabled him to win the race, though with the relatively slow time of 2:53:36. One hundred and eighty-two men started this marathon; one hundred and sixty-four finished it. Some of them were reduced to walking along the way, however.

Did anyone say that marathon running was just too darned dangerous?

It was the year of the Inferno in 1909; it was also the year that national newspapers caught on to the importance of marathon running. Quite a few brought forth physicians who declared that the attempt to run twenty-four miles was just too dangerous for anyone's health. The person whose career was altered the most was the winner of the 1911 Boston Marathon.

Who was Clarence DeMar and what made him so "mah-velous"?

Born in Ohio, Clarence DeMar (1888–1958) endured a truly difficult childhood. After his father died when young Clarence was eight, he often walked miles each day, delivering goods his mother marketed to keep the family afloat. After the family moved to Massachusetts, DeMar starred on the track and skiing teams at the University of Vermont, and then settled in to what might have been a rather dull life, working in a print shop in Medford, ten miles north of Boston. Wishing to keep his athletic strength, DeMar frequently ran to work, and then back home. This was his unorthodox training for the Boston Marathon, and to the end of his life DeMar eschewed what he called fancy and unnecessary training methods. The only way to be ready was to get out and run every day, he said.

DeMar won the 1911 Boston Marathon with a time of 2:21:39, the fastest record to date. He was tall but not lean, and he had an unorthodox running style, which was anything but elegant. His speed could not be denied, however, and it seemed likely he would win many other Marathons. Instead, DeMar practically disappeared from the racing world for more than five years. Only later did his fans learn that DeMar had been cautioned by his doctor, who declared he should not even go upstairs rapidly, much less run long distances.

When did Native Americans make their first appearance at the Boston Marathon?

A Canadian Indian named Tom Longboat (1887–1949) won the 1907 Boston Marathon with a time of 2:24:24. Journalists had been unimpressed by Longboat, especially because he did not give his utmost in practice (he also smoked a lot of cigarettes). On race day in 1908, however, Longboat proved all the critics wrong, and some of the newspapers commented that they had misjudged both this particular Indian and the athletic capacity of Native Americans in general. But the more dramatic appearance by a Native American came in 1912 and 1913, when the same Indian placed second.

Andrew Sockalexis was a Penobscot Indian from Maine. He placed second in 1912 with a time of 2:21:52, and on his return in 1913 he told the newspapers that

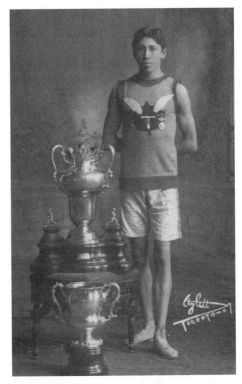

Tom Longboat was the first Indigenous runner to win the marathon in Boston.

the Penobscot girl he wished to marry had consented only in the event he won the Boston Marathon. Sockalexis placed second yet again, but he did get his bride.

How did the advent of World War I affect the Boston Marathon?

James Duffy of Ontario won the 1914 Boston Marathon with a time of 2:25:01. Just two months later came the assassin's bullets that killed the Austrian archduke, igniting World War I. James Duffy enlisted in the Canadian Army and died a hero's death at the Battle of Ypres in the spring of 1915.

America was not yet in the war, but the Marathon was squeezed by the big news that came from the warfront. This was not the first time: the 1912 Marathon suffered, for example, by coming just four days after the sinking of RMS *Titanic*. In 1917 the Marathon was held, but in 1918, it was dropped in favor of a running competition between the US Army and US Navy. Held at various points along the twenty-four mile Marathon route, the Army-Navy competitions proved a serious disappointment, and the idea of dropping the Marathon was never suggested again.

What was the first year in which people from far overseas made a powerful impression?

This had to be 1919, and perhaps it is not mere coincidence that it came just after the end of World War I. Participation in the Great War made Americans as a whole more aware of other peoples, and it was with some trepidation that Bostonians viewed the Marathon of 1919. Could Jimmy Henigan, the local hero, pull it off for "The Hub?" Sadly, the answer was no.

Three Finns dominated the 1919 Marathon. Carl Linder, who was born and raised in Finland but now lived in Quincy, came in first with a time of 2:29:13. He was followed by his diminutive countryman William Wick with a time of 2:30:15, and then by yet another,

How did long-distance running fare during the sports craze of the 1920s?

The spectators of the Boston Marathon grew in number each year, and the excitement about the event surpassed the interest in any other single sports event, but the Marathon was held on only one day of the year. Baseball ruled in the 1920s with Bostonians much more interested in how the Red Sox were doing than in any other sports story. About the only improvement that long-distance runners saw during the 1920s was the appearance of better footwear. The first advertisements for these brands of footwear also appeared, and a handful of top runners made some very small money by giving endorsements. In general, however, long-distance running was far, far behind "big" sports such as baseball, football, and boxing.

Otto J. Laakso (2:31.31), who lived in New York State. The Finns had pulled off the biggest set of victories seen since the Canadians made their dramatic appearance in 1900.

What made Clarence DeMar *the* runner of the Boston Marathon during the 1920s?

That DeMar was a superlative athlete could not be denied. But he had lost a half-decade of running, thanks to the advice of his physician, who declared it was too dangerous. And when Clarence DeMar entered the 1922 Boston Marathon, he was eleven years older than the man who had won it in 1911. Back then, DeMar had achieved something truly marvelous, winning the Marathon with the record time of 2:21:39. Newspaper critics asserted he'd be fortunate even to be able to reach the finish line in 1922.

Clarence DeMar proved them wrong, dead wrong. The thirty-three-year-old won the Marathon with the time of 2:18:10, setting a new course record. Journalists who crowded round DeMar after the race learned that he now ran to and from his job at the Medford print shop nearly every day.

Why did great runners like Clarence DeMar have to work all sorts of jobs?

There was no money in the Boston Marathon in those days—none. The winner received a laurel wreath, and perhaps a number of free drinks at Boston bars, and that was all. This remained the case until the 1980s.

What was the single most curious incident in Clarence DeMar's long running career?

The 1923 Boston Marathon featured De-Mar as the star. He had come back at the age of thirty-four. Could he pull it off again? DeMar was also being studied by a group of young scientists, eager to determine whether marathon runners had enlarged hearts. But Clarence DeMar suited up for the 1923 Boston Marathon in his usual nonchalant style. He even used the same shoes as in 1922. And it was the safety pin in one of those shoes that saved him.

As the lead runners approached Cleveland Circle, an automobile hit a bicycle, which swerved and ran over DeMar's shoe.

Known as "Mr. DeMarathon," Clarence DeMar won seven Boston Marathons and a bronze medal at the 1924 Paris Olympics.

157

DeMar only had a slight lead over Frank Zuna at this point, and to take the time to pull off the shoe might cost him the race. The safety pin held the shoe together just long enough for DeMar to win the race with the time of 2:22:37. The scientists then took him and the other top runners for X-rays, but this early attempt to understand the effects of running went nowhere: not until the 1950s would science catch up with what had happened in the field of long-distance running.

When did the town of Hopkinton replace the village of Ashland as the starting point?

Ashland had been selected in 1897, and the choice had been reinforced by the twenty-four mile distance, selected at the London Olympics of 1908. But in 1924, the Boston Athletic Association altered the distance to twenty-six miles and three hundred eighty-five yards. Given the longer distance, it made sense to alter the place where the race commenced, and Hopkinton replaced Ashland as the best-known town name associated with long-distance running. A long-time rivalry between Ashland and Hopkinton ensued, but by the twenty-first century, the two towns had learned to get along.

Clarence DeMar won this, the first of the longer Boston Marathons with the time of 2:29:40. He was, by now, running's equivalent to Babe Ruth. Reporters longed to know more about Clarence DeMar and how he performed what seemed like miracles, but they usually received frosty replies. To DeMar, it was quite simple: train longer and harder, and eat right. The Boston Marathon, in fact, became one of the first major sporting events in which many of the athletes did eat right, which meant a rich combination of protein and carbohydrates, and practically no sugar or sweets.

Could Clarence DeMar do it again?

In 1925, DeMar finished a disappointing second, and in 1926, he fell all the way to third, but he roared back in 1927 with a victory time of 2:40:22. He won again in 1928 with a finish time of 2:37:07, and after a dismal 1929 in which he came in ninth place, DeMar came back for one more astonishing victory. He won his seventh Boston Marathon in 1930 with a time of 2:34:48.

How did the Great Depression affect the Boston Marathon?

The Great Depression made life throughout the United States a good deal darker and grimmer than before. Sports, however, did not suffer to the same degree as financial institutions and the like. The reason, quite likely, is that people needed entertainment even more than before, and that sports were relatively inexpensive. The Boston Marathon costs its sponsors a great deal, but for the average citizen of Newton, Ashland, and Framingham, it cost almost nothing to go to Route 35 to watch the runners. Crowds actually increased during the 1930s.

Is there any way to know how DeMar would stack up against the marathon greats of our time?

As with most sports, attempts to compare the champions of one era with another are difficult. One can say this with confidence, however: no Boston Marathon champion of recent times has ever demonstrated a work ethic equal to DeMar's. This holds true for the American champions of the 1970s, and the Kenyans, who practically took over the sport in the 1990s. If he had the footwear available to modern runners, DeMar would, quite likely, have competed well against the great American champion Bill Rodgers.

Who was the next "outsider" to win the Boston Marathon?

One of the truly great aspects of the Boston Marathon is the extent to which the crowds cheer for outsiders. Right from the beginning, the Boston crowds had their favorites, but they never failed to exalt a foreigner. And when Paul de Bruyn (1907–1997) became the first German to win the Marathon in 1932 with a time of 2:33:36, Bostonians cheered him lustily. They hoped, of course, for another local man to change the pattern, for another Clarence DeMar. They did not find him (how could one possibly replace such a giant), but they found someone almost as good, John "The Elder" Kelley.

Born in Medford, Massachusetts, John Kelley (1907–2004) was one of ten children. He was an outstanding track and field athlete in high school, and he ran his first Boston Marathon in 1931. In 1935 Kelley won the Boston Marathon with a finishing time of 2:32:07.

How different was John "The Elder" Kelley from Clarence DeMar?

The two men paid tribute to each other, as great champions should, but they were cut from very different bolts of cloth. Clarence DeMar had a majestic presence, which was sometimes soured by outbursts of anger: this was especially true when fans mobbed him. John "The Elder" Kelley (1907–2004) was on the short side (five-foot four) and he lacked DeMar's athletic style. Whatever was missing was more than made up for by Kelley's enthusiasm, however: here was a person who was born to run and simply loved to do so.

Photos of John Kelley winning the Boston Marathon in 1935 can be contrasted with those of his victory in 1945, and little difference between the two can be found. In both cases, John Kelley ran with outbursts of enthusiasm. This was never truer than when he approached the finish line in 1945. Kelley became a crowd favorite of a very different type from DeMar. Fans did not expect Kelley to win every year; rather, they anticipated he would light up the race with his cheerfulness.

TARZAN

What were public sentiments where Native Americans were concerned?

Around the turn of the twentieth century it was expected that the Indians would disappear completely, that they would become so assimilated that no one could tell the difference. This did not happen, but Indians of the 1930s especially felt the ravages of the economic times, even worse than other ethnic groups. Indians were pleased when one of their own, Ellison Myers "Tarzan" Brown (1913–1975), won the Boston Marathon in 1936 and 1939.

A member of the Narragansett tribe, and a descendant of one of the few Narrangansetts to survive King Philip's War (see the chapter "Early Boston, 1630–1760"), Brown was a supremely fit bricklayer from Rhode Island. Handsome, dark, and toned, he was a crowd favorite, but he gained special strength from the numbers of Indians that came to watch: some pounded on drums to mobilize his energies. Tarzan Brown won with a record time of 2:33:40 in 1936, and improved on it with a time of 2:28:51 in 1939. Sadly, Brown's success at the Boston Marathon was not echoed in other parts of his life. Finding it difficult to obtain work, he drifted into alcoholism and divorce, and he died penniless in 1975. His is one of the saddest stories associated with Boston Marathon winners.

Did the advent of World War II change anything about the Marathon?

One did find, for the first time, a suspicion of outsiders. It became more important than ever for an American to win the Boston Marathon. Other than that, however, the event seemed much the same as before.

American desires for a local champion were thwarted, however, by an outstanding young talent from north of the border. The early 1940s belonged, at least so far as the Boston Marathon was concerned, to Gérard Côté of the province of Québec in Canada.

Who was Gérard A. Côté?

All Canadians who had previously won the Boston Marathon had been from the province of Ontario, and they nearly all fit the Canadian social model: earnest, quiet, and polite.

Gérard A. Côté, born in 1913, was a native of Québec, and he had an uninhibited style, both on the track and in the hotel celebrations that followed his events. He was, in fact, one of the first truly exuberant Boston Marathon champions.

The first francophone to win the Boston Marathon was Canadian Gérard A. Côté, who won in 1940, 1943, 1944, and 1948.

Côté ran his first Boston Marathon in 1934. He placed twenty-fourth that year, but he was just getting started. He won the event in 1940 with a time of 2:28:28, and he won again in 1943 with a time of 2:28:25. The following year, Côté won for a third time. His finish time was 2:31:50, and he was hailed as one of the greatest of all Boston Marathon champions. Unfortunately, Côté got into hot water almost immediately with the Canadian Army. He was part of the Canadian forces in 1944, and had not gained special exemption to run the Boston Marathon. Though he was excoriated in the Canadian newspapers, Côté showed no special embarrassment or shame: he later commented that he had to make best use of the good years available to him.

What was the Boston Marathon like in 1945, the year World War II came to an end?

April is known as the month in which the European war ended with the suicide of Adolf Hitler and the fall of Berlin to the Russians. In the United States, April 19 was a cloudy day with no showers, and John "The Elder" Kelley ran to his second Boston Marathon victory.

What one person defines the Boston Marathon better than any other?

This is not a scientific answer but an anecdotal one. If one can quote any authority, it might be Bill Rodgers (see p. 164), who won the Marathon in 1975, 1978, 1979, and 1980, and when he was asked about John "The Elder" Kelley, his answer was succinct: "He was the Boston Marathon."

Born in West Medford, John Kelley (1907–2004) ran his first Boston Marathon in 1928. There were 254 starters that year, and Kelley was one of the finishers, but he had to walk the last six miles of the course: he had lost his steam. This early difficulty did not deter Kelley, however. He took several years off to work on his stamina, and when he returned in 1934, he placed second. Kelley won immortal glory the following year, winning the 1935 Marathon. Nine frustrating years followed in which Kelley came in second several times. But he took the laurel again in 1945. By any rights that should have been it. But John Kelley was just getting warmed up.

How many more times did Kelley run the Boston Marathon?

He ran every single year between 1945 and 1981: the latter date marked his fiftieth time running the Boston Marathon. Kelley was never among the top competitors after 1950; on the other hand, his popularity and name recognition only increased. In all, John Kelley ran the Boston Marathon sixty-one times, won the laurel twice, and came in second seven times. No other runner comes close in terms of longevity of effort.

Why did the statue of John "The Elder" Kelley have to be turned around?

Located at the base of Heartbreak Hill in Newton, the statue shows the older John Kelley in his seventies, encouraging his younger self in his twenties or thirties. When the statue first was placed, it faced west, to welcome and encourage the runners entering the last six miles of their effort. Over time, it was found that many locals disliked the statue pointing west: it should face east, they declared, both to face the rising sun and to indicate the ultimate result of all the effort: Copley Square.

To what extent did foreigners dominate the Boston Marathon in the 1950s?

When one looks at the record, it seems unbelievable. A Korean won in 1950, and he was followed by a Japanese runner in 1951. A Guatemalan man prevailed in 1952, and he was followed by another Japanese runner in 1953, and a Finn in 1954. Japan saw yet another victor in 1955, and a Finn won in 1956. The long list of foreign winners was finally broken by John "The Younger" Kelly, who won in 1957. He was followed by a Yugoslav in 1958, a Finn in 1959, and then yet two more years of triumph by Finns in 1960 and 1961. Sometimes it seemed as if the Marathon was being run in some other country. Another Finn won in 1962; he was followed by two Belgians in a row (1963 and 1964), and then two more Japanese, who won in 1965 and 1966. A New Zealander took the laurel in 1967, and it was not until 1968 that America had a champion in Amby Burfoot of Connecticut.

Who was John "The Younger" Kelley, and are the two father and son?

They are not related. John "The Younger" Kelley was like the famous John "The Elder" only in that he was long and lean—stringy, some called him. John "The Younger" Kelley was the darling of most Bostonians in the 1950s; he was the only hope for the city to break free from the tyranny of so many foreign winners. John "The Younger" fulfilled their desires by winning in 1957, but America then went through another decade-long drought before Amby Burfoot won in 1967.

Who is perceived as being the "most perfect" of all runners of the Boston Marathon?

Abebe Bikila (1932–1973) was from Ethiopia, and in 1960 he won the Olympics marathon in Rome with the astonishing time of 2:15:16. Lean, a bit shorter than many African runners, Bikila was so well balanced in physique that he sometimes ran marathons in his bare feet. When he and fellow Ethiopian Mamo Wolde came to Boston in the spring of 1963, it was widely expected that they would finish first and second, and that everyone else would compete for number three.

John "The Younger" Kelley did not agree. He ran with the two Ethiopians in a practice, and while he came away deeply impressed, he knew that the weather conditions might be more favorable to a native son. Then, too, the Belgian runner Aurèle Vandendriessche was a real threat. An accountant by trade, Vandendriessche analyzed the race in every minute detail.

Ethiopian Abebe Bikila won both the Boston Marathon and the 1960 Rome Olympics. Sadly, he died in 1973 of a cerebral hemorrhage.

How much of a factor did the weather play on April 19, 1963?

The day started off rather cloudy. This was the first time that a helicopter monitored the event, allowing for aerial photographs. When the skies cleared, the weather was a bit humid, but overall it suited the Ethiopian runners just fine, and they got off to a fantastic start. Americans and other nationals trailed the two lead runners by more than six hundred yards. But a weather change set in around 1 P.M. A storm offshore sent thicker air inland, and the Ethiopians had trouble adjusting to the difference. They were so far ahead that the second cohort of runners felt little hope, but late in the game Vandendriessche passed Wolde, who had slowed to a walk. Hundreds of yards further, he met and passed Bikila. Vandendriessche ran to a remarkable victory.

Why do we remember the Ethiopians so fondly?

They were among the first Africans ever to run the Boston Marathon, and they are forever enshrined as the most popular. Gracious and charming, these incredible athletes left their mark on Boston, and helped pave the way for the entrance of the Kenyans two decades further down the road.

THE GREAT BOOM

When did long-distance running become fashionable for millions of Americans?

No one can date it precisely, but Frank Shorter's spectacular victory at the 1972 Olympics had something to do with it. Born in Germany but raised in upper New York State, Shorter felt a special connection to the Olympics of 1972, which were held in the city where he was born. Shorter was not expected to do well at the 1972 Olympics, but he burst past a field that included the defending Olympic champion Mamo Wolde of Ethiopia. Shorter came in at 2:12:19, two minutes ahead of the silver medalist. Shorter became the first American man to win the Olympic Marathon since 1908.

Though few sports historians point out this link, running may also have become more popular in the wake of the first Arab oil boycott of 1973, which made oil and gasoline much more expensive. And the appearance of new stores, dedicated solely to runners and their gear, was not far behind.

How important was Jim Fixx to the running boom?

Born in New York City, Jim Fixx (1932–1984) authored *The Complete Book of Running*, which was published in 1977. As a result, running boomed around the United States. It was especially popular in the cities on the East Coast, where many white collar workers feared they had become too sedentary. Between the various events of the mid-1970s and the publication of Fixx's book, running became the rage.

163

Why was the Falmouth Road Race so important?

Until about 1973, the Boston Marathon was still an event for elite runners. People came from all over the world to compete, but the local, everyday runner was practically shut out of the event. The Falmouth Road Race, run on the southwestern side of Cape Cod, was the shot in the arm that the Boston Marathon—and long-distance running in New England—required.

The brainchild of Tommy Leonard, the bartender at Boston's Eliot Lounge, the Falmouth Road Race was a seven-mile event that often displayed talent that would later win at the Boston Marathon. The Falmouth Road Race was the enthusiast's dream, participated in by many thousands of locals.

How did Bill Rodgers emerge as the favorite?

Born in Hartford, Connecticut, in 1947, Bill Rodgers was acquainted with long-distance running from an early age. He starred at the University of Connecticut where his roommate was Amby Burfoot, winner of the 1967 Boston Marathon. Burfoot saw Rodgers' incredible talent, and encouraged him to go further, but Rodgers had periods during which he burned out on running altogether.

It was in 1974, while working in a school for physically challenged adults, that Rodgers experienced a mini-crisis of his own. Low on funds, he saw his car repossessed, and found it necessary to walk to work. Within a matter of days, he was running both to and from, and found a renewed interest in the sport. By 1975 he was very much in the game.

What was so different about Bill Rodgers?

He ran with a looseness that had never been seen before. One can look all the way back to the champions of the 1930s and not find another runner with those easy, loping strides. Of course, Bill Rodgers had to work at it: this was marathon with a capital "M." But when he swept the field in 1975, it came as a stunner, especially when the final number was registered: 2:09:55. Rodgers had broken the previous record, and was now the fastest of all Boston Marathon runners.

How long had it been since Americans had dominated the Boston Marathon?

An Englishman won in 1970, and a Colombian prevailed in 1971. A Finn took the laurel crown in 1972, and John Anderson, in 1973, was the first American to win for some time. He was followed by an Irishman, who won in 1974, and then the field and circumstances suddenly changed with the dramatic appearance of Bill Rodgers.

Jack Fultz (1948–) won the 1976 Boston Marathon, and a Canadian prevailed in 1977, but in 1978 Bill Rodgers was back. He won with a finishing time of 2:10:13, and then repeated in 1979 with a time of 2:09:27. The small gain on his previous year indicates just how difficult it was to improve on one's time, once the two hours and fifteen minute barrier was broken.

How big was the boom that followed the 1975 Boston Marathon?

The boom had gathered force ever since Frank Shorter's victory in Munich, but Rodgers' victory in 1975 made it simply pop with energy. Millions of Americans, all across the country, put down their books, newspapers, and other diversions and became serious runners. Many improved their health as a result, but it can also be argued that many experienced injuries from the sport.

Perhaps the most important thing to come out of the running boom was an improvement in equipment. Running shoes had been around for some time, but they had never been truly popular; they now became the rage. Middle-class businessmen competed with one another in conversation, as to who was more conversant with the newest style in clothing and running shoes.

How big did the Falmouth Road Race become?

Falmouth was widely seen as the tune-up for the Boston Marathon. The great runners tended to go to Falmouth, and the reporters studied Falmouth results for clues as to who would prevail in Boston.

Was that it for Bill Rodgers?

No. He came back in 1980, to win one more time, this time with a finishing time of 2:12:11. By now, Rodgers held many of the records, and was the preeminent runner in the world. At the same time, however, he was trending to the downside of the hill. It is a cruel truth that many, if not most, marathoners have a handful of really good years, and that their performance then begins to lessen.

But the tail end of Bill Rodgers' sensational career also coincided with the rise of female runners. Women had entered the sport, and it would never be the same again.

WOMEN IN THE MARATHON

Why did it take so long for women to enter the Boston Marathon?

In hindsight, it seems rather strange. But prior to the year 1970, the majority of American physicians, observers, and lay persons believed women physically incapable of running twenty-six miles. We, of course, know that they are quite capable, but it took some time for the truth to become evident. Then again, prior to about 1970, there simply wasn't much in the way of athletic equipment for women: nearly all the major shoe companies and sportswear brands were aimed at men.

Who was the first woman to take the dare?

In 1967 Kathy Switzer (1947–) registered as K.V. Switzer for the marathon, deliberately making her name ambiguous, so no one could be certain she was female. About a third of the way into the course, she was practically assaulted by longtime BAA official Jock Semple. Furious that someone had violated the "no girls allowed" aspect, Semple pushed Kathy Switzer aside, only to be virtually attacked by her boyfriend, running alongside (all three later made up and became good friends).

Kathy Switzer was the first woman to run the Boston Marathon, which she did in 1967 by disguising she was a female.

The Kathy Switzer incident sparked a furor over whether women should be allowed to run. Quite a few traditionalists raised their heads to say that women were incapable or that they would only get in the way of the men, but it was fortunate for the cause of women's liberation that this was the *Boston* Marathon, a city known for progressive politics and attitudes where women were concerned. Bud Collins, longtime sportswriter for the *Boston Globe*, echoed the sentiments of many when he declared it was time for the Marathon to open up to women. And once the decision was made, the girls and women came in the hundreds.

If Kathy Switzer was the first person to take the dare, then who was the first woman to run in an official capacity?

The gates opened in 1970. This was the year when Sara Mae Berman of Massachusetts became the first woman to cross the finish line in an official capacity. She came in at 3:05:08, and was immediately joined by her husband, Larry, who had finished the men's race. Kathy Switzer also ran in 1969, coming in second to Berman.

How many women ran in the early 1970s?

It was, at first, only a trickle, but by the late 1970s it was a flood. Not only were women now in the Boston Marathon, but all sorts of handicapped individuals now had the opportunity to participate. Women continued to hold the headlines, however. When for-

Are there many hard-luck cases among former Boston Marathon greats?

Given that there was no prize money until the 1980s, there probably are quite a few such stories, and some of them have been forgotten. Patti Catalano had one of the hardest of all roads. Her third marriage dissolved just as her running career did, and in 1989, she was on the streets of Boston, sleeping in her car and trying to stay warm. Amazingly, she made a comeback. By 2005, she was in her fourth marriage with two children, and was beginning to compete in major races. Anyone that looked for a sob story from Catalano was bound to be disappointed. When questioned about her trials and travails, she nearly always responded that they were part of life, and that running marathons was not for the faint of heart.

mer anchorwoman Gayle Barron won the women's race in 1978, she shot to stardom, and one year later it was the opportunity of "Micmac" Patti.

Born in Quincy, Patti Catalano (1953–) was the daughter of an Irishman who had boxed in the US Navy and a Micmac Indian mother who had run away from home in Nova Scotia. The eldest of nine children, Patty had a decidedly hard time in life, caring for her siblings and seeking to live up to the high standards of her parents. Poverty alternated with mild prosperity, and during the good times she ate far too many donuts (she later suffered from bulimia). None of this mattered to her many fans in 1979, 1980, and 1981, however.

Micmac Patti, as she was called, was the outstanding athlete of the 1979 race. In superb condition, she showed a style that was hard to match. She came in second that year, and again in 1980 and 1981. Though she never gained the laurel crown, Patti Catalano represented a breakthrough for many young women.

THE 1980 DEBACLE

What made the 1980 Boston Marathon so ill-starred?

The trouble began during the winter of 1979 to 1980. The Soviet Union invaded Afghanistan in December 1979, igniting one of the sharpest, most intense periods of the Cold War. President Jimmy Carter announced a boycott of the 1980 Summer Olympics in symbolic protest of the Russian invasion (the 1980 Winter Olympics were held).

Marathon winner Bill Rodgers, who was now one of the most respected and admired voices in the running community, declared his opposition to the boycott: he wanted his shot at the 1980 Olympic Gold, and was incensed that President Carter had denied the opportunity to so many fine athletes. At one point, Rodgers announced he would wear a black armband in protest, but he did not make good on this threat.

167

How did the name Ruiz become a synonym for cheating in sports?

Millions of people watching on television were simply stunned by Ruiz's time. Numerous sports announcers choked back their words because they had never even *heard* of Ruiz. But the person "on the ground" was Bill Rodgers. Just twenty minutes earlier, he had won his fourth and last Boston Marathon. He was asked to present the trophy to the winner on the women's side. Rodgers later recollected that Ruiz did not seem very tired, and that she could not answer a number of questions he posed, on topics such as splints and times. Even so, Rosie Ruiz took the laurel wreath and the admiration of the crowd, while poor Jackie Gareau, who had run a fine race, was almost forgotten.

A week later, the suspicions of some were found to have merit. Though she never made a complete confession, it seems that Rosie Ruiz had not even started the Marathon, that she waited near one of the last entry points, perhaps a mile from Copley Square, and then ran in to seize the unwarranted glory. Stripped of her crown, which was awarded to Gareau, Ruiz became a byword for fakery in sports.

How many women showed up for the 1980 Boston Marathon?

Nineteen eighty was the "year of the women" so far as most Boston Marathon observers were concerned. More women entered than ever, and more of them had legitimate chances at achieving record times. Gayle S. Barron did not run, but Joan Benoit, the 1979 winner, was in good form. So was Patti Catalano (née Lyons).

Nineteen eighty was also the year of Bill Rodgers. Having already won three Boston Marathons, he could easily have retired to fame and glory, but he came back to run. Rodgers won the men's race with a superb time of 2:12:11. Most keen observers thought his performance terrific, but they also predicted it would be among his last. One just could not keep up that rate forever. But as sensational as Rodgers' run was, an even bigger story shaped up in the women's field.

Who was Rosie Ruiz?

Born in Havana, Cuba, in 1953, Rosie Ruiz (1953–) was a Cuban-American who lived in Manhattan. She was a popular person, had a number of friends, but most of those friends admitted they had never seen her engage in any truly strenuous athletics.

On April 19, 1980, the two favored runners were Jacqueline Gareau, a twenty-seven-year-old French Canadian, and Patti Catalano. Both had trained at great length, and they were equally fit for the rigors of the race. Almost at the last minute, however, Gareau was upstaged by Rosie Ruiz, who appeared out of nowhere to win the race with a time of 2:31:56 (Gareau came in at 2:34). If this was accurate, she had just set a new record.

FINANCIAL CRISIS

What happened to the Boston Marathon in the early 1980s?

Long-distance running had been on a tear for so long that no one believed it could possibly be endangered. But the Rosie Ruiz scandal raised eyebrows, and the sudden death of runner and author Jim Fixx in 1984, soured many people on running. It was not as if the sport were suddenly to go away, but the enthusiasm began to dim.

At the same time, the Boston Marathon experienced difficulty attracting the truly best runners. The New York City Marathon had recently turned professional, meaning prize money was allowed, and quite a few of the best runners said they would not run both. As a result, the Boston Marathon suddenly had fewer entrants than normal, and the finishing times were less than spectacular.

Was there any possibility that the Boston Marathon would fold?

If the Boston Athletic Association had remained in charge, there was at least an even chance that the marathon was doomed. In 1986, however, the BAA reached an agreement with the John Hancock Financial Services Company: the BAA would continue to manage the event, while John Hancock would be the underwriter. Prize money was awarded for the first time ever.

As one might expect, there were plenty of critics, people who felt the entire event was being sabotaged by pecuniary interests. Clarence DeMar was long dead, but one suspects he would have delivered withering criticism. Quite a few other major runners leveled shots at the new system, but others recognized that the time for magnificent amateur performance had passed. If the Boston Marathon was to continue, there would have to be prize money.

Who benefitted the most from the financial changes?

It's hard to say. No one special group seems to have benefitted. What is clear is that the prize money jolted some new enthusiasm into the old organization; the number of runners rose almost every year for the next two decades. Quite likely, it is mere coincidence that a new ethnic group began to dominate the Boston Marathon.

How large were the crowds by this point?

They surged during the first decade of the twentieth century. In 1909 nearly 300,000 spectators showed up to observe 182 men run, 162 of whom finished the course. The photographs from this time do not show dramatic or intense finishes; nor is the run to Copley Square celebrated. The journalists of that time seemed more interested in the mid-section of the course, and the photographs display runners who have not yet "broken from the pack."

It's a safe bet that ninety-nine percent of the observers hailed from the local area, but the Boston Marathon was beginning to attract national attention.

169

THE WOMEN'S AND WHEELCHAIR RACES

Why were women kept from running until the year 1972?

Hard though it is for us to believe, physicians and marathon organizers believed they were doing women a favor because they felt that the female body could not hold up under 26.2 miles of grinding punishment. A tiny number of women ran "illegally" during the late 1960s, and it was not until 1972 that women were officially part of the race.

How could anyone believe that women were "inferior" in this way?

Many things seem accurate until they are proven otherwise, and so it was with women running the Boston Marathon. The first women to officially run proved that females were up to the challenge, but no one at that time dreamed that so *many* women would one day participate. Nina Kuscsik of South Huntington, New York, was the first official female champion, coming in at 3:10:26 in 1972. That same year Olavi Suomalainen of Finland, won the men's race with a time of 2:15:39. The fifty-five minute difference between the two champions suggested that men did have a significant leg-up, and that it would be a long time before women became their equal. But, as with so many other aspects of sports and athletics, the prognosticators were way off.

Twenty years later in 1992, Olga Markova of Russia won the women's race with a time of 2:23:43. That same year, Ibrahim Hussein of Kenya won the men's race with a time of 2:08:14. If we use these twenty years as a rough guide, we see that the winning females shaved forty-seven minutes off their time, while the leading men improved by seven minutes. Men continue to enjoy an advantage, that of packing more muscle on to frames, but it seems possible that a Boston Marathon will one day witness a female runner with a better time than any of the men.

How long was it before foreigners began to take over the women's side of the race?

They have never done so to the same extent as what we see on the men's side. American women continue to place well in the Boston Marathon. But it was a mark of the times when Rosa Mota of Portugal won in 1987, 1988, and 1990 (with times of 2:25:21, 2:24:30, and 2:25:24 respectively). Olga Markova of Russia won in 1992 and 1993, and she was followed by Germany's Uta Pippig, who won in 1994, 1995, and 1996. The women's field showed more dominance by a handful of runners at the top than did the men's field. At the same time, however, one noticed more energy and enthusiasm in the crowds for the women than the men, who seemed like old hat.

How great a runner was "Catherine the Great" of Kenya?

Catherine Ndereba (1972–) ran to her first Boston Marathon victory in 2000 with a time of 2:26:11. She followed that up with another victory in 2001, this time coming in at 2:23:53. She returned to victory in 2004 with a time of 2:24:27, and on the eve of the 2005 Marathon, people debated what it would be like to have the first-ever four-time champion on the women's side. No man had accomplished it since Bill Rodgers.

Catherine ran her heart out in 2005, winning her fourth Boston Marathon with a time of 2:25:13. She became known as "Catherine the Great," and was hailed as the greatest female runner ever. To be sure, her amazing success stimulated plenty of competition, but no twenty-first-century runner has yet garnered four Boston Marathon laurel wreaths.

Who ever dreamed up the idea of having wheelchair participants in the Boston Marathon?

The decision was an outgrowth of the focus on people with disabilities, which moved

A silver medalist in the 2004 and 2008 Olympics and winner of the Boston Marathon, Catherine Ndereba is one of the best marathoners of her generation.

forward by leaps and bounds during the 1970s. Of course the wheelchair competition did not begin without controversy, and some aspects of controversy continue to dog it in our time. Robert Hall of Belmont won the first men's wheelchair competition in 1975 with a time of 2:58:00, and, not surprisingly, the trend was to ever-more rapid finishes. Wheel-chair contestants have a field day in the opening five miles, which are mostly downhill, and then face a tough climb in the last five. The men's wheelchair competition has shown plenty of international muscle with two different Frenchmen winning three times (1988, 1989, 1990), a Swiss winning a total of four times (1997, 1998, 1999, and 2000), and South African Ernst van Dyk winning a grand total of ten times (2001–2006, 2008–2010, and 2014).

THE BOMBINGS

Was there anything special to indicate that 2013 would be different from usual?

There was not. April 15, 2013, was a fine, warm day in the Boston area. Approximately 1.5 million people were ready to watch the event, while close to 33,000 runners lined up to participate. People from Africa continued their longtime domination of the event. Lelisa Desisa Benti of Ethiopia won the men's event with a time of 2:10:22, and Rita Jeptoo of Kenya won the women's with a time of 2:26:25. All seemed normal.

But then two bombs went off at 2:49 P.M. at or near the finish line in Copley Square. The first was shattering enough, sending debris through the air; the second sounded louder and was deadlier. What should have been the leisurely finish to the Boston Marathon became, instead, the scene of a terrorist attack. Three people were killed and 246 injured, roughly eighteen of whom lost limbs.

How did people respond to the bombings?

With shock, horror, and disbelief. Boston had been spared most of the worst of the terrorist events (although two of the planes that crashed into the World Trade Center had taken off from Logan). And if the terrorists were so determined to strike America, why would they choose something so harmless (and motivating) as the Boston Marathon? These questions were asked time and again in the days that followed the bombings.

Boston police, meanwhile, were joined both by FBI agents and the Massachusetts state police. Sections of Watertown were closed off for many hours, and the manhunt commenced. Four days later, the two suspects in the bombings had been apprehended. Tamerlan Tsarnaev was killed in a shootout with police, and his younger brother, Dzhokhar, was imprisoned. Both had been brought to America by their parents as refugees from Chechnya a decade earlier.

Boston has such a long, and largely successful, immigrant history. What went wrong with the Tsarnaev family?

That question has been asked many times, and has been answered most successfully by Masha Gessen in *The Brothers: The Road to an American Tragedy*. Her research indi-

Police try to maintain and aid victims immediately after the 2013 marathon bombing.

cates that the Tsarnaev family never successfully integrated into American society, that they remained essentially Chechen refugees, living in Cambridge, Massachusetts. The elder brother, Tamerlan, seemed to have a shot at the American dream. He was a fine athlete in his youth, but his life disintegrated through bitterness and the use of drugs. In 2012, Tamerlan was back in his home country of Chechnya for several months, and this seems to be the time when he was truly radicalized.

Plenty of mysteries about the 2013 bombings remain, not least of them being why the brothers did not create an exit strategy. Did they really believe they could lie low in their Cambridge apartment? The more one studies the event, the more peculiar it seems. This was not the case for the great majority of Bostonians, however. As the shock began to wear off, the people of Boston vowed to remain strong, and to show the world what they were made of.

Where does the expression "Boston Strong" come from?

One week after the bombings, Red Sox slugger David Ortiz gave a short, impromptu press conference. Unlike professional journalists, who approached the matter in a calm, dignified manner, Ortiz shouted "This is our f——g city. And nobody [is] going to dictate our freedom. Stay strong." This was enough to generate a movement in which Bostonians vowed the city would not be taken from them. If there had ever been thoughts of postponing the following year's Marathon, these were quickly quelled.

THE RED SOX

What makes the Red Sox the most interesting team in all professional baseball?

It surely is not the number of victories. Though they've done much better at the beginning of the twenty-first century, roughly eighty percent of Red Sox history has been marked with disappointment. Very few teams have lost so many important games, and almost none have endured as many "shockers" as the Sox. Yet the fan base remains as strong as ever.

If one had to put together a formula, it would go something like this: the Red Sox fan base is established on four sturdy pillars, which have carried it through generations. Ethnically, the Red Sox benefitted, from its earliest days, from the excitable patriotism of the Irish and Italians who flocked to see their games. Religiously, the Irish, Italians, and many other fans tended to be Roman Catholic, and they shared their enthusiasm for the team despite all other differences. Politically, Red Sox goers have traditionally been Democrats. Finally, Red Sox patriotism—and these days they even call it "Red Sox Nation"—has benefitted from its connection to Boston politics, the fortunes of the Kennedy family most especially.

Were they always known as the Red Sox?

No. In their first incarnation, around the year 1900, they were the Boston Americans. They also had in-town competition, from the Boston Braves. But once the Red Sox label was applied, perhaps around the year 1906, it stuck. Their most formidable foes in the early years were known as the New York Highlanders: only later did they become the Yankees.

Did they always play in Fenway Park?

Fenway is the park that defines the Sox, and what makes Boston a baseball town. Fenway was built in 1911–1912, but the first games—even the first World Series—were played at the

Huntington Avenue Grounds, right where Northeastern University has an athletic facility today. The Huntington could only hold about seven thousand fans, and it was necessary to expand. When April came in 1912, fans around Boston were thrilled to learn that the new stadium was complete: it was, at that time, the single largest baseball venue in the nation.

Fenway was supposed to see its first game on April 16, 1912, but there were two rain delays, and the first game was not played until April 19. News of the sinking of RMS *Titanic*, which reached Boston on April 16, also dampened enthusiasm; even so, the first game was played to a sold-out crowd, and the new Fenway could accommodate about 33,000.

What were the fans in those days like?

We don't have recordings of their voices, or many diaries either, so we rely on the still photographs produced at the time. The typical Red Sox fan appears to have been working-class, but with some middle-class aspirations, and he looked a whole lot fitter than can be said of many baseball fans of our time. He almost always wore a hat, and sometimes even a suit jacket, making for some incongruous photographs. That he was crazy about the Sox was obvious.

Very few women came to Fenway Park in the first two decades, but by the 1940s there were small congregants of females, some of whom acted as informal cheerleaders for the club. The most famous of these was Lolly Hopkins, who used her megaphone to inspire the players.

Were the Red Sox winners in those days?

They were indeed. The Red Sox (at the time, they were the Boston Americans) won the first World Series ever played in 1903. They won again in 1912, 1915, 1916, and 1918, making them by far the most successful ball club of the early twentieth century. In those early days, the ballplayers didn't make much money, regardless of which club they played for, and teams won or lost largely on the amount of energy supplied by their fans. The Boston fans were by far the most enthusiastic.

How on earth could Boston have been so foolish as to lose Babe Ruth, *the* ballplayer of the next two decades?

How could she have lost the seventeen-year-old Ben Franklin, who went on to display the single greatest collection of talents displayed in colonial America? There have been times when Boston benefitted, as when she acquired Alexander Graham Bell (a native of Scotland), but she has often lost great talent to other cities, states, and even nations. To the diehard Boston baseball fan, the trading of Ruth was an enormous sin, one that has never been forgiven. Many people call Boston's terrible drought, in terms of World Series, the "Curse of the Bambino."

Michael McGreevy, the owner of a saloon in the South End, was leader of the Royal Rooters, a singing group that came to every game, bringing their own brass band. Known as "Nuf Ced," McGreevy was famous for breaking up arguments at his saloon with those words. The Boston fan base was stronger than that of any other city, and there is little doubt that Boston was king of the baseball world between 1903 and 1918.

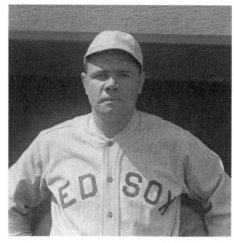

Babe Ruth in 1919, when he was still with the Red Sox.

Why were the Red Sox unable to sustain their success?

This is one of the greatest and hardest questions concerning the Red Sox. They won the 1918 World Series quite convincingly, and then, after a sub-par season in 1919, the owner chose to trade Babe Ruth to the New York Highlanders (soon to be renamed the Yankees).

Was Ruth really that important?

Generations of fans and baseball historians have posed this question, and the answer is a resounding "yes." Ruth was so talented that while with the Red Sox he was primarily a pitcher: his immense capacity for hitting had not yet been discovered. Soon after he was traded to New York, "The Babe," as he was known, began belting home runs. He took special pleasure in doing so whenever he returned to Fenway in Yankee pin stripes.

Ruth was a sensational talent, but like many great athletes, he also had the luck to be in the right place at the right time. He arrived in New York (Yankee Stadium had not yet been built) just as the game was changing. The balls were lighter, and they soared out of ball parks in ever-increasing numbers. Ruth was the hitter of the 1920s, but Lou Gehrig was not far behind. Between them, these two sluggers established the Yankees as the number-one team, while the Red Sox languished (and sometimes fell into despair).

THE LOWEST DECADE

How did Boston go from first-place to last, and do it so quickly?

Between 1903 and 1918, the Red Sox were always in contention, and they usually won their "big" games, compiling a 6–0 record in World Series. But soon after Babe Ruth was traded, the bottom simply fell out. Not only did Boston no longer have the phenomenal talent of Babe Ruth, but the Yankees had him, and Ruth made all the difference. Boston began losing. Numbers never tell the entire story, but they sure do help.

In 1918 the Sox went 75–51, and won the World Series. In 1919, they went 66–71, and came in sixth place in the American League. Some improvement was seen in 1920, when the Sox managed 72 victories, but in 1922 and 1923, the Sox managed the dismal record of 61–93 and 61–91, respectively, in dead last in the American League. It is not as if the Sox lacked talented players; rather, the enthusiasm of the club was at an all-time low. The Royal Rooters disbanded, and Fenway became a rather sad place during the 1920s. The worst was yet to come.

How much worse could things get?

In 1925, as the nation was starting to experience the "Roaring Twenties," the Sox managed only 47 wins as opposed to 105 defeats, and in 1926 they went 46–107. Things were so bad that people spoke openly of the end of an era, and how it might be nice if the Red Sox moved to another city. The trouble of course, was that no other city wanted to take them! Though the Red Sox never did as poorly again (they went 51–103 in 1927), attendance at games dropped dramatically. Frequently there were only 10,000 people on hand in a stadium built for 33,000.

What was it like when Babe Ruth and the Yankees came to town?

There were always some Bostonians who continued to like and admire Babe Ruth, saying that it was not his fault the managers had traded him. Ruth was seldom booed at Fenway, but there was a pit in the heart of thousands when he came to bat, and he seldom disappointed. Ruth crushed many homers in Fenway, and the Yankees nearly always left victorious.

It is important to note, however, that the great animosity that characterized Boston-Yankee relations had not yet come to the fore. Boston fans were disappointed, and sometimes angry, but they railed against their own city and the mistake of the Red Sox ownership rather than the Yankees.

Was the Great Depression good or bad for baseball?

When the Great Depression began in 1929, some people wondered if the game should even continue. Would there be enough fans to fill the stands, they asked? And the answer came soon enough. People went to the ball park in sizeable numbers because they needed to take their minds off their difficult circumstances. Baseball attendance did not boom during the Great Depression, but it did not fall off, either.

THE YAWKEY ERA

How and when did the Red Sox get their new owners?

In 1933 millionaire Tom Yawkey (1903–1976) purchased the Red Sox. He would hold the reins for the next forty years, and when he died, his widow (his second wife, Jean) would do so for yet another decade. These years, beginning in 1933, are therefore known as the Yawkey Era.

Yawkey was ambitious for his club, but he was a businessman with several other irons in the fire. The Red Sox were certainly a priority, but they were not the only one he had. And despite his best efforts, the 1930s showed little improvement, so far as Red Sox fans were concerned. The club went 43–111 in 1932, 63–86 in 1933, and 76–76 in 1934. In none of these years were the Red Sox in contention, and it was not until 1938 that they even managed to attain a second-place finish in the American League, 9.5 games behind the Yankees.

A 1938 photo of Tom Yawkey with his first wife, Elise.

Did anyone ever say it was time for the Red Sox to quit, to give it up?

Quite a few newspaper men said so, but the general public was not ready for the end. There was always the hope that next year would be better. And toward the end of the 1930s, the Red Sox finally got lucky in recruiting: they wound up with Ted Williams and Dom DiMaggio.

Ted Williams is well known, but who was Dom DiMaggio?

The younger brother of Joe DiMaggio, perhaps the greatest all-round player the game has ever seen, Dom DiMaggio (1917–2009) came to Boston in 1940. For the next decade, he was one of the standouts on the Red Sox team, even though he looked more like a college professor than a ballplayer. DiMaggio was on friendly terms with Ted Williams, who had arrived a year earlier.

THE WILLIAMS ERA

One sees plenty of photos of the elderly Ted Williams. He seems cranky, not charismatic. Am I right?

The elderly Ted Williams (1918–2002) had a chip on his shoulder, but it was nothing new. Throughout his truly remarkable career in baseball, Williams was the most temperamental of all the great stars. But he who looks only at the photographs of Ted Williams in old age can have little conception of how appealing, and handsome, he was as a young fellow. When he came to Boston in 1939, Williams was a bit shy of twenty. Six-foot-three and exceptionally lean, he was nicknamed "The Kid" and the appellation stuck.

Though he had pitched some in college, Williams quickly became known as a hitter, and he freely confessed that his single great ambition in life was to be known as the greatest hitter in the world. He was.

What was so different about Williams? Was it in the swing? Or in the eyes?

Even Williams never quite figured it out. He was irritated by those that said his great talent stemmed from his eyesight, something over which he had no control. If there is an answer, it is that Williams got the bat out and around the ball faster than anyone else at that time. Even Joe DiMaggio, who was a more complete player than Williams, never met the ball so fast or sent it on such a trajectory.

Another thing about Williams was his devotion to the sport. No one read as many books or memorized as many statistics as he, and no one analyzed his opponents to the same degree. All that hard work paid off in the season of 1941, surely one of the most remarkable the sport has ever seen.

Did Ted Williams and Joe DiMaggio dislike one another?

They got along fine. They were men of gargantuan talent who could not have been more different in personality. DiMaggio had a perpetually buttoned-down look, as if he could not bear either elation or depression, while Williams was a bundle of nerves and emotions. Williams came to dislike, even to loathe, the Fenway fans who booed him on many occasions. As a result, he vowed never to tip his cap to the fans, and he maintained this resolve right to the end of his long career.

How did baseball hit a peak during the season of 1941?

In May, Joe DiMaggio started a streak that ran all the way to fifty-six games: he hit safely in all of them. This record has never been broken.

In June, Ted Williams started cranking out hits and RBIs to such a degree that it seemed possible he would become the first player of the time to hit .400 for the season. Williams had plenty of detractors, those that said he could not keep it up, but when the season ended, he had a record of .406. No one had hit .400 or better in eleven years, and no one has ever done it since. Between them, DiMaggio and Williams set a style for aggression and skill that has seldom, if ever, been equaled.

Who was the better hitter?

In Williams' own opinion, he was the better hitter, but DiMaggio was the better, more complete player. DiMaggio could play well from any section of the ballpark. In terms of statistics, Williams had the more overpowering numbers, while DiMaggio delivered the more graceful performances.

How did the Red Sox do during that dream season for Ted Williams?

In 1941, the Sox managed a respectable 84–70, but still came in seventeen games behind the Yankees. And for those that wanted an immediate rematch, the Japanese attack on Pearl Harbor came as a rude shock. The war was on and many of the great players served. Williams entered the U.S. Navy in 1942, and soon became a pilot (the eyesight that served him so well on the ball field was effective in the air as well).

Ted Williams was a Red Sox through and through, playing his entire career with the team.

Was there any chance that baseball would be abandoned during World War II?

Many people thought it should be, that it represented too frivolous a use of energy in wartime. The person who disagreed with this the most strongly was none other than President Franklin D. Roosevelt. He had been the manager of his prep school's baseball team, and he clearly expressed his opinion that it was better for the morale of the nation that professional baseball continue.

Boston struggled through the World War II years. The club went 93–59 in 1942, but managed only 68 victories in 1943, and it went dead even (77–77) in 1944. Boston fans hoped and anticipated that the return of Ted Williams would bring an improvement of their fortunes.

What was that first postwar season like?

To judge by the fans' reaction and the anecdotal reports, 1946 was one of the most jubilant years ever seen in professional baseball. Americans were thoroughly tired of the war and sacrifice. They wanted some entertainment, and an increasing number of them listened on radio, while the ballparks, round the nation, filled up once more.

The Red Sox won 104 games in 1946, the largest number the club had ever managed. They finished 12 games ahead of their nearest opposition, and went all the way to the World Series, where they lost to the St. Louis Cardinals. This was disappointing, but many fans declared an end to their troubles had finally come, and that the coming decade would see a return to the halcyon days of the 1910s.

Did Ted Williams ever get back to hitting .400?

Neither he nor anyone else even came close. His 1941 season remains the single most successful of any modern American ballplayer.

How did the Red Sox do in the years that followed the magical season of 1946?

They came as quite a comedown. Boston won ninety-six games in 1948 and 1949, but in both cases came in second in the American League. In 1950, the Sox came in four games behind the Yankees, and some fans declared they would never see a true winning team in their lifetime. Williams went to the hospital after breaking some bones in 1950, and his hitting, while good, was never as good again.

Williams had the bad luck to be summoned for military service a second time, and he made an emotional farewell to Fenway Park in 1952. Many fans mourned his departure, while numerous journalists declared that the Red Sox were better off without him. In either case, the decision was made too early. After a year of service in the Korean War, Williams returned to Boston.

Did Williams realize by 1955 that he would never wear a World Series ring?

He did. When people brought this to his attention, Williams usually snapped. It hurt that he was still one of the best batters in the game, and that there was no chance he would make it to an American League Championship Series (ALCS), much less a World Series.

Boston went 84–70 in 1955, 84–70 in 1956, and then slipped to 82–72 the following year. The Sox had a dismal year in 1959, slipping to fifth place in the American League. And then, as if to top all the other bad news, it was announced that Ted Williams would retire at the end of the 1960 season.

What was it like in Fenway, on Ted Williams' final day?

Williams agreed to do a short promotional speech. Before the game began, he spoke to the crowd, and many in the bleachers groaned as he went into a typical Williams rant. "Despite what all those knights of the Typewriter Keys have said about me," and he gestured toward the press box, "being in Boston has been the greatest thing in my life." That was as close as Williams came to magnanimity.

Did the fans realize this would be Williams' last game?

Everyone knew this was Williams' last season, but they mistakenly believed he would go to New York to play in the last three games. Williams and the club manager worked out an agreement under which his last game would be on September 27, 1960.

Williams had four at-bats that afternoon, and on the last of these—in the eighth inning—he smacked a home run that was reminiscent of "The Kid" at his best. As he started to jog the bases, Williams heard the loudspeaker announce that this was indeed his final game. The fans suddenly were in on the secret. The cheers for Williams were thunderous, and he thought for a moment of tipping his cap, but he remembered his vow of nearly two decades earlier. Williams rounded the bases, headed straight for the dugout, and refused to come out, even when the crowd cheered and chanted for a full five minutes.

Was Williams really as ungracious as he appeared in that moment in his final at-bat?

Williams was an extremely temperamental person. He could soar higher than the average ballplayer, and he could descend to a surly anger that lasted for days. In retrospect, he knew he should have been more charming on his last day at Fenway, and he finally made it up to the fans, thirty-one years later.

How did the Red Sox do in 1960, Ted Williams' last year with the club?

It was a dismal year for the Sox. They went 65–89, and finished seventh place in the American League.

THE YASTRZEMSKI ERA

How different was Carl Yastrzemski from Ted Williams?

They had two things in common: an unorthodox left-handed swing and a mastery of left field at Fenway Park. Other than that, they were very different.

Carl Yastrzemski (1939–) was the son of a Long Island potato farmer, and when he first arrived in Boston some people questioned whether he would be truly loyal to the Red Sox. He soon proved them wrong, and he went on to become one of the most faithful persons ever to wear a Red Sox uniform.

What did critics say about the Red Sox in the early 1960s?

The criticisms were much the same as they had been for decades. Still led by Tom Yawkey, the Red Sox managers spent too much money on hitters and not enough on pitchers. The club, as a whole, gave too much attention to one or two leading stars, and not to a team effort. And the fans were a mercurial lot. On some days they cheered mightily, and at other times they booed.

The Red Sox of the early 1960s were the victims of a long losing streak, so long that no one on the club could even remember the 1946 American League pennant. As for the glorious days of the beginning of the twentieth century, those seemed so far off that they no longer counted.

One of the greats of the 1960s and 1970s was right fielder Carl Yastrzemski, who had 452 home runs in his career.

183

How badly did the Sox perform in this period?

One might think the Sox would do well. This was the time when John F. Kennedy, a native son of Boston, was in the White House. The Kennedy family was known for its passionate attachment to sports, and the Red Sox should have benefitted from the connection. But the club sank to 72–90 in 1964, and to 62–100 in 1965, the year it finished forty games behind the Minnesota Twins, which won the American League East. This was a truly dismal time to be a Red Sox fan.

Was there anyone that could make a difference?

Only Carl Yastrzemski had that capacity, and no one had yet seen him perform at his best. Yastrzemski's left-handed swing was nearly as good as Ted Williams'; unlike Williams, Yastrzemski had the ability to lift the whole team through his efforts. Just how he accomplished this remains a bit mysterious; perhaps the answer can only be given by someone who played alongside him in the 1960s. But when the "Impossible Dream" year of 1967 arrived, it was Yastrzemski who drove the whole effort.

For all the success of 1967, is it true that the Red Sox still flubbed the World Series?

The Red Sox went from72–90 in 1966 to 92–70 in 1967. They won the American League East, and then took the American League Championship Series, to win the pennant. In the World Series, the Sox lost to the St. Louis Cardinals, by four games to three.

Boston spirits were not downcast, however. The turnaround from 1966 was so dramatic, and Yastrzemski emerged as such a powerful motivator for his club that it seemed

Why was a Red Sox victory an "Impossible Dream"?

This was so because the Sox had languished for so long. In 1966, The Red Sox won 72 games and lost 90, enough for a ninth-place finish (dead last) in the American League East. Red Sox failures and defeats were, by now, so common that many sports writers wrote them out of the equation. If ever the Red Sox had been a force, it was no longer so, they declared.

And then came the "Impossible Dream" of 1967, the year in which the Red Sox, led by Yastrzemski (or Yaz), went on a tear. Time and again, they pulled victory from the jaws of defeat. Time and again, Yastrzemski made sensational catches at or near the wall, or drove in all runners with a resounding triple. Many veteran sports journalists believe that Yastrzemski lifted the Red Sox of 1967 to a greater degree than any single player had ever done, before or since. Yaz won the Triple Crown, for home runs, overall hits, and runs batted in. No Red Sox player had managed this since Ted Williams.

certain the Red Sox would soon accomplish the final victory, and go all the way to World Series success. But it was not to be. The Sox went 86–76 in 1968, for a fourth-place finish, and 87–75 in 1969, the year they finished 22 games behind the Baltimore Orioles.

By 1970, had many people given up on the Red Sox?

Yes. One felt it immediately upon entering Fenway. The crowd was smaller and less boisterous. A sullen spirit pervaded the park. The 1960s were over, and the special spirit given to Boston by the Kennedy family was less in evidence (John F. and Robert F. had both been assassinated and Ted was in poor form). It seemed quite possible that the club would move elsewhere.

Tom Yawkey was, amazingly, still the owner and chief spirit of the Red Sox, but he was in failing health. In the last years of his leadership, the Red Sox went for broke, and invested heavily in both the pitching and hitting departments, and for the first time in decades, they came up with some real winning talent.

Who were the newcomers to Fenway in the early 1970s?

Carlton Fisk was a Vermont native who grew up in New Hampshire. As the new catcher, he instilled his teammates with a massive fighting spirit. His sometimes ugly feud with Yankee catcher Thurman Munson gave an added intensity to Red Sox–Yankee games. Bill Lee was a talented California-born pitcher, who brought a much-needed zany spirit to the Red Sox. And Luis Tiant was a Cuban-born pitcher with an unusual wind-up, who delivered well in the clutch.

By 1973 the nucleus of a brand-new Red Sox could be seen, one that mixed power hitting with precision pitching. Yastrzemski was still the heart and soul of the club, but he was pleased, even delighted, to hand over some of the responsibility to the new talent. And when a group of new hitters came to Boston in 1974, it seemed as if the Red Sox would finally shake off the chains that had held them for so long.

How good were the newcomers, the boys of 1974?

Dwight "Dewey" Evans (1951–) had some snap to his bat, but it was as right-fielder that he really shined the brightest. Fred Lynn was a power hitter who would win a number of Golden Gloves for his inspired performances in center field. And Jim Rice—one of the first African Americans to really make it with the Red Sox—played left field.

All three of these "boys" had real potential, but it was Jim Rice that had the capacity to change everything. Not as tall as Carl Yastrzemski, nor as massively built as Babe Ruth, Rice had a nearly unique combination of forearm and wrist power: he hit home runs from the strength of his lower arms, rather than the use of his whole body. Rice had the power to lift the Sox.

How good were the Red Sox of 1975?

They represented the strongest combination of talent that the Sox had possessed in a half-century. If it was a matter of bat power only, the Red Sox had the potential to smack   185 their way past all opponents, including the hated Yankees. And for once the Red Sox bullpen was nearly as strong as its dugout.

The season began well for the Sox with Fred Lynn and Jim Rice stroking more home runs than anyone could remember. Even during the best of Ted Williams' years, the Sox had never possessed a "one-two combination" of this talent.

What was the World Series match-up in October 1975?

The Red Sox had done very well to reach their third World Series in a half-century (earlier ones coming in 1946 and 1967). Most people gave them little chance against the "Big Red Machine," as Cincinnati was called. The Reds had Johnny Bench, a legendary catcher, and Pete Rose, one of the most prolific hitters of all time. The Reds also had deeper talent in the pitching area. But the Sox matched them, run for run, and game for game, until the bottom of the ninth inning in the sixth game of the World Series. Cincinnati was up by three games to two, and just a few more outs would make them World Series champions. But it was Carlton Fisk, the Red Sox catcher, who came up to bat.

What was different about Carlton Fisk? Why was he such a standout?

Six-foot-three and incredibly strong, Carlton Fisk (1947–) was the driving energy of the 1975 Red Sox. Teammates and opponents alike were intimidated by this man, who seemed the very embodiment of a true Boston Red Sox (a native of New England). Fisk fouled off several pitches and then struck the very heart of one. He, and thousands of other people in Fenway Park, watched—helplessly and hopefully—as the ball headed toward foul territory, on the extreme left field.

Fisk watched, hoped, and prayed. So did millions of Boston fans watching on television. Even some of the Cincinnati Reds later claimed they hoped that this one amazing fly ball would stay fair. And, by half a miracle, it did. The ball hit the left field foul pole, resulting in a home run. Carlton Fisk's amazing drive won Game 6 of the World Series for Boston.

Was this the moment when baseball came back into its own?

Many sports historians say that this is the very moment, the precise moment, when baseball came back to rival football as the most popular sport in the United States. Until about the year 1960, baseball had reigned supreme, but the growing popu-

A recent photo of Baseball Hall of Famer Carlton Fisk, who was a star of the 1970s Red Sox.

larity of the Super Bowl threatened to make football the new national pastime. Carlton Fisk's amazing home run, on October 27, 1975, brought baseball back to the fore.

Boston went wild with rejoicing that night. The victory in Game 6 was not sufficient to bring the World Series rings, however. Cincinnati won Game 7, and the World Series of 1975.

What was the reaction by the Boston fans?

One would think that having come so close would lead to an immense letdown. This was not the case, however. Boston fans were certain that the team had done its best, and if it was not enough to defeat the Big Red Machine of 1975, it soon would be.

How important do we now believe Game 6 was?

For the Red Sox, it was merely one of a host of moments they remembered from the 1970s. But to baseball fans nationwide, the drama of Game 6 lingered for years. Just two months prior to that historic game, *Sports Illustrated* ran a cover entitled "The Baseball Boom," and one saw it for the next half decade.

THE SEASON OF 1978

What was so different about the Red Sox in spring training of 1978?

They looked like winners. The "kids" of 1974 had turned into real veterans, and their slugging power was something magnificent to behold. The pitching staff was deeper than ever before. Bill Lee was in one of his traditional funks—both psychological and physical—but the newcomer, Dennis Eckersley, showed signs of being the best starter the Sox had had in decades. All signs pointed to a favorable finish, but the experts— those that had been around Fenway for decades—warned of the traditional summer heat, followed by autumn weakness.

Who were the "foes" in 1978?

The Yankees, of course. The Baltimore Orioles were still a real threat, but nine-tenths of Red Sox concerns focused on the Yankees. The main reason was the deep pockets of New York owner George Steinbrenner, who was willing to spend almost any amount to bring great talent to his team. If the Red Sox had Dennis Eckersley, the Yankees had Ron Guidry, and if the Sox had Carlton Fisk, the Yanks had Thurman Munson. Even so, when all the statistics were totaled up, it looked as if this would be the Red Sox year.

How did the sluggers come out of the gate?

They blasted their way out with home runs that went faster and farther than ever before. Fred Lynn knocked quite a few, but the real standout was left-fielder Jim Rice, who with

187

a short twist of his wrist and forearm, could send a fastball flying into the stands. Early in the season it looked as if Rice might be able to compete with the all-time record in home runs for a season (61).

What were the early match-ups with the Yankees like in the spring of 1978?

They were downright nasty. A level of anger and frustration had built on both teams, and when they clashed it was truly memorable. The Sox won more often than they lost, but some observers wondered if someone might eventually get killed in a Yankees game. Jim Rice was the number-one hitter in the American League East, but Reggie Jackson of the Yankees was known as the best hitter in the clutch. And then, when the games between the rivals got close, both sides brought out their memorable relief pitchers: Luis Tiant for the Sox and Goose Gossage for the Yanks.

How well did the Red Sox do in the first half of the 1978 season?

At the All-Star Break, they were ahead of the Yankees by 14.5 games. It seemed no one could touch them. But then a series of injuries affected the team. Yastrzemski was out for a time, as was Carlton Fisk. When Fisk was not present, team leadership fell to Rick Burleson, the feisty shortstop who kept everyone on their toes. But, as had happened so many times before, the Sox began to fade toward the end of August. They were still three games ahead of the Yankees, and in decent shape to win the division, when the Yankees came to town early in September. What followed was a shellacking so terrible that some journalists called it simply "The Murder." The Yankees took five games out of five, and replaced Boston in first place.

Why would a season in which both teams won ninety-nine games be settled by a playoff of only one?

Very simply, the Red Sox and Yankees played a one-game playoff because the regular season ended in a first-place tie. Tiebreakers are always just one game.

Why, of all the games played at Fenway in the twentieth century, is this one the most remembered?

This is because the drama, stakes, and intensity were so high. It also happened to be one of those pleasant afternoons in early October with moderate sunshine and a warm breeze. Fenway was packed.

Who did better in this particular game: the old veterans or the young guns?

Jim Rice had been sensational during much of the season, but his bat was quiet on October 2. He kept hitting into double plays. Fred Lynn was highly effective in center field, but the real kudos properly go to Carl Yastrzemski who, quite simply, played his heart out. He had been there in 1967 and in 1975: he realized this was probably his last

How could the Sox have squandered a lead of 14.5 games?

This is one of the wonders of Red Sox history, that the team so often finds ways to snatch defeat from the jaws of victory. When questioned in the bleak aftermath of the five-game "murder," Dwight Evans replied that Boston still had twenty-odd games to play, and that anything could happen. Left unsaid was the painful fact that something already had.

Amazingly, though, the Red Sox found their feet in mid-October. They won twelve of their last fourteen games, and ended the season at 99–64 in an exact tie with the Yankees. As a result, a one-game playoff for the American League East division title was scheduled, and at 1:15 P.M., on October 2, the perennial foes met each other once more, at Fenway.

chance at post season play. And when Yaz homered in the second inning, to give the Sox a fragile lead, he looked, just for a moment, like the man who had carried the club back in 1967.

The Sox held a fragile 3–1 lead until the seventh inning, when of all people, Yankee shortstop Bucky Dent came to bat with two men on. Dent was anything but a fine hitter (his average was around .234). On this occasion, however, he took a fastball from Mike Torrez and lifted it well beyond the infield, and high enough that most Red Sox fans believed it would be an easy catch. Yastrzemski thought so: he pounded his glove. And then the worst of all Red Sox nightmares took place.

How could one fly ball turn into a home run that killed the Red Sox season?

One really had to be there to feel the depths of the Red Sox despair. As a radio commentator expressed it, the warm wind which had made the fans feel so good two hours earlier turned into a mild gust that helped that fly ball move toward the left field wall, and then suddenly, it was gone. Bucky Dent, one of the great underperformers on the Yankees, had a home run that brought three men home, and gave the Yankees the lead.

Was Bucky Dent's home run it? Or did the Sox mount one last attempt?

They came on strong at the bottom of the ninth inning. Two men were on, a base was stolen, and there were runners at first and third when Yaz came to the plate, for the fifth time in the game. The applause that greeted him sounded like thunder; it lasted for two solid minutes. He, and every fan, knew that this was the most important at bat of his long, illustrious career.

Yaz fouled several balls, and then aimed straight for a Goose Gossage fastball. He lifted it high, but not deep enough, and the third out was soon in a Yankee glove. Yaz,   **189** the best clutch hitter the Red Sox ever had in the twentieth century, was out, and the season was over.

Did people blame Yaz for the loss on October 2, 1978?

Only the least-knowledgeable of Red Sox fans did so. Those that knew anything about the game saw the man play his heart out, giving his all for the team. If anyone could have rescued the Sox on that dismal afternoon it was Yastrzemski, but even the greats cannot always save their team.

How bad was the effect on Red Sox fans?

This, the one-game loss on October 2, 1978, was by far the most punishing and destructive blow ever dealt the Red Sox. No earlier losses even came close. To have performed so well during most of the season, to have won 99 games, and then to stumble in the one-game playoff was deeply humiliating.

For once, the Red Sox fans blamed each other as well as the players. Perhaps they had not done enough to support their team, they thought. Perhaps more should be done to modernize Fenway Park: this question, too, was raised. But if they wanted to vilify someone, they almost always turned to Bucky Dent, the terrible person who had the audacity to lift a fly ball that, by the force of magic, turned into the game-winning home run.

How "good" were the other numbers: the attendance?

Attendance in 1978 broke all previous Fenway records with 2,320,643 tickets bought.

THE POST–1978 SLUMP

How long did it take the Red Sox to shake off the effects of 1978?

It took the better part of a decade. When the team came back in the spring of 1979, there were fewer fans, and the players, too, seemed in a sour mood. Some of them continued to perform well on an individual level, but the team ethos was very low.

One of the few bright spots of the season of 1979 was the career culmination of Carl Yastrzemski. He had never been a prima donna, a superstar; rather, he had always been a very workman-like player, who did more than he talked. But in August 1979, Yastrzemski homered for the 400th time, and in early September, fans waited eagerly on every Yaz at bat, eager to see his 3,000[th] career hit.

What was the magic moment, so far as Yastrzemski's career is concerned?

Yaz disappointed the fans several times. He was at hit 2,999, but he couldn't seem to connect for the 3000th. On September 10, 1978, he had four at bats, and got precisely nowhere. One night later, however, on September 11, he connected for a single, and was suddenly at the magic numbers of 400 home runs and 3,000 hits. No other Red Sox had

> ## Who was the greater Red Sox player:
> ## Ted Williams or Carl Yastrzemski?
>
> In terms of charisma, it was no contest. Williams was the most dramatic, and contentious of all Red Sox stars, while Yastrzemski was one of the quietest. But in terms of the numbers, and how much they contributed, it comes out almost to a dead heat. Williams played with the Sox from 1939–1960, and in that time he helped them reach one World Series. Yastrzemski played from 1960–1983, and in that time he led them to two World Series and one dramatic one-game playoff game against the Yankees. Perhaps the reason Williams still looks so well in comparison, is that Yaz had the bad luck to make the final out in all three of his most important games: in 1967, 1975, and 1978.

ever accomplished this. To be precise, however, no other American League player ever reached that goal, and as of the time of this writing in 2015, Yastrzemski still stands alone in his league, as the man who put 400 and 3,000 together.

How did the team do in 1979, and afterward?

Rather poorly. The Sox won 91 games in 1979, but only 83 in 1980 (these were good for third and fourth places AL East finishes). Nineteen eighty-one was a washout year for the entire sport, thanks to an ill-timed players' strike that threatened to erode the fan base. The Sox came in sixth in the American League East in 1983 with a dismal record of 78–84. This was the year Carl Yastrzemski retired, putting an end to one of the longest and greatest of all Red Sox careers. Unlike Ted Williams, whom he admired, Yastrzemski put on a great show on his final day, tipping his cap many times, and telling the fans he loved them and their fair city.

The Red Sox managed to win 86 games in 1984, but they fell to 81–81 in 1985, finishing 18.5 games behind Detroit for a fifth place finish that year. No one wrote about removing the Red Sox from Boston, but there was deep pessimism concerning their chances for the future. Yaz was gone, and the young lions of the 1970s had never lived up to their full potential. Jim Rice, for example, hit 44 homers in 1978, but he was down to 20-something a year by 1985.

THE WORLD SERIES OF 1986

What was different about the Red Sox of 1986?

They did not resemble the incredible juxtaposition of talent that had come out of the gate in 1978. But the Red Sox were a seasoned team, and in the spring of 1986, they un-   191 leashed the biggest surprise their opponents had seen in a long time: the fastball of Roger "The Rocket" Clemens.

Born in Dayton, Ohio, in 1962, Clemens came to the Red Sox at the end of 1985. Six-foot-four and filled with power, he simply overwhelmed opponents. On one afternoon in May 1986, he struck out twenty batters in one game, a feat never seen before. With Clemens' hurling power, and with the Red Sox bats coming out for one grand finale, it seemed that Boston really had a chance in 1986.

Roger Clemens (shown here later with the Astros) played for the Red Sox from 1984 to 1996.

Where were the Yankees in 1986?

For once, they were not a major factor. George Steinbrenner still owned the team, and he still emptied his pocket in search of talent, but the Yankees had a sub-par year, while the Red Sox moved from one victory to another. This was not a fantastic year, such as 1978, but a solid one in which the Red Sox kept improving. They won their first American League East division title since 1975, and moved on to the World Series where they faced the New York Mets.

Did the Red Sox and the Mets have a history, a rivalry?

They did not. Virtually all the ire Red Sox fans felt was directed against the New York Yankees, rather than the Mets. Because the Red Sox had only been in three World Series since 1919 they had actually never even faced the Mets. But if they could win in 1986 it would help that their foes at least hailed from New York.

How long had it been since the Red Sox played in Shea Stadium?

They never had done so. Some of them, as individuals, had played there in All-Star Games, but the Red Sox and Mets were strangers to one another. And, as it turned out, this did not make them any nicer to each other.

Who was the number-one hope for the Sox?

With Roger Clemens on the mound, the Red Sox believed they could win. The Mets felt the same way about Dwight Gooden. Between them, these were the best of the young guns of that year. Game 2 was heralded as a match-up between these two stars, but the rivalry never had a chance to heat up. Gooden was bounced early, as the Red Sox pounded the Mets, 9–3. Given that left-hander Bruce Hurst had narrowly beaten the Mets the night before, the Sox were up two games to none, having taken both games in Shea Stadium

Did Boston fans believe they were home free?

Just about. The next three games, after all, were to be played in Fenway. But the Mets rallied to win Game 3 by 7–1, and Gary Carter homered twice in Game 4 to lift his teammates to a 6–2 victory. The series was even at two games apiece. The Red Sox came back strong for Game 5, however. They tormented Dwight Gooden for a second time, winning 4–2. The scene then shifted back to New York, and Shea Stadium.

What went wrong in Game 6 of the 1986 World Series?

From the Red Sox point of view things went reasonably well until the tenth inning. They had a lead that the Mets erased, and the game was sent into extra innings. The Red Sox scored two runs in the top of the tenth, but the Mets tied the game again in the bottom of the inning. Then, with a runner on second base, Mets batter Mookie Wilson hit a weak dribbler that rolled between Sox first baseman Bill Buckner's legs, which scored the winning run. The Mets had tied the series at 3-3.

Buckner knew, when the game ended that he would be vilified. He was, indeed, traded the very next year, and his name is still essentially "mud" in Boston. But Buckner's was far from the only mistake.

Was there any chance the Red Sox would bounce back, and win Game 7?

One of the worst parts of being a Red Sox fan in the 1970s, 1980s, and 1990s was that the team almost never bounced back from ordeals like this one. The sense of futility dogged the Red Sox that night, and when they returned to Shea Stadium for Game 7, the crowd rose to deliver a standing ovation to Bill Buckner. The Sox lost Game 7 by 8–5.

Was that it for the "Gold Dust Twins"?

It was. Jim Rice and Fred Lynn (known as the "Gold Dust Twins"), had been with Boston more than a decade, and both had experienced considerable frustration. Rice was injured during the 1986 World Series, but he did not win the appreciation of the fans. Both men faded rapidly after the 1986 World Series, although Rice returned as batting coach, a position in which he excelled.

CLOSE BUT NO CIGAR

How did the Red Sox perform in the decade that followed the 1986 World Series debacle?

They did much better than one might expect. Given that Yastrzemski was now long gone, and that Jim Rice and Fred Lynn were fading rapidly, the Sox might have been expected to go dismal on the fans once again. Instead, with Roger Clemens providing the pitching power, and a group of youngsters using their bats, the Red Sox did quite decently.

The Sox won the American League East in 1988 with an 89–73 record. They were matched against the Oakland A's, who won 104 games that year, and had the makings of a dynasty in their clubhouse. The A's polished off the Sox in the American League Championship Series, by 4–0.

How important did Roger Clemens become to the Red Sox in these years, the late 1980s?

It seemed, at times, as if he carried the whole team. An enormous man, possessed of great inner and outer strength, Clemens won games when no one else could. What he did not possess—and this was sad—was the type of ebullient personality that could lift the spirit of his team. Clemens kept a grim face most of the time, and he became a symbol of the travails of the Red Sox.

Did spirits really have that much to do with the game?

Absolutely. One can say that the difference between a joyous or grim expression was important throughout major league baseball, but in a town like Boston that had experienced such heartbreak it was even more important than usual.

How did the Red Sox do in 1990?

It seemed as if this would be their breakthrough year. The Red Sox went only 88–74, but that was enough to clinch the American League East. They then flew to Oakland, to meet the A's for a rematch of the 1988 championship series.

Game One of the American League Championship Series (ALCS) pitted Roger Clemens against Dave Stewart of the A's. Everyone watching saw this as a meeting of the giants, and the Red Sox fans, watching on television, were deeply disappointed when Clemens could not handle the wave of Oakland batters. Stewart, on the other hand, shut down the Red Sox, and Oakland went on to take that game and the three that followed. The final result was that Boston was shut out, 4–0.

Was 1990 another heartbreak year for Boston?

Not really. It had none of the up-and-down drama of 1986, and no one could fault the Oakland A's for being the best team in baseball. But, as so often proves the case, the A's did *not* become the dynasty everyone expected. They lost the World Series that year, and didn't make it back until 2004. Red Sox fans were well accustomed to the idea of "wait until next year," but after 1990 they had to wait until 1995 before making it back to the post-season. Both the American and National leagues had, by then, split into three divisions with a wildcard entry for the team that won the most games without taking a division. The Sox had only an average year with eighty-six victories, but that was enough

Fenway Park as seen from the Green Monster.

to win the American League Division Series. In the American League Championship Series, they were creamed by Cleveland, three games to none.

As the millennium approached, was there any talk of moving the Red Sox from Boston?

Such talk had largely disappeared, but there was a lot of discussion about Fenway Park. Should the ancient lady be dismantled entirely, refurbished, or just allowed to slowly perish? John Harrington, who headed the Yawkey Trust, was convinced Fenway had to be demolished in order to build a brand new park just next door. He envisioned a new park that would seat 45,000, and bring in new corporate sponsorship through elite restaurants and mini-clubs available only to the wealthy.

The Yawkey family was legendary in Boston, but there was great resistance to the idea of demolishing the old ball park. Harrington eventually sold the Yawkey Trust's fifty percent share of the Red Sox to an outside organization, and the way was paved for a renovation of Fenway. Accomplished in 2002–2003, the renovation was just enough to make the place more manageable, and not nearly enough to take away the beauty of the 1912 structure. Fenway remained the great lady of all old-time ball parks: big enough to accommodate a crowd and small enough so that one could find his friends, regardless of where they were.

THE NEW MILLENNIUM

How different was Boston—and the Red Sox fans—in the year 2000?

The city was well on its way to becoming one of the gleaming "urban renewal" success stories, but tired old Fenway remained the single largest draw. More people, nationwide,

195

identified Boston with the Red Sox than with anything else. Attendance remained strong at the beginning of the new century, and after the thrilling events of 2003 and 2004, it reached new heights.

When Boston learned of the death of Ted Williams in July 2002, the fans—and the whole city—took a long retrospective of the man who defined the Red Sox six decades earlier. Williams had done his best to make amends, especially when he made a special appearance during the All Star Game of 1999, and Boston fans preferred to remember him as the greatest hitter of his time, rather than the ungracious hero who refused to tip his hat to the crowd.

What was so different about the Red Sox of 2003?

For the first time ever, the club looked multifaceted and multiethnic. The Red Sox were one of the last teams to embrace African Americans—and this cost them much in the 1950s and 1960s—but they were one of the first to recognize the talent that came from the Caribbean Islands. Cuban-born Luis Tiant was a great star in the 1970s, and Pedro Martínez, who came to the Sox in 1998, proved to be one of the best pitchers they ever had. Well-liked by the Boston fans, Martinez won twenty games his first year, and kept on doing well subsequently.

At the same time, the Sox had some relatively new sluggers. Manny Ramirez was a slugger who debuted with the Sox in 2001, and David Ortiz joined the team in 2003. Between them, these new fellows had as much slugging power as Boston had ever seen.

How well did the Red Sox do in 2003?

Boston did not capture its division, but it won the wild card, and entered the fight for the American League Championship Series (ALCS). The Red Sox bested Oakland (gaining revenge for the defeats in 1988 and 1990), and then started the series against the Yankees.

Red Sox–Yankee animosity was high in 2003, but it got even worse during the ALCS. There was a nasty brawl in Game 6, during which Yankees bench coach Don Zimmer (who managed the Red Sox in the late 1970s) was hit and thrown to the ground. This fracas was a low point for both teams, but Boston came out looking worse. And then came the ultimate humiliation, the loss in Game 7.

How could the Red Sox manager have left Pedro Martinez in the game?

That question has been asked a thousand times, and there still is no good answer. At the end of the seventh inning, the Red Sox had a three-run lead, and Pedro Martinez pointed to the sky, his traditional sign that his job was done. By any reasonable standard, he was correct. But Red Sox manager Grady Little surprised everyone by keeping Martinez on the mound in the eighth inning, and his thinking, or lack thereof, contributed to a disaster of epic proportions. Martinez had performed very well for over a hundred pitches, but he soon began to fall apart. The Yankees sensed the Red Sox confusion, and exploited it to the maximum.

In the tenth inning—with Martinez now gone—Yankee shortstop Aaron Boone stepped to the plate. Like Bucky Dent of 1978, Boone was a major underachiever, who had hit .100 in the series to this point. And like Dent, Boone proved to be a giant-killer. He slayed the Sox with a fine home run that won the championship series for the Yankees, four games to three. The loudspeakers belted out Frank Sinatra's "New York, New York," and Red Sox fans tasted one of the worst humiliations of many.

Was anyone ready to give up?

By rights, they should have been. Boston had provided so many possibilities, and had delivered on none of them since 1918. But the heartbreaking loss of 2003 did not set back the Red Sox; if anything, it pushed them to aspire for more. And when the team came out of spring training in April 2004, with a new manager, Terry Francona, many observers agreed that they looked like one of the best ever seen.

For the first time since the late 1970s, the Sox matched bat power with terrific pitching. And there was one very big improvement on the 1970s teams: the Sox of 2004 played as a team. They seemed to enjoy each other's company, something that was seldom said during the days of Fred Lynn, Jim Rice, and so forth.

How important was Johnny Damon to the Red Sox of 2004?

He was something really special, a medium-sized fellow with good bat speed but also a terrific base runner. Johnny Damon (1973–) was the firecracker of the team, setting up numerous victories either through his singles and doubles or his stealing bases. But to top all this off, Damon was everyone's favorite. The fans loved him, and so did his teammates. As a result, Damon became the trend-setter, right down to his hair style. His long locks were emulated by many other Red Sox, and the team of 2004 had a shaggy look, especially when compared to the trimmed and shaved Yankees.

How did David Ortiz come to wear a Red Sox uniform?

Playing for Minnesota Twins, David Ortiz (1975–) had been a real underperformer, but any scout could see his enormous po-

First baseman David Ortiz joined the team in 2003.

Why did the Red Sox fade in autumn on so many occasions?

Some sportswriters put it down to the weather, saying that July and August favor the offense, and that the crisp, cool weather of September and October is just right for the defense. Something else contributed, however—a sense of impending defeat. After the terrible losses of 1978 and 1986, the Red Sox began to expect to lose in the autumn, and that made the turnaround of 2004 even sweeter.

tential. After a lackluster 2002 season, the Twins released him. Ortiz then signed with the Sox before the start of the 2003 season. Not everyone liked Ortiz's casual attitude (he took more days off than any other Boston player). but his skill with the bat was undeniable. Then too, he was a gentle giant, who brought more laughter to the clubhouse than anyone except Johnny Damon.

Between them, Ortiz and Manny Ramirez were a one-two punch that was—for a few years—just as good as the legendary Babe Ruth–Lou Gehrig partnership. With Johnny Damon as leadoff hitter, and with the big guns just a couple of turns away, Boston had enormous hitting power. The question, to be sure, was whether they could keep it up for an entire season.

ROAD TO THE CHAMPIONSHIP

How did the Red Sox do during the summer of 2004?

They were only so-so in July, but around August 12, they began one of the great runs of their club's history, and one of the most memorable in the entire history of baseball. After a hard-fought win over Toronto, the Red Sox launched a run of twenty victories and only two defeats to come to within two games of the Yankees. The difference between the two clubs had seldom been more clear-cut, right down to the hairstyles.

The late Red Sox run was not sufficient to win the division, but as often happened they placed a wild card entry to the American League Championship Series. The Sox won 98 games in 2004, more than in any year since 1986.

What was the match-up with the Angels like?

No one took the Anaheim Angels lightly. The two teams had seldom met. But the Sox felt good about their pitching with Curt Schilling to hurl in Game 1 and Pedro Martínez in Game 2.

Schilling performed well to win the first, and Martinez did his best in the second, but the Angels brought out all their bats that evening. A 6-1 Red Sox lead turned into a game tied at 6–All, and there it remained until David Ortiz crushed a monster home run in the top of the tenth inning, to win Game 2 by 8–6. The Sox won the series in three games, and were on their way to meet the Yankees in the American League Championship Series.

Did anyone make an accurate prediction of the 2004 ALCS?

If so, they failed to broadcast and take credit for it. Instead, hundreds of thousands of fans in Boston and New York, as well as millions round the nation, watched in stupefied bewilderment as one upset and upstart led to another.

Curt Schilling (1966–) was assigned to stop the Yankees in Game 1, played in Yankee Stadium. A year earlier, when brought to Boston, he famously commented, "I'm not sure I can think of any scenario more enjoyable than making fifty-five thousand people from New York shut up." That was his challenge when he took the mound on October 12, 2004.

What happened to Schilling that evening?

The game was lost, by 10–7, but the worst news for Red Sox fans was that Schilling was hurt. He was diagnosed with a torn tendon sheath in his ankle, and the announcement was that he would need surgery, and would have to miss the rest of the ALCS championship. Red Sox fans greeted this horrible news with resignation.

Nearly as bad was that Pedro Martinez took a shellacking in Game 2 of the ALCS, and the Red Sox were suddenly down by 0–2 in the series. They returned to Boston, endured a rain delay, and then went out for Game 3, which turned into the nightmare of nightmares. Both teams pounded the ball that night, but the Yankees did so more successfully, and the final score was 19–8. The Yankees now led the ALCS series by 3–0, and almost everyone was reminded that no professional baseball team had ever won a series after losing the first three games.

How did the Red Sox get off the floor, climb out of that 0-3 hole?

In Game 4, played in Boston, the Dominican Duo of Manny Ramirez and David Ortiz came through, as they had so many times during the regular season. The Red Sox took

What were the big Red Sox songs of 2004?

Neil Diamond's "Sweet Caroline" and "Dirty Water" were the two best-loved songs of that run to the championship. The contrast between the two is part of what makes the duo so successful. "Sweet Caroline" is about innocence and joy, while the Standells' "Dirty Water" evokes the nastier, darker aspects of life in Boston, even while celebrating them.

Game 4 by 6–4, and then won Game 5 in the bottom of the fourteenth inning. That still left them down by 2–3, and facing a return to Yankee Stadium.

Why is Game 6 of the 2004 ALCS called the "Bloody Sock Game"?

It's entirely thanks to pitcher Curt Schilling, who postponed surgery and went out on the mound once more to face the Yankees. If Johnny Damon was the heart and soul of the Boston club, the man who kept the others laughing, Curt Schilling was the blood and guts, the person who inspired every person to do his best. Schilling was photographed from all angles that night, and the blood stains on his sock were clearly visible, but he pitched his way to a Red Sox victory, 4–2. The ALCS was now tied, at three games all.

Pitcher Curt Schilling spent the last years of his professional career (2004–2007) with the Red Sox.

Could anyone else have accomplished this?

We often ask these questions in retrospect, but in the light of that particular night, there was no other person who would have pitched the Red Sox to victory. Schilling's courageous performance made all the difference.

What was Game 7 of the ALCS like?

It was an incredible thriller with little doubt that the Red Sox would prevail. Johnny Damon had batted .100 in the series to this point; in Game 7, he hit not one, but two home runs, one of them a grand slam. Ortiz homered as well, and when the game ended, at 12:01 A.M., the Red Sox had beaten the Yankees to win the American League Championship.

No team had done this before. No baseball team had ever come from an 0-3 deficit to win a best-of-seven series. It can also be argued that the 2004 Red Sox accomplished something even bigger: that they finally erased the shame of 1978 and 1986. Of course they still had to win the World Series.

What was the World Series of 2004 like?

Compared to the ALCS and the challenges the Red Sox had faced, the World Series of 2004 was like a walk in the park. Matched up against the St. Louis Cardinals, whom they had faced in 1946 and 1967, the Red Sox won four games in a row, never allowing the series to become a real contest. The Cardinals had won 105 games that year, and in Tony La Russa they had probably the best manager in the business, but the Red Sox thrashed them: 11–9, 6–2, 4–1, and 3–0.

Had the Red Sox truly done it? Had they broken the "Curse of the Bambino"?

Only the most cynical of observers would argue against it. Even longtime foes, such as George Steinbrenner, admitted a certain satisfaction at seeing the Red Sox finally beat their demons, and win the World Series of 2004. And the celebration that welcomed them in Boston was simply out of sight.

A long line of cars, police motorcycles, and "Duck Tour" buses brought the World Champions from Logan Airport to Fenway on October 28, 2004. The Red Sox were treated like royalty, as most of Massachusetts took an unofficial holiday: very little work was performed in the Bay State that day. And just to make certain everyone truly understood the magnitude of the victory, the World Series trophy was sent, over time, to all the 350 towns and cities of the commonwealth.

REDEMPTION ACHIEVED

How did Boston and New England sports fans react to the World Series win of 2004?

Nothing in Massachusetts, or New England, sports history even comes close. An enormous collective sigh of relief was heard; some elderly persons declared they now could die at peace; and millions of younger ones declared that a new era was about to be inaugurated. For once the optimists had it right because the Red Sox won the 2004 series at the same time that the New England Patriots commenced their incredible run to the top of the National Football League.

How did the Red Sox do in 2005 and 2006?

The pressure was off: this was understood by everyone involved. The Red Sox had two rather mediocre years before beginning another ascent. All the members of the 2004 team were present in 2007, and the managers were nearly all the same. In 2007 the Red Sox won ninety-six games and clinched the American League East title: they then faced the Los Angeles Angels of Anaheim in the divisional championship series.

The Red Sox made short work of the Angels, winning three games in rapid succession, but the ALCS was a whole other matter. After losing a painful, close game, the Sox were down by 2–1 games in the ALCS and it was not until the fifth game that they regained their stride. Manny Ramirez put on quite a show in the Red Sox clubhouse, shouting at his teammates that they were not a "good" team but a "great" one, and that this was the moment to show it. *Sports Illustrated* commented in an understatement: "These are not your father's Red Sox."

How magnificent was the turnaround in the ALCS and then the World Series?

The Sox won seven consecutive postseason games, once they turned the tables on Cleveland. They beat the Indians, and then the Colorado Rockies in the World Series, by a combined score of 59–15. They also righted the course of baseball history, by becoming the first World Series champs since the Yankees of 1998 to also be the team that won the most games in regular season play.

Were the celebrations of 2007 as large as those of 2004?

Not even close. Boston, and New England, fans were becoming accustomed to victory. The Red Sox and the Patriots were on parallel lines. Fenway, too, was no longer in danger: it now was the queen of all ball parks.

How did the Red Sox do over the next few years?

They were so-so in 2008, 2009, 2010, and 2011. The last of these also saw the end of the management by Terry Francona, who had done so much for the Red Sox. But 2013 saw something quite different: an inspired run to a championship based on more than ethnic or athletic loyalty. Something larger was at stake.

How well did the Red Sox perform in 2013?

Boston won the American League East with 97 wins and 65 losses. Their first ALDS opponent was Tampa Bay, which afforded them little competition (Boston won by three games to one).

Where will the Red Sox be a generation from now in around the year 2040?

If most other things remain equal, the Red Sox will continue to be the darlings of downtown Boston. Their long struggles—through most of the twentieth century—were so painful that they created a deep aversion to any sort of repetition. No one suggests that the Red Sox will become "America's team" in the way the Yankees were during the 1920s, but they will remain among the favorites of the American League East.

And where ball parks and stadiums are concerned, there is little doubt that Fenway will continue to be number one. Other venues are larger and contain more amenities, but there is a religious-like feeling to the Fenway faithful that is duplicated in no other city. If the Red Sox were supported by Irish and Italian immigrants who were mostly Roman Catholic (in the 1910s and 1920s), they now are seconded by truly multiethnic supporters, who come from Eastern and Western Europe and the Caribbean Islands, who make baseball an integral part of their lives.

OTHER GREAT BOSTON SPORTS

How and when did Bostonians become so keen on sports?

The trend began in the decade that followed the Civil War. Many Bostonians spent time in army camps during the war, and they often played an early form of baseball as a diversion. Sports of all kinds also became one of the few ways that minorities could move up the social and economic ladder. Over time, sports and athletics became almost as important to the typical Bostonian as culture and higher education.

The cerebral nature of the Boston public can still be seen in its athletics, however. The game—whether baseball, football, basketball, or hockey, is hotly contested with the foe. Then, journalists of all kinds—professional and amateur—go at it, discussing and debating what happened. If Bostonians are keen on the results of sports—and almost everyone agrees this is true—they are equally keen on dissecting what happened, and postulating as to why.

What are the favorite sports of the average Bostonian?

It really depends on the decade, or generation, to which the person belongs. In the 1930s and 1940s, Bostonians were simply mad about baseball, and that did not mean just the Red Sox. Pick-up games were common all over the city and in the various suburbs. Basketball took a serious slice out of the baseball amateur sports during the 1950s, but it was the appearance of ice hockey that really jolted Bostonians out of their baseball complacency in a major way. During the 1940s and 1950s, the average Boston boy dreamed of becoming the next Ted Williams; in the 1960s and 1970s, he fantasized about being the next Gordie Howe.

Why do Boston sports reporters have such a negative reputation?

It is, in part, because of their tempestuous relationship with baseball great Ted Williams (see the chapter "The Red Sox"). Williams coined the expression "knights of the typewriter keys" and he obviously did so sarcastically. The contentious relationship between Ted Williams and the sports reporters led to almost two generations of negative emotions, where the press was concerned. It must be admitted, though, that Boston sports reporters sometimes seemed perverse in their attempt to play down the opportunities of the local teams. Sometimes the relationship was one of benign neglect, and at others it was practically poisonous. One team that required nearly two decades in order to attract the attention of the Boston press was the Boston Celtics.

What are some of the sports that upper-class Bostonians have typically enjoyed?

Tennis has long been a favorite, but to be a serious squash player remains the sign of having arrived in legal and medical circles. Boston physicians and attorneys spend more time on the squash courts than do their counterparts in any other major city. Too, the upper-class Bostonian dreams of placing first in the Head of the Charles Regatta.

Established by the Cambridge Boat Club in 1965, the Regatta is now in its fifties and shows no signs of slowing down. On the penultimate, full weekend in October, thousands of athletes (now representing fewer than thirty nations by last count) come out for the two-day extravaganza. The course begins at the Boston University DeWolfe Boathouse and ends at Christian Herter Park, meaning that the rowers move three miles up the Charles.

Was boxing ever one of Boston's favorite sports?

Only as the sport was just beginning. One of the first—and some say greatest—of all boxing champions was John L. Sullivan (1858–1918). Born in the South End of Boston in 1858, Sullivan was the son of recent Irish immigrants. He grew up hardy and tough, and as he began to win fights, he was nicknamed the Boston Strong Boy. Eventually he took his show to the road, and became the undisputed heavyweight champion boxer of the (Western) world from 1882 to 1892. Sullivan died at fifty-nine as the result of his numerous bouts and because of overindulgence in food and drink. Bostonians admired Sullivan throughout his lifetime, but by the time of his death they were becoming interested in other, less damaging sports.

The Boston Strong Boy, John L. Sullivan was the city's pride and joy in the boxing ring.

THE CELTICS

Why did it take so long for Boston to have a professional basketball team?

Basketball was invented in Springfield, Massachusetts, a mere ninety miles west along the Massachusetts Turnpike from Boston. Bostonians did not take to the sport right away, however. In fact, for the first three decades, basketball was more popular in the high schools and colleges of the Midwest than New England. Boston high schools practically abandoned the sport in the year 1925, and for the next decade and a half it was rare to find youngsters concentrating on the sport. One exception to the general rule existed, however, and that was the College of the Holy Cross in downtown Worcester.

Founded by the Jesuits in 1843, Holy Cross was a school that demonstrated equal passion for athletics and scholarship. The Jesuit fathers welcomed basketball, which they saw as a good way to keep the young men diverted during the winter months. Between about 1940 and 1945, Holy Cross developed the number-one college basketball team in New England, and many of its standout players later went to the Boston Celtics.

How did the Celtics get founded? And where does the name come from?

Walter A. Brown (1905–1964) of Boston was the founder and first owner of the Boston Celtics. He came from the family that traditionally fired the starting gun of the Boston Marathon. In 1945, Brown was manager of the Boston Garden, a sports arena that was lacking in regular attendance. Positioned right where the Old North End and the West End come together, the Boston Garden was a fantastic venue, but it needed more people in the seats and bleachers. Brown decided basketball was the best remedy.

In 1946, the Boston Celtics were formed, as one of the first teams in the brand-new National Basketball Association (NBA). The name came from a New York City-based traveling team, but it clearly fit both Boston and Worcester, where many of the early players came from. That first team, which played the season of 1946–1947 was composed entirely of white men, and most of them came from Irish backgrounds. It made perfect sense that they were named the Boston Celtics.

What has made the Celtics immortal?

Perhaps it's the seventeen different times they've won the National Basketball championship. Maybe it's the fact that the old Boston Garden was such a seedy, run-down place that it eliminated all show and pretense. Perhaps it's the thousands of cigars, smoked by Coach "Red" Auerbach during the glory days of the 1960s. And to those that listened on radio, it may well have been the inimitable voice of Johnny Most. But whichever is the most likely, and whatever combination exists, there is little doubt that the Boston Celtics are truly one of *the* teams of professional sports.

Why did basketball take such a long time to "make it" in Boston?

Boston has been a baseball town since the 1890s, and a hockey town since the 1920s, but basketball did not make a serious appearance until the late 1940s. Even then, plenty of veteran Boston sports writers passed over the Celtics, saying that the city was famous for its baseball team (which often lost) and its running of the Boston Marathon. Basketball was an afterthought, they said.

Basketball was invented in Springfield, Massachusetts, a mere ninety miles west along the Massachusetts Turnpike, but the sport did not win much honor or glory in its home state, at least not at the beginning. Midwestern schools and colleges took to basketball long before Boston, and as late as 1940, there was practically no basketball tradition within the city. The change came about as the result of the rise of the Holy Cross Crusaders..

One often hears of the Boston College Eagles and seldom of the Holy Cross Crusaders. Why is that?

The College of the Holy Cross is located forty miles due west of Boston in downtown Worcester. Holy Cross has a long and proud tradition, but Boston commentators give more attention to Boston College, the other Jesuit-founded college in the region. But in the 1940s, it was Holy Cross that took to the new sport of basketball, and when the Crusaders won the national collegiate championship in 1947, a new era in New England sports history was born. Boys of ten to twelve, who had previously dreamed of being linemen for football teams now spoke of their desire to be centers on basketball teams. The New England climate lends itself to basketball, and the emphasis began to shift. Of course it took more than one collegiate championship to make the difference: a first-class venue was required.

Who was Walter Brown?

A hard-hitting, fast-talking Irishman, Walter Brown was the son of the man who organized the first Boston Marathon. For two generations, Brown family members fired the pistol shot that announced the commencement of the race. In the mid-1940s, Walter Brown was owner of the Boston Garden, a rather run-down, yellow-brick art deco building located at the point where the Old North End and the West End met. Brown was a hockey man, who had the Boston Bruins and the Ice Capades as his major customers at the Boston Garden. But as World War II came to an end,

Walter Brown, founder of the Boston Celtics.

Brown worried about the relatively low attendance, and he was eager to sponsor a new sport to fill seats at the Garden. Brown was instrumental in the founding of the Basketball Association of America (BAA). Organized on June 6, 1946, the BAA had eleven teams, one of them being the Boston Celtics.

The name, incidentally, was not original with Walter Brown. Anyone who studied the history of professional basketball knew of "The Original Celtics," a barnstorming team out of New York City. Brown seems to have hit upon the new name in a moment of sudden inspiration. It was good to remind sports fans that there was a precedent for the name, and to associate the very Irish city of Boston with the "Celtics" was even better. Brown declared that his team would wear green uniforms, to remind fans of the connection with the Emerald Isle.

What were the names of the original eleven teams (of the Basketball Association of America)?

In addition to the Celtics, they were as follows: the New York Knickerbockers, the Providence Steamrollers, the Philadelphia Warriors, the Washington Capitals, the Toronto Huskies, the Chicago Stags, the St. Louis Bombers, the Cleveland Rebels, the Detroit Falcons, and the Pittsburgh Ironmen. Only a few of those teams have kept their original name and identity: the Celtics and the Knicks are most prominent in this regard.

What did that first team look like?

The Boston Celtics team of 1946–1947 was tall enough: the team members averaged six-foot-one. They did not look like the National Basketball Association (NBA) teams we know today, however. First, they were somewhat shorter. Second, they tended to have crew-cuts. And third, perhaps most important, they were entirely white. This surprised no one in 1946: Jackie Robinson had not even penetrated the color line in baseball. But to our modern eyes, those early Celtic teams really stand out in a visual sense.

How did the Celtics do in their first season?

They did poorly, but the same can be said for many of the other teams in the newly formed association. Basketball was in its early stages, and some of the rules and traditions we know today had not yet developed. Even so, we can shrug at the fact that the Celtics came in dead last in the Eastern Division of the Basketball Association of America with a record of 22–38 in their first season.

Was there a chance the franchise would fold?

There was an excellent chance this would happen. Three of the founding teams of the BAA did not make it past their first season. Owner Walter Brown had already mortgaged his home in Hopkinton (the town where the Boston Marathon begins), and it seemed possible he would lose his shirt. Brown was nothing if not dogged, however.

For the first home game of the 1946–1947 season, 4,329 fans came to Boston Garden. Perhaps this was not a great showing, but it was enough to give Brown reason for hope. For the first half-decade of team history, Brown shrugged off one financial loss after another, believing that his team would eventually make it in the eyes of the fans. There is a good reason why the long-retired Celtics number 1 jersey hangs in the Garden as a testament to Walter Brown.

Did the Celtics improve in the years that followed?

Not to any great degree. In 1947–1948, they came in third in the Eastern Division with a record of 20–28. In 1948–1949, they came in next to last with the record of 25–35. What did strike fans, and commentators, was that the franchise had legs. The fans kept coming, and Walter Brown kept pledging that his team would do better in future. In 1949, the National Basketball Association (NBA) was founded, and professional basketball was placed on a firmer foundation.

Why do we hear so little of the players from those early years?

Diehard Celtic fans can recite their names and positions, chapter and verse. But the Celtics in their first half-decade were not memorable. The teams were composed almost entirely of graduates from northeastern colleges and universities with Holy Cross and Boston College providing the majority. The Celtics kept losing. A big change was on the way, however: the Celtics were about to acquire the coach who would lead them to success.

How large a presence was "Red" Auerbach?

Born in the Williamsburg section of Brooklyn, in 1917, Arnold "Red" Auerbach (1917–2006) was a tough-talking, fast-smoking person who loved cigars. He arrived as the new head coach of the Boston Celtics in the spring of 1950. This was the same off-season when owner Walter Brown made franchise history by choosing a black player, Chuck Cooper, in the NBA Draft.

Auerbach was not an immediate hit with Bostonians. He had a vulgar streak that turned off many, and his red-hot intensity did not appeal to everyone. His players, however, saw something special in him from the very beginning. This man intended to win.

Where is the best place to see Red Auerbach, as he was in the days of Celtic greatness?

In a place where one would not expect. A bronze statue of Red Auerbach was unveiled in Boston's Quincy Market in September 1985. "Red" sits on a bench, facing the visitor. He looks like a permanent fixture, part of the scenery.

Did the Celtics perform any better in the early Red Auerbach years?

A difference was seen right away. In 1950–1951, the Celtics came in second in the Eastern Division with a record of 39–30. This was a big improvement, but they were eliminated by New York in the playoffs. The following season—that of 1951–1952—again saw the Celtics come in second, this time with a record of 39–27. They were getting better—this was obvious—but they did not yet possess the firepower to meet the best of teams on an equal footing. In 1952–1953, the Celtics came in third in the Eastern Division with the record of 46–25. The higher number of games won shows that the Celtics were getting better, but the fact they came in third shows that the division was getting better, too.

The Celtics came in second in the Eastern Division in 1953–1954 with a 42–30 record. They followed up with a dead tie (36 wins 36 losses) in 1954–1955. The Celtics improved to 39–33 in the 1955–1956 season. Auerbach had done plenty with the material he possessed, but the Celtics were about to receive a major jolt, a shot in the arm. This was provided by the 1956 NBA draft in which Red Auerbach selected Bill Russell.

What was so different about William Fenton Russell?

In a sport dominated by tall men, Bill Russell (1934–) was exceptionally tall, 6'9". Born in Louisiana, he worked his way up the ranks, and was an outstanding player at the University of San Francisco. Russell was chosen by the Celtics in the 1956 NBA Draft, but the team had to wait for his first appearance. This was not due to any vanity or hesitation on Bill Russell's part: he was the center for the United States Olympic team, playing in Melbourne, Australia.

Bill Russell made his first appearance in Boston on a cold day in December 1956. He was two months late, but he had a Olympic gold medal to show for his absence. Russell later recalled that the day was overcast, and that his first impressions of Boston were not

positive. There seemed to be a powerful undercurrent of racism in the city that had been so prominent in the abolition movement of the previous century. Minutes after descending from the plane at Logan, Bill Russell signed his first autograph, at the request of a ten-year-old. This is significant because it was one of the very few times he did respond to these requests.

How good was Bill Russell on the basketball court?

Chosen as center for the Celtics, Russell soon filled the position, to the outcries of many. Boston basketball fans were over-

Red Auerbach (right) sitting with Bill Rusell in 1956.

209

whelmingly white and working-class, and many of them resented Russell's appearance. Did Boston not have enough native talent, they asked? Russell was not always his own best advocate. Off the court, he was frequently aloof and moody: he made almost no effort to court Boston sports fans. On the court, he was nothing short of sensational.

Though he started off as a poor shooter, and never became a really good one, Russell was an outstanding center. His height and strength intimidated some opponents: his grim appearance at game time frightened others. Russell took up far more room and space on the court than his opponents, and he proved the best rebounder and shot blocker the NBA had ever seen.

How did Bill Russell get along with his white teammates?

The Boston Celtics had come some distance since the late 1940s—when the team was entirely white—but white players still dominated: one only has to gaze at the photographs to realize this truth. Numerous comparisons—most of them unflattering—were made between Russell and his white teammates, and it was inevitable there would be some friction. What is remarkable is that the friction did not last. While he had a hard time with Boston sports fans—some of whom never accepted him—Bill Russell did rather well with his white teammates: he and Bob Cousy formed an especially strong bond.

How did the Celtics do in Bill Russell's first year in Boston?

In 1956–1957, the Celtics placed first in the Eastern Division (the first time this happened) with the record of 44–28. They made it to the playoffs, where they took down the Syracuse Nationals in three straight games, which was sweet revenge because Syracuse had previously knocked them out three times. It was on to the NBA finals in which the Boston Celtics were matched up against the St. Louis Hawks.

The finals against St. Louis were marred in the opening game, when Red Auerbach and his opposite number exchanged punches. Auerbach later expressed regret at having spoiled the opener. The series was fantastic with both teams extending each other to the utmost. Boston won in seven games with a score of 125–123 in the last of seven.

How much better had the Celtics become?

One can argue that the arrival of Bill Russell increased the Celtics performance by a factor of one-in-four. It was not only his height and strength; Russell simply stared down his competition. With veteran Bob Cousy astounding audiences with his dribbling skill and assists, and with Russell blocking the shots of most opponents, the Celtics had, rather suddenly, become world class. As Red Auerbach expressed it, "We've been chasing this thing [the championship] seven years."

Was that first NBA championship followed by a second?

Not right away. The Celtics came in first in the Eastern Division in 1957–1958, winning forty-nine games and losing twenty-three, but they came up against the St. Louis Hawks in the NBA championship series. This time the Hawks prevailed in six games, and the Celtics were dethroned. The quality of Celtics' play remained high, however, and attendance at games in Boston Garden was up twenty-five percent over previous years. Walter Brown's long-shot bet on basketball had succeeded.

What was the 1958–1959 season like?

The Celtics came in first in the Eastern Division, and they advanced through the playoffs with relative ease. They met the Minnesota Lakers in the NBA finals, and beat them in four straight games, the first time this had happened. Owner Walter Brown seldom traveled with the team, but he was on hand to receive the NBA championship, the second his team had won. Most observers declared that this second NBA championship was a feat which the Celtics were unlikely to repeat. They were atop the world of basketball, and it seemed a long shot that they could remain in that position.

What was that first meeting like?

On November 7, 1959, the Philadelphia Warriors came to the Boston Garden to face the Celtics in the second game of the regular season. Russell had heard plenty about Wilt "The Stilt" Chamberlain, but he found all the advance publicity was immaterial when compared to the immense size of the man. This would be a battle between titans.

Boston beat Philadelphia that night, by the score of 115–106, but sports fans naturally looked to the individual statistics of the two leading men. Chamberlain outscored Russell by 30–22, but Russell had far more rebounds. Years later, Russell commented that Chamberlain's appearance was actually a benefit to his own career. Had Chamberlain—or someone like him—not appeared, Russell might have coasted for years. In-

What do basketball historians make of the long rivalry between Bill Russell and Wilt Chamberlain?

Those that watched the two during the 1960s thought it was something of a tie, but those that study the statistics are convinced that Russell was by far the more potent player. To be sure, Chamberlain could explode in the middle of a game, scoring more points than Russell, or anyone else in the sport. But Russell was far more consistent.

One of the most telling of all statistics is the one concerned with what we call "game seven." NBA championships, as well as World Series championships, are determined by the best of seven games, and if a series goes to Game 7, it is often truly memorable. One first-rate sports historian estimates that in his long career—high school, college, and NBA—Bill Russell played in eleven "game sevens," and that his teams won every single one of them.

stead, "Wilt was my greatest challenge, and toughest competitor. He won his awards. I won mine."

How did the Celtics perform in that season, 1959–1960?

Boston came in number one in the Eastern Division with the record of 59–16, and in the semifinals, the Celtics faced off against the Philadelphia Warriors. Russell did not outscore Chamberlain in those games, but he played well enough to see his Celtics win through, and Boston then defeated St. Louis in the NBA finals. This was a memorable year for the Celtics, who had now won three of four NBA championships in a row.

Where was Red Auerbach at this point in his career?

Right where he had always been: at Boston Garden. Auerbach seemed like a fixture at Celtics games. He had long been a smoker, but his "victory cigars" were now the toast of the town; when fans saw Red light one up, they felt confident of victory.

One aspect of Celtics basketball that had not changed very much was the fan base. The crowds (13,000 maximum capacity) that filled Boston Garden, night after night, continued to be white and working class. Celtics fans had accepted the fact that African American players were starting to dominate the game, but they still displayed marked favoritism to white players.

How did the Celtics look as the new decade dawned?

The Celtics went 57–22 in the regular season of 1960–1961, and they came in first in the Eastern Division. They went on to beat the St. Louis Hawks in five games in the NBA Finals. By this point, the crowds were accustomed to Celtic victory, but they remained keen for more of the same. And in 1961–1962, the Celtics went 60–20 during the regular season, and beat Los Angeles in seven games in the NBA Finals.

Red Auerbach hit the peak of personal and professional success in the early 1960s. Not only did he become the winningest coach of the NBA, but his legend spread far and wide: it seemed there was no way to beat Red and his Celtics. In 1962–1963, the Celtics won 58 games, lost 22, and beat Los Angeles yet again in the NBA Finals, this time in a total of 6 games.

When did the Celtics lose their founders?

Walter Brown died as he had lived: the owner and manager of Boston Garden. He had always been primarily a hockey man, but he grew fonder of the sport that he had previously labeled "boom ball." Brown died shortly before the Celtics went into training for the 1964–1965 season. He was granted uniform number one, and it was permanently retired.

Red Auerbach coached for another year, but he was wearing out. Years of playoffs, filled with twists and turns, had taken their toll, and he retired shortly before the 1966–1967 season commenced. That Red would retire was a big enough surprise, but the next question, quite naturally, was who would replace him?

Who was the first African American ever to become a coach in a major league sport?

Bill Russell. In 1966–1967, Russell became the first player-coach in Boston Celtics history, and the first African American to coach a major-league team (in any sport). Russell's critics—and there were many—claimed that his ego was so large that he could not bear to be coached by anyone but himself. And Russell did not turn in a superlative performance in his first year as player-coach.

Russell turned that around in a hurry, however. The Celtics were world champions in 1969, when they topped the Los Angeles Lakers by 108–106 in the last game of the NBA finals. For all the critics, Bill Russell had only scorn.

Who was the voice of the Celtics?

This was Johnny Most (1923–1993), yet another New York City native who came north to lend his talents to Boston. Most became the on-air voice of the Celtics in 1953, and remained there for the next thirty-five years. No one accused Most of having a soft or easy voice: rather, his voice was like the slam of a truck, dropping its back-end load. Most's enthusiasm was evident much of the time, but there never was a moment quite like the last play of the Celtics-Philadelphia game on April 15, 1965. Hundreds of thousands of people listened on radio, and many had slightly varying memories of his words, but the recording goes as follows:

"Havlicek stole the ball! … Havlicek saved this ball game! Believe me! Johnny Havlicek saved this ball game. The Celtics win it, 110 to 109." Though most of the listeners would have heard Johnny Most on many other occasions, this was the one that defined him in their eyes.

Where are there so many native-born New Yorkers in the history of the Boston Celtics?

It's one of the real surprises of Celtics history. Red Auerbach was born and raised in Brooklyn, and Bob Cousy and Johnny Most both grew up in Manhattan. Of the three, Cousy made the adjustment the most easily. He was from the city on the Hudson, but he became an honorary New Englander—and Bostonian—soon after the Holy Cross national championship win of 1947. Johnny Most was the grandson of a German anarchist, and he had the New York City accent to prove it. But Most adjusted very well to Boston, and the fans eventually accepted him as one of their own. The person who did not make the adjustment and never became part of Boston, according to Celtics fans, was Red Auerbach. The good news, however, is that Auerbach never looked back to New York City. Rather, he regarded Washington, D.C., as his real home, and this did not upset the Boston fans very much.

When did Bill Russell retire?

Arguably the most famous of all the Celtics, Bill Russell hung up his sneakers at the end of the 1969–1970 season. He had nothing left to prove. Eleven championship rings decorated his fingers, showcasing his remarkable career. It must be said, however, that Russell did not let bygones be bygones. He made it plain that he loathed many Bostonians, and despised their racist attitudes. Russell did not return to Boston for many years. Only as age mellowed him did Russell consent to re-

A photo of Bill Russell with Red Auerbach shortly after they won the 1966 NBA Finals.

turn to Boston Garden for a public ceremony to see his number retired. Wilt Chamberlain was in the audience that day, and Russell poured praise upon the only other person who really knew all he had been through. Between them, Russell and Chamberlain had experienced the best and the worst that celebrity could bring. It was no small thing to be that tall and that talented at a time when African Americans were breaking in to the sport. Russell had soft words for Wilt Chamberlain. One wondered what he would say about white Boston, however. But when someone in the crowd shouted out, "We love you, Bill," he said, "I love you too."

What did Russell say about the reasons for the Celtics' success?

Russell could be eloquent, and he was at his best when addressing this topic. There were key people—Walter Brown, Red Auerbach, Bob Cousy, Bill Russell, John Havlicek—but there were no stars, he declared. We were in this to accomplish things together, and we really looked out for each other.

How did the Celtics fare during the 1970s?

Clearly, the new decade was not as generous. The Celtics were now one of the great teams, rather than the greatest. The Philadelphia 76ers were their biggest, most persistent rivals, but the Phoenix Suns were competitive as well. It was painful to Boston fans when Philadelphia dethroned the Celtics in the spring of 1977. The following season was bittersweet in that John Havlicek retired. This meant virtually none of the players from the period of Celtic dominance were still around.

When did Larry Bird come to the Celtics?

The "Hick from French Lick" was drafted by the Celtics in 1979. Six-foot-six Larry Bird (1956–) was a Midwestern boy, through and through. After a difficult childhood, which included the suicide of his father, Larry Bird was a standout at the University of Indiana.

No Celtic draftee came with such expectation since John Havlicek, and Larry Bird—the quintessential country boy—had good reason to be wary of Boston and its crowds.

He made the adjustment quite rapidly, however, concentrating on practice and drill. He wanted to be ready for the season of 1979–1980.

How did the Celtics do in the first year of having Larry Bird?

The Celtics went 61–21, and ended up first in the Eastern Division by a margin of two games. They did even better in 1980–1981, winning 62, losing only 20, and coming in at first place again. That Larry Bird was a phenomenon was apparent to all. It didn't hurt that he was a dynamic white player in a city that still had not completely accepted the African American presence. Bird was soon joined by Kevin McHale, who also played forward, and by Robert Parish, who was the new Celtic center.

Hoops star Larry Bird enjoyed a full career with the Celtics from 1979 to 1992.

What were the NBA finals of 1984 like?

Fans and commentators naturally dispute over which were the greatest of all NBA finals, but those of 1984 were surely in the top half-dozen. Larry Bird and the Celtics faced off against Magic Johnson and the Los Angeles Lakers in one of the great contests of basketball history.

The Lakers took Game One, and they should have captured Game Two as well, but a costly turnover led to overtime, which the Celtics prevailed. The Lakers thumped the Celtics in Game Three, but Boston came back to take Game Four. Game Five was known ever after as the hottest game ever played in the NBA. Boston Garden was not air-conditioned, and the indoor temperature soared to 97 degrees, which the Lakers called something close to hell. Larry Bird was unfazed. He claimed he'd played in this kind of heat a number of times. Bird scored 34 points, grabbed 17 rebounds, and led the Celtics to a memorable victory. The Lakers still had some fight left: they took Game Six. But Boston prevailed in Game Seven, and Larry Bird—as usual—got a lot of the credit.

Did Larry Bird ever go too far? Was he sometimes obnoxious?

Not to the Boston fans—they thought him the greatest thing since sliced bread. But Bird did carry his self-exultation too far at times. The reason most other players—and teams—forgave him is that he had such a transparent good-guy look and attitude. It was difficult to get too angry at someone who called himself the "Hick from French Lick." Of course, there is usually an exception to the rule.

In 1985, Larry Bird and a fellow Celtics player got involved in a brawl in a Boston pub. The full details were never disclosed, but it seems likely that Bird threw some punches. Most Boston fans forgave this, but a minority held it against him for the rest of his career.

What was the greatest of all Celtic years?

Virtually all observers concur that 1985–1986 was the best Celtic season, ever. The Celtics were 40–1 at home, and 27–14 on the road. They played to sold-out crowds in the Garden, and stared down their opponents, time after time. When it was time for the playoffs, the Celtics mowed down the Chicago Bulls in three straight games, even though the dynamic Michael Jordan scored 63 points for the Bulls in one of them. In the Eastern Division semi-finals, the Celtics beat the Atlanta Hawks by three games to two, and they moved on to the Eastern Conference finals, where they beat the Milwaukee Bucks. And when it was time for the NBA finals, the Celtics took down the Houston Rockets, four games to two. The season ended, appropriately, at the Boston Garden, and the score in that last game was 114–97.

Who played sixth man in that immortal year, the season of 1985–1986?

The Celtics were already a powerhouse with Dennis Johnson and Danny Ainge as guards, but when they brought in Bill Walton as the sixth man, the crowds practically went wild. Though he'd played for the Portland Trail Blazers (guiding them to an NBA championship in 1977), Bill Walton had suffered from a host of injuries, and his career seemed over. A last-minute trade brought him to Boston, where he was an immediate hit with Celtics fans. Not only was Bill Walton as Irish-American as they come, but he had a reputation as something of a flake, a West Coast free spirit who followed the Grateful Dead. Under ordinary circumstances, Walton's oddities might have turned off the Boston crowd: in the magical year of 1985–1986, it only made him more popular.

What could the Celtics do to top the season of 1985–1986?

Nothing could equal the sensational way they thrashed their opponents in that memorable season, and other teams began to catch up with the Celtics. Larry Bird and his fellows were still a major force in the NBA, but they could not dominate the way they had in previous years.

Is there anything more that can be said about the amazing rivalry between Larry Bird and Magic Johnson?

Here's what can be said. Johnson–Bird is akin at Frazier–Ali, Williams–DiMaggio, and Bill Russell–Wilt Chamberlain. The NBA fan of the 1980s was treated to something truly spectacular, two amazing, great talents who gave their all at the same time. This is why the Bird–Johnson rivalry is so special because one can measure their statistics, records, and championships from the same time period. And that of course, leads us to the wonderful, tantalizing question: who was greater?

When did Larry Bird's career begin to fade?

He'd been injured a number of times previously, but the season of 1989 was like torture for the Hick from French Lick. Bird underwent double ankle surgery, and he could not play the entire season. When he was on the court, he looked just as good as in the past, but this was a sleight of hand. He really wasn't up to his former heroics.

Bird retired in 1992. His career statistics were little short of phenomenal.

What happened to Boston Garden?

To the die-hard Celtics fan, the demolition of Boston Garden—which took place in 1997—was one of the greatest errors, even heresies, that the city has ever known. The average basketball fan simply loved the crowded, run-down condition of the Garden, which had long since entered Boston lore. But that which delighted the typical Boston sports fan had a way of infuriating players from other teams, and by the early 1990s, it was apparent that the Garden would have to go.

The new Boston Garden (seating capacity 20,000) was constructed in 1993, and many fans admitted that it was greatly superior. Nostalgic fans continued to lament, however, and when the bulldozers arrived in 1997, there were almost riots to save the old place. The fans did not prevail—the old Boston Garden came down—but pieces of stone and brick were sold, so that longtime fans could own their "piece" of the Garden. That the demolition of the Garden took place as the Big Dig was underway is one of the congruities of the time. The old Boston was being carved up to make room for the new.

Celtic championship banners hang proudly at Boston Garden.

217

What were the Celtics like, as of the year 2000?

They had become an afterthought in the NBA, but they remained big news in Boston. The typical Boston Celtics fan had only become more confirmed in his allegiance to the team.

How did the Celtics pull off their "miracle" season in 2007–2008?

Danny Ainge (1959–), who was a major star from the days of glory in the 1980s, was now general manager of the Celtics, and he was keen for a revival of Celtic greatness. Many Celtics fans were impatient by this point. They pointed to sixteen championship banners floating from the rafters, and demanded to know when the seventeenth would arrive. Ainge had something up his sleeve. The Celtics had such a bad year in 2006–2007 that they were able to draft Kevin Garnett and Ray Allen. Even so, the new season would be a major fight, as the Celtics attempted to erase many years of failure.

The Celtics went 66–16 during the regular season. This was the biggest single turn-around in NBA history, an improvement of 44 wins over the previous season. They moved through post season play to meet the Atlanta Hawks in the NBA finals.

What does the future hold for the Boston Celtics?

It's difficult to predict. The Celtics have such an amazing track record, so replete with triumph that it is difficult to envision them establishing yet another dynasty. Stranger things have happened, however.

What has remained constant, through good years and bad, is the Celtics fan. Fans are still the hard-working, occasionally hard-drinking Bostonians who like sports rough and tough. And when the Boston Celtics are not in their best form, fans can always watch the Boston Bruins.

NEW ENGLAND PATRIOTS

Why did it take so long for Boston—and New England—to get a professional football team?

Football is not as natural to the sons of Boston as it is to, say, those of Houston, Texas, or Montgomery, Alabama. Once they became accustomed to the sport, New Englanders took it up with enthusiasm, however.

In 1960, the Boston Patriots were formed as one of the first teams of the American Football League (AFL). They had no stadium of their own, and for the first decade of team history, they played in places like Nickerson Field and Fenway Park. Meanwhile, many other NFL teams were building major, impressive stadiums, and they naturally attracted larger crowds. The Boston Patriots were not a strong team. They floundered during the early years of the franchise, usually coming in either in the middle of their division or near the bottom. A turning point was registered when the Patriots got their own stadium in the town of Foxborough, about twenty-five miles southwest of Boston. Schaefer Stadium opened on August 15, 1971. The new stadium had a seating capacity of about 55,000.

How did the Patriots perform in their new venue?

The first few years were disappointing. The Patriots went 6–8 in 1971, and fell to a dismal 3–11 in 1972. The following year was a little better, with the Patriots winning 5 and losing 9, and in 1974 they went 7–7. It's worth noting that these were especially painful years for Patriot fans because the Miami Dolphins, who were founded around the same time, won almost every single time they faced the Pats. Nineteen seventy-five was an especially disappointing year with a 3–11 record, and finally in 1976, the Patriots came close to victory. They went 11–3 during the regular season, and looked strong in the early playoffs, but they lost the divisional playoff game to the Oakland Raiders, 24–21.

Did anyone at the time compare the Patriots to the Boston Red Sox?

They did not. The Red Sox, after all, had first been formed in 1903, and had more than half a century to get their act together, while the Patriots were still a young franchise. The average Boston fan continued to support the Pats, and was exposed to much disappointment. If the Miami Dolphins showed up the Pats during the early 1970s, then the Dallas Cowboys, on their way to becoming "America's Team," were everything the Patriots were not toward decade's end. Some sports enthusiasts declared that Boston was a sporting town, one where the fans really cared, but that it never would become a winning one.

How important was Steve Grogan to the Patriot teams of the 1980s?

Grogan (1953–) should have been the answer to the prayers of Patriot fans. Born in Texas, he was a truly physical player, one who rushed for many touchdowns. When he came to the Patriots in 1975, Grogan injected some enthusiasm, and he clearly became the team leader. But his performance in the air was disappointing. Throughout his career, he threw more interceptions (208) than touchdowns (182). Grogan's yards per game were often impressive, but he did not captain the team to as many victories as one hoped, or might have expected.

What was the nadir for Patriot fortunes?

Nineteen eighty-one was perhaps the most dismal of all Patriot years. They went 2–14. The following year (1982) was a little better as the Pats improved to 5–4 in a year cut short by the players' strike. Even that mediocre performance was enough to send the Patriots into the playoffs as a wild-card contender, but they got smashed by their longtime nemesis, the Miami Dolphins with a score of 28–13.

Nineteen eighty-three was an average year for the Patriots, who went 8–8, and things were a bit better in 1984, when they went 9–7. The year that really made fans perk up their ears was 1985, however, when the Pats went 11–5, and entered the playoffs as a wild-card contender. They beat the New York Jets in the wild-card playoff (26–14), and took the divisional playoffs by beating the Oakland Raiders 27–20. Almost everyone believed the Patriots would stumble at their next game, which was the American Football Conference (AFC) Championship, played at Miami. To the amazement of many, the Pats beat Miami *at* Miami (this was the first time ever) by a score of 31–14.

What was the build-up to Super Bowl XX like?

The Patriots were the afterthought. The commentators could not get enough of the Chicago Bears and their formidable coach, Mike Ditka (1939–). Under Ditka's leadership, the Bears looked as if they would become a new super-dynasty. Quarterback Jim McMahon (1959–) was the lion of the hour. An eccentric, enthusiastic, and highly likeable person, McMahon stole the show, even before the game began. A large crowd gathered at the New Orleans Superdome for the game, on January 26, 1986.

What was the game like?

It was a rout. The Patriots actually scored first, getting in a field goal, but by the beginning of the second quarter, the Bears' offense had worn down their Patriot opponents. Time and again, the Bears seized the ball, and McMahon delivered on almost all his big opportunities. The final score was 46-10. New England's humiliation was complete, and it seemed likely that the Bears would be *the* story of the next half-decade.

Did the Chicago Bears deliver on their great potential?

One of the few small satisfactions for the Patriots fan was that the amazing 1985–1986 Chicago Bears team did not dominate football for the next half-decade. Mike Ditka remained one of the most successful and respected coaches, but Jim McMahon faded rapidly, and the Bears had only an average record through the early 1990s.

Where did the Patriots go after this painful humiliation?

Remarkably, they did not collapse. Substantially the same team performed well during the 1986 regular season, going 11-5. This time, however, the Patriots lost early in post-season play, going down to the Broncos by the score of 22–17. The following year (1987) was a disappointment as the Patriots sank to 8-7; 1988 was a ho-hum 9-7, but a real crusher came in 1989 when the Pats sank to 5-11. Almost all of the players who had done so well in the 1985 regular season now were gone, and the Pats fell to an incredibly humiliating 1990 season, when they went 1-15.

Was that terrible season (1-15) enough to send the fans packing?

It *should* have been the case. By 1990, however, the Patriot team owners had done a good job of promoting their stadium for other uses. Rock concerts—notably those of U2 and the Rolling Stones—brought lots of people to Foxborough, and they sometimes attended a double header, going to a rock concert on Saturday night and the football game on Sunday afternoon. By the beginning of the 1990s, the Patriots had a rather solid fan base, one which would not go away.

How did the Patriots rebound from the terrible season of 1990?

They did better in 1991, rising to 6–10, but in 1992 they fell to a crushing 2–14. It was at this point that the Patriots finally got the kind of coach who could make a difference. Bill Parcells (1941–) was already known as one of the rough, tough coaches whose knowledge of the game was equaled by his ability to control (some said manipulate) the players. Under Parcells, the Patriots rose to 5–11 in 1993, 10–6 in 1994, and then fell

Before coaching the Pats from 1993 to 1996, Bill Parcells led many other teams, including the Air Force's Falcons.

back to 6–10 in 1995. Nineteen ninety-six was Bill Parcells' breakout year as the Patriots improved to 11–5 during the regular season.

How did the Patriots perform in post-season play?

Their record was strong enough that they only had to play in the division once, and they crushed the Pittsburgh Steelers, 28–3. The Patriots then won the conference championship by defeating the Jacksonville Jaguars by 20–6. The post-season performance was reminiscent of 1985, when the Patriots had played above their heads. And, as in 1985, the Patriots of 1996 faced a truly formidable team in the Super Bowl: the Green Bay Packers.

To be sure, these were not the Green Bay Packers of the 1950s and 1960s, but they seemed likely to establish a new dynasty, and their quarterback, Brett Favre, was already winning favorable comparisons with quarterbacks from virtually all decades. Commentators agreed that the Patriots had to do something very special to keep even with the Packers, and that they needed something of a miracle in order to win.

What was the game like?

Super Bowl XXXI was played at the New Orleans Superdome on January 26, 1997. The Patriots surprised everyone by making two fast strikes down the field, and going up 10–0. But the Patriot strength lasted only half-way into the second quarter, and by half-time it was evident that Green Bay had too much muscular strength on the ground. The game never turned into a rout, as had happened in 1986, but the Patriots had too much ground to make up. They made the game interesting at times, but there was never a question that Green Bay would win, and the final score was 35–21.

Patriot fans did not go into a fit after the Super Bowl. They knew their team had done its utmost, and that it was hard to match one as powerful as Green Bay. Patriot fans anticipated much better things in the future, and the game of 1997 kept many of their hopes alive as Boston sports entered their second century.

What did Patriot fortunes look like at the turn of the twenty-first century?

Perhaps they were not dismal, but they certainly did not look promising. The Patriots seemed doomed to be one of the perennial contenders that faded in the stretch. Few observers predicted great things for the Patriots, however.

One sign that some people missed was the appearance of Bill Belichick (1952–). Sometimes known as the "hooded man" or the "man in a hood," Belichick was one of the great over-performers on the coaching

The current coach of the Patriots is Bill Belichick, who took leadership of the team in 2000.

circuit. Uninterested in appearance, he dressed down rather than up, and his face usually showed his preoccupation with facts and figures. What few people realized was the extent to which he understood the game.

When did Tom Terrific make his first appearance?

Born and raised in California, Tom Brady (1977–) was an all-round athlete who seemed condemned to a mediocre career (he later joked that his greatest fear was having to work as an insurance salesman). Brady had to fight for each and every start at the University of Michigan, and he was one of the last draft picks of the 1999 NFL Draft. The man who became his great rival—Peyton Manning—was a standout at the University of Tennessee and was first in the NFL Draft of 1998.

Brady came to the Patriots in 2000, and soon became the number-two quarterback. Given that Drew Bledsoe was both a popular and successful quarterback, there was little likelihood that Brady would ever have a real chance. That situation changed on September 23, 2001, however. Drew Bledsoe was injured in the game, and Tom Brady came on to make the first throws of his NFL career.

What was Brady's first year like?

Brady was uneven, throwing plenty of interceptions, but his talent soon became apparent. Not only was he cool under pressure—some said he was the coolest they had ever seen—but he could scramble from the pocket and run with the best of them. One thing that was notable from that very first season was that Brady could inspire his teammates: with him at the helm, they believed they could win. This was something the Patriots had seldom had, and when they had possessed it, it was only for brief periods.

The Patriots made it to the playoffs for the first time in several years, and they surpassed expectations, making it all the way to the Super Bowl, to face the St. Louis Rams. Going into the game, the Patriots were two-touchdown underdogs, and almost everyone expected the St. Louis offense would cream the Patriots. What they saw, however, was something quite different.

What was so different about the NFL season of 2001–2002?

The terrorist attacks of September 11, 2001, altered the schedule of professional football: no games were played on the Sunday that followed the attacks. As a result, it was expected that the NFL would have a truncated season. But NFL leaders decided that this was not the moment to lose even one week because of the enormous revenue that was pouring in. The season was therefore extended by a full week, and the Super Bowl was played in February (not late January) for the first time.

Was there any chance Brady would fare as badly as Drew Bledsoe?

One can argue that there was not that much difference between them in terms of talent. But Brady showed a winning style, right from the very beginning. He quarterbacked

223

for only the last two minutes of the game, and then had his first official start one week later. Brady and the Patriots thrashed Peyton Manning and the Indianapolis Colts, 44–13.

At what moment did Tom Brady enter the ranks of the NFL immortals?

Brady had already shown plenty of guts, but the deciding moment clearly came in the last two minutes of Super Bowl XXXVI. With the game tied at seventeen apiece, and with no timeouts remaining, Brady and the Patriots had one last chance with 1:32 left on the clock. According to commentators like John Madden, this clearly was the time to keep the ball on the ground, to run out the clock, and send the game into overtime. Brady thought otherwise.

We will never know precisely who was responsible for the call, Brady or Coach Belichick, but there is little doubt that this was the moment that cemented their alliance. Brady elected to throw the ball. He went 5/6, taking his team sixty yards down the field, and he brought the Patriots into field goal position with just seven seconds remaining. Now it was the moment of Adam Vinatieri.

How important was Adam Vinatieri to the Patriots of 2001–2002?

He had already proven himself worthy of his difficult role, but when Vinatieri (1972–) sent the ball skidding between the posts with exactly zero left on the time clock he moved into Patriots immortality. Vinatieri became known as a clutch player on the same level as Tom Brady, and New England won its first Super Bowl, by 20–17.

What did the commentators say about that?

They admitted, for once, that Brady and the Patriots had completely flummoxed them. The St. Louis Rams, too, admitted that they could not understand the end result. The Rams outgained the Patriots by nearly 150 yards that day, and still lost the game.

Even if Tom Brady and the Patriots had not gone on to other successes, this would have been sufficient. Boston and New England had their first football championship, and millions of fans felt that the pain they had endured during the days of Steve Grogan, Drew Bledsoe, and others had been erased. The Patriots came home to a thunderous welcome in Boston; more than 1.25 million people turned out to celebrate in festivities that began the moment the Patriots landed at Logan, and lasted all day long.

How did the Patriots do the following year?

The 2002–2003 season was something of a disappointment, but no one grumbled. The Patriots had already accomplished the unthinkable, and it was anticipated they would do well again. And so it was in 2003–2004, when the Patriots went all the way to the Super Bowl, where they met the Carolina Panthers.

Carolina was one of the newer teams of the NFL, and it had a Cinderella-like season to reach first the playoffs and then the Super Bowl. The two teams met at Reliant Stadium in Houston. The game commenced with a schizophrenic scoring pattern. Neither team showed excellence in the first or second quarter. Both stumbled through long sections of no scores at all, with occasional frenetic bursts of energy.

How did New England pull out its second Super Bowl victory?

The Carolina Panthers were up 22–21 in the fourth quarter, but the Patriots scored a surprise touchdown to go up 27–21, and then made a special, two-point conversion for 29–22. That seemed as if it should be enough, but Carolina mounted one last comeback, to send the game into overtime. New England won in overtime, thanks to a fantastic kick by Adam Vinatieri, who again proved to be worth his weight in gold to the Pats team. The final score was 32–29, and Tom Brady was Super Bowl MVP again.

There's no denying Tom Brady is a rock star quarterback who has been at the helm for four Patriot Super Bowl Championships.

The celebrations of 2004 were loud and boisterous. Perhaps 1.5 million people attended the parade that brought the Patriots from Logan Airport to Fenway Park. Even so, there was something less ecstatic about the celebrations than those of February 2002. The Patriots had shown what they could do, and the typical Boston sports fan actually became more demanding, not less. If the Patriots could pull off two Super Bowls, then surely they could accomplish another, and become a dynasty. Commentators shook their heads at this, pointing out that New England did not have the offensive depth to make a dynasty. Little did they know that Bill Belichick was already ahead of the fans: he wanted a dynasty just as much as they did.

What was so special about the coaching of Bill Belichick?

Thousands of sports fans have posed this question, and the various answers tend to be controversial, to say the least. Like Vince Lombardi, Tom Landry, and Don Shula before him, Bill Belichick was a remarkable coach, one who got his players to perform to the utmost. Belichick seldom revealed any of his secrets; he wanted to have a new wrinkle for each game. But he became one of the most familiar sights on Sunday television: the man in the hooded suit.

It's safe to say that no previous NFL team ever handled its prize talent as well as the New England Patriots. The Tom Brady–Bill Belichick combination became the most formidable and envied in the NFL.

How did the Patriots fare in the following season?

They had a good—but not great—regular season in 2004, and in February 2005, they met the Philadelphia Eagles in Super Bowl XXXIX. The Pats prevailed, 24–21, to become third-time World Champions. By now, it was fair to compare them with the Pittsburgh Steelers of the late 1970s.

How big was the rivalry between Tom Brady and Peyton Manning?

The good part is that the rivalry was never personal. Brady and Manning liked each other right from the start. Sports commentators, however, made much of the fact that Manning had always been heir to the Manning family tradition, while Brady was a surprise champion, one who seemingly came from nowhere. Between 2002 and 2007, Brady gained the upper hand in the long rivalry. What he did not expect (perhaps no one did) was that another Manning would rise to challenge him.

How did New England perform in the regular season of 2007?

The New England Patriots had a year that changed the record books. Previous to this, only one team in NFL history (the Miami Dolphins of 1972) had ever gone undefeated. Their record was 14–0. The NFL season had changed, been lengthened to 16 games, and in 2007, the Patriots went 16–0. Sometimes they crushed their competition; at other times they merely escaped them; but the undefeated record placed the Pats in NFL history, and had people everywhere saying that it would be splendid for New England to go 19–0, meaning all the way through the playoffs and the Super Bowl.

The Patriots defeated first the Jacksonville Jaguars, and then the San Diego Chargers. When they arrived in Phoenix (the game was to be played at the University of Phoenix Stadium), the Patriots seemed like royalty who were about to be crowned for the fourth time. To go undefeated in the regular season, and then to win the Super Bowl, would put them beyond even the Pittsburgh Steelers of Terry Bradshaw's time.

What was the one thing that all Patriots fans wished to forget?

As Super Bowl XLII approached, Patriot fans wished to blot the last game of the regular season from their memory banks. The Pats had prevailed, defeating the New York Giants 38–35, but it had been a narrow, painful, squeaker, and quarterback Eli Manning had shown himself as cool as Tom Brady under pressure. The Giants came in at 10–6 during the regular season, and they threaded their way through the playoffs. Most commentators placed the Patriots as the favorite by two touchdowns, however.

How did Super Bowl XLII proceed?

The Giants started the game with a spectacular drive, but had to settle for a field goal rather than a touchdown. They held the lead for some time, but in the fourth quarter, New England had a narrow, 7–3, lead in what was up to that moment one of the lowest-scoring of all Super Bowl contests. The fourth quarter turned into a real brawl, however, and Eli Manning connected with one of his receivers in what is considered one of the great catches of all Super Bowl history. The Giants prevailed by 17–14, pulling off what is considered one of the biggest upsets.

Did Boston figure prominently in New England Patriots advertisements?

No, and it's a rather sad thing. The Patriots decided, by the year 2000, that they had to appeal to all of New England, and that to showcase Boston would limit their fan base. Technically this was the right decision, but it meant that Boston was seldom displayed in Patriots advertising. The hard-core Patriots fan did not care about it very much, but the sports historian could only shake his or her head. Gone were the days when one city could claim a New England team.

Tom Brady was not at his best in Super Bowl XLII, but he was not blamed. The Patriots were so clearly the number-one team of the first decade of the new century that it was hard to fault them for anything. Tom Brady, meanwhile, had gone on to fame in other areas. His marriage to Brazilian supermodel Giselle Bündchen, made him one of the most visible—and perhaps envied—of all football players. The general feeling in Boston was that the Patriots would soon be on top once more.

How long did it take before the Patriots were again challengers for the top position?

The New England Patriots of 2008 and 2009 were not what their predecessors had been. Few of the stellar team of 2007 were still around when the regular season of 2010 commenced. In part this was because of trades, but it was also the result of age: many of the best Patriot standouts retired. In 2010, Tom Brady started poorly, losing the first two games, but then went from strength to strength. Brady, clearly, was back, and the Patriots seemed almost as good as the amazing team that went undefeated three years before.

Much to the surprise of most observers, the New York Giants also contended for the top spot. Most observers believed that 2007–2008 was an anomaly, and that Eli Manning—the younger brother of the more famous Peyton—had had his moment. Eli Manning and the Giants were only so-so (9–7) during the regular season, but they moved through the playoffs with ease, to face the Patriots in Super Bowl XLVI.

What was the build-up to Super Bowl XLVI like?

In Boston—and New England—the feeling was that the Patriots could, and would, exact revenge for the defeat in Super Bowl XLII. Tom Brady had had an excellent regular season, and if he could meet and beat Peyton Manning on such a regular basis, it seemed very likely he would overwhelm Eli. The Giants were careful not to attract much attention: their goal was to beat the Patriots twice in a row.

How did the game begin?

Played at Lucas Oil Stadium in Indianapolis, the game started off with a bang. The Giants jumped out to a 7–0 lead, but the Patriots came right back with seventeen unan-

227

Defensive Tackle Linval Joseph tries to stop Tom Brady from passing during a Super Bowl XLVI play.

swered points, to go up 17–7. As the game entered the fourth quarter, the Patriots were in a strong position. What many people did not realize was just how tired the Patriot defenders were. And when the Giants came back for another rush in the fourth quarter, they pulled off a series of minor miracles.

What did the football establishment predict for Super Bowl XLIX?

Most observers believed that the Patriots would win. One could, of course, argue that the Pats of 2015 were not the Pats of 2005, or even those of 2010. *Sports Illustrated* expressed it this way:

> The Patriots are the NFL's gold standard, a franchise as consistent as a metronome. Coaches leave, free agents depart, stars retire or are unceremoniously traded, and Brady and Belichick stitch together winning season after winning season … The NFL isn't supposed to work this way.

Sports Illustrated, January 26, 2015

How did Super Bowl XLIX begin?

The Patriots and Seahawks seemed unevenly matched. The Patriots had more firepower and finesse, while the Seahawks had more strength on the ground. Early in the fourth quarter, the Seahawks were up by 24–14, and Patriot fans felt tightness in their chests. Everyone realized that Tom Brady and the Patriots would be graded by the results of this game. Either they would go down as a great team that somehow managed to lose three Super Bowls (while winning three others) or they would become the great team, the one that won four Super Bowls.

Brady did not seem to feel the pressure. He guided his team downfield (sometimes it seemed as if they glided), brought them into scoring position, and then delivered a blistering four-yard strike for the touchdown. Now it was 24–21 with 7:55 on the clock.

Could Seattle have done more to prevent the Patriots' comeback?

Under normal conditions, the answer is yes. But the Patriots' blood was up. They forced the Seahawks out in four quick maneuvers, and then regained possession. Brady again led his team down the field, again delivered to the end zone, and suddenly the score was 28–24 with only 2:02 remaining. Brady, clearly, had done his work, and now it was up to the Patriot defense.

Now Seattle showed its stuff, barreling down the field in a remarkable possession of its own. They got to the Patriot one-yard line, and then inexplicably tried a pass when they should have run the ball. Did the Seattle coach make a terrible blunder? Definitely, but it was the kind that happens when one is under severe pressure. New England won the game, 28–24.

What were the celebrations in 2015 like?

They actually had to be postponed by a day because of severe winter weather. Bostonians remember 2015 as the single worst winter they have seen since the 1980s, and there were times when the snow plow crews ran out of places to put the snow. The celebrations were ecstatic, however. To every New England fan, it was abundantly evident that Tom Brady was *the* best quarterback ever, and that between 2001 and 2014 the Patriots had established *the* dynasty of the twenty-first century. The real question was whether outsiders would agree.

Most of them did. There are still those that argue for Terry Bradshaw as the most accomplished of all quarterbacks, and those that declare Roger Staubach had the purest form. There are those who argue for the Pittsburgh Steelers as the most dominant of all teams, and others who assert that Vince Lombardi was the greatest coach. But for the modern fan there is little doubt that Tom Brady and the New England Patriots are number one. Will they continue in that position? Will New England win a fifth Super Bowl? These are the questions that drive Monday morning quarterbacks.

THE BOSTON BRUINS

How did Boston become such a strong hockey town?

Even with the climate as we know it, it makes sense that young boys of Boston would like to play ice hockey. But in the much colder temperatures of decades past, it made even more sense. Many, if not most, neighborhoods had rinks, and the ice grew so thick during the winters of the 1940s and 1960s, especially, that it was a natural fit for the young boys and men of Greater Boston.

When were the Bruins organized as a team?

This happened in 1924, when the Boston Bruins became the first American team to enter the National Hockey League. Till that time, the sport was entirely dominated by Canadians, and even after Boston and other American cities gained teams, hockey remained a stronger spectator sport in Canada than the United States. This would change after World War II, however.

The Bruins got off to a difficult start: they went 6–24–0 in their opening season. They soon developed a reputation as a hard-hitting team, however. One of the first Bruins' stars—Eddie Shore—developed a bad reputation as a shover in hockey games: on one occasion, several Montréal players (back then they were the Montréal Maroons) ganged up on him and gave him a thorough beating.

Did the Boston Bruins profit from being relatively close to Canada?

Yes, not only did the Bruins manage to recruit many Canadians over the decades, but the New England population got jazzed up about hockey. Today hockey is seen as one of the most expensive sports to play, at the high school level especially, but in the 1940s and 1950s, young New Englanders could organize pick-up games with little more than skates and a puck.

Then too, the Bruins were able to observe the techniques that made the Canadians such formidable hockey players. Even so, it was not until 1929 that the Bruins really contended, and that was the magic year they won the Stanley Cup for the first time.

How did the Bruins fare during the Great Depression?

The 1930s were hard on virtually all teams of the National Hockey League (NHL). The crowds in Boston Garden were decidedly

It might be said that Bostonians are as proud of their Bruins as they are of their patriotic history. Here, the George Washington statue sports a Bruins jersey.

small. At least the Bruins made it through that decade with their identity intact, however: the same cannot be said for some other professional hockey teams. The Montréal Maroons folded, and were replaced, a bit later, by the Montréal Canadiens.

How is the Bruins–Canadiens rivalry different from, say, the Red Sox–Yankees rivalry

It's a different type of intensity. It's true that Red Sox fans really loathe the Yankees, who they see as overpaid spoiled brats (and that sentiment is on a good day). But the Bruins-Canadiens rivalry is more white-hot. Bruins fans know how many times Montréal has spoiled their chances, and there are times when the two teams seem ready to murder each other.

Was it any easier in those days because of the smaller number of teams?

One can argue this either way, but most of the veteran Bruins would probably say it was more difficult in their time. The six or so teams in the NHL in 1929 knew each other extremely well, and if one team managed to get hold of another team's "number," the dominant team could win for years, if not decades. The Bruins pulled out an exceptional win in the Stanley Cup finals of 1930.

Eddie Shore was the dynamo that prodded the Bruins forward in 1929, and for many years after, he remained the Bruins' exemplar of skill *and* bad sportsmanship. A full decade passed before the Bruins assembled a really great team, however, and in was in the 1940–1941 season that the Bruins won twenty-three straight games, and finished first in the Eastern Conference. They won the Stanley Cup that year, for their third in all.

How did the Boston Bruins win their third Stanley Cup?

In 1940–1941, the Bruins lost only eight regular season games on their way to a romp through the NHL. They swept the Detroit Red Wings 4–0 in the NHL finals.

What was the equipment like in those early years of professional hockey?

The regulation wear was not too different from what we know today, but the practices and pick-up games were played in all sorts of unconventional and ill-fitting regalia. Then too, there was not as much color in the uniforms of the various teams of those days. But

---

What makes the competition between the Bruins and Canadiens so intense?

The Montréal Canadiens have long been the toughest opponents for the Bruins, and the men from Montréal enjoy a substantial plus in the win-loss category. That makes any victory over Montréal all the more sweet for Boston fans.

231

this did not bother the players one bit. They considered their sport the toughest around, and looked down on nearly anyone who tried to play, or act, fancy.

What were the crowds in Boston Garden like in those days?

During the 1940s and 1950s, Boston Garden was not filled to capacity: neither the Bruins nor the Boston Celtics, who were formed in 1946, played to sold-out venues. But the enthusiasm among the people that did come was high. One thing that was notably absent in those early years was the violence and super-enthusiasm that is often seen today. Hockey was a tough sport, but it was also seen as a civilized one. Quite a few professional hockey players had rather short careers, and then went on to work in white collar jobs.

Hockey legend Bobby Orr played ten seasons with the Bruins.

How different was Bobby Orr?

Born in Ontario, Bobby Orr (1948—) came to Boston in 1966, and soon became a legend in his own time. Standing six-foot, and of about an average build for a professional hockey player, Orr was the fastest man on skates that the hockey world had ever seen. He did not revolutionize the sport in his first season with the Bruins, as is sometimes claimed, but he soon became the invaluable sixth man, meaning he could move from offense to defense with incredible speed. Though he was Canadian-born, Bobby Orr was soon taken in as an honorary Bostonian, and he was the amazing crowd pleaser who pulled in packed crowds, night after night.

Thousands, perhaps scores of thousands of young men in and around Boston tuned in to see the games on television, or went to Boston Garden. Many of these young men nursed a brand-new dream, that of becoming a hero in professional hockey. The 1940s had belonged to baseball with young Bostonians aching to be the new Ted Williams, and the early 1960s belonged to the Celtics with many Bostonians keen to become the new Bob Cousy. But by 1969, or thereabouts, Bobby Orr was the standard that many young Bostonians aspired to.

What was the greatest of all years for the Boston Bruins?

Various team players would have varying responses, but for the average fan there is little doubt that the season of 1969–1970 was the most exciting of all. The Bruins sailed

What is the most famous photograph in the history of professional hockey?

Beyond doubt it is the one that shows Bobby Orr, completely off the ground in the millisecond that followed his scoring the winning goal in the NHL 1970 finals. That one photograph, which is sometimes called Superman-in-Flight, did more for the Bruins, and professional hockey, than any number of paid advertisements. Of course it didn't hurt that the Bruins' surprising Stanley Cup win in 1970 came at roughly the same time that American moviegoers flocked to see *Love Story*, a film that had a Harvard hockey player as its leading man.

through the playoffs on the way to the finals, where they faced the St. Louis Blues. The Bruins won in seven sensational games, and the most famous photograph in the history of professional hockey was taken in the last of them. Bobby Orr flew through the air, right in front of the opponent's goal, his hair streaming wildly. Orr scored the game-winning goal, and he ensured his immortality.

How important was the weather to the success of the Bruins in those days?

Inside the hockey rink, one is oblivious to the weather outside. But the outside temperatures have an obvious effect on how thick the ice becomes, and the thickness of the ice in those days—the late 1960s and early 1970s—had much to do with the sport's appeal. Bostonians had been baseball watchers since about the year 1903, and they had slowly become basketball observers since 1946. Hockey was around for a long time before the majority of Bostonians took it to their hearts, but once they did, Boston became one of the great cities in the nation where professional hockey was concerned.

Why did Orr not remain with the Boston Bruins for his full career?

He should have. Orr was one of those amazing talents—like Ted Williams, for example—who should remain in one town and with one team so that his greatness can be fully appreciated. But Orr was experiencing a lot of physical difficulties, especially with his knees, and, displeased with the latest contract offer, he moved to the Chicago Blackhawks for the remainder of his career. Bostonians should have been outraged to see this great talent depart (as had Babe Ruth), but they sensed that they had the best part of the deal. Orr's best years, and virtually all of his stellar achievements, were in Boston.

What happened to the Bruins in the decade that followed Bobby Orr's departure?

They contended and acquitted themselves well, year after year, but they were not a major threat for a long time to come. The Montréal Canadiens, especially, had their number after about the year 1978. But the Bruins—and most other American hockey franchises—were about to receive one of the biggest shots in the arm that was possible in any sport.

233

How many Bostonians watched the thrilling Olympics hockey series against the USSR?

The answer is necessarily anecdotal, but it seemed as if every television set in Greater Boston was tuned to the Olympic Winter Games, held in Lake Placid, New York. The winter of 1979–1980 was when the Soviet Union invaded Afghanistan, igniting an especially tense period of the Cold War. Bostonians, and many of their countrymen, watched with eager anticipation as the US Olympic hockey team took on the formidable Russians in February 1980.

Virtually every sharp-eyed observer concurred that the Russians should have destroyed the Americans in the game played on February 22, 1980. But the young American team, which had several Bostonians on the roster, defeated the Russians 4-3 in what has since been called the "Miracle on Ice." The Americans went on to beat Finland in the finals, and American ice hockey took an enormous leap forward in popularity.

How did the Bruins perform in the aftermath of the Olympics, which brought such attention to the sport?

The 1980s were a crowded decade, where Boston sports were concerned. The Celtics had an outstanding time; the Patriots came close in 1985; and even the Red Sox, usually at the bottom of the barrel, made it to the World Series in 1986. Less attention was paid to the Boston Bruins than before. And the change in weather toward the decade's end diminished some of the enthusiasm for the sport.

The winters of 1981, 1982, and 1983 were truly ferocious in New England, and Greater Boston especially. This was perhaps the all-time high where the sport was concerned, when new rinks were constructed, and when hockey seemed it might even overtake baseball one day. But the weather change that set in during the year 1988 reversed the trend. Even though New England has had a handful of truly ferocious winters since—those of 1993, 1996, and 2015—the overall trend has been one of growing warmth. As a result, there have been fewer pick-up games, and a smaller overall fan base for the Bruins. And the Bruins did not always help their own case. A heartbreaking Stanley Cup loss to Edmonton in 1990, set the Bruins back for years to come.

What was the lights-out moment for the Boston Bruins?

During the 1988 Stanley Cup finals—a series in which Boston was not doing well—the lights at Boston Garden went out completely: this was in Game 3. The game was suspended, and both teams started at the same position and with the same score, but this time in Edmonton, Alberta. The Bruins lost this fourth game of the series, and succumbed to extreme disappointment.

What happened to the Bruins in the late 1990s?

Perhaps it was a combination of nostalgia and neglect. Boston Garden saw its last game in May 1995, and was soon replaced by the new TD Garden. Bruins fans registered se-

The TD Garden in Boston, home of the Bruins, was opened in 1995 and has been renovated in 2006, 2009, and 2014.

vere disappointment with the change. At the same time, the Bruins went downhill. In 1997, they missed the playoffs for the first time in thirty years, and by 1999 they were at the bottom of their division.

How wonderful was it that the Bruins won the Stanley Cup in 2011?

It's hard to describe just how much it meant to the people of Boston. First came the quarterfinals of the Eastern Conference, and, as so many times before, the Bruins faced off against the Montréal Canadiens. To that point, their long rivalry was marked by twenty-four Canadiens victories and only eight Bruins wins in postseason series.

Montréal took the first two games of the quarterfinal, by 2–0 and 3–1. Boston roared back, winning Game 3 in overtime (5–4) and Game 4 by 2–1. The Canadiens captured the next game by 2–1, but Boston took the series by 4-3 in the sixth game. There was much rejoicing in Boston: the Bruins had moved past their arch rivals.

Why was it so special for the Bruins to defeat the Philadelphia Flyers in 2011?

The previous season had witnessed a genuine meltdown by the Bruins in the seventh game of their series with the Flyers. Boston came back thoroughly prepared, and the Bruins took down the Flyers in four straight games: 7–3, 3–2, 5–1, 5–1. The Bruins victory made a very strong statement: these were not the Bruins of 2010!

The Bruins went on to defeat the Tampa Bay Lightning in seven games, and then faced the Vancouver Canucks in what was expected to be a wipeout for the latter team. Van-

235

couver took the first game (1–0) and then the second (3–2) but Boston exploded for eight goals in the third game, and shut out Vancouver (4–0) in the next. Vancouver managed one more win in Game 6, but the concluding game of the series went to Boston (5–2).

How wild were the celebrations in Boston?

They were calmer than one might expect. The crowds were big on June 11, 2011, as the Bruins paraded from the TD Garden through town, carried by a parade of Ducks, and the enthusiasm was high. Boston had experienced a thirty-nine-year drought, and now the Stanley Cup came back to New England.

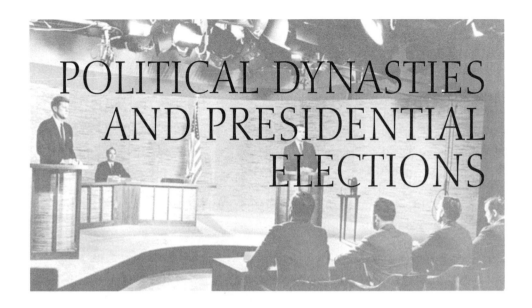

Can anyone explain why Boston is so important to American politics?

To a large degree, this is a mystery. To be sure, Boston is one of the great American cities, but the same can be said of Los Angeles, Miami, Philadelphia, and half a dozen others, and none of these cities have spawned anywhere near the political dynasties that have risen in Boston. The only city that comes close is New York.

What makes Boston politics different from those of other major American cities?

This, too, is somewhat subjective, but it may be the rich combination of an intelligentsia and a politically informed working class. Bostonians tend to be more "up" on political events than their contemporaries in other American cities, and they almost certainly argue with each other over politics to a greater degree. This has long been the case: Boston is a contentious place.

COLONIAL AND REVOLUTIONARY POLITICS

What were pre-Revolutionary Boston politics like?

They were dominated by a handful of families, which provided the governors, town clerks, and leading members of the legislature for roughly three generations. One can call Boston the cradle of liberty—and this is true in that the town gave birth to the American Revolution—but its politics were oligarchic, tending even to aristocratic in nature.

Who was the first great master of Boston politics?

The master was Samuel Adams (1722–1803) and the unfortunate recipient of his teaching was Governor Thomas Hutchinson (1711–1780). The two men knew each other well, and heartily disliked one another. Hutchinson seemed to have the upper hand, until the Stamp Act was passed by Parliament. The moment Bostonians learned of the Stamp Act, they became willing to follow Sam Adams and his unofficial group of followers, the Sons of Liberty.

Adams was the first to utilize the Boston mob; if he had any predecessors, they are anonymous to us. Between 1765 and 1775, Adams turned the Sons of Liberty and the mob (sometimes the two were roughly the same) into the most powerful change agent yet seen in the American colonies. Years later, when America won its independence, Sam Adams calmed down—if that is the right expression—and became a highly respected citizen interested in law and order.

Thomas Hutchinson was governor of the Province of Massachusetts Bay from 1769 to 1774.

Was it inevitable that John Adams would rise to the vice presidency?

Not at all. John Adams (1735–1826) was thoroughly respected in Boston, and Massachusetts, but this did not make him a shoe-in. Had either Alexander Hamilton or Thomas Jefferson been in a position to "campaign" for the vice-presidency, they might have succeeded.

Of course there were no actual campaigns in 1789. American democracy was in its rough, crude beginnings, and the decision was made entirely by the members of the Electoral College, who, quite naturally, chose George Washington unanimously. Thomas Jefferson would have been a poor choice for the vice-presidency because he, too, was a Virginian, and Alexander Hamilton was already viewed as being very close to Washington. People looked northward, for a New England man to balance the ticket, and John Adams was chosen.

Did John Adams enjoy being vice-president of the United States?

Not at all. Like the great majority of the men who have served in that capacity, John Adams was frustrated by the high profile and low means of his job. He could be held responsible to some degree if things went wrong, but he could make almost no decision without President Washington, who was held in such high regard that he probably would *not* be blamed.

Adams watched as the political infighting in New York and then Philadelphia (the nation's capital was not Washington, D.C., until the year 1800) became more intense.

What was the relationship between John Adams and Sam Adams?

They were second cousins, and members of a very large clan that dated back to the founding of the Massachusetts Bay Colony. Both John and Sam Adams grew up with a chip on their shoulder, meaning they felt it necessary to improve the financial fortunes of their respective families (in this regard, John Adams fared much better than his cousin). Both were patriots from an early moment in the Revolutionary struggle, but they had very different ideas about how the new nation should develop. Throughout his life, Sam Adams was primarily a democrat (with a small "d") interested in the growth of representative democracy. Throughout his even longer life, John Adams was primarily an aristocrat, believing that the better-educated should govern.

From an early date, he was a strong federalist, meaning a person that believed in the power and authority of the federal, as opposed to state, government. This meant that Adams and his boss, George Washington, saw very much eye-to-eye, and it gave Adams a major leg-up where the election of 1796 was concerned.

Was there any sort of campaign in 1796?

There was not. John Adams, the sitting vice-president, was selected by the members of the Electoral College, and his rival, Thomas Jefferson, became vice-president under the curious formula that existed at the time (the runner-up became vice-president, regardless of how bitter or nasty the campaign had been).

John Adams was inaugurated in Philadelphia in March 1797. Southerners generally disliked him; New Englanders generally respected him, while not showing him much love; and the occupants of the Middle States—New Jersey, Philadelphia, and Delaware—seemed not to care very much. Adams took office, however, at a time of growing concern for the future of the nation.

One sometimes hears of the XYZ Affair, but it never makes sense. What was it all about?

In 1797, President John Adams sent three commissioners to treat with the government of Revolutionary France. The Directory government—as it was called—had acted in a most unfriendly manner toward the United States, seizing many American merchant vessels. The three American commissioners asked to see French diplomat Talleyrand, to present their credentials, but they were brought to three unidentified Frenchmen—who were named in the documents as Mr. X, Mr. Y, and Mr. Z. Much to the surprise of the American commissioners, a hefty bribe was demanded, even before negotiations commenced.

Charles C. Pinckney of South Carolina, leader of the three American diplomats, rebuffed the three Frenchmen with these words, "No, not a penny." In popular parlance, this soon changed to "millions for defense but not one penny for tribute." As a result, when the three commissioners came home, they were hailed by the public, and President John Adams was pressed by Federalists and Republicans alike to lead the nation to war against France.

It seems ironic. Had France not assisted America during the Revolutionary War?

It is one of the many oddities that surround the diplomacy and politics of the 1790s. Some historians label that decade the most politically contentious of early American history. President John Adams was no lover of France. He had been quite unhappy while serving as a special ambassador in the early 1780s. Adams could have boosted his own popularity greatly by asking for a declaration of war: it would probably have ensured his reelection in 1800. But of all the many things people can accuse John Adams of insincerity or pandering were not among them. Adams allowed a limited, undeclared naval war to begin.

How did Bostonians feel about the undeclared naval war against France?

They were all for it. Bostonians had a long history of regarding France with suspicion. The great exception to the rule came during the Revolutionary War, when France sent sailors and soldiers to fight in the American cause. But once they heard of the demand for a bribe, by XYZ, Bostonians were rather keen for a fight, and they were delighted that USS *Constitution* had been built in Boston Harbor in 1796–1797.

As president, John Adams did not do great things for Boston. He did not need to in that federal patronage had not yet become part of American politics. Even so, the men and women of his hometown complained that he seemed *too* even-handed, too unwilling to do anything for the Commonwealth of Massachusetts.

What was the election of 1800 like?

John Adams was now the incumbent president, and he announced his desire to be elected again (there was, at that time, no constitutional limitation on the number of terms a president could serve). His vice-president, Thomas Jefferson, announced his candidacy. So did Aaron Burr and Alexander Hamilton.

The average voter had no say in what transpired. None of the candidates won a clear majority in the Electoral College and the election was, therefore, thrown into the U.S. House of Representatives, where all sorts of bribery and kickbacks were possible. The political mess that followed (there is no other way to describe it) ended with Thomas Jefferson being selected as the third President of the United States. John Adams was held to a one-term presidency.

Was John Adams upset by his loss in 1800?

Neither John nor Abigail Adams (1744–1818) really liked Washington very much (the nation's capital had just transferred to the city on the Potomac), and they had many sour grapes about Thomas Jefferson's election. John and Abigail went home to Braintree, to take up gardening, philosophy, and to enjoy the last quarter of their lives together.

Bostonians did not register any great disappointment with John Adams' election defeat. It had been nice, of course, to have a fellow Bostonian in the White House, but they had not seen any substantial benefit during his term in office. Bostonians, therefore, greeted the beginning of Thomas Jefferson's first term with a certain resignation, and the belief that the Federalist Party would soon regain the presidency.

Abigail Adams is well-known for her marriage to the nation's second president; her letters indicate she was an early feminist.

THE ERA OF GOOD FEELINGS

What is the single most distinctive aspect of American politics bequeathed by Boston?

One can certainly answer that the town meeting is distinctive, but it belongs to New England as a whole rather than Boston in particular. Cynics would be quick to say that political cronyism is a major bequest by Boston to the nation, but the same charge can be leveled at Philadelphia and New York. The single most distinctive Bostonian contribution, therefore, is the art of the gerrymander.

In 1812, one of the first political cartoons in American history appeared in the Boston newspapers. Governor Elbridge Gerry performed the first gerrymander in American history, redrawing the lines of the congressional districts on the North Shore in Essex County. The result was distinctly favorable to his political party. Though Gerry's name is not well-known—either to Bostonians or other Americans—he started a political process that continues today.

What happened to the Federalist Party in Massachusetts?

As late as 1812, the Federalist Party won nearly all the local elections in and around Boston. When Caleb Strong (1745–1819) was elected Massachusetts governor in 1812, he felt strong enough to declare that the Massachusetts militia would not be employed anywhere outside of the Commonwealth. But the War of 1812 proved the Federalists' undoing.

Throughout 1814, Massachusetts and Connecticut elected officials expressed their displeasure with the Madison administration and the ongoing War of 1812. In November 1814, delegates from various New England states convened in Hartford, Connecticut, to consider how they might persuade President Madison to give up the war. Among the various considerations was the idea—however sketchy—that the New England states might secede from the Union and form their own, brand-new nation. Not only did the end of the War of 1812—the peace treaty was signed on Christmas Eve—make secession unnecessary, but the Federalists became damned throughout the entire nation. The Federalist Party virtually collapsed in the three years following 1815.

What was the Era of Good Feelings?

Historians generally pass over it rather quickly, for the simple reason that it is not controversial. When Virginia-born President James Monroe came to Boston for a visit in 1817, the populace greeted him with great enthusiasm. Just a few years earlier, he would have been derided, and perhaps even damned as a Republican, but the collapse of the Federalist Party brought a halt to divisive politics.

For the next half-dozen years, Bostonians breathed a sigh of relief as they turned away from national politics. They had plenty to occupy them on a local level. But as the election of 1824 approached, Bostonians again became concerned, and they again had a local son to present to the nation. This was John *Quincy* Adams, the eldest son of John Adams.

What had John Quincy Adams done to this point in life?

The better question to ask is what hadn't he done? The precocious John Quincy Adams (1767–1848) started his political life early, as his father's confidential secretary. He moved on to become ambassador to Czarist Russia, and one of the leading members of the delegation that brought the War of 1812 to an end. John Quincy Adams then served as secretary of state, during which time he helped establish a firm boundary between the United States and British Canada. Few men have ever gone to the White House as well prepared as John Quincy Adams.

John Quincy Adams ran for president in 1824. This was the first time voters had the opportunity to participate, and we therefore have the vote count from the various states. John Quincy Adams came in second to General Andrew Jackson in the popular vote, but no one won a majority of the popular vote, and the election was therefore

Was this the first time that the recipient of fewer popular votes won the White House?

It was indeed, and some political historians believe that it was a bad way for us to begin our tradition as a truly representative democracy. Since the election of 1824, three other men have won the presidency while amassing fewer popular votes. They are Rutherford B. Hayes, Benjamin Harrison, and George W. Bush.

thrown into the U.S. House of Representatives. After many ballots, the House gave the election to John Quincy Adams.

What was John Qunicy Adams like as president?

He was remarkably like his father—filled with high ideas and ideals that did not translate well. Perhaps the best-read and most-educated of all the men ever to reach the White House, John Quincy Adams proved singularly inept in running the nation. He was not a terrible president (no great catastrophe struck the nation during his one-term presidency), but one struggles to point out even one major accomplishment.

President John Quincy Adams

How different was the election of 1828 from that of 1824?

In a word, it was *very* different. All the major contenders in 1824 were from the Republican Party, and the Federalists were now as dead as the proverbial nail in the coffin. But the new Democratic Party had arisen, and General Andrew Jackson was nominated. He ran a very different campaign in 1828, attempting to skewer John Quincy Adams, who was the Republican nominee.

General Jackson and his many friends painted John Quincy Adams as an effete Easterner; Adams did his best to portray Jackson as an illiterate Westerner. Both sides resorted to all sorts of shenanigans, and this was the first time that both parties promised disaster to the nation if they did not succeed. In the end, it was Jackson over John Quincy Adams by a substantial majority. Boston and Massachusetts, unsurprisingly, voted for Adams. Some of the smaller towns in western Massachusetts went for him by enormous margins.

Was that it for John Quincy Adams and the family dynasty?

No. Just three years later, John Quincy Adams ran for the U.S. House of Representatives. With his family seat at Braintree, Adams won election to the congressional district representing the immediate south shore of Greater Boston. Adams was the only American president ever to win an election after being in the White House, and he remained in the U.S. Congress till his death in 1848.

John Quincy Adams was more successful and better-loved as a congressman than he ever had been during his White House years. He made a point of championing unpopular causes, and was one of the few representatives from New England to speak out strongly against slavery. Though he once had been president, his congressional colleagues showed no deference: they fought against him as hard as anyone else. He won their respect, however, and at the time of his death, he had largely exorcised the negative sentiment earned by his White House failures.

Having supplied two sons for the White House, did the Adams family call it quits?

They did not. The leaders of the Adams family recognized that they were not ideal presidential candidates, that they lacked the common touch. They therefore went into other branches of politics and diplomacy, and did quite well. Charles Francis Adams (1807–1886)—son of John Quincy Adams—was a congressman until President Lincoln named him ambassador to Great Britain. Crossing the Atlantic in 1861, He became the point man of the Lincoln administration, keeping both Britain and France out of the Civil War.

Henry Adams (1838–1918)—son of Charles Francis Adams—never won election to anything, and he detested any sort of pandering to voters or national whims. Henry Adams turned out to be an extremely astute observer of the national scene, however, and his history of the United States during the administrations of John Adams and Thomas Jefferson turned out to be one of the best political books of the nineteenth century. In his autobiography, *The Education of Henry Adams*, he leads the reader on a rather dark trail, through the benefits and demerits of being an Adams family member.

THE FITZGERALDS

Almost everyone knows something about the Kennedys. But who were the Fitzgeralds?

As historian Doris Kearns Goodwin has artfully shown, the Fitzgeralds were the predecessors to the Kennedys and it is nearly impossible to envision the Kennedy success without that of their grandfather. John "Honey Fitz" Fitzgerald (1863–1950) was a Boston Irishman who worked his way up the political ladder of Boston during the late nineteenth century, and capped his success with election as mayor of Boston in 1906. His nickname "Honey" comes from the fact that he had a melodious voice, and would often break into song while on the campaign trail. Fitzgerald was the first Boston Irish politician to break beyond the bounds of his fellow Irish: he successfully appealed to other ethnic communities within Boston. Many of the photographs of Honey Fitz show him in campaign mode, and they often display him making hay of the fact he was such a good family man: his wife Mary Hannon Fitzgerald and his eldest daughter Rose often accompanied him.

If Honey Fitz was so good a politician, why do we seldom hear of him?

This is because he was succeeded—actually pushed out—by an even more skillful man, who copied his methods and then surpassed him. This was James Michael Curley (1874–1958), the most prominent politician of Boston between about 1912 and 1948. During a long career, Curley was twice elected governor of Massachusetts, twice a member of the U.S. House of Representatives, and an astonishing four times mayor of Boston. Curley would doubtless have had even more terms as mayor, had the Massachusetts legislature not passed a law preventing the mayor of the city of Boston from succeeding himself in office. Thwarted by this law, Curley won election four times, and then had to move out of City Hall in order to allow four years to pass before he could once again enter the lists.

Of course, no discussion of James Michael Curley would be complete without accounting for the fact that he twice went to jail. The first time was early in his career; the second occasion came in 1949, when he went to federal prison for corruption. Curley served only six months of his sentence before he was pardoned by President Harry S. Truman. Triumphantly returning to Boston, Curley entered City Hall, and made a grand statement to the effect that more had been accomplished in the twenty-four hours since his return than in the six months of his absence. This was one of the few times that Curley misread the city and its mood. His lieutenant-governor, who had competently managed the ship in his absence, then chose to run against him, and to the surprise of many, Curley lost in 1950. Though he continued to try, his political career was well and truly over.

Where did the Kennedy clan stand on James Michael Curley?

They respected Curley but did not like him. They remembered that he ousted their grandfather, Honey Fitz, and though the Kennedys copied Curley in some respects, they never warmed up to him.

THE KENNEDYS

Everyone knows the name Kennedy. But when did this first become the case?

Bostonians knew the name of Joseph P. Kennedy (1888–1969) because he was so successful a businessman, banker, and breaker of the rules. Vowing to become a millionaire by the age of twenty-five, Joseph P. Kennedy succeeded, but he stepped on many toes in the process. Not long after that, he became a bootlegger, running alcohol during Pro-

---

Did any subsequent mayors of Boston stand as high as James Michael Curley?

Some of them were quite effective in public policy, but none attained the type of fame and notoriety he possessed. The one that came closest was Mayor Kevin White, who occupied City Hall between 1968 and 1984.

hibition. He might have remained only a local success were it not for his marriage to Rose Fitzgerald, daughter of Honey Fitz.

The couple wed in 1914, and soon raised a large family, first in Brookline and later in Manhattan. Right from the beginning, the Kennedys were a family of outsized ambition: one could almost see the ambition in the bright good looks of the children, who went to the best schools, and were expected to excel. Joseph Kennedy became head of the Securities and Exchange Commission during the Great Depression. President Franklin D. Roosevelt believed that the best way to catch a thief was to hire one, and Kennedy and his staff wrote legislation that made the sort of insider trading from which he had benefitted illegal. Kennedy did so well in this post that President Roosevelt nominated him as ambassador to Great Britain, and the entire family moved to London in 1940, at the height of the danger posed by the German "Blitz."

Is this where the many photos come from—such as the one where the entire Kennedy family met Pope Pius?

Yes. The Kennedys were world-class charmers, right from the start. The photogenic family loved to travel, and to meet with dignitaries, and Joseph Kennedy did his best to ensure that his children would have a major head start in politics (indeed in life). About the only thing that the photos do not display is the world-weariness and downright defeatism that dogged Joseph Kennedy during World War II.

Joseph Kennedy had made a life out of beating the odds, but he did not believe Britain could defeat Germany, or that the United States should make any effort to rescue its English-speaking cousin. Kennedy spoke to the press too many times, and he registered his pessimism, which in a time of war was dangerously close to treason. President Roosevelt recalled Kennedy and demanded his resignation.

Is there any good reason why the Kennedys and Roosevelt were not close?

They came from very different milieus. Even though both were "Harvard" families, the Roosevelts had a much longer lineage: they were Dutch patrons who made their money in the eighteenth century. The Kennedys, by contrast, were Boston Irish who rose with startling speed, but who had not yet caught up in terms of social grace (with Rose Kennedy being the major exception to the rule). Beyond this, however, President Roosevelt was furious with Joseph Kennedy for his defeatism, and the two parted ways in anger. Years later, Joseph Kennedy still vented about the "sonafabitch" who killed his son.

How could this be? Franklin Roosevelt sent men into battle, but he never killed anyone himself.

In 1944 Joe Kennedy, Jr., the eldest son and brightest spot in the senior Kennedy's eye, was killed while on a bombing mission over Nazi Germany. Joe Kennedy did not have to take that assignment; he volunteered. Joseph Kennedy, Sr. was never quite the same again, and to the end of his days he cursed Franklin Roosevelt as the person that "sent" his son to his death.

So John F. Kennedy was not the eldest? How did he fit into his father's plans?

The spotlight had always been on Joe Junior, the one expected to fulfill the family destiny. After his death in 1944, Joseph Kennedy, Sr. looked at his next-eldest son, John F. Kennedy with more interest and concern. The second-eldest son had graduated from Harvard in 1940, written a fine book called *Why England Slept*, and had become a real war hero, serving on a PT boat in the Pacific. Even so, John F. Kennedy was always in the background till his brother was killed: soon thereafter, he had to take on the mantle of expectation.

What was John Kennedy like in 1945—the year World War II ended?

The photographs from the time show an extremely lean, even flimsy-looking John Kennedy. He had injured his back while playing football at Harvard, and then injured it again during World War II. There was a skinny and even frail look to him—but everyone that actually knew him agreed he was tough. This was the sickly, rather weak son who had languished in Joe Junior's shadow, but he was now ready to become a leader.

In 1946, John F. Kennedy ran for and won election to a congressional seat in East Boston. He was a Democrat in a Democratic year, but most observers agreed that two things won the election for him: his war-hero status, and the efforts of his sisters, cousins, and

The crew of the PT-109, which JFK commanded in the Pacific Theater during World War II. He is standing at the far right in this photo. Kennedy commanded several PT boats during the war.

aunts. The Kennedy ladies were an important part of the formula that won his election in 1946, and they repeated their efforts through every one of his subsequent campaigns.

Did Bostonians realize they had something quite special in John F. Kennedy?

Not in the first five years of his career. The U.S. Congress was filled with handsome veterans of World War II, and John Kennedy stuck out mostly because of his wealth. Opponents correctly declared that he'd never had to worry about money for a moment in his life, but they failed to make the argument stick. Kennedy proved very good with his poorer constituents.

If John Kennedy ever made a "wrong" move in his early political years, it was his wedding to Jacqueline Bouvier (1929–1994). The wedding, held in fashionable Newport, Rhode Island, was a major step on the social ladder, but it risked alienating him from his old-style Boston roots. Kennedy's new wife was not an asset in the first years of the marriage: over time she turned out to be a real strength.

Why did John Kennedy move so quickly up the ladder for a U.S. Senate seat?

Kennedy family advisers anguished over it to a great degree. Their concern was that John was too young for such an august post; at the same time, they feared his World War II luster would eventually wear off. John Kennedy therefore ran against Henry Cabot Lodge for the open Senate seat from Massachusetts. It was a major gamble, but the Kennedys—the ladies, especially—outdid themselves on the campaign trail, and in November 1952, Kennedy won in a squeaker. At this point, he had actually outperformed his elder brother, Joe Jr., whom everyone had expected to reach the Senate in 1956.

How important was "old" Joseph Kennedy at this point?

He was the maker and breaker of deals, the purse that funded the family fortunes. Political opponents sometimes accused John Kennedy of being a mere cipher for his father, but if this ever were true, it became less so with each passing year. Senator Kennedy won high points for his political style, and the publication of another book, *Profiles in Courage*, helped along his career. The moment at which John Kennedy became fully his own man was probably the Democratic National Convention of 1956, when he tried for, and narrowly lost the vice-presidential nomination. Years later, John Kennedy mused that his elder brother probably would have won that contest, and then would have been submerged by the Eisenhower and Republican high tide of the autumn of 1956.

As it turned out, John Kennedy's narrow loss in 1956 probably helped his political career. He was soon in contention for 1960, and in that magic year—magic for Bostonians, especially—Kennedy entered and won several primaries on his way to victory at the Democratic National Convention. Nominated at the tender age of forty-three, he became one of the youngest men ever to seek the office. His Republican opponent was another veteran of the Congressional class of 1946: a hard-working, talented, and passably handsome fellow from California named Richard Nixon.

How important was John Kennedy's speech to the American bishops in Houston?

No Roman Catholic had ever been elected to the presidency. The only one that ever made the attempt was Alfred Smith, who was swamped by Republican Herbert Hoover in 1928. Some of the impressions mainline Protestants had concerning Roman Catholicism were very much the same as they had been thirty-two years earlier. Right or wrong, many Protestants thought of Catholics as emotional, unpredictable, and given to drink. Herbert Hoover had been the "dry" candidate in 1928, while Alfred Smith was "wet."

John Kennedy knew the odds as well as anyone. Though he'd seldom experienced prejudice on a personal level, he'd seen its effects on many older members of his families (the Kennedys and Fitzgeralds). Kennedy, therefore, appeared before a large group of Protestant bishops in the summer of 1960, assuring them he would not take his marching orders from the Pope. Kennedy's presence had a lot to do with his success, and the issue of religion was not raised again in the 1960 campaign.

How did the presidential debates of 1960 become so important a part of American political history?

Television was only a decade old in 1960, and many Americans did not own a set. Plenty of them went to the homes of family and friends on those autumn nights in 1960, to ob-

The televised Nixon–Kennedy debate during the 1960 presidential campaign is considered a historic event that proved how television could significantly influence voting. The fact that Nixon was visibly sweating during the program turned off many potential voters.

serve the first presidential debates. What they saw was an accurate reflection of the social and political leadership of the nation, and they were the first American voters to be able to hold a television "picture" in their minds.

Nixon came in as the favorite. A bit older than Kennedy, he was extremely seasoned, having served as vice-president for eight years under President Dwight D. Eisenhower. Nixon was a hard-worker, what we today would call a policy "wonk" and he knew how to show his knowledge. What he lacked, according to his opponent, was "class." John Kennedy was respectful of Richard Nixon in public, but extremely dismissive of him in private, referring to him as a graceless individual who would come apart under pressure (this prediction eventually proved accurate).

In the three televised debates, Nixon and Kennedy proved about equal on substance, but Kennedy ran away with the events in terms of style. Handsome, trim, even debonair, he simply spoke better and let the camera adore him (while Nixon seemed to fear the camera). Radio listeners declared the debates a narrow tie, but television viewers called it a hands-down victory for the senator from Massachusetts.

PRESIDENT KENNEDY

What was it about Kennedy that made people love him so?

Novelists and psychologists can probably address this better than historians. Kennedy possessed a very real charisma, a style that endeared people to him. He was good-looking, articulate, and clean-cut, but he also symbolized a youthful and dynamic approach to the world. Even some who had voted against him admitted that they rather liked to see this young man—all of forty-three—and his young family in the White House.

On January 20, 1961—a very cold day at that—John F. Kennedy was inaugurated in Washington, D.C. Robert Frost, known as New England's poet, spoke at the inauguration, and the combination of the old Robert Frost and the youthful John Kennedy made for a memorable event. Kennedy had already won big points in terms of style; the question now was whether he would govern as a Bostonian, an Irishman, a Roman Catholic, or as a true American who combined all of the above.

How did Bostonians feel about Kennedy's election?

They were thrilled. For perhaps half a century, Bostonians had felt forgotten by the national current of politics, as Roosevelts dominated the White House, and Republicans controlled the U.S. Congress. John Kennedy was thoroughly Irish in ethnicity, but he was also a Harvard man, who could throw around concepts as readily as any Boston Brahmin. He was rich enough that he did not need the presidential office, yet ambitious enough that it was the center of his focus. Though some old-line Yankees maintained reservations about the man in the White House, the great majority of Bostonians were delighted.

Was the Kennedy presidency helpful to the people of Boston?

It feels a bit like heresy to say that the answer is "no." The Kennedy presidency brought glamour to Washington, D.C., and increased respect from other nations of the world, but John Kennedy did not do anything special for his hometown. Indeed, there were times when it seemed he could not care less. Where Kennedy did help his home town was in the area of public renown. Harvard and MIT both sent numerous professors to work in the Kennedy administration. One of the most perceptive comments on Boston's relationship with the new president was offered by Walter Muir Whitehill, dean of the Bostonian historians of the time.

"When I began this book," Whitehill wrote, "a native Bostonian was president of the United States. He was the first since John Quincy Adams, for nobody could claim that Calvin Coolidge, although twice governor of Massachusetts, was other than a Vermonter.... Many of us rejoiced in the vision, literacy, imagination, and energy that John F. Kennedy brought to his high office. Since November 22, 1963, his stature has not decreased."

Did Bostonians feel a closer tie to President Kennedy than the people of other major American cities?

If they claimed that they did, they fooled themselves. Kennedy, like Franklin Roosevelt, belonged to the entire nation. By the time of his death in November 1963, he had risen well above majority leader or even political number one: he had become the most beloved president of modern times. The only president to whom Kennedy can be compared is Franklin D. Roosevelt: the former used the medium of television as skillfully as the latter exploited the medium of radio.

That Bostonians grieved Kennedy's death is beyond dispute. He—and the Kennedy family—soon took on a larger-than-life quality with everything good and wonderful being attributed to them. Some of this has not changed. While the people who actually shook John Kennedy's hand are few in number, and while that number decreases with each passing year, Kennedy's legacy remains secure. He was the most charismatic person ever to occupy the White House.

THE KENNEDY SENATORS

How different were John F. and Robert F. Kennedy?

They were very different in personality and style, but remarkably similar in personal toughness. The difference is that John F. Kennedy usually concealed his inner toughness, while Robert F. displayed his for the world to see.

In the two years that followed President Kennedy's death, his younger brother Robert F. Kennedy (1925–1968) became the new recipient of the family destiny. Even though their youngest brother, Ted Kennedy, had already been elected to the U.S. Senate in 1962, it was

Robert who assumed the leadership. Robert Kennedy won election to the U.S. Senate, representing the State of New York in 1964. Once in the Senate, Robert Kennedy became a major opponent of President Lyndon B. Johnson, and he eventually morphed into a vigorous opponent of the Vietnam War.

Was Robert Kennedy thoroughly identified with Boston?

He was an even less dutiful son than his brother before him. Though he went to local schools, to Harvard and to Harvard Law School, Robert F. Kennedy did not display any particular love for Boston. If anything, he was more closely identified with Manhattan, where he raised his large family. In one way, however, Robert Kennedy did win immortality in Boston, and that was his connection with American youth.

Robert Kennedy was a first-class campaigner.

Boston was, and remains, the city of choice so far as college-aged people are concerned, and Kennedy's appeal to youth carried over to maintain his connection with Boston.

How did Bostonians react to the assassination of Robert Kennedy?

In June 1968, minutes after he declared victory in the California Democratic primary, Robert Kennedy was shot and killed by Sirhan Sirhan (the assassin did not seem to hate Kennedy so much as American politics in general). Bostonians mourned Robert Kennedy's death, but he was "less" a part of them than his elder brother had been. There was, too, a certain weariness where grief was concerned. John F. Kennedy's assassination had been followed by that of Malcolm X (1965), and by that of Martin Luther King, Jr. (1968).

If ever Americans had had a royal family, it was the Kennedys, however. No previous political family, including the Adams, even came close. Speculation, therefore, focused on the Kennedys, and on who would replace Robert as the leader. Of course it could only be the fourth of the Kennedy sons: Edward Kennedy, better known as "Ted."

Why does Ted Kennedy generally not receive his due?

This has finally changed. In the early twenty-first century, after forty years in public service, Ted Kennedy finally won the accolades he deserved. They were a long time in coming.

Born in Boston, Ted Kennedy (1932–2009) was the youngest of the eight Kennedy siblings. In conversation and style, he was often the afterthought, and few people thought he would ever reach a top position. Like many younger siblings, Ted Kennedy used his physique to make up for the attention he did not receive. Built like a linebacker in his youth, he was handsome in a manner quite different from that of his elder brothers. John F. Kennedy was debonair; Robert F. Kennedy was rumpled in a way that worked; and Ted Kennedy seemed like everyone's favorite fellow at the bar, the one who entertained the crowd, and then went home alone. It must be admitted that he made some serious mistakes in life, and that these almost cost him the fanfare of what it meant to be a Kennedy.

What were Ted's biggest mistakes?

While at the University of Virginia Law School, he cheated on a final examination, having a friend take it for him. Much more seriously, Ted was the center of a controversy surrounding the death of a young woman in the summer of 1969. Widely considered the front runner for the Democratic nomination in 1972, Ted was at a party on Chappaquiddick Island off the coast of Cape Cod. He left in the company of Mary Jo Kopechne, and she was never seen alive again. When Kennedy phoned police, six hours later, he seemed disoriented, perhaps even drugged. Ted had always had critics, those that claimed he was irresponsible and immature. Their claims now seemed justified.

In 1972, Kennedy stuck to business in the U.S. Senate, and played no part in the presidential campaign. When he won re-election in 1976, however, Kennedy began to eye the White House. And when incumbent President Jimmy Carter showed weakness, Ted made his bid official. Standing on the steps of the newly finished John F. Kennedy Library, Ted declared his candidacy, implicitly laying claim to the mantle of his older brothers.

What happened in the Democratic primaries of 1980?

Something unthinkable happened: a Kennedy lost. Ted Kennedy lost all the early primaries and caucuses to incumbent President Jimmy Carter, but he staged a strong rally in the middle of the primary season. At first Ted made strong second finishes, but he eventually won a total of ten primaries, and was able to insert many of his plans into the Democratic platform at the national convention. As he conceded defeat, on national television, Ted made a truly inspired speech, the kind which might have made a big difference earlier in the campaign. He sounded a very low note minutes later, however, when he refused to shake President Carter's hand. As Ted departed the stage that August day, it seemed as if the Kennedy legacy was finally finished.

What kind of a comeback did Ted Kennedy make?

He made a fantastic recovery, and did so over the course of many years. Massachusetts residents had long since decided that Ted Kennedy was their man, where the U.S. Senate was concerned, and they turned out to vote for him in 1982, 1988, and 1994. What was really noticeable, however, was the extent to which Ted Kennedy now was identified both with the city of Boston and progressive Democratic politics: in this one man, the two seemed to become one.

In campaign after campaign, and issue after issue, Ted Kennedy was the national standard-bearer, the person who fought for one cause after another, believing that the Democrats could win. In 1994, when Bill and Hillary Clinton brought national health care to center stage, Kennedy wearily proclaimed that this was the moment when Americans would obtain what he had so long desired. But it was not to be. Not only did health care die a slow, painful death in the U.S. Congress, but Ted Kennedy actually had real competition for his Senate seat.

Ted Kennedy, shown here in 1987, dominated Massachusetts politics for years, though he did get some strong Republican competition from Mitt Romney in the 1980s.

How did Mitt Romney rise to become Ted Kennedy's competition in 1994?

Mitt Romney hailed from Michigan, but he moved to Massachusetts and made a fortune as an executive of Bain Capital Inc., a company that profited from the rapid turnovers in the New England economy of the late 1980s. Extremely rich, and as handsome as John F. Kennedy at his best, Romney was a dream candidate so far as Massachusetts Republicans were concerned. For the first time they had a real chance to beat Ted Kennedy.

In the senatorial election of 1994, Mitt Romney pulled ahead in the polls and seemed likely to win. A series of debates were branded as "ties," but Kennedy did better with the audience, using his long-established Massachusetts ties to cement the relationship. Kennedy won the 1994 election by a narrower margin than in previous years, and in the aftermath he pledged to be the "hardest-working Kennedy" the voters had ever seen. He did not disappoint.

How long did Kennedy serve as the "Lion of the Senate"?

He had become the "Lion of the Senate" during the 1970s, when his thick mane of hair and his richly textured voice earned him the nickname. Over the years, as his hair turned white and his voice went up the scale, Kennedy became even more committed to what he considered the Massachusetts agenda with universal health care near the top of the list. Kennedy did not succeed in his fondest projects, but his hands were all over the Senate legislation of the 1980s, 1990s, and early 2000s: it is no exaggeration to say that he was one of the most successful, and popular, of all U.S. senators.

What does the future hold for the Kennedy family?

There are more Kennedys than ever because they tend to believe in large families with lots of children. But the Kennedy mystique, which still has some power, is more broadly felt in the nation as a whole, and is not confined to Boston, or even to New England.

ALL POLITICS IS LOCAL

Who was Tip O'Neill and how did he become such a favored man in American politics?

Born in East Boston, Thomas P. "Tip" O'Neill (1912–1994) came from a Boston Irish family that had done better than most. He grew up in the political era of James Michael Curley, and learned some oratorical skills by watching the great mayor, but their personal styles were quite different. Where James Michael Curley seemed like everyone's friend, Tip O'Neill really was everyone's friend.

Tip started off in the Massachusetts legislature, and soon moved to the U.S. Congress. When he became Speaker of the House of Representatives in 1977, he worked with a fellow Democrat, Jimmy Carter, in the White House. Tip and Carter were not especially friendly, however.

What was Tip O'Neill's most famous hour?

It was in adversity—not success—that Tip O'Neill (1912–1994) won the greatest applause. In 1980, Republican Ronald Reagan won the White House from Jimmy Carter, and eight years of Republican dominance in Washington commenced. Reagan and O'Neill came from rather different backgrounds, and they had very different priorities. Reagan intended to cut back government—which he saw as much of the problem—and O'Neill wanted government to play the role of intermediary between business and labor.

Fortunately, Reagan and Tip O'Neill liked one another personally. Though they contested fiercely in the political arena, the two men could both unbend and enjoy each other's company, sometimes at the White House. On one matter the two men became bitter, however, and that was the Big Dig. Three times, the U.S. Congress passed the funding measure; only on the third attempt did Congress muster the two-thirds majority necessary to overcome the presidential veto.

Why did Reagan and Tip O'Neill contest so fiercely over the Big Dig?

Intended to revitalize downtown Boston, the Big Dig was conceptualized in the early 1980s. A great deal of federal money was needed to bring the project into reality, and Tip O'Neill naturally fought for what

The Cambridge-born Tip O'Neill was speaker of the House from 1977 to 1987.

255

he believed would be good for Boston. To Reagan—the fiscally conservative Republican—the Big Dig was purely a Massachusetts concern, and he felt that the taxpayers of that state should foot the bill.

Tip O'Neill retired from Congress in 1988, leaving a legacy as broad as his shoulders. Ronald Reagan departed Washington, D.C., in 1989, confident that his legacy had reshaped the American political landscape. Both men were products of their times, and both fought for what they saw as the right cause.

GOVERNOR DUKAKIS

How did a second-generation Greek immigrant become heir to the Massachusetts political leadership?

If one asked Michael S. Dukakis, he was no one's heir: he accomplished it on his own.

Born in Brookline, Dukakis (1933–) was an excellent student at Swarthmore College. He served in the U.S. Infantry, and then turned to politics. By the early 1970s, he was the major hope for Massachusetts Democrats, a liberal with a progressive agenda, whose last name was *not* Kennedy. Dukakis won election as Massachusetts governor in 1976, and then again in 1982. He showed himself a solid, middle-of-the-road politician, whose rather boring personal habits (he was the soul of convention) contrasted with his lightning-fast brain.

Dukakis did not invent the Massachusetts miracle—as it was called—but he was in position to take advantage of it. Between 1982 and 1988, hi-tech companies poured billions of dollars into Massachusetts, most of which ended up in five-story office buildings along Route 128. Boston did not participate fully in the enormous run to prosperity, but it was not too far behind. Dukakis trumpeted this as he announced his candidacy for president of the United States in 1988.

Yet another Bostonian running for president? Does Boston hold the record?

It does indeed. John Adams, John Quincy Adams, and John Kennedy all hailed from Boston, and several other men from that city have tried to win the White House.

At the beginning of the campaign, most prognosticators wrote Dukakis off, saying he was too short, too ethnic (Greek), and not interesting enough to be a real candidate. Dukakis confounded them all, beating

Michael Dukakis campaigning in 1988.

several other candidates, including Reverend Jesse Jackson to win the Democratic presidential nomination. When the Democrats held their national convention in July, Dukakis held a ten-point advantage over Vice-President George H. W. Bush. Ted Kennedy gave a riveting speech at the convention, deriding Bush as an absentee vice-president who had not been around for the major policy initiatives of the Reagan administration (*"Where was George?"* Kennedy bellowed). That was the high point of the campaign, however.

What went wrong with the Dukakis campaign for president in 1988?

Just about everything. Dukakis made the foolish mistake of being photographed in a U.S. Army tank (he just did not have a military presence). He also stumbled badly in the first presidential debate, seeming too cerebral and calm. Worst of all, however, was that Dukakis did not strike back against a set of attack ads, all revolving around the release, or furlough, of a Massachusetts prisoner. While on furlough, Willie Horton attacked and raped a woman; the Bush campaign exploited this time and again, suggesting that Dukakis was asleep at the switch when important decisions were made.

Not until the final three weeks of the campaign did Dukakis strike back. He finally accepted the label of liberal, saying he was a liberal in the tradition of John F. Kennedy and Franklin D. Roosevelt. It was too little, too late. Dukakis won a total of ten states, but he was simply swamped in the Electoral College and George Bush swept to victory and the White House.

How frequently was Boston mentioned in the political debates of 1988?

Michael Dukakis, naturally, touted the Massachusetts miracle, as evidence that post-industrial states could achieve new levels of prosperity. Vice-President Bush had a Boston quip of his own, however. On a campaign trip to Boston, Bush gestured to Boston Harbor, and asked Governor Dukakis to clean up the environmental mess. There was just enough truth in the accusation—a thimbleful—that Bush could claim victory in this particular exchange.

What Vice President Bush did not mention—and perhaps he was wise not to—was the environmental risk Boston experienced on a daily basis. This was thanks not to Governor Dukakis or his administration, but to a changing energy market. Bostonians, and New Englanders, had become keener on natural gas in the previous decade, and several shiploads filled with the combustible gas passed through Boston Harbor each day. In 1978, *60 Minutes* ran a special program on the danger posed to hundreds of thousands of Boston residents. Though they knew of the danger, Bostonians did not pay the matter much attention.

Could the results have been different? Could Dukakis have won?

Very likely not. 1988 was a good year for Republicans all around, and Dukakis was swimming against the stream. He made a rather poor candidate, and later was lambasted in political circles. On the positive side, Dukakis never took his defeat that hard. He seemed to be that rare man in American politics, a stoic. In later years, Dukakis taught political science at Northeastern University.

SENATOR KERRY

Was it even remotely possible that Massachusetts would find another man to run for the presidency?

There are times when it seems ludicrous that one state would present so many men for serious consideration. If one draws a straight line between the Adams family compound in Quincy and the Kennedy birthplace in Brookline, and includes the birthplaces of Michael Dukakis and Ted Kennedy, it seems as if Massachusetts has it all over the other states. There was yet another Bostonian who wished the nation's top job, however: his name was John F. Kerry.

Born in Colorado, John F. Kerry (1943–) went to private schools in Massachusetts, to Yale University, and then to Harvard Business School. Wherever he went, Kerry was noticed for his height (six-foot-four), intelligence, and extraordinary ambition. A fine speaker when he exerted himself, and an excellent athlete, Kerry seemed well-positioned to take at least a section of the political mantle once enjoyed by the Kennedys (he briefly dated one of the Kennedy sisters).

How did Kerry rise in the Democratic Party?

He was a member of the legislature, and then lieutenant-governor under Michael Dukakis. Given that "The Duke" was an uninspiring presence, it was natural that Kerry would receive a lot of attention, and he made the most of it. Upon winning election to the U.S. Senate, Kerry became one of the most reliably liberal votes in the Senate, right alongside his good friend Edward Kennedy.

In 1990, as the United States contemplated war with Iraq, Senator Kerry gave a lengthy speech on the floor of the U.S. Senate. As a Vietnam veteran, he spoke with special knowledge, he said. Everyone knew that 57,000 Americans had died in Vietnam, Kerry declared; much less-known was that almost twice that number had committed suicide in the decade and a half since the war ended. Kerry and the Democrats did not win this particular debate, but Kerry's speech heralded his arrival as one of the young leaders of the party.

John Kerry was a U.S. senator representing Massachusetts from 1985 until he was named U.S. secretary of state in 2013.

How did Kerry rise to become the Democratic nominee in 2004?

2004 was a year in which the political scene was particularly disheartening. Americans were deeply divided over the progress of the war in Iraq, and President George W. Bush was neither a good speaker nor particularly empathic. This seemed like the right year for John Kerry to run. He ran into plenty of difficulties, however. Vermont Senator Howard Dean was much more attractive at first, and it seemed at times as if the Kerry campaign would run out of energy, swamped by sheer boredom. Kerry was nothing if not persistent, however, and he prevailed in the primaries to secure the Democratic nomination.

Perhaps the major reason that voters sided with Kerry was that he was a legitimate war hero. He had served in Vietnam, and won several medals. This was good news to Democrats, who feared being boxed out by Republicans on national security issues. Kerry understood the importance of his medals, and his acceptance speech at the national convention began with, "Lieutenant John F. Kerry, reporting for duty!"

What went wrong in the early part of the 2004 campaign?

John Kerry and his running mate, John Edwards, seemed in good shape. But a series of political attack ads, which suggested he was not a hero, and that he despised his own country, reversed the situation. Kerry proved singularly unable to hit back. Perhaps he believed his war record spoke for itself, but he would surely have done better to respond.

The two presidential debates showcased very different political styles. Incumbent President George W. Bush was dismissive of both his opponent and the process; Senator Kerry was respectful but impressive, as he marshaled tons of data in his responses to questions. Most observers believed that Kerry won both debates, though not by commanding margins.

How did the election of 2004 turn out?

Most informed Americans knew that the race would be close, and that the final result might depend on who won the state of Ohio. As it turned out, incumbent George W. Bush won the popular vote by 51%-48% and by a squeaker in the Electoral College, with Ohio making all the difference. Many Kerry supporters demanded he ask for a recount in Ohio, but Kerry demurred. For the third time in twenty-four years, a Massachusetts man had come close, but had not made it to the White House.

Could it have been different? Did Kerry use his Boston connections to the maximum extent?

Yes, Kerry could have won under slightly different circumstances. No, he did not employ his Boston connections, precisely because he feared being branded as a typical Massachusetts "tax-and-spend liberal."

GOVERNOR ROMNEY

Was Mitt Romney a native of Massachusetts?

No. Born in Michigan, he was the son of the very popular Republican Governor George Romney (1907–1995), who made an abortive run for the Republican nomination in 1968. Mitt Romney grew up in Michigan, but some of his most formative years were spent on missionary trails. Like most young Mormons, he left home at an early age to proselytize in foreign nations. Even at this early stage, one could see something special in Mitt Romney. Blessed with extreme good looks and a charming demeanor, he was a very charismatic man.

Later in life, Mitt Romney (1947–) moved to Massachusetts, where he became president and CEO of Bain Capital Inc. a company that specialized in taking over failing companies, putting them right side up, and then selling them for considerable profit. Mitt Romney's personal wealth soared during the 1980s: he was one of those that truly profited from the so-called "Massachusetts miracle."

What led Mitt Romney to challenge Ted Kennedy for the Senate seat in 1994?

In part it was arrogance: Romney seemed to think he could accomplish anything. No previous Republican contender had even come close to unseating Ted Kennedy. But 1994 was a Republican year, and Mitt did well in the debates. What weakened him going down the stretch was the enormous attachment many Massachusetts voters felt for the Kennedys. Even if Ted was the least impressive of the three brothers, he still reminded many people of John and Robert. Romney did well enough in the final vote, however, to persuade many that he was a rising star of the Republican Party. Wisely, he did not make another attempt for statewide office until 2004, when he announced his candidacy for governor of Massachusetts.

This attempt was less quixotic than the previous. Massachusetts loved the Kennedys, but it had a strange penchant for electing Republican governors to preside over a heavily Democratic legislature. Romney won convincingly, and took office in 2003.

Mitt Romney served as governor of Massachusetts from 2003 to 2007.

How did Mitt Romney and Ted Kennedy become political allies?

Virtually no one expected it. The two had fought a rather bitter senate campaign in 1994. But politics makes strange bedfellows, and in 2005, Romney and the ageing Ted Kennedy joined forces to bring about the

2006 Massachusetts Health Care Reform Law Designed to ensure that most state residents had health insurance, the program was one of the first of its kind, and—by most measures—was considered a success. Like so many other things in Massachusetts politics, however, the initial cost was soon surpassed, and the taxpayers picked up an ever-larger bill.

Ted Kennedy was at Governor Romney's elbow as the health care bill was signed, and Romney used this to trumpet his bipartisan ways; by 2007, it was obvious he wanted to make a run for the presidency. Choosing not to run for governor again, Romney concentrated on the Republican primaries, and soon became embattled in a fierce set of political fights.

How badly did Romney stumble in the 2008 primary season?

Critics liked to point out how much money Romney spent to win a total of three primaries, and then come in second or third in most of the others. Arizona Senator John McCain won the Republican nomination, and Romney was consigned to the sidelines. But when John McCain lost the 2008 general election to Democrat Barack Obama, Romney began to speak of another run.

How did Romney do in the Republican primaries of 2012?

He was a much-improved candidate, but it was generally admitted that it was the weakness of the field in 2012 that allowed him to advance toward the nomination. Throughout the process, Romney displayed some real strength. His family was Kennedy-esque in good looks and energy. Romney had real difficulty connecting with the average voter, however. It was, in part, his incredible wealth, and also thanks to an enduring aloofness. While Romney had

---

How rich was Mitt Romney?

Though it was seldom discussed, the Romney family wealth was just as large as that of the Kennedys, and it had been gained in an even shorter period of time. Some estimates put Romney's overall wealth at $700 million, some even higher. As the 2000 presidential campaign approached, it was apparent that Romney had the deepest pockets—by far—of any candidate.

Yet just as the nomination seemed to be his for the taking, Romney stumbled. He made some unfortunate remarks just ahead of the Iowa caucuses, and when asked about his record on civil rights, he mistakenly claimed that he watched as his father marched "with" Martin Luther King in the 1960s. When interviewers demonstrated that he had not been present, Romney stumbled in explaining the difference between literally being present and his figurative presence (presumably from the television set). Romney's inability to admit that he misspoke cost him numerous voters, just as the campaign season began.

a great smile, there seemed to be little behind it. In a year when they did not expect to unseat incumbent President Obama, Republicans elected Romney as their nominee.

Like John Kennedy, decades earlier, Mitt Romney faced questions about his religion. Would he be loyal to the Mormon Church—officially the Church of Jesus Christ of Latter-day Saints—or to the nation's interests, some people asked? Romney never addressed these questions as successfully as Kennedy had in 1960, but the national mood was different, and many young voters, especially, affirmed that religion made little difference when choosing a new president of the United States.

What was the match-up between Obama and Romney like?

It was interesting. The voters saw a relatively young African American with ties to Boston and Cambridge because of his days at Harvard Law School, and a relatively older Anglo-American, whose ties to the Boston area were established during his thirties and forties. Both men played on their associations to major East Coast cities, but neither did much campaigning in Boston or Massachusetts because they knew the outcome. That liberal Massachusetts would vote for Barack Obama was close to a certainty.

The televised debates were a little disappointing. Both Obama and Romney were such cerebral personalities that the national audience seldom got a good feel for what the person was like. And in a situation like this in which neither candidate connected especially well, the voters chose to stay with what they knew: in this case, Barack Obama. He won the general election by a convincing popular vote of 54 percent, and he won handily in the Electoral College.

After the Election of 2012, did anyone point to other Boston—or Massachusetts—affiliated politicians?

For once, there seemed to be a dearth of likely candidates for the national level. But given the Bay State's incredible success record where presidential politics were concerned, no one was about to write off Massachusetts. Since the founding of the nation, Massachusetts had provided four presidents—John Adams, John Quincy Adams, Calvin Coolidge, and John Kennedy—and in the brief space between 1988 and 2012, it provided three serious challengers for the office: Michael Dukakis, John F. Kerry, and Mitt Romney.

THE BULGERS

How could two men of such different character come from the same family?

This question has been asked many times. It seems strange that a highly respected Massachusetts politician William Bulger would be the younger brother of the notorious murderer James J. "Whitey" Bulger, who was number one on the FBI's most wanted list. But such are the incongruities of family, whether in Massachusetts or elsewhere.

Whose career comes first?

It is easier to commence with the career of William Bulger (1934–). Born in Dorchester, he was the third of six children born to Irish-American parents. William Bulger graduated from Boston College High School, and started his studies at Boston College before going to serve in the Korean War. Returning home after the war, Bulger graduated first from Boston College and then Boston College Law School. He was clearly a man on the way up, and the voters of South Boston elected him to the Massachusetts House of Representatives in 1960.

In 1970, Bulger ran for and won election to the Massachusetts Senate, where he spent the majority of his long career in public service. Bulger came to be speaker of the Massachusetts Senate almost by accident, but once there, he established an iron grip over that legislative body, becoming the single most effective Boston politician since Mayor James Michael Curley. The two men were frequently compared in terms of political skill, but not in terms of charm: Bulger did not have Mayor Curley's easygoing, surefooted style.

Why did William Bulger leave his comfortable position as speaker of the Massachusetts Senate?

His position was comfortable because he made it so—chasing out virtually all opposition. But in his early sixties, Bulger was offered another type of job, and one which—incidentally or not—had a higher pay grade. Bulger was nominated and then approved to become president of the University of Massachusetts. The general feeling was that the former speaker would know how to bring the "bacon" home to the higher education system.

Bulger did reasonably well in his tenure as president of the University of Massachusetts. In 2003, he stepped down after pressure was applied by Governor Mitt Romney (this was one of the few times Bulger experienced the kind of political pressure he was so skillful in applying to opponents). The reason was that Bulger had refused to cooperate with the FBI during the investigation of his elder brother, Whitey Bulger.

How serious was the career of Whitey Bulger?

Born in Everett, Massachusetts, James J. "Whitey" Bulger (1929–) was one of the

A mugshot of Whitey Bulger taken when he was being sentenced to serve time at Alcatraz.

most successful and notorious criminals of the late twentieth century. Just how he got started in racketeering, prostitution, and blackmail is not well established, but by the 1970s, he was a prime informant for the FBI, which managed to bring down a well-established criminal family in Charlestown, Massachusetts. The FBI gave Whitey Bulger a pass for a long time, but in 1994 he went into hiding when he learned his arrest was imminent. It was no small matter that he fled at the very time when his younger brother was tapped to be president of the University of Massachusetts.

How did Whitey Bulger manage to hide out for so long?

For sixteen long years, Bulger kept out of view: for ten of those years he was on the FBI's most wanted list. Bostonians—as well as the rest of the nation—were astonished to learn in June 2011 that Bulger had been captured by the FBI in San Diego. For more than a decade, he and his longtime girlfriend had managed to keep out of view, primarily by using cash rather than checks, and by avoiding cameras. Neighbors claimed they had seen no suspicious behavior on the part of Bulger or his girlfriend, but the FBI found a treasure trove of cash, as well as plenty of guns. The irony is that Bulger was captured without a fight.

The FBI brought Bulger to Boston. Part of Boston Harbor had to be closed in order for the agents to bring Whitey Bulger to the waterfront federal courthouse; his arraignment was one of the most spectacular sights in Boston (rivaled only by the arrest and deportation of Anthony Burns in 1854). In 2013, Bulger was found guilty on thirty-one crimes, and involved in eleven murders. He received several life sentences.

COLLEGES AND UNIVERSITIES

How many schools, colleges, and universities are there in Greater Boston?

More than in any other American city. A large number of people that fall in love with Boston are those who attend a college or university there, arriving at the age of eighteen, and despite suffering some homesickness, sticking it out to graduate four years later. The twice annual student arrival—first in early September and then in mid-January—is one of the biggest events in Boston's year.

Can you provide some example of the depth and scope of the schools and programs?

Let's begin with an alphabetical sample, and then move to the specifics. Andover Newton Theological School is first in most lists of Boston colleges and universities. One of the oldest and most distinguished of American seminaries, Andover Newton was established in 1807. Moving just a bit down the list we find Babson College. Located in Babson Park, which is itself part of the town of Wellesley, Babson was founded by millionaire Roger Babson (1875–1967), one of the first and most successful of all American statisticians. Babson holds the dubious distinction of being one of the few economists to predict the Great Depression of 1929–1941, and he did so with astonishing accuracy. And now, moving to the third letter of the alphabet, we find Cambridge College, one of the newest and most successful of the many Boston educational institutions. A combination of business school and community resource, Cambridge College has been turning heads for more than a generation.

Has it always been this way? Has Boston always been number one in higher education?

Actually, Boston has long been number one in high school education as well. The Newton public schools are considered one of the best in the entire nation and the Boston Latin

School is the country's oldest high school. Of course, it's not always a hit or a home run. Quite a few youngsters have gone to Boston to attend college, decided it was not for them, and gone on to thrive in other pursuits. Even so, if one looks for inspiration for one's youngsters, a college education in Boston is usually considered one of the safest of bets.

For how long has Harvard University been the nation's premier collegiate institution?

Yale graduates would, doubtless, contest Harvard's position as number one, but to Harvard men (and there were no Harvard women till the 1970s) it was always obvious that their college was at the top. Not only does Harvard possess enormous strength in its professoriate, but the libraries and museums are simply unmatched. A serious scholar could easily spend a half-century attempting to learn the bulk of what was available at Harvard, and in the end he or she would surely conclude that it was a hopeless task.

For example, if one is interested in botany, Harvard's collections are unmatched. If one prefers zoology, the museum started by Louis Agassiz has no rival. And if one prefers to go through long boxes of archival material, the Harvard University archives seem to go on forever.

How many great names from arts and letters are connected with Harvard?

This list would go on for many chapters. But the most sensible way to demonstrate Harvard's greatness is to make a shorter list of those that managed—even if for a few brief years—to be "on top" of the knowledge in the field.

Samuel Eliot Morison (1887–1976) is at or near the top of almost everyone's list. Born and raised in Boston, he went the short distance across the river to attend Harvard, and graduated in 1908. From that basic beginning, Morison became "Mr. Harvard" during his long tenure as professor, researcher, and prolific author. Anyone who examines Morison's three-volume history of Harvard knows that he is in the hands of a great talent. One of the few that could puzzle out the originals in Latin and Greek, Morison also found time to author Pulitzer-Prize winning books on Christopher Columbus and John Paul Jones (he was working on Ferdinand Magellan at the time of his death). Thanks to a strong connection with President Franklin D. Roosevelt, who was also a member of the Class of 1908, Morison became the official historian of U.S. naval operations during World War II. Though he traveled far and wide, Morison

Though S. E. Morison is indeed "Mr. Harvard," this statue is on Commonwealth Avenue in downtown Boston.

lived in the same third-floor house all of his life. His long career is a testament to the love that many Bostonians have for their city, and for the college just across the Charles River.

Is there another such person who left an indelible imprint?

Indeed, there are so many. But one of the first that comes to mind is Louis Agassiz, the father of American zoology and geology. Born in Switzerland in 1807, Agassiz first came to the United States in the 1840s. He rose to become professor of zoology and geology at Harvard, and was instrumental in founding several of Harvard's world-renowned museums.

HARVARD

How is it that Boston—and Cambridge—came to have the first American college?

In retrospect, it is not that surprising. The Puritans prided themselves on religious purity, and they believed it derived from reading the Bible (as opposed to their Catholic foes who read the Bible in Latin). The Puritans were the culmination of nearly a century-long tradition in which various Europeans worked to translate the Bible into their different languages. So it makes sense that the Puritans would want a college, one to turn out any number of ministers.

Harvard University was established in 1636. Since then, it has been not only a highly respected institution of learning, but also a great influence on the history of the United States.

What are the specifics of the founding of Harvard College?

John Harvard (1607–1638)—whose magnificent statue greets tourists in Harvard Yard—left all of his books and a fair amount of money for the founding of a college, and the new institution was named in his honor. To be sure, the college had yet to find teachers, or even an administrative center, but the first class entered in 1637 and graduated in 1642. They are known as the Immortal Nine, the first graduates of Harvard: Benjamin Woodbridge, George Downing, John Bulkley, William Hubbard, Samuel Bellingham, John Wilson, Henry Saltonstall, Tobias Barnard, and Nathaniel Brewster.

John Harvard, who died tragically young, left a bequest to establish Harvard College.

Nearly all of these men went on to successful careers, but the two that stand out the most are George Downing and William Hubbard. The former went back to Old England, and was a renowned diplomat (Downing Street in London is named for him). The latter became the "teacher" or minister at Ipswich, and he was the author of a number of books, principally having to do with early New England.

Nine graduates is such a small beginning. Did the number of graduates rise soon thereafter?

No. There were years, such as 1644 and 1648, during which there were no graduates. But the trend was definitely upward, and the names of the graduates serve almost as a guide to the history of the Massachusetts Bay Colony. Names such as Angier, Rowlandson, Moodey, Crosby, and Mather are found among the early lists. The original class of 1642 was not surpassed in terms of size, until 1661, when there were twelve graduates.

During the first century, the Harvard class was arranged in order of social distinction, rather than academic achievement. The concept of the "gentleman C's" (giving a

---

Who is the first Harvard graduate to have been killed in the service of his country?

In 1690 Daniel Denison, who graduated in July of that year, enlisted in the naval force sent against Québec City. He sailed with the fleet in August, and did not return. Though we have no specifics of what happened to Denison, he is honored as the first Harvard graduate to fall in combat.

passing grade to a failing student from a wealthy, donor family) was alive and well in the seventeenth century.

What subjects were taught at Harvard in those early days?

The curriculum was definitely dated: aspects of it traced all the way back to the Middle Ages. Latin and Greek were considered the most important subjects with Hebrew and Bible studies not far behind. For its first century and a bit more, Harvard was primarily intended to produce ministers for the Commonwealth of Massachusetts. The men that graduated from Harvard in those early days tended to live long lives, and to be renowned as the minister of Springfield, the minister of Westfield, and so forth.

One of the best examples of the well-rounded Harvard man is Edward Taylor (1642–1729), who earned his bachelor's degree in 1671. Taylor went to the frontier town of Westfield, where he served as both the minister and the resident physician for decades. One of his few breaks from duty was when he traveled to Boston and Cambridge to witness Harvard graduations. When Taylor died in 1729, he had earned a master's degree, and was known as one of the most successful of all country parsons. What was not known, and did not become known for another century and a half, is that Taylor was also one of the finest poets early New England produced. His "Meditation" poems, which he composed before each supper, have been studied ever since they were first discovered in the late nineteenth century.

Is Edward Taylor from the same social group as Samuel Sewall, the longtime judge and diarist?

They were cut almost from the same bolt of cloth. Both men graduated in 1671, and they kept in touch for the rest of their lives. If Taylor provides our knowledge of the inner life, especially where poetry and religion are concerned, then Sewall gives us a big window through which to see the day-to-day secular life of Boston. Sewall's diary, which is preserved in the Massachusetts Historical Society on Boylston Street, informs us of military, political, and social events. He seems to have been invited to almost every major celebration, and to have attended virtually all the funerals of the rich and powerful. Even beyond that, however, Sewall had the common touch. He seems to have been on good terms with just about everyone, except for the occasional tenant who refused to pay the rent (Sewall was a major landowner as well as shipping merchant).

When did Harvard begin to change its curriculum?

The great changes in science, and in physics especially, took place in England, France, and Germany between about 1675 and 1725, but Harvard did not adjust its curriculum until the 1750s. Leading the way in the new scientific knowledge was Professor John Winthrop IV, the great-great-grandson of Boston founder John Winthrop. In 1768, Winthrop made a pioneering observation of the Transit of Venus (this was accomplished on a ship off the coast of Newfoundland) and from that date forward, Harvard began to catch up with its European contemporaries.

As for America, Harvard had no competition until 1693, when the College of William and Mary was founded in Virginia, and it took until 1701 for Yale to make the crude beginnings of what later became a great university. Therefore, as late as 1775—the year the American Revolution commenced—Harvard was still the great college in the American colonies.

HARVARD IN TRANSITION

How many students graduated Harvard in 1775? And, did any of them become Loyalists?

Harvard had a bumper crop of forty graduates in 1775, and rather few of these young men rose to become either prominent Patriots or noteworthy Loyalists. Harvard was academically liberal in 1775, but still socially conservative: only recently had the college abandoned the practice of listing class members by social rank. Even the most well-to-do of Harvard men recognized that Boston and Massachusetts were headed toward independence, however, and Harvard did not become a bastion of Tory sentiments.

In 1783, the year the Peace of Paris ensured American independence, Harvard graduated thirty young men, many of whom went on to lives of social and economic distinction. Rather few of the Harvard graduates of this time went into the ministry: a practice of Harvard men going into business, long-distance trade most especially, had been born.

How do we know so much about the weather in Boston in August?

Boston has always had plenty of record keepers: the task seemed to cross the Atlantic with the Puritans. But thanks to a handful of men who attended one Harvard commencement after another, we have an unusually good idea of the weather in Boston and Cambridge at that time of year.

Reverend John Pierce (1773–1849) graduated from Harvard in 1794, and proceeded to attend no fewer than forty-six commencements. Of course it helped that he was the pastor of a church in nearby Brookline: he did not have to travel far. Through Pierce's diary of the various commencements he attended, we have an unparalleled view of the weather of that time.

What does John Pierce's diary reveal to us about the weather?

That it was—much like today—extremely variable. For a sampling of commencements, we begin with 1808. Pierce comments that the commencement on August 31 suffered from extreme dust, there having been but one rain shower in the previous four weeks. Something similar was recorded for August 25, 1813, when Pierce attended his twenty-ninth commencement. In 1815, when the commencement was held on August 30, the day was clear, but unusually hot. And even in 1818, when Pierce attended his thirty-fourth consecutive Harvard commencement, he recorded that "There having been only small showers for five weeks, it was exceedingly dusty." Looking for some variety from the general theme, we turn forward, all the way to 1826, the year when Pierce attended his forty-second commencement, and finally we see an alternative, "The day was uncommonly fine. For the last twenty days it had rained in every one but three; so that the dust in the sandy soil was completely laid."

One thing that Reverend John Pierce did not experience was the great change that takes place today. Harvard commencement in our time is usually held on the last of June or the first of July, and the parents of the graduates marvel at the great beauty of the grassy lawns. What they do not know is that just three days later, when all the students have departed, the Physical Plant of the Harvard Corporation immediately begins to tear up those same grounds in order to remove and replace outworn pipes. The grass is then reseeded, and when parents return on the first of September, they find things looking unusually fine.

Did Harvard have any real academic competition in the early decades of the nineteenth century?

Neither Harvard nor Yale was very large, but between them they practically monopolized the best high school graduates. The day of the major state colleges and universities did not arrive till the decade that followed the Civil War.

When did the Hasty Pudding Club come into being?

The first program, conducted by members of the Class of 1846, was *Bombastes Furioso*. The tickets declared that it was for the "Benefit of the Alligator." The play featured Artaxominous, the King of Utopia; Fusbos, his minister; Bombastes; and Distaffina. Only four actors were needed to bring this production to the stage. But if one moves forward a full decade, to the year 1854, then there are no fewer than four plays featured: *Boots at the Swan, Milliner's Holiday, Two Bonnycastles,* and *Who'll Lend Me a Wife?* No fewer than thirty-two actors were required for these productions, and though numerous parts

The building formerly owned by the Hasty Pudding Club was bought by Harvard University; the Hasty Pudding Theatricals still make use of it, however.

were female, the actors themselves were all men. Other featured pieces included productions of *Othello* in 1869 and *My Young Wife and My Old Umbrella* in 1871.

Did Harvard make much noise during the Civil War?

Harvard was extremely patriotic during the Civil War: many of its finest young men went off to serve, and some of them never returned. One of those who did return, and who went on to become one of the icons of Harvard, Cambridge, and Boston was Oliver Wendell Holmes (Class of 1866). The son of a physician, poet, and man of letters, Holmes Jr. served with distinction at the Battle of Antietam, where he was wounded. His father went looking for him in a story made famous by a contribution to *Harpers Weekly*, called "My Hunt after the Captain."

The really big changes for Harvard lay just ahead. Charles W. Eliot (1834–1926), member of the Class of 1861, did not serve in the Civil War: he was in Germany, studying aspects of higher education. Soon after he returned from Europe, Eliot became the twenty-sixth president of Harvard, and, it is safe to say, the institution was never the same again.

Would Eliot's former classmates—those of the Class of 1862—have recognized the institution thirty years later?

Many of them, of course, did come back to Harvard, for Commencement Days especially. The grounds looked similar, and the physical setting was not greatly different. Inside the classroom and the laboratory, however, a true revolution was taking place.

Eliot recruited the brightest and best of America's young intellectuals, bringing them to Harvard. Notable among them were William James, who was the first tenured professor of philosophy, and his brother, the novelist Henry James. Also Charles Eliot Norton—a distant relation of the Harvard president—and George Santayana, among others.

Did Harvard play an important role in World War I?

Many young Harvard men—both recent graduates and some that were in their thirties—served in World War I. Not only was it seen as patriotic, but the typical Harvard graduate of that time would have likely thought it shameful to attempt to escape service. Of course there were some exceptions to the rule, but generally speaking, Harvard men played a considerable role, especially in the first deployment of the International Red Cross.

One of the oddest anomalies of military service was that of Samuel Eliot Morison, member of the Class of 1907. Though his academic career was already advancing, Morison enlisted for duty in World War I, and served as an infantry private. By odd circumstances, Morison advanced so much in the public esteem that when World War II arrived, he was made an honorary rear-admiral, and given the task of writing the official history of the U.S. Navy in that conflict. Morison therefore became the only person to have been a private in the First World War and an admiral in the Second.

How important was Harvard to the nation during the Great Depression?

President Franklin D. Roosevelt created a loosely affiliated group of advisors that was called the "Brains Trust." As a Harvard man, FDR clearly enjoyed having Harvard graduates close to him; he hired plenty of young men from Yale and Columbia, too. The beginning of the Great Depression was one of the lowest times for Harvard because neither the university nor its many famed graduates had any answer to the peril of the times. But as FDR and his cabinet established one New Deal program after another, Harvard became to be seen as part of the solution. And World War II did nothing to diminish Harvard's importance; rather, the school on the Charles became more famous than ever.

Was there any fear that the G.I. Bill of 1944 would diminish Harvard's enrollment?

This seemed distinctly possible. Young men coming home from the war might well have looked to other schools, and diminished Harvard's pool of applications. Instead, Harvard participated in the G.I. Bill, and thereby gained more applicants than ever.

The golden age of Harvard was in the 1950s. This was a time when Harvard undergraduates looked on their professors with admiration and sometimes adulation, and when the words of any Harvard bulletin or program were perceived as nearly indisputable.

What happened to Harvard during the 1960s?

The place looked the same, but the attitudes were distinctly different. Many famous, even renowned, academicians presided at Harvard as ever before, but the student body was skeptical of many of their pronouncements. Harvard Yard was the scene of many youth protests throughout the 1960s, as students demonstrated against the complacency of the elder generation. Of course, the same can be said for many other campuses around the nation; the difference being that the parents of these Harvard students paid increasingly steep tuition.

Where does Harvard come by its wealth?

The basis for its wealth was laid during the mid-nineteenth century. The Civil War did much to advance the cause of Harvard, that of its endowment most especially. But it was the explosive growth of mutual funds throughout the late twentieth century that saw Harvard gain the extreme wealth it possesses today. As of 2015, the Harvard endowment stands at roughly $37.6 billion. To put that in perspective, the Harvard endowment is greater than that of all the other major Ivy League colleges and universities put together.

Is it really possible for a child of working-class parents to attend Harvard?

It is probably more possible than at any earlier time in the nation's history. One simply has to be top-notch in practically all the categories that Harvard considers. In 2015, there were 35,000 applicants of whom roughly 1,950 were accepted, for an overall acceptance rate of six percent. Assuming that this daunting statistic does not turn one off, there is always the second matter of how to pay the $45,000 in tuition and fees. The large majority of students who make it to Harvard, however, do not fail or turn away because of funding: there are vast scholarship opportunities.

Is there any area of the arts and humanities or the sciences and engineering in which Harvard does not excel?

There was a brief time—in the early 1990s—when it seemed Harvard might lag in one area: that of generating new ideas in the computer industry. For a brief time, ambitious youngsters favored starting up companies of their own rather than attending Harvard. This changed by about 2005, however, and a Harvard education is now viewed as equal to a Stanford one, even where computer engineering is concerned.

What was the most ebullient part of Harvard's long story?

The Ivy League does not lack for ebullience: one only has to watch a Harvard-Yale game to witness the enthusiasm. But for sheer recklessness and joy, it is difficult to match the late 1960s, when Timothy Leary, professor of mathematics and drug enthusiast, spread the word that college students should "tune in" (to a higher consciousness), and "drop out" of the grind of classes, grades, and competition. Just how many Harvard students followed Leary's advice is unknown, but he surely had an effect on the 1960s generation.

Was there any "low" moment for Harvard in the twentieth century?

If so, it surely came in the late 1980s. Harvard was under increasing pressure from students and alumni to divest from South Africa. The university was also criticized for its cooperation with, first, the Carter Administration, and then the Reagan administration in the development of new weapons, primarily missiles. Harvard students expressed disenchantment with their school.

MIT

Given that Harvard had such a stellar, outstanding reputation, why was MIT necessary?

Up to the 1840s, Harvard was still primarily a vocational school for the training of Protestant ministers: the large majority of graduates became New England clergymen.

The beautiful campus of the Massachusetts Institute of Technology includes Building 10 and the Great Dome, shown here, which was constructed in 1916.

The founder of the Massachusetts Institute of Technology (hereafter referred to as MIT) believed it necessary for Boston to have a first-class technical school, one where the training of engineers and scientists would be the first priority.

William Barton Rogers (1804–1882) was the third son of an Irish refugee who arrived in Philadelphia in 1798. All four Rogers children attained a high degree of professional success. Rogers grew up in Philadelphia and Baltimore, and taught in Williamsburg and then Charlottesville (both in Virginia) before becoming a Bostonian in his thirties. Once he made the move north, Rogers became convinced that Boston needed more technically skilled graduates, and he wrote his first proposal for a technical school around 1846. Fifteen years passed before the Commonwealth of Massachusetts gave its approval, chartering what became the Massachusetts Institute of Technology.

Did MIT always occupy its current, very grand headquarters on the Charles River?

Even in an area accustomed to the hustle and bustle of Harvard Yard, there is something quite unusual about the solemnity and grandeur of MIT. The main campus is located right on the north side of the Charles River, and when one stands either atop the Prudential Center or the Hancock Tower, MIT occupies the central location, the area to which one's eyes are drawn. But the answer is no: for its first forty-nine years, MIT was located in buildings in what is now Copley Square.

Though MIT possessed its formal name right from the charter beginning in 1861, many people referred to it as "Boston Tech" during its first half-century. MIT was then located in a handful of rather large, four-story Victorian buildings in Copley Square. At that time, the Rogers Building, which was named for founder William Barton Rogers was the last imposing building on Boylston Street.

Did natural events play any role in the eventual relocation of MIT to the north side of the Charles River?

The Great Fire of Boston (see the chapter "Nineteenth-Century Boston") did not really harm MIT, but it came close enough that the surrounding area was devastated. MIT managed to recover from this disaster, but the school went through some very shaky financial times during its first three decades, and on several occasions it was rescued only by major financial gifts by leading Bostonians.

Rather than natural events, it was a major bequest by a man who wished his anonymity preserved that brought about the relocation to Cambridge. George Eastman (1854–1932) the founder of Eastman Kodak Company, purchased and then handed over roughly fifty acres of prime real estate to MIT, allowing for the move from the north side of Boston to the south side of Cambridge.

Is it true that Harvard wished to incorporate MIT?

Not once, not twice, but a total of five times, Harvard administrators attempted to persuade their MIT counterparts to join the great institution in Harvard Square. Harvard President Charles W. Eliot led the attempt on several occasions: he made his first attempt in the 1870s and his last in 1905. The history of higher education in America might not have been altered profoundly, but it would surely have been somewhat different if Harvard had ever succeeded in the attempt.

Speaking of Charles Eliot and Harvard, are there any great stories about his MIT counterpart?

Yes indeed. William Barton Rogers was as instrumental to the founding of MIT as Charles W. Eliot was to the rise of Harvard as a leading American university. Barton was there at the founding of MIT, but he resigned the presidency in 1870, only to return to the top post in 1878, at the request of the MIT trustees. Rogers was in the process of handing over the presidency

Charles W. Eliot was president of Harvard from 1869 to 1909.

a second time when he died, during a ceremony handing out degrees to the graduates, on May 30, 1882.

How big a difference was made by the shift from Copley Square to Cambridge?

In terms of physical space, the difference was obvious and immediate. MIT now had room to expand. Thanks to a handful of major bequests, MIT also launched the building of some truly magnificent quarters. The transition from Copley Square to Cambridge was formally made in June 1916. Though few of the graduates of that year realized it, their careers, and the fortunes of their alma mater, were about to be changed by American entry into World War I, which happened ten months later. MIT supplied a good many officers for the American effort in World War I; when World War II began, MIT would supply much of the technical know-how that resulted in the Allied victory.

Do many MIT students of our time know the long history of their school?

Given that MIT has a primary focus on the future, and that it is intimately involved with creating material structures for the twenty-first century, it is likely that rather few of the present-day students know much of their school's past. An MIT student will often reply to questions on that subject, declaring that it is the Harvard person's job to know the past, and that M.I.T students concentrate on the future.

But if one questions an archivist or MIT scholar, the answer is that the years when the school was called "Boston Tech" were extremely fruitful. During the forty-nine years it occupied the old quarters in Copley Square, MIT graduated a total of 6,602 young men (no women in those days), of whom 6,284 earned the bachelor of science degree, 289 earned a master of science degree, 3 earned a doctor of science degree, 23 earned a doctor of philosophy degree, and 3 graduated with a doctor of engineering degree.

When did MIT move in the direction of an alliance between government and industry?

Outgoing American president Dwight D. Eisenhower warned his fellow citizens of the dangers of the "military-industrial complex" in January 1961, but it had already been around for a full decade. World War II was the catalyst that brought about close cooperation between the United States government and a handful of Massachusetts corporations with MIT acting as the good shepherd of the process. A handful of significant inventions from MIT helped the Allied effort in World War II, and once the Cold War began, MIT was among the top three or four of all institutions of higher education that helped further the efforts of the military-industrial complex.

MIT students of the 1950s did not protest their school's affiliation with the government. The Cold War seemed so desperate a battle between the forces of communism and capitalism that the great majority of M.I.T students were solidly behind the government. It took the advent of the Vietnam War, a new concern on college campuses, to bring about the student protests that demanded change.

277

How different were the MIT students of the 1960s from those of the 1950s?

They were profoundly different from those of the 1950s. Both the casual dress (and long hair) and unconventional attitudes of the MIT students clashed with their rather conservative professors and the university administration. One can say that this was true of many colleges and universities of the 1960s, but it was more evident at MIT, where the typical student went from wearing a business suit to blue jeans. In November 1969, as American involvement in the Vietnam War neared its most controversial phase, a majority of MIT students went out "on strike" against the administration. MIT president Howard W. Johnson (1922–2009) bowed to the student pressure, and MIT divested itself of the so-called Instrumentation Laboratory, where many weapons systems had been developed. Johnson later wrote a telling memoir of his presidency, entitled *Holding the Center: Memoirs of a Life in Higher Education.*

Was this the first major success on the part of 1960s student protests?

No, but it was among the most meaningful of all their successes. MIT had long been a leader in developing weapons systems. The university held contracts for the development of the Polaris submarine, the Poseidon, and the Apollo (space) program. All those contracts had to be fulfilled, but no new ones were entered upon.

How important was MIT to the start of the computer revolution of the 1970s?

One can certainly argue that the University of California at Berkeley, and the start-up corporations of Silicon Valley were more important, but MIT led the way on the East Coast. Computer science entered the popular lexicon in the mid-1970s, and it became one of the most important programs of study at MIT during that latter part of that decade. Hundreds, perhaps thousands of MIT graduates have since made major contributions to the field of computer science, and the great network of high-tech firms just outside Boston—in the area of Route 128—have benefitted significantly.

When did MIT become well known for its number of Asian students?

As late as 1965, the typical MIT student was white, American-born, and male. The shift began in the 1970s, when a trickle of Japanese students arrived in Cambridge. They were followed by many of their countrymen, and by large numbers of Chinese.

BOSTON COLLEGE
AND BOSTON UNIVERSITY

Which is older: Boston College or Boston University?

They both date from the optimistic part of the nineteenth century, a time when Bostonians believed most future problems would be solved by the expansion of higher education. Officially founded in 1863 by the Jesuits, Boston College dates to1827, when Bishop Benedict Joseph Fenwick first held classes in his cathedral basement. Boston University was chartered in 1869, though its history goes back to 1839, when it was the Newbury Biblical Institute.

Boston College occupies a set of low hills in Newton, and the route of the Boston Marathon passes practically through the campus. Boston University is primarily located along the Charles River in West Boston, but the campus has allied schools throughout the Boston area.

A Jesuit bishop, Benedict Joseph Fenwick (1782–1846) founded Boston College.

What was Boston College like in its early years? Did the students experience any discrimination?

Founded by a Jesuit (a member of the Society of Jesus), Boston College was as bedrock Roman Catholic as an institution could be. There was no outright discrimination against the students of Boston College; rather, the old-line Boston Yankees looked down their nose at Boston College, saying it would never rival Harvard, or other institutions that dated back to the seventeenth century. This assumption has largely been proved wrong. While thousands of young college students doubtless would prefer to attend Harvard or MIT, they are not dismayed when an acceptable letter comes from Boston College or Boston University.

The Boston College curriculum in the first half-century of the school's existence was dictated by Roman Catholic beliefs. Both the professoriate and students suffered somewhat during the first half of the twentieth century, as old-line Catholic beliefs held back a certain amount of intellectual development. This changed dramatically in the 1960s. Enrollment grew from 2,700 in 1945 to nearly 10,000 in 1965.

Can one tell a B.U. student from a B.C. one?

At games, of course, one can do so from the colors (maroon and gold for B.C.; scarlet and white for B.U.). But away from the gym or football field, there is little difference between B.U. and B.C. students these days. Both come from an academic tradition that is liberal and progressive; both see Boston as the best city in the nation; and both aspire to the law, business, and science: in that order.

What was Boston University like in its early years? Was there an athletic rivalry with Boston College?

Boston University was decidedly Protestant in character and expression. B.U. profited more from the scientific and technological changes of the late nineteenth century than Boston College did. And yes, a lively athletic rivalry between the two schools developed by about the year 1900. Boston College usually defeated B.U. in football and basketball, while B.U. dominated in baseball and track.

OTHER SCHOOLS

What makes Northeastern University so different from other schools in the Greater Boston area?

It's the cop-op program. Northeastern students typically spend five years (not four) earning their degrees. The "co-op year" is the time these students spend in local businesses or government institutions, serving internships that help them gain jobs after graduation. Northeastern is also different from Boston University or Boston College, for example, in that it is entirely centered within the city of Boston. Northeastern students are perceived—rightly or wrongly—as the most hard-working college students in the area, and as the ones that like to party the most.

What are the most important numbers, or statistics, concerning Northeastern?

In 2015 there were 19,700 undergraduates and 13,300 graduate students. Tuition and fees came to $45,500, and room and board was another $23,000. These seemingly unsupportable numbers become more manageable when one realizes how much financial aid is available.

When did the Mass College of Pharmacy come into its own?

As one might expect, the rise of the pharmaceutical industry created new opportunities for the Massachusetts College of Pharmacy and Health Sciences (MCPHS). The 1980s were the decade that saw the sudden rise in demand for various medications. Located on Longwood Avenue, close to Kenmore Square and Fenway Park, the MCPHS is one of the best deals, from a financial point of view, to be found in higher education. MCPHS graduates rank at the very top of their fields in terms of earning power, a decade after graduation.

Why is the Fletcher School of Law and Diplomacy so little known?

This depends, to be sure, on the family one grows up in. For families with a tradition of foreign service or diplomacy, Fletcher is simply the school, even more important than Harvard. Undergraduates often arrive in Greater Boston not knowing the name of Fletcher: by the time they depart, they usually understand its importance.

Many, if not most, of the classes at Fletcher are taught by former diplomats and consuls: men and women who truly know the world of international diplomacy. The Fletcher program tends to turn out a well-rounded individual, one who is able to balance American interests with those of other parts of the world. Fletcher is proud of its tradition, which dates back to the Cold War, but it looks forward to an era of greater international cooperation.

LESSER–KNOWN SCHOOLS

Why is the New England School of Acupuncture such an important part of the educational landscape of Greater Boston?

Because Greater Boston residents are advocates of acupuncture. Perhaps this is because Chinatown has been an integral part of Boston for three generations; then again, it may be connected to the fact that Boston had a "China trade" dating all the way back to the 1790s. In either case, however, Bostonians regard acupuncture as one of the most efficacious of all medical treatments. To be sure, there are some medical hardliners who swear they will never even consider acupuncture as an alternative: for every one of these, there are at least three others who practically swear by their acupuncturists. The New England School of Acupuncture is in Newton.

Are there any "New Age" colleges or universities in Boston?

None of them actually use that label, but Lesley University, located in Cambridge, comes close to fitting the bill. Lesley, which had 1,492 undergraduates and 2,930 graduate students in 2015, has turned out more music teachers and expressive therapists in different modalities than almost any other school in New England.

What are some of the most highly regarded religious schools in the Boston area?

Andover Newton Theological School, which is located in Newton, is one of the oldest and most venerated of religious academies. Eastern Nazarene College in Quincy is also highly regarded. Plenty of others exist, including the Episcopal Divinity School in Cambridge and Gordon-Conwell Theological Seminary in Hamilton. One comes to appreciate the diversity by examining names such as the Hellenic College Holy Cross Greek Orthodox School of Theology in Newton. Boston is perceived as a very secular place, but there are pockets that are strongly religious.

What is the difference between Babson College and Bentley University?

They are only about three miles apart, and both are at the extreme western end of Greater Boston. Babson College is a relatively small school. Founded by Roger Babson (1875–1967), one of America's premier statisticians (he predicted the market crash of

1929), Babson turns out mathematical scholars who often go on to work at high-priced Wall Street firms. Once a Babson person, always one, they say, and Babson graduates are distinguished by hard work and low profiles.

Bentley University was founded about the same time, but it has advanced to much larger proportions. There are 4,200 undergraduates and 1,300 graduate students (as of 2015). Tuition and fees are roughly $44,000, and room and board come to another $14,500.

Why don't more Babson and Bentley graduates stay in the Boston area?

Quite a few do, but a majority of the best jobs available in their fields tend to be in Greater Manhattan. Babson and Bentley graduates, therefore, tend to remain New Englanders, but to live in the extreme southwestern part of the state of Connecticut.

Roger Babson, the founder of Babson College, was an economist who predicted the stock market crash of 1929.

282

MUSIC, RADIO, AND MUSEUMS

What was music in early Boston like?

The Puritans made plenty of music, but nearly all of it is lost to us. Their secular music was of the homemade variety, and their church music exists only in a handful of hymnals that have survived. We know, however, from the diary of Judge Samuel Sewall that most Puritan meeting houses (their name for churches) had a preceptor, who set the pitch, and presumably kept the choral group in line.

Where did the Puritans obtain their first hymnals?

They brought over one from Holland, published in 1613, but they soon wrote and printed their own, the Bay Psalm Book. Printed in Boston in 1640, this was one of the first books of Puritan New England.

Did the Puritans frown on music as something that might lead a person to the devil?

They expressed various thoughts on the subject. It's true that some of their leaders believed almost any type of self-expression—music included—was unnecessary and potentially harmful. At the same time, however, the Puritans were interested in keeping up with the times, and the Shakespearean era was filled with musical developments. Quite a few Puritans in Boston, therefore, frowned on music in a general way, while enjoying it in private.

Benjamin Franklin, born just about the time when the Puritan era yielded to the Yankee one, later wrote that his father was an accomplished violinist, and that music was one of the most enjoyable aspects of life on Milk (later Franklin) Street. We can say, however that music was not part of the public scene in Boston. When colonial soldiers marched off to combat, for example, they did not sing.

When did the first musical instruments cross the Atlantic?

There had to have been earlier shipments, or else the Franklins would not have had their violin, but the first record of musical instruments comes to us from diaries and ships' logs of the early eighteenth century. There were no music stores as yet, and these instruments were sold either in book stores or dry goods stores.

Was there no such thing as a formal, orchestral concert in colonial Boston?

Not in an official way. The colonial elite—the men and women portrayed in the paintings of John Singleton Copley—enjoyed music in their homes, and some even hired musicians on a permanent basis. But there were no concerts. Not only were there few professional musicians in town, but the audience was, as yet, too small. To the best of our knowledge, the first concert with an orchestra was performed in 1771, by the musicians of King George III's 64th Regiment, then stationed in Boston.

Did the American Revolution help or hinder music in Boston?

Almost certainly it helped the spread of music. The fife and drum corps that we admire from Revolutionary times were matched by British musicians, and a larger percentage of the total population came to admire music in its rudimentary forms during the Revolutionary War. It helped, too, that the foremost Boston composer of the time, William Billings (1746–1800), brought out his compositions in several books and pamphlets published during this time. By the time the Revolutionary War ended, the old Puritan ambivalence about music had largely disappeared. This does not mean there were lots of musicians, however.

Why was theater more acceptable than music during the eighteenth century?

If the Puritans were ambivalent about music, they were dead-set against theater, which they viewed as one of the speediest paths to the devil. But the end of the Revolutionary War witnessed a change of heart, and theater moved past music in the 1780s and 1790s. One reason is that theater troupes came from England to America, but rather few musicians followed suit.

When the first wave of musicians did arrive, early in the nineteenth century, they tended to be enamored of German classical music, which was then in its third or fourth generation. Old England, too, modeled many of its early compositions and musical programs on German ones, not least because King George II sponsored Handel.

What were the first musical societies, or groups, formed in Boston?

The Handel and Haydn Society was formed in 1815, at a time when admiration of all things German was at its height. The early patrons of this society were upper-class Bostonians, men and women whose Puritan ancestors would have frowned on such activity.

A chorus rehearsal of the Handel and Haydn Society in 1903. The society dates back to 1815 and is still active today.

The years immediately following the War of 1812 were a time of cultural expansion for Boston, and the city leaders were keen to sponsor new musical groups. Mayor Samuel A. Eliot did much to encourage interest in classical music.

Was there already a division between those that loved classical, and those that admired folk music?

Which style of music a person preferred became one of the ways that rank and class were determined in early nineteenth-century Boston. Classical music became identified with the city's upper class; and folk music—that practiced in the home and on the street—became viewed as somewhat vulgar. We don't know that much about the musical programs of the 1830s and 1840s, but we believe that an audience was forming, one that wished to emulate the best of Romantic Period music from Europe.

Why did the Yankees of the 1830s depart from their ancestors' beliefs (where music is concerned)?

In part this was because of the quality of music that suddenly became available. Germany, which was not yet unified as a nation, had the largest number of musicians and fledgling orchestras; handfuls of itinerant Germans brought the early beginnings of romantic music to Boston. There they found a new audience, composed of Boston Yankees whose grandparents had despised almost anything "foreign." The Bostonians of the 1830s, however, were eager to acquire culture anywhere they could find it. Mayor Samuel A. Eliot was instrumental in having the first concerts performed, even though the musicians lacked a permanent home.

285

How important was Jenny Lind?

Johanna Maria "Jenny" Lind (1820–1887) was a blockbuster in every sense of the word, the person who brought European music to American ears. Though she performed more recitals in Manhattan, it is those she gave in Boston that birthed a new audience.

Born in Sweden, Lind was an outstanding vocalist who was first trained in her homeland and then in France. She sang in opera for many years, but in 1849 she commenced a new career as a recitalist and no less a figure than P.T. Barnum engaged her for an American tour. She arrived in New York in the autumn of 1850, and commenced a series of recitals that took people's breath away. Her seven recitals in Boston demonstrated both her immense talent and the fact that the city on the bay was ready for formal European music.

Soprano Jenny Lind was from Sweden, but it was in Boston that she brought her talents to American ears for numerous performances.

What buildings, or institutions, grew up as a result?

Boston Music Hall opened its doors in 1852, with many highbrow Bostonians declaring that this was where Jenny Lind should have performed, two years earlier.

Did the Transcendental and Abolitionist movements have anything to do with the spread of music?

Given their lofty goals, one would think so. Most of the records of their meetings that remain do not mention music, however, and we are forced to imagine that these were rather dull affairs, filled with fine speeches but lacking entirely in musical tone. Though the Transcendentalists and Abolitionists were the kind of people who could have found music uplifting, it tended to be the soldiers of the Civil War—the grunts in the field, as we now say—who really made music more popular.

Do we know the names of any of the Civil War composers?

Most of the songs sprang up from the soldiers themselves, and no one ever claimed that it was "his" or "her" song. Surely the best-known of the Civil War songs was "John Brown's Body," which seems to have been developed by a Massachusetts regiment. In 1861, Julia Ward Howe (wife of Samuel Gridley Howe, founder of the Perkins School for the Blind) was inspired by the singing of "John Brown's Body." She quickly composed her own version, which became "Battle Hymn of the Republic." The opening words still have the power to move us.

Mine eyes have seen the glory of the coming of the Lord
He is trampling out the vintage where the grapes of wrath are stored
He hath loosed the fateful lightning of His terrible swift sword,
His truth is marching on!

How quickly did formal music take off after the Civil War's conclusion?

The Boston Conservatory was formed on February 11, 1867, with the Belgian violinist Julius Eichberg (1824–1893) as its leader. Just one week later, on February 18, 1867, the New England Conservatory of Music was established, with Rhode Island native Eben Tourjee (1834–1891) as its first leader. The two groups competed for a rather small audience in the early years with the New England Conservatory of Music coming out on top. Very likely this was because Tourjee was a masterful promoter, as well as a fine musician. He purchased the large Saint James Hotel in Boston's South End, and attempted to fill its five hundred rooms with musicians.

Boston Music Hall, the interior of which is shown here in a period newspaper illustration, was first opened in 1852.

What was the National Peace Jubilee?

Organized by Patrick S. Gilmore (1829–1892), the National Peace Jubilee of 1869 was intended to celebrate the current state of peace, as well as to discourage anyone from taking action that might threaten it. Boston went all-out for the Peace Jubilee: an enormous building, combining wood and canvas, was erected near the site of today's Copley Square. Thirty thousand people fit underneath the structure. The orchestra was one thousand in number, and the chorus ten thousand.

Sadly, the Franco–Prussian War began just a year later (in 1870) and Boston felt compelled to make a second statement on the blessings of peace. For this second occasion in 1872, a structure was erected that could seat 50,000 people. The chorus numbered 20,000, and the orchestra 2,000. Equally impressive was the number of top-flight composers who came to lead their own pieces. Johann Strauss and Franz Abt both were present.

Who founded the Boston Symphony Orchestra (BSO)?

Henry Lee Higginson (1834–1919) was a Boston Yankee who served in the Civil War and rose to the rank of colonel. He joined his family's merchant concerns, and later did well in banking. In 1881, Higginson became the sole founder of the Boston Symphony Orchestra. In the charter, he laid down the rules. This was to be a place for fine music, but there would be venues for a larger public to attend. Higginson knew quite well that his core constituency was composed of about five thousand families, most of whom lived either in the Bacon Hill area or Boston's West End. They would be the concert-goers, the holders of season tickets, but the new Boston Symphony Orchestra would attempt to reach the masses, at least at some point down the road.

Is there a difference between the Boston Symphony Orchestra and the Boston Pops?

They are very closely linked, but are not synonymous. The Boston Pops was formed four years after the BSO (in 1885), and its name suggests the connection with a "popular" audience. Some historians believe that the word "pops" comes from the uncorking of champagne and wine bottles, associated with the beer garden concerts, but this remains unproven. The Boston Pops quickly became the popular arm of the Boston Symphony Orchestra, intended to bring baroque, classical, and romantic music to a wider audience. In the first two decades of its existence, the Boston Pops performed largely to the same group of Boson Brahmin families that attended the Boston Symphony Orchestra concerts: the early twentieth century would be the dividing point.

How powerful was the German influence in the early years of Boston music?

It can hardly be overstated. In music, philosophy, and higher education, Germany served as the model for many upper-class, East Coast Americans at the end of the nineteenth century. The curriculum changes instituted at Harvard University were largely inspired by President Charles W. Eliot's time in Germany. The musical programs of the Boston Symphony Orchestra and the Boston Pops were inspired by German music and musicians. Indeed, Boston became the most popular place for German singers and musicians to relocate.

Who was Karl Muck, and why is his story so tragic?

One of the great Wagnerian conductors, Muck (1859–1940) was born in Germany and came to Boston in his thirties. Muck rose to become musical director of the Boston Symphony Orchestra in 1906. He served for two years, took a hiatus, and then returned as director in 1912. At the height of his career, Muck was perhaps the most influential musical director in the United States. The outbreak of war with his native Germany caused Muck considerable pain, not least because he was on friendly terms with Kaiser Wilhelm II. Even so, very few people suspected Muck of pro-German sympathies, and there was a general feeling in Boston that it was better to leave things alone. This attitude changed when the United States entered World War I in 1917.

Critics pointed out that the Boston Symphony Orchestra no longer played "The Star-Spangled Banner" at the end of its concerts. One would imagine that liberal Boston would have supported Karl Muck, but there was a general call for his head, and he was arrested and even interned as an undesirable alien. There was much extreme feeling in Boston in 1918–1920; even so, one is ashamed—in retrospect—over how Muck was treated. Deported from the United States, he returned to Germany to serve as musical director of the Hamburg Philharmonic.

Did the Boston Symphony Orchestra expel all its foreign-born musicians?

Had it done so, the orchestra would have been half-empty. There was a general consensus, however, that the musical director should not be a German. Leadership, therefore, passed to French-born Pierre Monteux (1875–1964) and then to Russian-born Sergei Koussevitzky. The latter became one of the great directors of the BSO. Truly a master of European musical style, Koussevitzky was interested in American expressions of romantic music: he patronized and commissioned works from several men who later became influential, including Aaron Copland. Koussevitzky's remarkable career happened

Boston is such a liberal place today. Was this not so during World War I?

Most of the United States went through a xenophobic period in which foreigners, especially Germans, were suspected of all sorts of crimes and misdemeanors. Plenty of Bostonians sympathized with Karl Muck, but their voices were drowned out by those who cried he was a foreigner, and could not be trusted.

to overlap with that of another man whose name would become virtually synonymous with classical and romantic music in Boston, Arthur Fiedler.

FIEDLER AND THE BOSTON POPS

Who was Arthur Fiedler, and how did he rise to prominence?

Born in Boston, Arthur Fiedler (1894–1979) came from an Austrian family with a long, deep tradition in music. The family name derives from the Austrian word for fiddler.

His father moved to Boston, where Arthur was born. Emanuel Fiedler was a member of the Boston Symphony Orchestra for twenty-five years, and he was known for his skill with the violin. The whole family moved back to Europe shortly before the commencement of World War I, and Arthur Fiedler was, for a time, prevented from returning to Boston. When he did make it back, he entered the BSO as a violinist, and started his own rise in the field. Though he clashed at times with BSO musical director Serge Koussevitzky, Fiedler made his way through talent and determination (both were needed in the super-competitive world of Boston classical music). He organized the first free, outdoor concert performances on the (also known as the Charles River Esplanade). Partly as a result of their success, Fiedler was named the eighteenth conductor of the Boston Pops in the winter of 1930.

Did anyone suspect that Arthur Fiedler would occupy the august position of conductor for so long?

Not one. Fiedler's amazing career as conductor commenced in February 1930, and ran right to his death in July 1979. No other conductor in the United States has enjoyed such a run.

Was Fiedler that much more talented than his contemporaries?

They certainly did not think so. As Fiedler gained national, and then international fame, his critics quieted, but they maintained that he was only one of a group of highly talented conductors, and that his skills were nothing that special. Fiedler was well aware of their envy, and he took it personally, feeling it necessary to outdo himself on each and every occasion in order to be beyond the reach of their criticism.

What Fiedler possessed in great abundance was energy and enthusiasm: he loved to bring classical music to a larger audience than in previous generations. During the 1930s, Fiedler enlarged on his summer performances on the Charles River Esplanade; these free concerts became favorites of the public, and helped many Bostonians put aside their cares and concerns, if only for one evening. By about the year 1940, Fiedler, along with his fellows at the BSO and the Boston Pops, had greatly increased the Boston audience. Originally, the BSO depended on the patronage of about five thousand families in Greater Boston: by 1940, this figure had increased to perhaps twenty thousand.

Conductor Arthur Fiedler led the Boston Pops for many years.

When did the Boston Symphony Orchestra begin playing at Tanglewood?

In 1937, musical director Serge Koussevitzky began taking the BSO west, to the Berk-shire Hills of western Massachusetts for summer programs. This soon became a lasting tradition, and many thousands of western Massachusetts residents became great fans of the BSO. The classical music fare at Tanglewood was considered "light," by the rigorous standards of the BSO, but this proved something of a relief for many of the musicians. Over time, Tanglewood became the second home of the BSO, and classical musicians were joined by many popular and folk singers.

How did Boston classical music fare during World War II and the Korean War?

At the beginning, both wars were expected to bring about the death of classical music in Boston, especially because so much of the Boston Symphony Orchestra programs centered on German composers. But the Boston audience of 1941 proved quite differ-ent from that of 1914: the Bostonian of the former date proved able to separate the idea of Germans as the foe from the Germans in their midst. As a result, both the BSO and the Boston Pops fared reasonably well during World War II. Arthur Fiedler, meanwhile, gained great applause by enlisting in the U.S. Coast Guard during the war. It turned out

291

his only duty was to make a sweep of Boston Harbor, and only once a week, but his patriotism won him the lasting affection of many Bostonians.

Was Fiedler, in the 1940s, already the dynamic presence that so many people remember from the television broadcasts of the 1960s and 1970s?

He was a younger incarnation of that same bundle of energy. Fiedler was enormously popular with his Boston audience, but not always friendly with his own musicians. His daughter later wrote a telling memoir, *Papa, the Pops and Me* in which she described some of the demons that drove her famous father. Though he had the affection of millions, especially when television broadcast the Boston Pops, Fiedler never felt secure among his fellow musicians. At home, he was an autocrat, expecting everything to be in its proper place, and for his children to be seen, and not heard.

What was the single greatest moment of Arthur Fiedler's long career?

There are many occasions that one can point to, but the single outstanding moment has to be the evening of July 4, 1976. It was the Bicentennial Year, and the Boston Pops advertised heavily to bring out crowds for the annual free concert at the Hatch Shell, on the Boston Esplanade. No one anticipated the size of the crowd that attended, however.

At least 400,000, and perhaps even 500,000 people came to the Charles River on the evening of July 4, 1976. The great majority were on the southern side of the Charles River Basin, where the listening was best, but perhaps 100,000 gathered on the north bank, where they had to strain to pick up the notes. The weather was sublime; the concert was magnificent; and the Boston Pops, which was already known to millions of Americans, suddenly became a sensation to the nation as a whole. Would this have happened without Arthur Fiedler, and his relentless attempt to bring classical music to the masses? It is barely conceivable.

How did the Boston Pops ever find a replacement for Arthur Fiedler?

During his lifetime, there was not the slightest chance: everyone understood that Fiedler would remain in the post till his death. He passed away in July 1979, and the Boston Pops faced the big challenge of finding someone to fill Arthur Fiedler's shoes.

After considerable search, the Boston Pops selected John Towner Williams (1932–). Born two years after Arthur Fiedler began his career as conductor, Williams was forty-eight when chosen, but he had the

Well known as the composer of music for such movie blockbusters as *Star Wars* and *E.T.*, John Williams took over the Boston Pops from Arthur Fiedler.

means and talent to make the Pops proud. Associated with filmmaker Steven Spielberg, Williams had already produced the film scores for *Superman, E.T.: The Extraterrestrial,* and *Star Wars.* Here was a conductor with the talent required.

How did the Boston Pops fare during Williams' time as conductor?

Very well. In the first two or three years, there was plenty of nostalgia for Arthur Fiedler, and many people who said that the Pops was not the same without him. As it turned out, however, Fiedler's single greatest contribution had been the July Fourth concert on the Esplanade, and this was just as much of a success during the 1980s. It helped that July 4, 1986, was celebrated so widely, round the nation, and that the fireworks over the Charles River were such a sensation. But from a purely musical basis, it was hard to fault John T. Williams as conductor: he was a worthy successor to Arthur Fiedler.

FOLK AND ROCK MUSIC

How early was Boston part of the folk music scene?

American folk music is almost as old as the nation itself, but it was not till the twentieth century that sound recordings were made: much of the earlier folk music is, therefore, lost to us. A thriving folk tradition sprang up throughout New England in the 1920s, however, and the advent of the Great Depression in the 1930s made it even stronger. This is because so many people lived out of doors during the Depression, and lived from hand-to-mouth. Free folk music was one of the few treats available to people in such circumstances.

New York and the Midwest are strongly associated with the folk music of Bob Dylan; Boston and New England had to wait till the early 1970s for a comparable folk hero. He arrived in the form of James Taylor (1948–), one of the most skillful guitar players ever seen in America.

How closely is James Taylor associated with Boston?

Most of the images associated with Taylor's music are related to rural scenes rather than urban ones, but one often feels the New England scenery as background. Born in Boston in 1948, Taylor is the son of a prominent Boston physician. The family moved to Chapel Hill, North Carolina, three years later, and Taylor spent his formative years in the South. Returning to the Boston area, he attended Milton Academy, by which time he had already written his first composition.

Taylor suffered a serious mental breakdown while in high school and soon after recovery he began writing at a furious pace. His second, breakthrough album was *Sweet Baby James.* Released in 1970, it revealed Taylor as a brand-new talent, one whose penetrating voice could challenge even the loud music of the rock bands of that time (it is a curiosity that his career rise came at the same time as that of Aerosmith).

How can one radio station—WBCN—receive so much attention, flattery, and notoriety?

People have asked that ever since WBCN first came on the air, during the winter of 1967. Right from the beginning, WBCN was the place where Boston musical tastes were changed.

Founded nine years earlier, WBCN was originally a classical music station, benefitting from an interest in FM radio. But by 1967, WBCN was in such poor shape financially that its manager allowed a handful of local rock-n-roll and folk devotees to take over a section of his programming. This soon turned into a full-fledged rock-n-roll station, but not of the type we envision today.

Talented musician and composer James Taylor, who gained fame with songs like "You've Got a Friend" and "Handy Man," is a native Bostonian.

How different was the music scene in 1967, from, say, what we know in 2016?

Almost fifty years separate the two dates, but even that half-century cannot fully convey the profound difference between the state of popular music in the late 1960s, and what we experience today. In 1967 rock-n-roll was almost a decade old, but to its many devotees, the art form seemed woefully misunderstood. Many listeners applauded the energy in the music without any real understanding of the lyrics. The first days of WBCN were determined to change the situation.

The deejays of 1967 tended to be long-haired, in their mid-twenties, and incredibly enthusiastic. The recent appearance of *Sgt. Pepper's Lonely Hearts Club Band,* one of the Beatles' most successful albums, released a new energy in rock and folk music. Boston was where most of the major concerts were held, but Cambridge, its poorer sections most especially, tended to be the home of the musicians.

What were the first songs played on WBCN?

Though these can be listed, it's more illuminating to discuss the type of groups whose music was played in that opening year. The J. Geils Band was already alive and kicking, and WBCN helped lift its cause by playing its early hits. Aerosmith might have remained a local, rather than national, band had WBCN not taken the band under its wing. And Bruce Springsteen got his early start by being played by the radio jocks of WBCN.

The Vietnam War was still in progress as WBCN was founded, and the early jocks felt free to discuss it—and the societal changes that accompanied it—in great detail. Unlike most AM stations, WBCN delighted in free-form discussions that went on long past the allotted time. Then too, WBCN was practically made for night owls, and given that Boston had roughly 200,000 college students, it was a match made in heaven.

Was WBCN the first major radio station to hire women?

Some others may have come before it, but WBCN definitely became the forefront of women seeking equal opportunity and pay (as well as fun!). Debbie Ullman was the first female deejay at the station, and before the 1970s were out, the staff was about equally composed of men and women. One did not detect any significant difference in the programming: WBCN was known as the exciting, progressive place in the Boston radio market.

When did the shift in headquarters take place?

The original WBCN headquarters and sound room were in a three-floor walkup on New-berry Street, and that was where many of the station loyalists were happiest. In 1973, however, the station moved to the fiftieth floor of the Prudential Building, on the same floor as the famous Skywalk Observatory. Thanks to glass windows, the shock jocks of WBCN could be seen by the typical, perhaps conservative, middle American, husband, wife, and children on the balcony.

Within a handful of years, even the longest-lived WBCN employees admitted that the move to the Pru was a success: perched fifty floors up, WBCN emitted a super-clean sound that brought in ever-more listeners. Then too, the high-profile address made it easier for the station to receive publicity from other markets. WBCN was at the top of its form in the mid-1970s. By then, Aerosmith and Bruce Springsteen, and others, were national standouts, and WBCN profited from its long and deep connections.

Was there ever a low point for WBCN?

A sudden change of ownership, in the winter of 1979, led to the firing of nearly two-thirds of the staff, and a subsequent worker's strike. 1979 was not a good time in the labor movement as a whole, but the WBCN strikers won, thanks to help and support from numerous other union groups in the Boston area. Some listeners noticed that WBCN was never quite the same again, however; the fun-loving place of the early 1970s had turned into the grimmer, more profit-conscious rock-n-roll factory of the early 1980s.

It has to be said, however, that the early 1980s also witnessed a profound movement of rock-n-roll into the mainstream, and that this was accomplished in a most uncompromising way. The Cars became the outstanding Boston group of the early 1980s, and both the local music scene and the music on the airways took over in a way never before seen. Of course, such incredible success is usually followed by a drop off, and it came in the appearance of MTV.

How important was WBCN to the Boston music scene?

The station 104.1 FM was originally founded with a classical format, but a lack of subscribers forced a turnover in 1967, and BCN, as it was known, soon became the center of the popular music scene in Greater Boston. Of course there were plenty of other stations, but most concentrated on Top Forty hits, and did not play the new music that was cropping up in and around Boston. A small establishment, "The Boston Tea Party" was at 53 Berkeley Street, and locals often went there to listen to great performers for less than $5.

BCN was famed for the willingness of its deejays to play extended albums, from cover to cover, and for the astute analysis offered by the crew. At a time when Boston was filled with start-up rock bands, and when the drug and free love scenes were coming on strong, BCN was the center for many listeners.

How did the J. Geils Band become so identified with working-class Boston?

The members of the J. Geils Band all came from elsewhere, but Boston in the late 1960s was their venue, and their sound echoed that of Boston's working class. Formed in 1967, the J. Geils Band got off to a slow start before being signed with Atlantic Records in 1970. From there they went from strength to strength. "Whammer Jammer" was followed by "Must of Got Lost," which was succeeded by "Love Stinks" and "Centerfold." J. Geils always considered Boston its first home and Detroit its second: the group succeeded with the same kind of working-class crowd in both cities.

Most of us have heard of Aerosmith. How did the band get its start?

Steven Tyler (1948–) was born in Manhattan, but his family summered on Lake Sunapee in New Hampshire, giving him a taste of Yankee and New England ways from an early age. After a tempestuous youth, Tyler moved to Boston in 1970. He and his friends started off at 1325 Commonwealth Ave, and Aerosmith's first advertisement was a banner atop a big building in Kenmore Square. Right from the beginning, Tyler and his fellow musicians decided to identify as a Boston band, one which brought the edge of hard metal to what had previously been the soft sounds of the late 1960s.

How and why did Aerosmith make it big?

If there is a cleavage between traditional and New Wave rock listeners, Aerosmith was the group that bridged the gap. Many listeners found the music too darned loud, and some objected to the lyrics, but there is little doubt that Aerosmith found its audience in the twelve- to eighteen-year-old market.

Sometimes called "The Bad Boys from Boston," Aerosmith soared into the music scene of the early 1970s with hits such as "Dream On," and "Walk This Way." Most of the group members did not hail from Boston originally (Steven Tyler was from New York City, for example) but they became thoroughly identified with Boston.

Although born in the Bronx, Aerosmith singer Steven Tyler adopted Boston as his home in 1970.

How and why did the group Boston become such a sensation?

No one predicted it. As late as the autumn of 1975, many observers lamented the lack of new talent, declaring that the great days spawned by Aerosmith were over. And then in the summer of 1976, was released one of the biggest best-selling albums of all time. The rock group Boston turned out an album of the same name.

Band leader Tom Scholz was originally from Toledo, Ohio, but the other band members—Fran Sheehan, Brad Delp, Barry Goudreau, and Sib Hashian—all hailed from Boston. The album sang primarily of youthful exaltation, but enough lyrics were about Boston—and Massachusetts—to make the listeners feel at ease.

What are some of the most memorable of the lyrics of Boston?

Well, we were just another band out of Boston,
On the road to try to make ends meet,
Playin' all the bars, sleepin' in our cars,
And we practiced right on out in the street.

297

The Sixties were gone, but Boston's first album made it feel as if a new version of the past had just begun. The enthusiasm that led to the sale of ten million albums worldwide testified to the desire of Bostonians to feel that a more utopian time was on the way. And, unlike the rock groups of the Sixties, Boston seldom infuriated or even irritated the parents of the teenagers who bought the album.

Could the group Boston keep it up?

They waited so long (two years) before releasing their second album that it seemed they would be a one-hit wonder. *Don't Look Back,* released in 1978, was a solid hit, but did not convey the excitement of the first album. The group then waited until 1986 to release their third album, *Third Stage.* Memorable for the hit "Amanda," *Third Stage* accomplished little else.

What Boston had already accomplished, however, was to make the city cool and hip once more. By the late 1970s, Boston was the destination for all sorts of musicians and groupies.

How big were The Cars?

Though their time at the top was short, The Cars remain one of the most beloved groups from the late 1970s. Neither Ric Ocasek (1949–) nor Benjamin Orr (1947–2000) came from Boston, but when they came together to form The Cars, they were in Boston, and the group and the city became inextricably combined in the popular imagination. Their first big hit, "Just What I Needed," was released in 1977: it quickly became the song most in demand on all the major Boston radio stations.

The Cars went on to release "My Best Friend's Girl" in 1978, and "Good Times Roll" in 1979. By then, they were regarded as the coolest kids on the block. The black clothing of the artists, their sleek and metrosexual look, became the rage in popular music.

How active was the pop music scene in Boston around the year 1980?

It could hardly have been more exciting. The city had many bands, but most of them were small, and the numerous clubs—especially the Rathskeller—featured out-of-town groups. Blondie was a New York band that thrived in Boston, as

Ric Ocasek wasn't from Boston, but he teamed up with Benjamin Orr and started the group The Cars in Boston.

> ## One does not automatically connect Boston with the disco craze. Is there a connection?
>
>
>
> **Y**es indeed. Though Chicago was perhaps number one in number of discotheques, Boston was tailor-made for success in the great number of college students. Then too, perhaps the single most successful artist to emerge from the disco craze was a native Bostonian.
>
> Donna Summer (1948–2012) was born LaDonna Gaines in Boston in 1948. In the late 1970s, she became the single most successful artist of the time with songs such as "Love to Love You Baby," which came out in 1975. By 1995, she had eleven gold and two platinum singles, and eight gold and three platinum albums.

did the Ramones, and a number of other punk groups. But the really big action was still on the way: it arrived in March 1981 in the form of U2.

U2 was an Irish band, not an American one, but it found its most receptive audiences in the United States as a whole and Boston most especially. In their first appearance in Boston, U2 found an audience that demanded three encores, setting the stage for a very successful 61-show tour.

What explains the phenomenal success of U2 in the Boston area?

First and foremost—U2 had a truly distinct sound. They built on the success of punk, but they went well beyond it. Second, though many audience listeners did not realize it—U2 was a Christian rock band, an anomaly in the industry. And third, Boston's fourth and fifth generations of Irish thrilled to lyrics that spoke of oppression and violence. "Sunday Bloody Sunday," about the Irish uprising of 1916, was especially popular in Boston.

U2 started off strong and just kept getting better—at least as far as Bostonians were concerned. By the time the group played in Foxborough, at the home of the New England Patriots, U2 had become an honorary Boston band.

Can anyone name the height of Boston success, so far as rock-and-roll is concerned?

Very likely it was close to the end of the 1980s. Old rock groups such as the Rolling Stones made what seemed like the last of their tours through the Boston area, while newer ones were booming. The rock scene had never been so exciting, or so prosperous. But the very success of that time played its role in bringing about a steep decline.

Who were Click and Clack?

Click and Clack, or Tom (1937–2014) and Ray Magliozzli (1949–), were Cambridge natives who came to WBUR on a lark in 1977, and never really went back. For ten years they volunteered, as their two-hour show rose to fame; they became one of the most recognizable, and best-loved of all Boston voices. Every Saturday afternoon, the brothers, who called themselves "Click and Clack, the Tappet Brothers," offered homespun advice on transmissions, tires, the clutch, and everything in-between. When Tom, the elder brother, died in 2014, it was one of the saddest of moments for Boston radio.

How did the Wahlberg family become so big, where popular culture is concerned?

The Wahlbergs are a Roman Catholic family from Dorchester, and they are as surprised as anyone by their incredible success. Donnie Wahlberg (1969–) formed New Kids on the Block in Boston in 1985. All five of the group's performers—Wahlberg, Jonathan Knight, Jordan Knight, Danny Wood, and Joey McIntyre—came either from Greater Boston or Worcester, and their sound had a sharp Boston edge.

Mark Wahlberg (1971–) was Donnie's younger brother. He helped form Marky Mark and the Funky Bunch in 1991. The group showcased Wahlberg as only the second white American performer to imitate black artists in hip-hop performance, and the album *Music for the People* was very successful. Mark Wahlberg became controversial for his

WBUR staff at an on-location broadcast. WBUR is Boston's Public Radio station.

occasional acts of violence, but he successfully transitioned from pop music to television and the movies. He has appeared in a large number of films.

How different is the story of WBUR (from that of WBCN)?

WBUR (90.9 FM) is Boston's Public Radio station. WBUR has a strong progressive bent, and many of its best programs focus on ways to improve the lives of the common person. "Click and Clack"—known officially as "Car Talk"—has been entertaining Saturday afternoon audiences for three decades. The hosts listen patiently as callers describe their various struggles with auto mechanics, and what problems to avoid. Click and Clack are always sympathetic, but one of their trademark responses is, "Drive it off a cliff!"

MUSEUMS, LIBRARIES, AND ARCHIVES

How many museums are there in Greater Boston?

Somewhere between sixty and eighty, but this does not take into account all of the smaller ones that receive little notice. Bostonians have been collectors for almost three centuries, and the area is rivaled only by Greater Manhattan in that regard.

What is the best known of all museums in Boston?

It's a close run between the Museum of Fine Arts (MFA) and the Boston Museum of Science. Which wins out usually depends on the age of the people asked: older patrons tend to prefer the MFA and younger ones tend to idolize the Museum of Science.

Museum of Fine Arts.

301

How did a Boston museum gain so much art from distant parts of the world?

The answer lies in the deep pockets of New England collectors, especially those of the late nineteenth century. The most eccentric, and perhaps most interesting, of them was Isabella Stewart Gardner, who ended up founding a museum of her own, but her efforts were equaled by at least a score of other middle-aged Bostonians, who combed the libraries and museums of Western Europe in the 1880s and 1890s. Few of the treasures were really "bought for a song," but many European collectors were struggling financially, and they ended up selling to Bostonians and New Yorkers.

The Museum of Fine Arts, better known as the MFA, first opened in Copley Square on July 4, 1876, in order to celebrate the nation's centennial. The original building was eventually deemed too small, and the new one, at 465 Huntington Avenue, was built in the early 1900s. Opened in 1909, the MFA is one of the largest of all American museums—four acres—and its collections are stunning. Impressionist painting clamors for attention, but so do Japanese and Chinese ceramics. The MFA possesses the largest collection of Early American silver (Paul Revere's objects on the list), and the paintings of John Singleton Copley are among the most popular.

Can anyone really see all that the MFA has to offer?

Not in a weekend, not even in a week, can this be done properly. Plenty of arts-minded Bostonians make four trips a year to the MFA, have done so for decades, and claim they still have not seen the entire collection. The MFA has a full-time staff of 570, and a volunteer staff in excess of 1,300.

Is there any key to seeing as much as one can, for the least amount of money?

In most cases, the answer is to arrive early, but with the MFA the answer is to come late in the afternoon on Wednesday, when the museum is free. This is also the case on several holidays, with Memorial Day high on the list.

How does the Museum of Science stack up to the MFA?

The two museums are so different that they really cannot be compared. The MFA caters to those interested in classical art, while the Museum of Science is intended for someone interested in the present and the future. Located at 1 Science Park, right on the border between Boston and Cambridge, the Museum of Science is an enormous complex that employs 358 permanent personnel, 201 part-time employees, and a volunteer staff of more than 700.

What are some of the major exhibitions that have brought newcomers to the Museum of Science?

The Ramses II exhibit, in the summer of 1988, was a blockbuster. The museum was jammed virtually every day of the week. One might imagine that this kind of exhibition would go to the MFA, but the Museum of Science has first-class preservationists, and Egypt entrusted many of its treasures to the museum for a few short months.

What are some of the lesser-known museums of Greater Boston?

One of the most interesting, the Boston Fire Museum, is located at 344 Congress Street. Boston has a long tradition of fires and firefighting, with the Great Fire of 1872 being the disaster most remembered. The Boston Fire Museum is open at no charge, but it draws only 3,500 visitors per year. Some lament the fact, while others rejoice that such a special place—filled with helmets, trucks, and memorabilia dating back to 1905—is not jammed with tourists.

Paul Revere House surrounded by modern buildings today, is open to the public.

Another of the less well-known museums is hiding in plain sight, at 1 Faneuil Hall. The fourth floor of the building houses the Ancient and Honorable Artillery Company of Massachusetts. Founded in 1638, the Ancient and Honorable has a membership list—past and present—that reads like a "Who's Who in American History." Roughly 40,000 visitors come to the museum, which is offered free of charge.

What is the single biggest attraction, so far as children are concerned?

Almost certainly this is the New England Aquarium, located on Central Wharf. Though some might question whether this is a museum or an entertainment park, the New England Aquarium has introduced more young people to the maritime world and its creatures than any comparable place on the East Coast. The Aquarium has 1.3 million visitors each year.

I hear that the USS *Constitution* and the Paul Revere House come under the same banner. Is this true?

They are both part of the Boston National Historical Park, which is centered in Charlestown. When the Charlestown Navy Yard shut down, there was a consequent loss of employment in the area, and the development of a national park was a good answer to the situation. Founded in 1974, the Boston National Historical Park has the Bunker Hill Monument and the USS *Constitution* at its center, but the park extends outward to include the Old State House, the Old South Meeting House, and the Paul Revere House. Nearly three million people visit the park annually, all of them entering at no charge. Of course it's another matter when it comes to parking.

What is the oldest library or archive in Greater Boston?

This honor goes to the Massachusetts Historical Society (MHS), on Boylston Street. Founded in 1791, by proud Bostonians who wished to commemorate their town's history, the MHS started as a very parochial institution, but grew over the years to where its journal—the *Proceedings of the Massachusetts Historical Society*—published on almost all aspects of Boston and New England history.

The MHS primarily serves the needs of serious researchers, at the college and postgraduate level, but no person with a genuine research need is turned away. The MHS has been preserving history for more than two centuries, and its letter boxes and archival sections are jammed, but it also has a number of outstanding paintings, primarily portraits of the colonial era.

What is the oldest-operating subscription library in Boston?

This is the Boston Athenaeum, located at 10½ Beacon Street. Founded in 1807, the Athenaeum was designed primarily as a reading room for the highly educated Bostonian, especially him who enjoyed reading newspapers brought from long distances. The Athenaeum possesses a 700,000-volume library, but it also has a number of valuable pieces of art. Few tourists stumble on the Athenaeum; those that do are asked if they have a special research request.

What are some of the intriguing museums set outside the city itself?

The John F. Kennedy Presidential Library and Museum, located on Columbia Point, is one of the biggest attractions. Designed by I. M. Pei, and dedicated in 1979, the Kennedy Library is a mass of glass and supports, which sometimes looks more like a cathedral than a museum. Administered by the National Archives and Records Administration, the Kennedy Presidential Library and Museum possesses 32 million documents, the great majority of which are directly related to the Kennedy presidency. By an odd twist of fate, the Kennedy Library also wound up with the papers of Ernest Hemingway.

The Kennedy Library is only a few miles south of downtown Boston, but it points in the direction of Quincy, Braintree, and Boston's South Shore; these areas are noted for the Adams National Historical Park. And of course, no visit to the area would be complete without a tour of *Mayflower II*, the replica of the ship that brought the Pilgrims in 1620, and Plymouth Rock. Another direction in which the historical compass points is west-by-northwest, on the way to Lexington and Concord.

How much can one see of the battlefields of Lexington and Concord?

Minute Man National Historical Park straddles the two, and the ambitious tourist can see a lot of the area over which the British regulars and American minutemen fought. Patriot's Day, celebrated on the nineteenth of April, is the big celebration each year, but tourists can see some of the historic houses throughout the spring, summer, and fall months.

The Old Manse is a home built for Reverend William Emerson, grandfather of Ralph Waldo Emerson. It was also, for a short time, the home of Nathaniel and Sophia Hawthorne. Locally one also finds the Concord Museum and the Concord Historical Society Resource Center.

Is there any part of Boston's long, illustrious history that is *not* commemorated sufficiently?

The Transcendental poets and philosophers are honored because so many of them lived in Concord: lacking that connection, it is difficult to see how they receive their due. Bronson Alcott, one of the founders of Fruitlands (see page 97), and his daughter Louisa May Alcott are well known to readers, but there are few monuments to suggest their importance. Overall, it's fair to say that Concord still gives primary place to its Revolutionary soldiers, rather than the men and women of the pen who followed a half-century later.

The abolitionist leaders, too, receive short shrift. The magnificent sculpture by Augustus Saint-Gaudens of the men of the 54th Massachusetts Infantry Regiment, is not equaled by any comparable monument to the men and women of the abolition movement. One of the few notable exceptions is a monument of Harriet Tubman and four other abolitionists in West Boston.

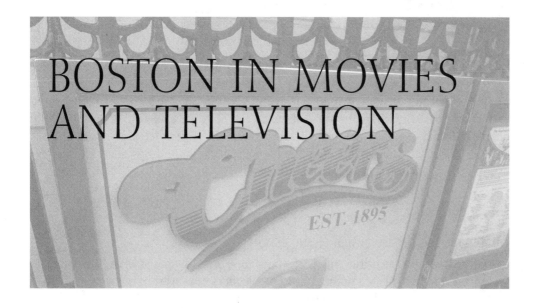

BOSTON IN MOVIES AND TELEVISION

Where does Boston stand in comparison to other major American cities, where the media is concerned?

There is a four-way tie at the top, with Manhattan and Los Angeles usually edging out Boston and San Francisco. Even though Miami and Chicago have plenty of dynamic action, and lots of scenes that display well on camera, it's usually the big four that seize the most media attention.

Of the four, Boston has one distinct and powerful advantage: its streets and city squares are a fascinating combination of the old and the new. Los Angeles, by contrast, films beautifully where boulevards and coffee shops are concerned, but doesn't have quiet nooks and side streets. This is a major reason that Boston—ever since the development of moving pictures—has been one of the most featured of American cities.

BOSTON ON TV AND IN THE MOVIES

How many movies have been filmed in and around Greater Boston?

At least a score have reached the big screen, and perhaps ten times as many smaller ones were filmed and never made it to wide release. If one counts all the documentaries that have been filmed, and the numerous pieces on the TV news show *Sixty Minutes* and elsewhere, the number could well reach a thousand.

What is it about Greater Boston that makes film companies go there, time and again?

First and foremost is the scenery: the Charles River Basin, Harvard, and the skyscrapers of the city itself. Second is the number of young people in Boston, eager to act as extras in any film. And third is the fact that Massachusetts offers some of the most attractive terms to filmmakers: not only in Boston, but the Bay State as a whole.

In the first two decades of American cinema, Boston came in second to Philadelphia as the East Coast city where the greatest number of films were made (like Boston, Philly has both history and a vibrant present). By about 1960, Boston fell behind Los Angeles and San Francisco. But when a memorable movie comes out of Boston, it tends to remain in the public mind for a very long time.

LOVE STORY

What made this particular film so successful?

Certainly it was not the critics, many of whom took broad swipes at what they called its saccharine quality. This did not matter to moviegoers, however; in the winter of 1970, they were eager for good news, and a story that carried a universal message.

Ryan O'Neal (1941–) plays Oliver Barrett IV, the great-great-great-great-grandson of a famous colonial leader for whom Barrett Hall at Harvard is named. Barrett IV goes to Harvard (of course) where he becomes an All-Ivy hockey star, shooting the puck with great skill. It was fortuitous that hockey was the rage in Boston at the time the film was released. Ali MacGraw (1939–)—widely considered one of the most beautiful women of the time—plays Jenny, the daughter of an Italian immigrant who has made good in Rhode Island. Ray Milland plays Oliver Barrett III, the rather bland and sometimes forbidding person whom his son calls simply "Sir."

How did *Love Story* fit into the spirit of the times (the late 1960s and start of the new decade)?

There is very little real rebellion in *Love Story*: rather, there is frustration and doubt where one's place in the world is concerned. Oliver Barrett IV knows he can have a life much like that of his father, but he knows how many sacrifices—emotional ones, especially—will go into that choice. Jennie, by contrast, seems free to choose what she wants.

By the spring of 1970, when the film was released, many young Americans were nostalgic for what their parents had possessed: a world in which inner values and outer performance seemed to match. This was not the world they knew because of the Vietnam War and several years of youth rebellion. *Love Story*, therefore, appealed to the desire for a simpler life in which the basic human emotions balanced the frenetic drive for material success.

What is the tragedy in *Love Story*?

Jenny develops a rare blood disease. Once she is in the hospital, Oliver Barrett IV meets his own demons in a more profound way. Here was love, and now it is disappearing before his eyes. The most memorable conversation in the film is between father and son. Oliver Barrett III comes to the hospital to express his sadness at his son's loss. Oliver Barrett IV replies with that inimitable, yet also cryptic line, "Love means never having to say you're sorry." That the line coincides with the audience's sentiments is beyond doubt, but the present-day viewer wonders what, precisely, is meant. Does "love means never having to say you're sorry" mean that love redeems all human failures? Or is the son condemning his father for not having given him that kind of love? The line is successful, even today, because it leaves the viewer wondering.

THE PAPER CHASE

What is the premise of the 1973 movie *The Paper Chase*?

The action takes place at Harvard Law School, where first-year student James Hart (played by Timothy Bottoms (1951–) is eager to do well. He is not well-versed in this super-competitive world, however, and his most embarrassing moments take place at the hands of formidable Professor Kingsfield (played by the veteran actor John Houseman [1902–1988]). By chance, Hart comes into contact with Susan Fields, the divorced daughter of Professor Kingsfield. As their romance develops, Hart begins to see the immense personal sacrifices that are necessary for one to achieve success in the world of Harvard Law, Cambridge, and Greater Boston. He continues to make the moves necessary for a successful first year, but when the final grade is sent, he tosses it into the air. His romance with the professor's daughter has shown him there is more to life than striving for material and professional success.

How did Boston audiences respond to *The Paper Chase*?

For viewers over the age of twenty-five, the movie was ho-hum, meaning that they'd heard its message before. But to a younger crowd, certainly anyone under the age of twenty, *The Paper Chase* was a revelation. Here, for one of the first times, the super-competitive world of high academics was exposed as being just as cut-throat as the business world that was to follow. Rather few young Bostonians switched their career plans, or life goals, as a result, but the movie had a powerful impact: it was perhaps the most-discussed film of that year.

Why did it take so long for *The Paper Chase* to make it to television?

The national bicentennial came in-between, and Boston, known as the Cradle of

The late John Houseman played the brilliant yet intimidating law professor specializing in contract law in *The Paper Chase*.

Liberty, naturally got plenty of media coverage in 1976. Then too, the end of the decade seemed a better time to launch the television series. When it came to CBS in September 1978, *The Paper Chase* was a major hit.

James Hart was, again, a first-year student at Harvard Law. This time he was played by James Stephens (1951–). Professor Kingsfield was again portrayed by the redoubtable John Houseman. Two other first-year law students—named Willis Bell and Franklin Ford III—were played by James Keane and Tom Fitzsimmons, respectively. Though there were numerous female roles, no female actor managed to stay in them for very long. It was a very male-centered program.

What are some of the most inimitable lines from *The Paper Chase*?

Virtually all of them were uttered by Professor Kingsfield (John Houseman). In a hard, cold voice that seemed way beyond snobbish, he called out the roll, and then picked on one student after another. His best line, however, was in the opening that preceded each program. "You come in here with a skull full of mush ... and, *if* you survive, you leave thinking like a lawyer."

Houseman held center stage for all seven seasons of the show. It didn't matter what the students were up to, whether they fell in or out of love, got high grades or low, Professor Kingsfield jerked them around like puppets. And to their great humiliation, he sometimes exposed what they had dreaded all along: that he cared not a jot about them. Audiences were astonished at the level of cruelty sometimes expressed, but they kept coming back for more. There was something truly irresistible about *The Paper Chase*.

Did *The Paper Chase* bring more young people to Boston colleges—or fewer?

The late 1970s and early 1980s were a time of economic recession in the United States, and almost any young person who could go to college or university did so. Boston did not exactly boom during this period, but the perennial applications to Harvard, MIT, and Harvard Law remained high. What *The Paper Chase* ensured is that young people had much to discuss with their parents. Were any of the teachers like Professor Kingsfield? Was the competition really that intense? Parents wanted to know.

THE BOSTONIANS

How many films have been made with the word Boston in the title?

Surprisingly few. As described above, there are scores of films that have been made in Boston, but they usually have names and titles that lack the proper name itself. One of the few that did do so was *The Bostonians*, released to the wide screen in the late summer of 1984.

The Bostonians is based on Henry James' novel of the same name. It is set in the anxious, tumultuous times prior to the Civil War, and words such as abolition and slave-driver are frequently employed. Even so, there is a great desire on the part of proper

Bostonians not to offend their white Southern kin, and this is part of the plot that drives the novel and movie.

Did Bostonians like *The Bostonians* very much?

Not really. The film was not a great hit, either in Boston or the nation as a whole. It received critical acclaim, however, for its portrayal of an earlier time, and for the timeless theme of competition in love. The archetypal prim, Boston lady, Olive Chancellor (played by Vanessa Redgrave [1937–]) is hopelessly, helplessly in love with her young protégé, Verena Tarrant (played by Madeleine Potter). Complicating matters, Chancellor's cousin from South Carolina is in town, and he, too, shows great desire for Miss Tarrant. The social mores of the time do not allow for female love, yet the cousin, played superbly by Christopher Reeve, also realizes he will not attain his object.

The Bostonians is not really a Boston film; rather, it belongs to the antebellum era, and New England in general. What is wonderful, what stands out, is the way the camera lingers on its subjects. There is an autumnal feeling to *The Bostonians*, a sense that the characters will soon be submerged in the horrors of civil war.

ST. ELSEWHERE

How did a hospital show make it to prime time on American television?

The same program would not have made it a decade earlier. By the early 1980s, the American population was growing older, however, and the earliest of the baby boomers approached the age of forty. They were therefore more interested in hospitals, medicine, and health than earlier, and *St. Elsewhere* made quite a splash.

St. Elsewhere came to NBC in the autumn of 1982 just as *Hill Street Blues* was coming to prominence as the number-one police drama of the time. The two series seemed to piggy-back one another, even though *Hill Street Blues* usually commanded a much larger audience.

What is the premise of *St. Elsewhere*?

To smart and sharp Bostonians, it was obvious: this was not a hospital you would send your relatives to. The fictional hospital of St. Eligius was located in Boston's South End, and its overworked staff treated the homeless, the desperate, and the drug-induced. Television viewers from more rural areas never really got the premise because the hospital seemed perfectly okay to their eyes: only Bostonians and New Yorkers with access to many of the best hospitals in the world, would look down on the place.

The *St. Elsewhere* cast was first-rate. Dr. Donald Westphall (played by Ed Flanders [1934–1995]) is the prim and proper director, who has worked his way up the hard way and resents every unnecessary expense. Dr. Ben Samuels (played by David Birney [1939–]) is the kindhearted but often ineffectual surgeon who cannot persuade the director to increase expenses to meet the daily needs. A jolt of comedy is provided by Dr.

Victor Ehrlich (played by Ed Begley, Jr. [1949–]), a young physician who is astonished by the level of chaos he finds.

Could *St. Elsewhere* have made it if it had been filmed in some other American city?

Only Chicago would fit the bill, and the Windy City did not have a big enough audience in those days. Boston was the perfect location for this decaying urban hospital because of the age of the city and the makeup of its population. Very likely, the same program would not be set in Boston today because the city has changed so much.

Ed Begley, Jr., played the young Dr. Victor Ehrlich on *St. Elsewhere*.

SPENSER: FOR HIRE

What led to the rise in private detective TV dramas?

The concept of the private eye—he or she who would track one's enemies, and perhaps one's spouse—had been around since the 1950s, but it hit with special force during the 1980s. A major crime wave hit the bigger American cities, beginning around 1984 and culminating with previously unheard of numbers of murders in 1989 and 1989. As a result, programs such as *The Equalizer* that were set in Manhattan were popular. Boston had its special private eye in Spenser, who debuted on CBS in September 1985.

The viewer never learns Spenser's last name, and it never seems to matter. Spenser, played by the ruggedly handsome Robert Urich (1946–2002), is a dashing private eye who lives in Boston and is often seen in his charming red vehicle, dashing through the narrow streets of East Cambridge and Charlestown. His girlfriend is Susan—played by Barbara Stock (1956–)—but the more impressive and popular sidekick is "Hawk" (played by Avery Brooks [1948–]).

Does the viewer get a good look at Greater Boston in *Spenser: For Hire*?

The camera never lingers as long as one would like, but the occasional view is worth the wait. One sees Boston as it was in 1985–1988, when the worst of the dirt and grime of the 1940s and 1950s had disappeared. One does not see the truly cleaned-up city that appeared by the year 2005, and it's worth noting that the Big Dig had not yet taken place.

The street scenes, too, are revealing. Spenser seems to corner his foes in the tightest of spots, those that highlight the last remaining sections of nineteenth-century Boston.

CHEERS

When did *Cheers* first come on the air?

Cheers came on air for the first time on September 20, 1982. *Cheers* appeared at a time of general malaise in the nation as a whole, and Boston in particular. The economic recession that began in 1978 showed no signs of relenting: if anything, economic and financial matters were even worse. Then too, Boston had suffered through two of the worst winters in recent memory, and though no one yet knew it, two more were coming.

The famous Cheers sign outside the bar where the television sitcom was set.

Cheers gathered only a small audience share in its first two weeks, but the critics were, for once, full of praise. The writing was sharp and punchy; the delivery was first-rate, and *Cheers* seemed tailor-made for the times.

Who are the big stars on *Cheers*?

Sam Malone—played by Ted Danson (1947–)—is a handsome ex-athlete who looks for a new woman every month but who knows down deep that he will never find contentment. This does not prevent him from enjoying life: he lives it to the hilt. Diane Chambers—played by Shelley Long (1949–)—is the object of his affections when he is not looking to the other side of the bar. When Long left the show, Kirstie Alley (1951–) filled the romantic role as Rebecca Howe. Carla Tortelli (played by Rhea Perlman [1948–]) is the caustic, slightly bitter female lead. Over time, *Cheers* also found terrific secondary actors including Frasier Crane (played by Kelsey Grammer [1955–]) and Woody Boyd (played by Woody Harrelson [1961–]).

What is the premise of *Cheers*?

Though no one ever says it explicitly, the 1960s are gone, and the era of free love and hope for the future seems dead as well. No longer do the young and middle-aged look to a utopian future; instead they have their feet firmly in the mud, snow, and ice of downtown Boston. If these are the worst of times, they can also contain some of the best of fun, and the cast of *Cheers* shows the viewer that life is good, even when the shot glass is empty.

How did viewers take to *Cheers*?

They simply loved it. *Cheers* was one of the few aspects of popular culture—in the 1980s—about which there was no controversy. One either watched it and loved it, or one totally ignored it.

How big a wind-up was there to the last series of *Cheers*?

American television has never seen such a built-up. The only one that even comes close was the conclusion of *M.A.S.H.* in the winter of 1983. As *Cheers* fans learned that this was their one last season, they clamored for extra-special romance and intrigue, and got plenty of the former and little of the latter. There was even the possibility that President Bill Clinton would make a guest appearance on the last episode: this did not happen.

Cheers' last episode aired on Thursday, May 20, 1993. Sam and Diane (who comes back after a long time away) plan to move to the West Coast, but he backs out at the last minute, and she heads west alone. "One for the Road" is one of the most-watched episodes of all television history.

GOOD WILL HUNTING

How did one small film make two such big stars?

Matt Damon (1970–) and Ben Affleck (1972–) both got their start in *Good Will Hunting*, one of the biggest movie surprises of the year 1998. The two came to this enviable position by way of a set of trials.

Damon was born in Cambridge. His parents divorced when he was two, and he spent years feeling like an outsider. He attended Harvard, but left before graduating: he was

Ben Affleck (left) and Matt Damon first made it big with *Good Will Hunting*.

already at work on the screenplay for *Good Will Hunting*. Ben Affleck was born in Berkeley, California, but his family came east when he was two. He, too, was a product of a divorced family, and when he first met Matt Damon, around the age of eight, the two struck up a fast friendship.

What is the storyline of *Good Will Hunting*?

As the film begins, the viewer is surprised to see that the lead man is in hiding. Will Hunting (played by Matt Damon) works as a janitor at the Massachusetts Institute of Technology (MIT) even though he has brain power that exceeds most of the finest students there. Just how Will came to this juncture is not explained; instead, the film takes the viewer to his private life, which is a series of barrooms, heated conversations, and unexpressed love between Will and his best friend Chuckie (played by Ben Affleck).

In the first twenty minutes, the viewer thinks this is a film about wasted youth, but Will responds to an inner drive, and solves an incredibly complex algebraic problem put on the blackboard in a classroom at MIT. The professor searches in vain among his students, only to learn that the problem has been solved by the youthful janitor.

How frequently does one see Boston—and Cambridge—in the film?

Not only are there some fine shots of the scenery, but *Good Will Hunting* accomplishes something rarely seen in other films: it manages to portray both the seedy and the magnificent of Boston. One moment the camera is on the fine gardens and grounds at MIT, and in the next it is in a run-down neighborhood that has seen better times. Both Will and Chuckie are products of South Boston (the section of town that saw such turmoil during the 1970s), but mild poverty and continual discontent (not race) are the primary foes.

The film does just fine in its first forty minutes, but it is the encounters with Skylar (played by Minnie Driver [1970–]) and Dr. Maguire (portrayed by Robin Williams [1951–2014]) that really take it to the next level. Will meets Skylar, a British orphan who is about to graduate from Harvard, on the same night he administers a beating to a rival in a neighborhood brawl. Will faces jail time, but is reprieved by Professor Lambeau, who arranges for both individual tutoring, and for counseling, to be provided by his college roommate, Dr. Maguire.

How good an actor was Robin Williams?

In 1997 Williams was at the very top of his game. He plays Dr. Sean Maguire, who teaches psychology at the very humble Bunker Hill Community College. Located less than two miles from MIT, Bunker Hill is the antithesis of the grand universities: it is a state school that serves primarily underprivileged Boston youth. Will is surprised to find Sean Maguire in this setting. Was he not a classmate of Professor Lambeau? And thereby begins a long dialogue between the two, over the merits of success and personal fulfillment.

The high point of their conversations is when Will learns of the death of Maguire's wife from cancer. Maguire does not regret his marriage or the pain of losing his wife; nor does he lament the fact that he teaches at lowly Bunker Hill, when some of his fellows are at MIT and elsewhere. What Dr. Maguire conveys to Will is that love is greater, and more important, than success.

How big a success was *Good Will Hunting*?

It was the film of the winter of 1997, and it brought two Boston boys to the forefront. Matt Damon and Ben Affleck were on their way to super-stardom.

THE PERFECT STORM

Why did it take Hollywood producers so long to see the gold contained within the fishing industry?

The Perfect Storm would not have succeeded in an earlier era. It is too gritty, too working-class oriented. But as the twentieth century yielded to the twenty-first, a new slice of the movie audience was discovered, one that reveled in working-class drama. Hollywood recognized that Boston had an audience of its own, but wanted to gain a big market share: the result was *The Perfect Storm*.

To what degree is the film based on reality?

In October 1991, three storms collided off the east coast of the United States. Any one of these storms would have caused some disaster; the way they merged led to a megastorm. Of course, people were on the watch for such observances because the phrases "global warming" and "climate change" had just entered the popular lexicon. Not many people died in the super-storm of October 1991; what is remembered are the incredible rain showers that lasted for days. At the same time, however, a great drama was being played out on the Grand Banks off Newfoundland.

Bostonians were long familiar with the importance of the Grand Banks: the fish from that region provided the basis for the city's early prosperity. And when Hollywood

---

Why haven't we heard of Gloucester before this?

Gloucester is one of the "might have been" towns of Boston's North Shore. When the Puritans first arrived in 1630, it was about an even chance whether they would locate within Greater Boston or slightly to the north. And even after Boston became the capital of the colony and then the state, Gloucester was important for its part in the fishing industry. The annual blessing of the fishing fleet takes place in town, and Gloucester is also known for the special quality of its light, which has led to numerous artists taking up residence there.

316

decided to make a film of the super-storm of 1991, Bostonians cooperated, but it was the men and women of Gloucester who really made the film a super-hit.

THE CRUCIBLE

How important is *The Crucible* to the American identity?

Even those who dislike the subject or the way it has been handled admit that this is one of the most fundamental of all American stories. Written by Arthur Miller in 1953, *The Crucible* is set in seventeenth-century Salem, but has undertones that take the reader and viewer right into contemporary times. *The Crucible* examines the crucible of religious faith and its worst and its best, and holds it up as a mirror so that present-day Americans can question their own consciences.

How many high schools have performed *The Crucible* over the previous half-century?

It's beyond counting. It's a rare high school that has not performed *The Crucible* at some point, and some high schools have done so a number of times. *The Crucible* ranks right up there with *Oklahoma* and *Man of La Mancha* as one of the most performed of all plays.

Does one see, or feel, Boston in the 1997 version of *The Crucible*?

One does not see modern Boston, but one feels seventeenth-century Boston in the filming, which was done mostly on Hog Island. Closer to Boston than Salem, Hog Island is one of the most unspoiled areas in the region, and the film conveys the cold, darkness,

as well as occasional rays of brilliant light that mark the area. The indoor scenes are powerful enough, but when the entire village runs to the waterfront in order to bathe (and wash away sin), the viewer is nearly overwhelmed. No other film of the late twentieth century does so good a job in showing the lives of our seventeenth-century ancestors.

Who leads the cast of *The Crucible*?

Daniel Day-Lewis (1957–) plays John Proctor, the unfortunate man caught between two loves. He is devoted to his wife, Elizabeth Proctor (played by Joan Allen [1956–]), but he is in the crosshairs of the mischievous temptress Abigail Williams,

Actor Daniel Day-Lewis played John Proctor in the film version of *The Crucible*.

played by Winona Ryder (1971–). When John does not accept her advances, Abigail leads the teenage girls of Salem Village in a genuine witch-hunt that threatens to overturn the very social and religious foundation of Puritan New England.

Who turns in the most memorable performances in *The Crucible*?

Daniel Day-Lewis and Winona Ryder are both first-rate, but the show is stolen by Paul Scofield (1922–2008), who plays Judge Danforth, and by Peter Vaughan (1923–)—a veteran British actor—who portrays Giles Cory. Both men are superb in bringing the seventeenth-century Puritans to life. Scofield is memorable in his role as a man of rectitude who is brought low by his suspicions, while Peter Vaughan is simply sensational as the irreverent villager who refuses even to plead (guilty or not guilty). As a result, Giles Corey was pressed to death by stones.

STREETS, SQUARES, AND NEIGHBORHOODS

Is there any one spot on which one can stand and declare that this is the heart of Boston?

There are in fact so many such places that it is difficult to make the final count. But if one wishes to nail it down, it's better to proceed in a fashion such as what follows.

Standing in front of the Museum of Fine Arts, one feels that he or she is in the very heart of cultural and artistic Boston. Standing in front of One State Street gives the impression that one has arrived in the very center of the financial heart of Boston. Entering Fenway Park means, of course, that one has arrived at the epicenter of athletic Boston. And this leads, surely enough, to the question: What is the heart of political Boston? It should be 100 Federal Street, but Bostonians have disliked the building itself ever since it appeared in 1971. It could be the Massachusetts State House, but that building belongs to the Commonwealth, not the city. And so one is left with the distinct impression that Boston—a city that contains many worlds—does not possess a heart to its political self.

What is the most famous, or best known of all the streets of Boston?

It's a real toss-up. Beacon Street is best known by those who are interested in the Federal history and architecture of Boston. Tremont Street has the deepest echoes for those that love the colonial period. Red Sox fans are most familiar with Yawkey Way. But if one compiles the long list of the streets of Boston and looks for the one that crops up the most—both in literature and the popular imagination—the answer is Comm Ave (Commonwealth Avenue).

Comm Ave runs from Boston Common due west, and the alert pedestrian can enjoy more good things along the route than in any comparable section of Greater Boston. The Mall, a beautiful green section in the middle of Comm Ave, has many sculptures, including the intriguing one of African American poet Phillis Wheatley.

319

A private garden on Beacon Street helps beautify the famous neighborhood. Residents have a lot of pride in their homes and yards here.

What is the best-known of the many public squares of Greater Boston?

Copley Square is definitely number one. There one can find everything ranging from the magnificent Boston Public Library to the most old-time of record stores. Copley Square also is where the Boston Marathon comes to its end. But if Copley is number one, then Kenmore Square is not too far behind.

Kenmore Square stands just a few hundred yards east of Fenway Park, and Red Sox fans flock to the bars and nightclubs. Kenmore is also well known for its hotels. It's the combination of students, Red Sox fans, and tourists that make Kenmore Square so popular a place: the Square is better known than any other landmark to many of Boston's college students

What is the most difficult traffic intersection in Greater Boston?

Twenty years ago, the answer would have been impossible because there were so many difficult ones. The Big Dig cleaned out a lot of them, however, and today, Greater Boston is not so much difficult as challenging (see the chapter "The Modern Metropolis"). One definitely has to keep one's eyes open at all times. That said, the three different approaches to Boston Common see the greatest amount of traffic, and, presumably, the largest number of traffic accidents. Many are the tourists who drive toward the Common, mistakenly thinking they will find parking. Get in the left lane and one quickly passes the Common parking garage, meaning that one has to go round the entire Common, braving the traffic once more in order to find a safe haven. But for all the difficulties, the tourists keep coming. The locals usually approach this area on foot.

What is the most dangerous street or thoroughfare in Greater Boston?

Entrance to the Boston Public Library.

Beyond a doubt this is Storrow Drive, which parallels the Charles River. Whether one gets on in the western part of the city, or is an afternoon commuter, heading home from the eastern section, Storrow Drive is hazardous. GPS definitely makes a difference, but one has to be constantly alert. On the northern side of the Charles River, Memorial Drive is safer than Storrow, but traffic often moves very slowly. Again, the locals have the advantage, as they can plan ahead. Bostonians are famous for phoning each other at all times of the day, alerting family and friends which streets to use, and which to avoid.

What is the most relaxing section of Greater Boston in which to drive?

There really isn't one. Boston has its quieter sections, but the competition for space on the road, and in the parking lots, is nearly constant. One therefore does not look for the best part of town in which to drive but rather for the few times when the city is calmer as a whole. And Sunday morning is definitely the best.

The tourist who wishes to drive Greater Boston does well to show up early on Sunday morning, and to familiarize himself with the streets when competition is at a minimum. By 1 P.M. the situation changes, with many cars on the road, but they are proceeding more slowly than is usually the case. And finding a parking place on the street, while not a snap, is much more possible on Sunday.

What is the worst time and place for driving in Greater Boston?

Any time after 3 P.M. on a weekday is bad, and the worst areas tend to be in the Financial District. Many highly paid bank personnel consider the ability to scoot out of town at five minutes prior to 3 P.M. the most significant side benefit of their jobs. Then too, the competition to get on the highways and head to Cape Cod—known simply as "The Cape"—is intense on Friday afternoons.

How many cars enter and exit Boston on any given weekday?

There are half a million vehicles parked within Greater Boston overnight, and many of
them rev up each morning. But concerning inbound traffic from the suburbs, the number might well be in excess of one million.

What is the section of Boston that has changed the most, so far as pedestrians are concerned?

There was a time when the Old North End and Chinatown were the very worst parts of
the city because of the congestion and noise. This has changed considerably since the
Rose Kennedy Greenway was completed in 2008. The Greenway allows pedestrians to
take breaks during their long afternoons in Boston, and it's much easier to move from
Faneuil Hall to the New England Aquarium than before. The designers of the Greenway
were skillful and efficient: they have made the eastern part of Greater Boston much
more pleasurable for the pedestrian.

How have the neighborhoods changed over time?

Perhaps the best example is the Old North End. During Puritan times, the North End
was the center of Boston's commerce; it became known as the roughest and toughest
part of town. When the Irish began to come in the 1840s, the North End was the logical place to settle, and the great-great-grandchildren of the Puritans moved out of that
locality, mostly headed toward the West End. Forty years later came another ethnic
change: the Italians moved in as the Irish moved out (many of them moved to Dorchester and South Boston). And in the 1970s and 1980s, the Old North End began to be
populated by Asians and Africans, the most recent of the newcomers.

Of course this begs another question: Which neighborhood has changed the least,
over time? And the answer is Beacon Hill. From roughly 1750 forward, Beacon Hill has
been the center of life for the most well-to-do and culturally astute members of the city
population. Apartments and houses change hands, of course, but the new owners tend to
be very much like the old ones, socially, ethnically, and in terms of material possessions.

Why does Boston—one of the smaller American cities—have so many distinct neighborhoods?

Oddly enough, it is Boston's very smallness that made this possible. The land area of Greater Boston is much smaller than that of Greater New York City, for example. And Boston was settled in fits and starts with the downtown region and Charlestown being the first. As a result, each "new" neighborhood felt the need to distinguish itself from the downtown. The Old North End, which remains the most visibly distinct part of Greater Boston, was the first to really set itself apart. The South End (not to be confused with South Boston) came later. Other localities—such as Brighton, Allston, and Dorchester—enjoyed long periods of political independence, when they were self-governing. As a general rule, the longer that a locality was separate, the more entrenched its political and ethnic identities became.

What has traditionally been the most difficult part of the city?

Dorchester and South Boston have usually been the last to profit in financial terms, and the first to suffer when the local economy goes south. Given other circumstances, Dorchester could have been the maritime and commercial center of the region, but the Old North End got that role. This does not explain all the reasons that Dorchester and Southie are so tight-knit, but it's a good place to begin.

For outsiders, Roxbury has long been considered the most dangerous part of Greater Boston. At the time of this writing (2015) Roxbury is in better shape than for many years, but during the 1970s, it was considered the most likely place for a person to be mugged.

Can a person get everywhere he or she wants by taking the subway?

Just about. Boston had the first subway system in the nation, completed in 1897, and the city is interlaced with subway stops. The outsider, or tourist, however, often finds the subway ride too much on his or her first trip to the city. He or she is advised, therefore, to drive the streets, but to do so with care. The driving itself is not so bad: it's finding the parking place(s) that is so difficult. In this case, too, Boston is much better than in the past: the city is served by a number of parking garages.

Is there any reliable way to find a parking spot on Boston streets?

If there were, thousands of people would soon compete to take advantage of it. But if one comes from out of town, perhaps arriving at Logan Airport, the key is surely to rent a small, compact car. Sport utility vehicles are popular with commuters, but people who really want to see the city use the smallest type of car possible in order to thread their way through the narrow streets.

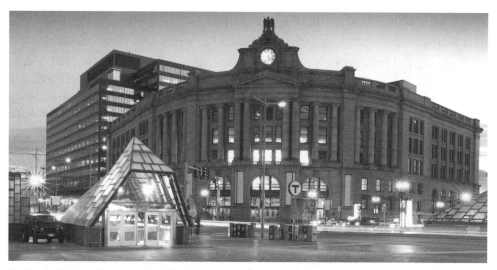
The South Station in Boston was built in 1898 and is the largest train station in the area.

Which parts of the city are worst in terms of dead-end traffic and cars that barely move?

It depends on the time of day. At 8 A.M. all of the major entrances to Boston, Mass Pike and Route 3 especially, are jammed, and it can be a frustrating commute. At midday, the areas around Government Center and the Back Bay are filled to capacity. And for the 4 P.M. rush hour, the toughest spots are in Chinatown and the Financial District.

How did Boston commuters survive in the decades prior to the Big Dig?

That's one of the great unanswered questions. No one knows how many Boston commuters went slowly mad, exasperated by their experiences on the Central Artery, or in the mass of tunnels beneath the city. Anecdotally, one can report that many Bostonians endured this for decades, and did so without any negative effects, while some others swore off the automobile entirely, and would only use the train or subways. What was so maddening—and what can still provoke rage today—is the short physical distances involved. There are times, particularly in mid-day, when it really is faster to jog across the Boston Common than it is to drive around it, and this is true even though the Common constitutes forty square acres.

Is it likely that Boston will ever become a city that is truly "easy to drive"?

No. And this should provoke no hand-wringing. American cities—from Los Angeles to Miami—keep getting larger and more filled with cars. It's difficult to envision a scenario under which driving around Boston becomes easy, but there are times when it is pleasurable.

Sunday is definitely the best day to visit Boston. Parking spaces—while not plentiful—can be found. Double parking is often tolerated for a handful of minutes, and these are all that is required for the father and mother to orient themselves, while giving the kids in the back seat a breather. Bostonians are not avid churchgoers these days, and there is little traffic till around 11 A.M. And in the afternoon, one finds a relaxed quality to Boston that is difficult to equal.

SQUARES

How did Boston ever come to have so many squares?

Some of the squares are unofficial (simply areas where four streets come together), but many others were planned. Kenmore Square, for example, formed because the area is located at the intersection between Fenway Park and the Longwood Medical Center area, which is famous for its many clinics and hospitals.

The more Bostonians experimented with public squares, the more they liked them, and Greater Boston simply throngs with squares, many of them named for prominent local citizens. Squares also form an excellent way of giving directions and meeting people. When in Manhattan, one reflexively gives the street and cross-street; when in Boston, one usually names the square that is close at hand.

What is the best-known square in Greater Boston?

It's a toss-up between Kenmore Square and Harvard Square, on the north side of the river. Kenmore Square is better known to locals, while Harvard Square is world famous. If one could put the attributes of these two squares together, he or she would possess the means to attract virtually everyone.

What is the most fashionable square in Greater Boston?

Copley Square used to claim this distinction, but ever since about the year 2000, Harvard Square has been number one. Of course one can use the subway to move from one to the other in a very short time, so it's possible to enjoy the best of both.

What used to be the least-fashionable part of Greater Boston?

Located at the intersection of Washington and Park streets, this was the so-called Combat Zone. It gained its name by virtue of the many men in uniform that came to patronize the area. There was an excitement to the Combat Zone—not entirely because of its connection to sex—but very few people lamented when the area changed, and simmered down in the 1990s.

If one has only six hours to spend in Boston, what areas should he or she be sure not to miss?

As long as these are daylight hours and the sun is shining, one does best to stay outside. There's enough to see on the Common and in the Back Bay that three hours of walking, combined with three hours in restaurants is sufficient to gain a sense of what Boston is all about. But if the skies are grey, or the town experiences rain, it's best to seek out either the Museum of Fine Arts or the Museum of Science.

NEIGHBORHOODS

What are some of the best-known neighborhoods of Greater Boston?

Allston, Brighton, Southie, The South End—there's no lack of neighborhoods, all of which possess their distinctive flavor. One lesson the neighborhoods confer is that Boston was not settled in a hurry, and that its people did not venture out of their prescribed areas. These days Boston is a freewheeling and friendly place, but as of about the year 1920, people lived in their compact neighborhoods, and seldom ventured into others.

What is the most dangerous neighborhood of Greater Boston?

As long as the sun is shining and there are people about, Greater Boston is quite safe. Once darkness falls, Roxbury is known as the most dangerous part of the metropolis, but its reputation has improved a great deal in recent years. The high point of danger in and around Boston came in the late 1980s, when crime was endemic. Since about 1995, Boston has become much safer.

ALLSTON

For whom is Allston named?

Allston may be the only locality in the United States named for a portrait painter. Washington Allston (1779–1843) was born and raised in South Carolina and came north to study at Harvard, where he remained, becoming one of the leaders of the Romantic artistic movement in America. He died in Cambridge in 1843.

When the town was named, no one anticipated that Allston would become a true mecca for students at Boston's many colleges and universities. Today, Allston has a population of about thirty thousand, over half of whom are graduate or undergraduate students.

What are some of the least-known neighborhoods of Greater Boston?

East Boston and Charlestown—which are side-by-side—are at the top of this list. Many tourists come to Boston several times before learning that there is an East Boston, and many others do not realize that Charlestown has a distinct identity of its own. Hyde Park and Jamaica Plain are well known to locals, but many outsiders do not realize that these make up part of Greater Boston.

What kind of housing do the students occupy?

Allston has row upon row of three-deckers, most of them built between 1880 and 1920. To arrive in Allston at the wrong time of year—which is to say in late August—is a nightmare, but he or she who comes even a month earlier often has a field day. The apartments are larger than those in Cambridge or Kenmore Square.

Allston is marvelously quiet at noon, and the afternoon is not bad, but the sounds from student stereos pick up each evening. Numerous major parties take place each weekend, and it can be difficult for the typical adult resident to thread his way through the noise and distractions.

BACK BAY

Where does the name come from?

What we now call the Back Bay was originally a tidal wasteland, located just to the west of the peninsula, that the Indians labeled Shawmut. Thanks to the tides, which were sometimes over seven feet, the area acquired an unhealthy and unlikable reputation.

Brownstone homes in the Back Bay neighborhood.

327

This changed in the first half of the nineteenth century when a land reclamation project began.

The work went on for more than twenty years, but when it was complete the unhealthy section of Boston had turned into its most desirable location. Brownstones were constructed during the Civil War era, and thousands of Bostonians moved from the Old North End and the South End to Back Bay, presumably to live in comfort. Some of the most affecting biographies from this period—notably Samuel Eliot Morison's *One Boy's Boston*—sing the praises of life in Back Bay and Beacon Hill.

Was there ever a time when Back Bay was not fashionable?

For a short time in the late 1970s Back Bay took on a dirty and rather tired look. Students found it easier to rent apartments in Back Bay, and real estate prices either stayed in one place or retreated a little. Once the recovery began, around the year 1984, however, its progress was rapid. Back Bay became one of the most desirable parts of Greater Boston.

What is the single greatest sight to be seen in Back Bay?

There are actually two. The first, which is truly sublime, is the reflection of nineteenth-century Trinity Church in the glass structure of the Hancock Tower. One sometimes stumbles about Back Bay for hours, seeking just the right light and position for photography, only to find it coming together in a matter of seconds with the church and the tower forming the center.

The second sight, which is more breathtaking than sublime, is the Charles River Basin. Like the Hancock Tower, the Charles River Basin is best seen in late afternoon. If one is lucky, the sun may go down at just the right time, affording a magnificent sunset.

Where do Back Bay and Beacon Hill come together?

They meet at the foot of Boston Common, right about where the Arlington Street Church stands today. The two neighborhoods share affluence, distinction, and ease of movement. There are residents of both communities who seldom travel, and who when asked, reply that there is no need. They already possess all the good things of life. And on a sunny afternoon, when the light sparkles up and down Beacon Street, they may well be correct. On the other hand, there's nothing quite so bad as a winter wind that sweeps up Beacon Street. It was to escape those winter blows that many of the regulars went to "Cheers," the place "where everybody knows your name."

BEACON HILL

How did a hill turn into a neighborhood?

Very slowly. Beacon Hill is where the first Puritans arrived in 1630, and it was still quite noticeable at the time of the American Revolution. The decades that followed saw a leveling of the hill, however, as landfill was needed for other parts of the city, notably Back

Bay. As a result, the hill, which marches along the west side of Boston Common, is not as high today. That does not prevent it from being one of the most desirable addresses in all Massachusetts, indeed New England, however.

Was there ever a time when Beacon Hill was neither fashionable nor rich?

Yes. In the three decades that followed the American Revolution, Beacon Hill was known as an area for prostitutes. One of the most affecting memoirs was written by Lucy Brewer, a nineteenth-century Massachusetts girl who claimed first to have been a prostitute on Beacon Hill, and then a U.S. Marine aboard the USS *Constitution* (scholars continue to debate the veracity of the latter claim).

What is the grandest sight to be seen in the Beacon Hill neighborhood?

Several areas and sights lay claim, but all are superseded by the magnificent monument directly across the street from the Massachusetts State House. Executed by Augustus Saint-Gaudens, the memorial to the 54th Massachusetts Infantry Regiment (composed of black soldiers and white officers)

BRIGHTON

Is it true that Brighton was once a farming community?

Perhaps because it is about 250 feet higher than downtown Boston in elevation, Brighton managed to resist, or hold at arm's length, the trend toward suburbanization. Brighton had numerous farms as late as 1850, and many orchards as late as 1890. It was an area to which the well-to-do hastened for the weekend, to get away from the bustle of downtown.

What is the ethnic makeup of Brighton in our time?

For at least three generations Brighton was Irish and Roman Catholic, but since about the early 1990s it has become increasingly Asian. Numerous people have left Chinatown and moved to Brighton.

What is the best-known cultural connection to Brighton?

Published in 1996 *Infinite Jest* is David Foster Wallace's dystopian novel, set in Brighton. The book isn't so much about Brighton as the absurdities of American culture in the late twentieth century, but Brighton serves very well as the physical location.

What is the difference between Brighton and Allston?

There are several, including proximity to the Charles River, but perhaps the single most important difference is found in school or university allegiance. Brighton is Boston College territory, smack next to the old Jesuit school, and Allston is primarily Boston University territory.

BROOKLINE

Is Brookline really its own town, or is it really just the western part of Boston?

Brookline is so merged into the western part of Boston proper that it is sometimes difficult to tell the difference. Geographically, however, the difference is evident in the landscape that moves upward, to the hills that separate the western part of the city from the suburbs. The clothing and attitude of the populace changes as well because one moves from student housing to the homes of the wealthy and well-to-do.

Brookline was an independent locality for decades, before being annexed to Boston in 1874. Its first residents were farmers, and they were followed by businessmen who wanted to live out of the hustle and bustle of the big city. The wealth that characterizes Brookline today is largely the product of Wall Street speculation, and the rise in the price of real estate. Brookline was a much humbler place when John F. Kennedy was born there in May 1917.

What was the first name for what we now call Brookline?

During the colonial and Revolutionary periods, it was known as Muddy River, and was considered the outermost part of Boston. Even in those early days, it was fashionable to get out of town, especially during the summer months, and some of Boston's leading citizens had farms and fields in Brookline.

Is the Kennedy mystique even stronger in Brookline than in other parts of the city?

Even though the Kennedys and Fitzgeralds lived in Brookline only a few years, this locality claims the Kennedys and their mystique more strongly than any other section of Greater Boston. This is where Kennedy was born in a modest three-floor home. And this is where the Kennedys—and Fitzgeralds—began their ascent to wealth and fame.

The Fitzgeralds were already well known because of John "Honey" Fitzgerald, the crooner who was mayor of Boston for two terms. The Kennedys were relative upstarts,

---

Is there such a thing as the "typical" Brookline family?

If so, their career would almost certainly revolve around medicine, higher education, or some combination of the two. Brookline has, perhaps, more medical doctors and doctors of philosophy than any other location in Massachusetts, and its residents are keenly attuned to the opportunities that exist in those fields. Of course there are the unusual ones, the surprises, but it still is rather rare to hear of a Brookliner who became a professional wrestler. Much more likely is that he or she would become an opera singer.

but the wedding of Joseph P. Kennedy and Rose Fitzgerald—in 1914—began what became America's most famous dynasty. Never mind that the Bushes have held the White House longer, or that the Clintons have spent longer at the top of Washington politics. The Kennedys are America's royalty, the number-one political family.

What would Brookline's fame be like if Michael S. Dukakis had won the presidency in 1988?

These days we regard Dukakis as an afterthought, but he looked strong in the summer of 1988. Had he succeeded, and beaten George H.W. Bush for the White House in November of that year, Brookline would be number one, among all American towns and localities in the production of presidents.

CAMBRIDGE

Is Cambridge actually part of Boston?

Not on the maps and not in political jurisdiction. But the proximity of Cambridge and Boston (it is only eight minutes by subway between Harvard Square and Kenmore Square) makes the former intrinsically part of the latter. For thousands of college students, and literally millions of alumni, there is no substantial difference between Boston and Cambridge.

If that is so, how did they become different cities with different names?

Cambridge first appears in the Puritan records in 1631 with the name of Newe Towne. In 1638 the tiny beginnings of Harvard College were seen, and by 1700, Cambridge was a separate community from Boston. In those days, virtually all the major leaders of Puritan Boston went by barge, horse, or foot to Cambridge, to observe the annual Harvard commencement.

What really gave Cambridge a new independent self, however, was the same event that granted the nation its political independence. During the nine-month Siege of Boston (1775–1776), the British occupied Boston, while the Patriots—led by General George Washington—were centered in Cambridge. Perhaps some self-promotion was part of it, but Cambridge became known as the "loyal" place (loyal to the cause of American independence), while Boston was associated with Loyalists and Tories.

When did Cambridge become an incorporated city?

This took place in 1846. By then, Cambridge had a distinct identity, and some worthy Cambridge types considered it beneath themselves ever to travel to Boston (and vice-versa). This extreme parochialism may seem distasteful and immature, but it was part of the American cultural inheritance from England. There are Oxford men and women who "never" travel to Cambridge, for example.

I know of Cambridge and even of East Cambridge, but what is Cambridgeport?

Located on the extreme eastern side of Cambridge, Cambridgeport was named in earnest hope that the area would become the important new maritime port for the Boston area. This never happened, and now about the only vessels passing through are those that carry natural gas. The name stuck, however, and Cambridgeport became part of the local vocabulary (many early runners of the Boston Marathon identified Cambridgeport as home, for example).

When did Harvard take on the physical dimensions that we know today?

Harvard has been a distinct place since the late seventeenth century, but its oldest building today (Memorial Hall) dates to around 1870. Harvard took on the look, aspect, and dimensions we know today in the late nineteenth century, during the presidency of Charles W. Eliot (served 1869–1909).

Everyone knows that Harvard Square is an exciting place. Has it always been so?

For thousands of college students—as well as many of their professors—Harvard Square is "the place" in all of Cambridge. It has to be said, however, that the Square is not as dynamic as in, say, 1970 or 1980. During the late 1960s, Harvard Square was known for its many student protestors; during the 1970s, it was known for its amazing collection of boutique shops, some focused on clothing and others on music records. Today's Cambridge suffers—as does Boston as a whole—from the concentrations in the music industry which limit the expression of many young talents.

CHARLESTOWN

One thinks of Charlestown as part of Boston. Is this correct?

Politically, yes. Institutionally, yes. But in their heart of hearts, the people of Charlestown think of themselves as quite different, even a world apart from Boston. It has been this way since Puritan times. Charlestown, after all, was settled by the Puritans a few short months before they crossed to Boston.

What is the most distinct aspect of the architecture of Charlestown?

Crossing from Boston, or coming down from the town of Everett, one immediately feels a difference. Charlestown may not be rich, but its residents carry on a very dignified way of life. Little things—such as the corner of building lots and the edge of a stone wall—matter a great deal in Charlestown, one of the most heavily zoned localities in all Massachusetts. The clothing of the people is not much different from that of the other side of the Charles and Mystic rivers: it's the pace of those people that shows the difference. Young people may drive swiftly through Charlestown in high-powered cars: residents over the age of fifty walk with a slowness and ease that is the envy of their Boston neighbors.

How important is the Bunker Hill Monument to the identity of Charlestown?

Construction began in 1825—the fiftieth anniversary of the battle—and was completed in 1843. Numerous men and women of Charlestown played roles in the construction, and their great-great-grandchildren remember it with pride. The Bunker Hill Monument is one of the steepest climbs in all Massachusetts, but he or she who perseveres is rewarded with a magnificent view of the city. Bunker Hill is also the site of numerous military gatherings throughout the year.

The Bunker Hill Monument in Charlestown.

How important is the USS *Constitution* to the identity of Charlestown?

The USS *Constitution* belongs to the nation, the federal government, and the U.S. Navy, in that order, but the people of Charlestown consider themselves its honorary owners. Launched from Boston in 1798, *Constitution* is the most famous of all American warships, and one of the few that can claim that it never lost a fight.

What is the most exciting part of Charlestown?

For history buffs, it is the Charlestown Navy Yard. Though the U.S. Navy officially closed its activities there in the 1970s, the Navy Yard is home to the USS *Constitution*, the world's oldest commissioned warship. Only about ten percent of her timbers are original, but she has been lovingly restored. The tours given of the ship are a constant draw to families; children marvel at the tight quarters, while parents exclaim over the success of this vessel, which is often called the world's "most fortunate ship." Launched in Boston in 1797, *Constitution* never lost a battle. There was a time in the 1840s when people called for her to be torn up for scrap; in response, poet Oliver Wendell Holmes, Sr., penned these lines:

> Ay, tear her tattered ensign down!
> Long has it waved on high,
> And many an eye has danced to see

That banner in the sky;
Beneath it rung the battle shout,
And burst the cannon's roar;
The meteor of the ocean air
Shall sweep the cloud no more.

Suffice to say that *Constitution* was not broken up, and that she remains one of the things Bostonians are most proud of.

What was the most disgraceful moment in Charlestown history?

Though the shame belongs to Boston as a whole, there is little doubt that Charlestown takes most of the blame for the events of August 12, 1834. Anti-Catholicism had reached a fever pitch in the Boston area, and a mob, a majority of whom were Charlestown residents, gathered at the Ursuline Convent in Charlestown. The ten Catholic nuns and forty residents—some of whom came from Boston's Unitarian families—were commanded to depart, and the convent was set afire. Condemnation came from all quarters, and some people were charged with the crime, but none were ever found guilty.

King's Chapel at the bottom of Tremont Street is frequented by visitors every day of the year.

What is the most surprising thing about Charlestown?

The absolute beauty of the streets. Charlestown is very small, but she has managed to keep more of her original homes and street layout than any other part of Greater Boston. Driving the streets makes one remember the 1980s TV series *Spenser: for Hire* which showcased Robert Urich driving the streets of Charlestown in a sporty red car. With all that, there is still one more marvel, and one that is seldom seen.

The Charlestown cemetery, Phipps Street Burying Ground, which is open only on certain days, is perhaps the most venerable to be found in the United States. Copp's Hill Cemetery in the Old North End, and King's Chapel Cemetery Burying Ground on Tremont Street are better known, but the Charlestown cemetery has many stones cut by someone known only as the "Charlestown Carver," a person whose work lives on.

CHINATOWN/FLATIRON DISTRICT

How did Boston become such a magnet for Chinese immigrants?

The influx started as early as the 1930s, and built to a crescendo in the 1970s. The first Chinese immigrants tended to be working or middle class, and they quickly established new businesses, with laundry and food service being the most common. By the 1990s, however, Chinatown had a distinct population of wealthy and well-to-do Chinese with more arriving all the time.

What kind of festivals are held in Chinatown?

Chinese New Year, which usually falls in late January or early February, is the biggest, but Chinatown delights in all sorts of spectacles. The Boston Dragon Boat Festival on the Charles River comes to Boston via Chinatown, and in the summertime there are all sorts of parades and processions. The growing popularity of traditional Chinese medicine, including acupuncture and herbs, has made Chinatown both more visible to traditional Bostonians, and more popular.

DORCHESTER

How does Dorchester come by its tough and gritty reputation?

In recent times, Dorchester gained this reputation from a number of working-class artists who hailed from there, and then made good in Hollywood. Donnie and Mark, the Wahlberg brothers, have made Dorchester more visible to millions of fans, both through their music and films. In truth, however, Dorchester has long been one of the toughest and most blue collar parts of Greater Boston. As one exits off Route 3, and enters Dorchester, he or she is struck by the number of signs, most of them having to do with plumbing, roofing, carpentry, and tailoring services. Of course that's not the entire story. One also finds monuments to the colonial past, such as the one that indicates where General Knox's cannon, which was hauled all the way from Fort Ticonderoga, were placed in March 1776.

Dorchester vies with South Boston for being the most Irish of all the bedroom communities of Greater Boston. These days the two towns enjoy a friendly but rough-spirited alliance; in the early twentieth century, they competed to see which local politician would dominate, and win City Hall.

What are some the clearest signs that one is in Dorchester?

The housing is distinctive. Built in the 1890s and the first two decades of the twentieth century, Dorchester's three- and four-decker houses are usually chocolate brown along the sides, edged with dull white trim. One knows in a flash that "this is not Brookline," for example. The clothing of the people of Dorchester is also noticeable: one sees more firemen, policemen, bricklayers, and masons than in any other part of Greater Boston.

Has Dorchester participated in the boom in housing prices?

Yes indeed. It's a rare neighborhood, or even street, in Greater Boston that did not see prices double between 1985 and 2000, and many are on the verge of doubling again. Dorchester may not have the niceties of numerous other neighborhoods, but it is superbly positioned on the south side of Boston with easy access to the big city, and a nearly straight ride to the Cape. In Boston that is no small matter.

What is the most modern and up-to-date section of Dorchester?

Whether one takes Morrissey Boulevard or Route 3, he or she is struck by the openness of the scenery. A quick left-hand turn brings the driver to Columbia Point, home to the University of Massachusetts at Boston, the John F. Kennedy Presidential Library and Museum, and the Massachusetts Archives. This is a bright spot in town, but there's a lonely feeling, too, brought on by proximity to the waters of Massachusetts Bay, which has seen many a vessel go down, and many a crew lost.

EAST BOSTON

How can there be an "East Boston" when the only thing east is the Atlantic Ocean?

It's one of the many incongruities that make Boston special. In some cases, it's only locals who know about East Boston, and it's quite possible that ten percent of all Bostonians have never even crossed to the side called "East." East Boston dates to the time of the Puritans and the real estate hunger of Judge Samuel Sewall, who owned much of the area. Over time, East Boston became the most industrial part of the entire city, something testified to by row upon row of empty warehouses. As recently as 2000, East Boston seemed like an afterthought, an addition that would eventually be discarded. But the success of the Big Dig brought more visibility to East Boston. The neighborhood has a quiet feeling. Even as thousands of cars move on Storrow Drive, and as hundreds of thousands of people mill through Downtown Boston, one can feel at peace in the "East."

How does one get to East Boston?

It was never very easy, and it has become—if anything—even more complicated. The person who comes barreling in from the west, intent on reaching Logan Airport, sails through the Ted Williams Tunnel on the way to the airport, heedless of the hefty toll. The discriminating tourist, and budget traveler, threads his way past Government Center to take the William Callahan Tunnel, which is toll-free.

Who are the people of East Boston?

They are primarily immigrants and the children of the same. Time was when East Boston was primarily Irish, and then largely Italian, but no one can quite count all the various ethnic varieties of today. One finds Haitians, Cape Verdeans, Asians from half a dozen nations, and quite a few Africans. Rents are lower here than on the west side, and East Boston is amassing a reputation as a good and safe place in which to live.

Is there any chance the factories will return?

The buildings stand empty today, a sad commentary on our post-industrial society. That the buildings will again see the manufacture of shoes, textiles, and so forth is unlikely; that those buildings will be used for something is almost a certainty. Greater Boston never tires of reinventing itself. East Boston may well be the next part of the city that sees gentrification.

What is the most exciting time of the year to be in East Boston?

New Year's Eve and the Fourth of July are the best times. A tugboat, anchored right off the park that decorates East Boston's waterfront, is the location of the fireworks that light up Boston Harbor. Again, it's worth noting that there are many Bostonians—who live in the city proper—who have never used the William Callahan Tunnel to go to East Boston.

JAMAICA PLAIN

Does the name come from a connection to the Island of Jamaica?

Probably not. Although it's romantic to speculate on Boston skippers sailing to Jamaica and back, it's more likely that the name derives from a corruption of the name of one of the Indian chiefs who lived in the area.

Why is it that so many people who move to Boston wind up in Jamaica Plain?

The neighborhood has long welcomed newcomers, and students flock to it as much as they gravitate to Somerville, ten miles to the north. Newcomers to Boston often find their first housing in Jamaica Plain, and move two or three years thereafter: this is a neighborhood that welcomes young couples, but loses them soon after graduation or the birth of their second child.

Kenmore Square is easily recognized from afar by spotting its practically iconic CITGO sign.

KENMORE/FENWAY

How can a residential area be so defined by a sporting place?

In most cities this would not be possible. Boston, however, lives and dies by the success or failure of the Red Sox. Hundreds of thousands—perhaps millions of people—know Boston primarily as the home of the Red Sox, and they wouldn't even come into town if not for them.

How much fun do people have in Kenmore Square?

It's not quantifiable, of course, but if one drives through the dozen or so major city squares, he or she gets the distinct impression that Kenmore Square people have the most fun. This is where record stores boomed in the 1970s and 1980s, and where rock bands have performed to sold-out crowds for decades. The subway stop in the middle of Kenmore Square is one of the most popular, and recognizable; thousands of college students are photographed by friends as they exit and enter.

How important is the CITGO sign to the identity of Kenmore/Fenway?

Given that Boston is such a heady (intellectual) place, one is often surprised to learn how "big" the CITGO sign is to the identity of the people of Kenmore Square, and of the city as a whole. Located at 660 Beacon Street, the CITGO sign is sixty feet by sixty feet, and is lit by many thousands of efficient bulbs. People from out of down often use the CITGO sign as a navigational landmark, and Bostonians often compare its brilliance at night to other night lights. The CITGO sign is doubly important for sporting and athletic Bostonians, however.

The very best view one can have of the CITGO sign is from inside Fenway Park. No one can count the number of fans who have laughed, cried, or booed on Red Sox nights, while looking at the CITGO sign. For runners of the Boston Marathon, the first sight of the CITGO sign indicates they are within two miles of the finish line, and that is terribly important to morale, as they struggle through the last set of obstacles.

How much music has been made in Kenmore Square?

When we combine the street musicians with the serious bands, and account for the many groups that never made it big, we conclude that Kenmore Square has more musicians, per square foot, than any other area in New England. And when we look round the entire nation, we see only a few places, notably in San Francisco and New York, where as much music has been made.

SOUTH END

Is there really a difference between Southie (South Boston) and the South End?

It's a little like asking if there is a difference between the Tower of London and Westminster Abbey. Locals may forgive a person for making the error, but they don't look kindly on it.

The South End is what used to, in fact, be the southern end of the peninsula that the Native Americans called Shawmut. It runs from Downtown Boston to the West End, and it is where the high-rise buildings of the central part of the city yield to the three- and four-story buildings of the neighborhoods. The South End is a delightful place for walking—made even better by the neighborhood gardens—but it is a place haunted by the past.

SOUTH BOSTON (SOUTHIE)

Is South Boston the most Irish of all Boston localities?

Traditionally this has been the case, and Southie politicians have carried the Boston Irish brand far and wide. In recent years, however, South Boston has become a magnet for numerous other minorities. Professionals with young children are also drawn to the neighborhood.

How strong is the connection between South Boston and St. Patrick's Day?

Just a generation ago, St. Patrick's Day was the festival of South Boston, and nearly everyone wore the green on March 17 (there is a slight conflict between this holiday and Evacuation Day, the day the British left Boston in 1776). While there remains plenty of enthusiasm for St. Patrick's Day, South Boston is beginning to look more and more like a melting pot, with room for more than just the Irish.

West End

Of all the different Ends, one hears the least about the West End. Why is that?

The West End has the lowest profile of all Boston neighborhoods, meaning it is the least well known. One of the few famous names from the locality is that of Leonard Nimoy, the legendary actor from the television series *Star Trek*.

West Roxbury

Where does the "West" come in?

West Roxbury forms the extreme southwest corner of the Greater Boston area, and is distinct enough from Roxbury proper to deserve the designation of neighborhood. Entering West Roxbury from the west, one is struck by the sudden transition from suburb to small city. Located on the northern side of the Neponset River, West Roxbury is blessed by row upon row of sycamore trees, some of which are quite old. The two-decker homes of the suburbs yield to the three-deckers of the town, and the street gets tighter, even as the traffic increases.

Do residents of West Roxbury suffer from any sort of identity crisis because they are not part of Roxbury itself?

This would have been true except that Roxbury proper was, for almost thirty years, considered the most dangerous part of Greater Boston. More homicides and physical assaults were recorded in Roxbury than in any other part of the metropolis. As a result, the residents of West Roxbury held their title with pride, and differentiated themselves from the town proper. Today there is less need for differentiation, but the residents are quite clear that they hail from West Roxbury.

What kind of businesses make it, and thrive in West Roxbury?

One finds a fascinating mixture of old-line Yankee bakeries, Asian eateries, and New Age stores. Even though a good many residents of West Roxbury work in the trades—plumbing, electricity, and so forth—one does not see the evidence, as one does in Dorchester.

The Islands

Why are the islands of Boston Harbor so little known?

The real Boston enthusiast knows a great deal about the various islands, but to the average tourist and visitor, they remain the least explored of all parts of the metropolis. So it has been almost since the beginning.

The fifty-odd islands of Boston Harbor are so spread out, and of such little value from a commercial viewpoint, that many people can afford to ignore them. But on the rare occasions when one does venture into Boston Harbor—whether on a sail or power boat—

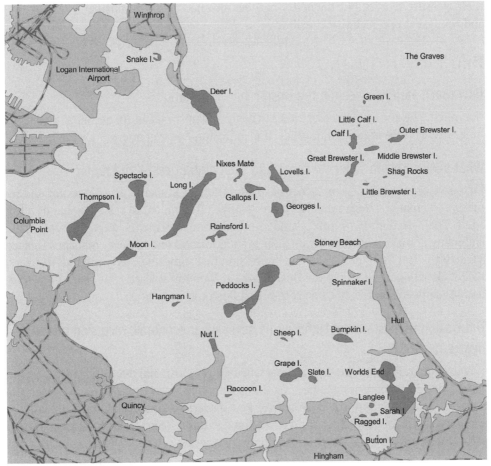

Winthrop
Snake I.
The Graves
Logan International
Airport
Deer I.
Green I.
Little Calf I.
Calf I.
Outer Brewster I.
Great Brewster I.
Middle Brewster I.
Nixes Mate
Lovells I.
Shag Rocks
Spectacle I.
Little Brewster I.
Long I.
Thompson I.
Gallops I.
Georges I.
Columbia
Point
Rainsford I.
Moon I.
Stoney Beach
Peddocks I.
Spinnaker I.
Hangman I.
Hull
Nut I.
Sheep I.
Bumpkin I.
Grape I.
Slate I.
Worlds End
Raccoon I.
Langlee I.
Quincy
Sarah I.
Ragged I.
Button I.
Hingham

Some of the larger islands in Boston Harbor are shown on this map. There are more than fifty in all, but most are too small to be of any practical use.

the islands can serve as a revelation. Here, just a few miles from the hustle and bustle of the big city are areas which have changed very little in the previous three centuries.

Was there ever a time when the islands were recognized as important?

Sailors—both commercial and pleasure-seeking—have long known that the islands of Boston Harbor are beautiful (in a stark fashion), but even they seldom go ashore: it is enough for them to pass by. The person who did the most to change this viewpoint was Edward Rowe Snow. Born in nearby Winthrop, Snow (1902–1982) wrote a large collection of books about Boston and its many localities. Snow revived many stories that had virtually faded. Through his prolific writings, one learns that the islands were primarily used as prison holds: whether for Native Americans during King Philip's War or for Confederates during the Civil War. Perhaps the islands could have become known for their pleasure resorts, but the better beaches afforded by the peninsular towns of Hull and Nantasket removed that possibility.

Price of Housing

How much variety is seen in the Boston housing market?

Not much. The entire area seems either to go up and up, or to stay in one place for a short time. There has been no significant decline in Boston housing prices since the 1960s.

What allows Boston sellers to command such high prices—and rents?

First and foremost it is the presence of so many college students. During junior and senior years, many college students prefer to live off-campus, to taste the life of a full adult. Their need for two-, three-, and four-bedroom apartments keeps the rents high, and many of these students stay on after graduation. No one has ever managed to keep a true statistical list, but one gets the impression that somewhere between one-third and half of all college students in the Boston area stay on for at least a few years after graduation (some, of course, become committed Bostonians for life).

Did Boston real estate not suffer in the seven-year economic recession which began in 2008?

It really didn't. People's incomes contracted; jobs were lost; and many individuals fell on hard times. Recessions tend to be good times for colleges and universities, however; the students kept coming to the Boston area. Few owners or landlords suffered during the economic crisis of 2008–2015. And when the economic recovery commenced, around 2014, the results for real estate were simply spectacular.

Which neighborhoods fared the best in 2014–2015?

Citywide, the median price of a home was $349,000 in 2005, $369,000 in 2010, and a whopping $529,000 in 2015. Back Bay saw the most spectacular gains, with the average price of a home rising from $621,000 in 2005 to $825,000 in 2010 and then to $1.181 million in 2015.

Which neighborhoods fared the worst?

Hyde Park saw a twenty-six percent decline in the price of the median home: from $287,000 in 2005 to $169,500 in 2010, and to $211,250 in 2015. Mattapan went from $225,000 in 2005 to $61,450 in 2010, but made a major rebound, rising to $190,000 in 2015.

Can anyone predict the future for Boston real estate?

One imagines that the bubble will burst one day, but people have been saying that since the late 1970s. The chances are that Boston real estate will continue to be one of the best investments a person, or family, can make.

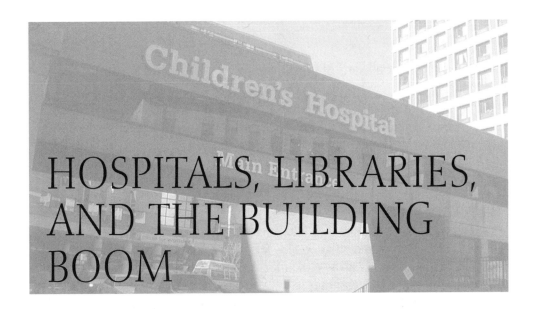

HOSPITALS, LIBRARIES, AND THE BUILDING BOOM

How important is the practice of medicine to the fiscal health of Greater Boston?

Perhaps one-quarter of everyone employed in Greater Boston—from nurses and doctors to X-ray technicians, and groundskeepers—are employed in some aspect of the medical field, making it far and away the number-one employer. It was not always this way, to be sure, but the astonishing advances in medicine over the previous half-century have made necessary—and useful—a staggering array of occupations that did not even exist prior to, say, the year 1950.

Was it in some way inevitable that Boston would become so important in the health care industry?

Boston has a long and distinguished tradition in the medical field; even so, few would have guessed at the enormous concentration of resources now available in the Greater Boston area. Then too, even the grandparents of today's Bostonians would not have suspected that so many diseases would become either curable, or manageable.

Is there any part of the city that has more hospitals and medical centers than the others?

For whatever reason, Jamaica Plain stands out as the number one spot in Greater Boston. Quite likely, there was still building room there longer than was true for the inner city. By about 2000, Jamaica Plain had more medical establishments—of all various sorts—than any other part of Greater Boston. Even so, the typical outsider—he or she who did not know the city well—continued to think of the area near Longfellow Bridge (the general home of Massachusetts General Hospital) as the place to go.

Is Boston famous for all sorts of breakthroughs in medical treatment?

One can make a long list, and argue that Boston—while not always first in line—often employs the new methods and techniques with great skill. It helps, of course, that Boston has so many recent graduates from the top-notch medical schools in Cambridge, and that so many talented young people want to stay in the Boston area. It might be, too, that the Puritan-Yankee obsession with record-keeping and the taking of notes has helped Boston become what it is: one of the meccas for medical treatment in the entire United States.

Is there a heavy price to be paid for all of this?

There is indeed. Massachusetts typically ranks either first, second, or third in the nation in health care costs, meaning that roughly forty-seven states spend less, on a per capita basis. Part of this is because of the extraordinary care that is available; the costs also stem from the fact that the residents of Massachusetts are very well educated on health care issues. The typical Massachusetts man or woman may well know more about the various diseases—and treatments—than his or her contemporary in almost any other state.

When was the turning point, the moment at which Bostonians became more aware of the social costs of drinking and driving?

For the Massachusetts legislature, the turning point was 1979, the year that the legal age for drinking was raised. But the typical Massachusetts resident clung to the notion—or sentiment—that one should be free to choose his or her own poisons. In terms of pop culture, the mid-1980s represents an important turning point. The debut of *St. Elsewhere* on CBS showcased a hospital that looked very much as if it were in Boston, and for the first time the doctors and nurses—rather than the drunk drivers and careless citizens—were the heroes. *St. Elsewhere* did not remain on TV very long, but it heralded a new approach in popular culture, to the importance and value of hospitals.

Are Boston physicians—and nurses—as highly paid as one often hears?

They are among the most highly paid in the nation. It's not always easy to obtain statistics on salaries, but one can look at the long list of physicians who live in the general

Is there anything to the old saw that Massachusetts drivers are the worst in the nation?

They used to be. Until the legal drinking age was raised to twenty—in the winter of 1979—Massachusetts had one of the worst records in the nation, and one of the highest percentages of automobile-related fatalities. This has changed for the better. It can still be said, however, that the winding streets of Boston with their many one-ways and frequent turns, do still contribute to a high percentage of automobile accidents.

area, and make a reasonable guess that some of them, at least, have moved to Boston to take advantage of the high salaries. For example, in 2006 there were 541 people registered and legally able to practice in the area of psychiatry, and that was only in the city of Boston, not including the many suburbs.

It must be said, however, that the pressures are nearly as great as the rewards. Medical schools do not keep, or at least they do not publish, the long roster of failures: those that successfully graduated and began to practice, but could not sustain the incredible pressures exerted by hospital administrators and health insurance companies.

Can anyone make a complete list of all the hospitals, clinics, and research establishments in Boston?

The trouble is that the list is constantly changing. But as of the year 2006, Greater Boston possessed the following: Arbour Hospital, Arbour-HRI Hospital, Beth Israel Deaconess Medical Center, Boston Medical Center, Bournewood Hospital, Brigham and Women's Hospital, Cambridge Health Alliance, Caritas Carney Hospital, Caritas St. Elizabeth's Medical Center, Chelsea Soldiers' Home, Boston Children's Hospital Cranberry Specialty Hospital, Dana-Farber Cancer Institute, Erich Lindemann Mental Health Center, Faulkner Hospital, Franciscan Hospital for Children, Hallmark Health System/ Lawrence Memorial Hospital, HealthSouth Braintree Rehabilitation Hospital, Jewish Memorial Hospital, Kindred Hospital, Lemuel Shattuck Hospital, Massachusetts Eye and Ear Infirmary, Massachusetts General Hospital, McLean Hospital, Milton Hospital Transitional Care Unit, Mount Auburn Hospital, New England Baptist Hospital, Newton-Wellesley Hospital, Northeast Specialty Hospital, Quincy Medical Center, Radius Specialty Hospital, Shriners Hospital for Children, Spaulding Rehabilitation Hospital, Floating Hospital for Children, Tufts-New England Medical Center, Veterans Administration Healthcare System Jamaica Plain, Veterans Administration Healthcare System West Roxbury, and Youville Hospital & Rehabilitation Center.

Is it possible that one metropolitan area has this many medical services?

Pound for pound, Boston is definitely in the top three, nationwide. In absolute numbers, there are far more physicians and nurses in Greater Manhattan, but in terms of specialty care, Boston is second to none.

Does this suggest that Bostonians are in some way "less healthy" than average?

Two generations ago, one could make that argument. Bostonians were known as unhealthy eaters and high consumers of alcohol. Major changes have taken place, however. First came the public awareness of the negative results of drinking and driving, and then came the famous Framingham Heart Study, which demonstrated, year after year, the importance of a balanced diet, and of cutting back on fats. As recently as 1960, the typical Boston physician tended to be male, grouchy, and slightly overweight; today she is more likely to be female, gracious if intense, and completely conscious of the importance of diet.

Does one imagine that the "health care complex" will continue to grow in size?

That's always one of the conundrums where Boston is concerned. Whenever we ask whether a certain industry will continue to grow, we have to ask ourselves if there is the physical space available. For the moment, however, Boston seems to have found an industry that takes up less physical space—on a pound-for-pound basis—than the earlier ones of its history. Docks and wharves, as well as manufacturing establishments, generally require more room than hospitals, not less.

HOW BOSTON BECAME A "MEDICAL TOWN"

Did early Bostonians put two and two together where health was concerned?

The early Puritan settlers of Boston did not: they believed in socking away as many calories as possible. And given the health conditions of the time, they may have made the right move. The portraits that survive from the seventeenth century show Bostonians to be slightly on the heavy side, but nothing that we would call serious. Thanks to the rigors of the climate, they tended either to die rather young, or to survive to phenomenal ages. The greatest dangers to public health in their time were simple: fire and water. More Bostonians died—on a monthly basis—from drowning or from house fires than anything else.

What was the greatest medical scourge in their lives?

Plenty of early Bostonians died from tuberculosis—which they called consumption or the wasting disease—but the illness that really struck terror in the population was smallpox. The pox had been around for centuries, but it was especially virulent in the seventeenth and eighteenth centuries, and neither Bostonians nor their cousins in Old England had any remedy. Boston was hit by smallpox time and again. At least six minor epidemics were recorded between 1650 and 1710, but the truly great one, the one Bostonians remembered for decades, was the epidemic of 1721.

Roughly 1,200 Bostonians died in the epidemic of 1721, and the town population was held back for decades thereafter. Only in the aftermath of this terrible plague were Bostonians willing to examine some real alternatives, and when Dr. Zabdiel Boylston declared he had a new, controversial, remedy, many people flocked to see him. It helped that Reverend Cotton Mather—the most learned and well-published man in town—stood behind the doctor, saying his remedy was efficacious.

Speaking of the Mathers—father and son—were they supporters of the new science?

Reverend Increase Mather (1639–1723) and his son Reverend Cotton Mather (1663–1728) were both pastors of the Old North Church (the father was also president of Harvard College for a time). Between them, father and son had the largest personal library in North America, and they were voluminous readers and writers. Father and son both had a real interest in the new science of medicine, but this does not mean they automatically jumped to support it. When Reverend Cotton Mather came out in support of the inoculation—as practiced by Dr. Boylston—opinions began to change.

What is the difference between inoculation and vaccination?

Given the choice between the two, almost anyone would choose the latter, which dominates medicine in our time. But in 1721, fully a century before vaccines were available, Dr. Boylston was ready to inoculate those courageous enough to visit his office. Inoculation involves pulling back a

The Mather Family tomb in Boston's Copp's Hill Burying Ground is the resting place for four generations of the prolific and controversial family.

small section of the skin, and directly placing an infected puss inside. Vaccinations tend to leave us with little more than a sore arm, but inoculation often gave the patient a minor case of the disease, and left him smallpox free for the rest of his days. The trouble was that the dose had to be just right, and in his eagerness to provide protection, Dr. Boylston may have given too strong a dose. Even so, only six of his patients died from smallpox, out of a total of 280 who received inoculation, and this was vastly better than the ratio shown by those that went without.

Why did someone throw a bomb—or grenade—in Cotton Mather's window?

The handmade grenade did not injure anyone, but the message was clear: stick to the tried-and-true methods of the past. The trouble was that those methods had not saved any lives. Courageously refusing to back down, Cotton Mather continued to argue for inoculation, and the results spoke for themselves. Within a generation, the majority of Bostonians were believers in, and recipients of inoculation.

The same cannot be said of all colonial America, however. As late as 1759, when Reverend Jonathan Edwards—the famous minister of Northampton, Massachusetts—went to Princeton, he found many people reluctant to receive inoculation. As he took up his duties as the second president of the College of New Jersey—today's Princeton—Reverend Edwards received an inoculation in order to persuade his fellow townsmen. He received too high a dose, and died at the age of fifty-five, far too young.

What was the life expectancy for a Bostonian in the years just prior to the Revolution?

Again—it all depended on how one weathered the childhood diseases. If one made it through chickenpox and scarlet fever, as well as several others, one tended to emerge with a very strong constitution. Learning how to swim finally became part of life in Boston in the eighteenth century, and there were fewer deaths by drowning. With some luck, a man or woman might well make it to his or her seventies. But there were all sorts of other illnesses that claimed lives—diphtheria and cholera leading the list.

When the British occupied Boston in 1775–1776, did they prove healthier or more sickly than the Bostonians?

The British had more and better doctors, but their soldiers came from some of the poorest families of the English motherland. British soldiers did not have a good survival rate during the Revolutionary War. American soldiers, too, struggled with all sorts of illness and disease, but there was a growing medical corps and medical tradition in North America. Soldiers on both sides succumbed during the smallpox epidemic of 1775–1776, but that was just about the last major one of its kind. The Continental Army did not have a great many doctors, but it had rather good ones, and American medicine emerged stronger, not weaker, at the end of the Revolutionary War.

How was the Massachusetts General Hospital founded?

In the decade immediately following the Revolutionary War, Bostonians assumed the lead, nationwide, in terms of founding new organizations. The Massachusetts Medical Society, the Massachusetts Humane Society, and a number of others were chartered, particularly by leading Bostonians: men who had witnessed the horrors of war, and did not wish to see them repeated. But as for a real hospital, that had to wait until 1811.

Reverend John Bartlett of Marblehead led the charge, enlisting about fifteen leading Massachusetts men in the drive to found a hospital. Massachusetts General Hospi-

This is how Massachusetts General Hospital looked in 1846.

tal received a charter from the Great and General Court in 1811, but seven years passed before the new establishment opened its doors. Located at the intersections of Blossom, Allen, and Fruit Streets, the new hospital boasted both a traditional medical wing, and a section devoted to the care of the mentally ill.

Was this the first time the mentally ill received their due?

The level of treatment was not very good, by our standards, but Boston was perhaps the third town in North America to afford them any treatment whatsoever. There is little doubt that some of the early treatments represented little more than "quarantine," and Massachusetts hospitals developed a dual tradition over the next century: hailed for their understanding of mental illness, but not applauded for their treatments.

Over the next decade or so, Massachusetts General Hospital became the place for Bostonians to go for physical ailments, and McLean Hospital, which was originally housed on the same grounds, became the place for mental health treatment. Not until about 1895 did McLean Hospital move to the suburban town of Belmont. Even so, McLean and Massachusetts General are governed by the same board of directors.

Did the Civil War provide any breakthroughs in terms of medical treatment?

How one wishes this were the case! Civil War physicians, especially surgeons, were challenged in the most extreme manner, meaning they had to meet the needs of great numbers of people, all at once. Medicine did not make much advance during the Civil War, which is rightly remembered as a time of "sawbones" doctors performing all sorts of amputations. As is often the case, however, tragedy leads to breakthroughs. Many of the physicians who lamented the primitive conditions under which they labored during the Civil War became the agents for change in the decades that followed. At Massachusetts General Hospital, it was Dr. Edward Coles (a former Union Army surgeon) who pioneered in the development of better methods. Other Mass General luminaries include Dr. Henry Jacob Bigelow, who witnessed the first employment of ether, and who was still at Mass General when the first X-Ray was taken there (in 1896).

Is the early twentieth century when diabetes became more prevalent?

There is no doubt that sugar entered the American diet in a substantial way around the year 1900, and that it was followed by an even greater flow after around the year 1950. Bostonians of around the year 1900 tended to get plenty of physical exercise, limiting the devastating effects of diabetes, but Bostonians also tended to drink more than their contemporaries. The combination of even a mild drinking habit plus the new appearance of sugar products made for a terrible combination.

Did the doctors tend to stay a long time?

They did. The typical Mass General physician of the late nineteenth century tended to arrive while in his early thirties, and to remain until retirement, which often came in his early seventies. This was an exciting time in medicine, and the breakthroughs came even faster as the twentieth century approached. Massachusetts General learned a great deal about infectious diseases during the Spanish-American War, and it tended to be the young men—and women—they taught who made the most of that knowledge during World War I. About the only major disease that Mass General had no answer for was the terrible influenza epidemic of 1918–1919, and the same can be said of all other American hospitals.

Nurses, too, tended to remain at Massachusetts General. The first class of nurses graduated in 1886, and many of these young women would remain in Boston for the rest of their lives. The graduates of, say, the year 1900 would witness enormous changes, but there were still some diseases for which the only answer was palliative care.

What is the state of medicine in Greater Boston today?

As of 2015, Boston is at or near the top of anyone's list, when hospitals, clinics, and medical centers are discussed. Though it has plenty of competition—from Beth Israel Deaconess, Brigham and Women's Hospital, and others—Mass General remains at the very top. In a study issued by *U.S. News and World Report*, Mass General was one of the gold star hospitals nationwide.

Mass General ranked eighth in cancer care; fifth in cardiology; second in the treatment of diabetes; first in ear, nose, and throat care; third in gastroenterology; fourth in geriatrics; fourth in gynecology; sixth in nephrology; second in neurology and neurosurgery; fourth in orthopedics; fourth in pulmonology; and sixteenth in urology.

Is hospital care for children on the same high level?

Boston Children's Hospital ranks first for cancer care, first for cardiology, first for diabetes care and gastroenterology, second for neonatology, first for neurology, third in orthopedics, fourth in pulmonology, and first in urology. One can state with confidence that this is one of the "best" cities for children with serious health challenges.

Boston Children's Hospital is one of the finest in the nation and ranks first in many specialties.

THE BUILDING BOOM

Why were the 1960s so good to developers and architects?

Boston was not rich during that decade, but the city—and its various constituent parts—were more willing to take risks than before. The death of President John F. Kennedy was a major blow to the city, but leaders in finance, politics, and the arts all vowed to recover. No better way seemed possible than to give Boston a new set of public buildings.

How long had it been since Boston experienced a major construction boom?

It had been a very long time. There had been a small boom during the 1920s, but it did not fundamentally alter the shape or size of public Boston. And between roughly 1935 and 1960, there had been no major redesign in the city's architecture: the citizen of 1960 viewed the same skyline—or lack thereof—as his father and grandfather.

Which was the first of the major new buildings?

The Christian Science religion did not have a large number of adherents, but its headquarters had been in Boston for more than half a century. Christian Science leaders announced in 1960 the beginning of construction of what would be one of the largest places of worship to be found anywhere in New England.

How soon after President Kennedy's death did the Kennedy family begin planning his museum?

In 1964, the very name Kennedy was practically gold, as far as public interest went. Robert F. Kennedy, brother of the slain president, and Jacqueline Kennedy—the widow—formed a committee soon after the president's death. Their desire was to honor President Kennedy's memory with a library and museum in Cambridge.

The Kennedy family did not turn to local Boston firms. Influenced, perhaps, by Mrs. Kennedy's interest in all things European, the Kennedys turned instead to the iconoclastic designer and architect I.M. Pei. He was already known as the designer of the courtyard of the Louvre in Paris, and he was now asked to draw up plans for the library and museum to honor Boston's most famous citizen.

How many different organizations were involved in planning the Kennedy library?

The announcement of I. M. Pei (1917–) as the chief architect came in December 1964. At that point, both Harvard University and the World Bank—which did much fundraising for the project—were firmly on board. But the project ran into difficulties right from the beginning.

351

Cambridge residents did not want a new library and museum in their city; the fear they expressed was that Cambridge would be overrun by visitors, and that the more austere—and renowned—buildings of Harvard and MIT would be overshadowed. Then too, there was the fear that the selling of all sorts of garish souvenirs would detract from the pristine surroundings. Pei and his team were well accustomed to difficulties such as these; they pushed forward.

Where would the Kennedy library and museum have been located?

The plan was for it to be on the north bank of the Charles River, right where the car barns of the Massachusetts Bay Transportation Authority (MBTA) were located. Money was raised, and the MBTA pledged to be out of its quarters by the year 1970. But the protests by Cambridge locals proved more than Pei anticipated. He was, after all, dealing with a community that thrived on controversy.

The assassination of Robert Kennedy in June 1968 was a major blow to the hopes of the organizers. So too was the marriage of the former Mrs. John Kennedy to the Greek millionaire Aristotle Onassis. Pei still hoped for success, but the change of personnel at Harvard (President Nathan Pusey left in 1971) left him virtually stranded. It was time to look for another site. Mrs. Kennedy-Onassis recognized the danger that the project might be tied up for twenty years in court. It made sense, therefore, to find a new location.

How did the committee, or group, hit upon Columbia Point?

The Point was, by then, one of the few areas in Greater Boston where a major structure could be built. Once the tentative plan was broached, many people expressed support because they believed tourist traffic would be directed around the city. Others liked the fact that President Kennedy's library would be practically on the water, the element he loved so much. Of course, there was not universal support, or admiration of the plan.

What did Pei aim for in the design of the Kennedy library?

Pei wanted a structure that would echo his great success at the Louvre. He envisioned a building that would take advantage of various geometrical shapes, balancing extreme modern architecture with the harmony of Columbia Point's natural setting. Work commenced in March 1976.

The extreme eastern side of Columbia Point is built on landfill, and pilings had

The John F. Kennedy Library was designed by renowned architect I. M. Pei.

to be sunk in order to reach rock. Construction materials had to travel a long distance to the site, and costs soon overran the early projections. Pei later declared that his years on the Kennedy Library were the most trying, and costly—in terms of time spent—of his long career.

What did the Kennedy Library look like when it opened?

Dedication day was October 20, 1979. The hundreds of participants, and thousands of spectators were treated to a postmodernist display of metal and glass. When photographs were taken from a southern angle, the library and museum appeared stunning because of Boston in the background. But when the same camera was turned on the library from a northern viewpoint, the results were disappointing.

How has the Kennedy library fared since it first was opened?

The John F. Kennedy library has never really won over the people of Boston: it remains one of the least visited of their grand sites. For the out-of-towner, however, the Kennedy Library is often a major hit. The biggest complaint, issued by many people from both camps, is that the library is too cold and austere. Given that it fronts directly on Boston Harbor, the library needs something warm and cozy to lure in the visitor. Instead, it often seems like a white battleship, more forbidding than welcoming. Similar things are sometimes said of the John Hancock Tower, but in that case the dominant color is blue.

THE PRUDENTIAL TOWER

Why do life insurance companies play so large a role in determining the Boston skyline?

It's pretty much an accident. Life insurance companies were more profitable during the 1960s and 1970s than ever before. Millions of aging parents of baby boomers wanted to protect their families. As a result, both the Prudential Insurance Company and John Hancock Financial had cash to spend. And as it turned out, both wanted to establish monuments to their success.

The Prudential Center—known to Bostonians simply as "The Pru"—came first. It was built between 1962 and 1965. The goal was to replace what had been an eyesore area with something truly spectacular. And when The Pru opened in April 1965, 25,000 people visited on the first day. They came away with mixed feelings and reports, however.

What were the major criticisms of the Prudential Center when it first opened?

Most visitors liked the shops, and room for expansion. Those that went to the top floor—the fifty-second—to take in the Skywalk Observatory were truly thrilled. But the view that is so grand from the top of The Pru is not reciprocated by those that examine the building from an outside view. The extra-large overhang on the windows gives The Pru a shuttered look, and there are times when it seems very much out of place. Oddly enough, it was construction of the Hancock Tower and Observatory that made The Pru seem better.

THE HANCOCK TOWER

Why did the John Hancock company decide to build so close to the Prudential Center?

John Hancock already had a small-sized tower of about fourteen stories in Copley Square, and its directors decided to surpass their Prudential rivals. Ground was broken in 1968, but it took years for the sixty-story tower to appear. And, just as the tower was close to being opened, Boston experienced a major wind storm that brought down a number of windows. For months, Bostonians laughed at the pretensions of the Hancock company, which had erected a monstrosity with sheets of ply board covering the empty window spaces.

When the Hancock Tower opened in 1976, the critics were not silenced, but they certainly did become quieter. Purists would continue to loathe the building for decades, but the majority of Bostonians came to like, and sometimes even adore, the sixty-story, 790-foot tower. The major reason was the almost surreal blue color of its exterior, which allows the viewer to compare it with the bright blue water of the Charles River Basin. An added plus is that the reflection of Trinity Church can often be seen on the west side of the Hancock Tower, leading to perhaps millions of photographs taken over the decades.

WHAT'S NEXT?

Can anyone predict the future for Boston buildings?

The architects, designers, and masons doubtless have many projects in the works, but they continue to run up against the obstacle that has bedeviled their predecessors. Boston has nearly run out of room. If Boston was like Manhattan, a city of skyscrapers, things might be different. Much of Boston's charm derives, however, from the relatively low skyline, and the quality of light that comes into the heart of the city. Given the number of historic, artistic, and cultural organizations in Boston, it is likely that the city will continue to embrace its architectural past, while occasionally adding something new.

UNIQUE BOSTON

When did daily life in Boston first attract notice to be commented upon?

The diary of Samuel Sewall (1652–1730) is one of the most remarkable sources for the understanding of Puritan Boston. From Sewall we learn that the seventeenth-century Puritans were great imbibers, that there were almost as many taverns as churches and places for public meetings. Puritan Boston had many taverns with names such as the Green Dragon, the Red Lion Inn, and so forth, but the single most popular seems to have been the Blue Anchor. Located right in the heart of what is now downtown Boston, the Blue Anchor was where the ministers, magistrates, and merchants met, for ale, beer, and conversation.

Because Samuel Sewall was a member of Boston's upper-class, we have less insight into the daily lives of the less fortunate. From the pages of his diary we learn, however, that Bostonians of 1690, or thereabout, were just as concerned with a livelihood and earning their daily bread as those of, say, 2015. Today we call them all "carpenters," but in Puritan times there were at least a dozen names for such men: joiner, welder, and so forth. The building trades were the largest in town, but the merchant trade, which dominated the docks and wharves, supplied Boston with many necessities. Bostonians would not have had molasses, sugar, or tea if not for the merchants, sailors, and ships.

What was daily life in Boston like in the years just prior to the American Revolution?

For many Loyalists, the decade prior to the Revolution was a golden age, which never was seen again. And it's true that the lives of the well-to-do were both interesting and enlivening. We know this from the number of concerts that were held, the number of carriages that were constructed and sold, and from the list of delicacies on sale in many stores. He or she who had money in the pocket could purchase just about anything.

At the same time, however, the number of people on the Poor List, and those supported by the various churches grew. The merchant trade declined during the years that

Bostonians resisted the new tax laws from Old England, and the Revolution itself was nothing short of a disaster for the people of the town. When the British sailed away in March 1776, they took more than one thousand Loyalists, most of whom never returned. Regardless of whether one likes or detests their politics, these upper-class men and women had brought a new sophistication to eighteenth-century Boston, and the place took a long time to recover from their absence.

What were the sights and sounds, as well as the smells, of Boston in the year 1800?

Boston was still a rather quiet place. The population was less than twenty thousand, and though there were lots of horses and wagons in the streets by day, the place became almost silent at night. The smells of that time would offend our nostrils a great deal, but Bostonians seldom, if ever, comment on them in their letters or diaries.

There were almost no real apartment houses in Boston in 1800: people lived either in their own homes or with relatives. There may have been a homeless population, but these men and women were not registered on any list. Bostonians—in and around the year 1800—may well have believed they had reached a pinnacle, and that the town would not have to change much in the future. We, of course, know that they were mistaken.

How big a difference did it make that Boston became a city in 1822?

The difference was qualitative rather than quantitative. Bostonians were quite attached to the idea of living in a town, rather than a city, and the change was difficult for many of them. New offices had to be constructed and new town officials, including the first mayor, were elected. The single biggest difference was that the city could be regulated to a greater degree; all sorts of new rules and regulations were voted in, and Boston took on a more modern appearance.

It was at this same time that the great work of landfill began in earnest. During the 1820s, sections of the Bay Back were damned, and by the 1850s, many of them were filled in. Most people saw the positives in this change—the city became more spacious— but they did not anticipate the traffic that would soon come their way. As the saying goes, "if you build it, they will come."

For how long did the suburbs manage to remain that way, separate from the city itself?

They held out for a good long time, sometimes as long as three generations. Places like Brighton, Brookline, Charlestown, Roxbury, and so forth all had real and significant identities of their own. But the pressure to be incorporated into the growing city of Boston was in front of them all the time. Each suburb or neighborhood that became part of Boston meant a diminution in the identity of that region, and Greater Boston became poorer culturally, even as it was enriched financially.

How did the city of Boston carry itself during the Civil War years?

These were—in the minds of many Bostonians—the best of all possible times. Once the decision for war was made (once the Confederacy fired the first shots in 1861), most Bostonians became firm Union men and women. The city took on a wartime look, even though there was not the slightest danger of any outside attack.

Boston had always been a prim and proper place, but the attitude and carriage of the "proper Bostonians" was consolidated during the Civil War years; from 1865 onward it was possible to detect a person's social status largely as the result of his or her clothing. Of course there were some imposters who could pretend to be better off, or poorer than was really the case, but they were the exceptions to the rule. The proper Boston man of the late nineteenth century wore a top hat, a long coat, and often smoked a cigar. The proper Boston lady was known for the elegance of her speech and the variety of her wardrobe.

What were the sights and sounds of Boston in and around the year 1880?

They had changed a good deal, even from thirty years previous. The single biggest change was the sound of the railroads. The iron monsters, as some people called them, created all sorts of sounds, many of which were pleasant just so long as one did not live too close. But the advent of the railroads did not mean the end of horses. Far from it. Here is how one official Boston report described the impact of horses on the Boston streets in and around the year 1880.

> The great and universal noise in the city was the pounding of iron horseshoes on the street pavements. That sound began before dawn when the milk carts came by thousands into the city from the outlying farms. By nine o'clock the tens of thousands of horses including those that drew the cars of the horse railways, the carriages of the physicians and merchants, the tip carts of the street cleaners and the long drays of the sugar refiners and the wool merchants were on the move. The horses of the street railways dangled bells from their collars. Dray horses had bells. Therefore much bell music was mingled with the pounding street noise.

Was Henry James one of those "prim and proper Bostonians?"

The James family actually hailed from New York City, but they were true cosmopolitans, who came to know Boston, New York, Washington, D.C., and London to an equally great degree. Henry James wrote *The Bostonians*, published in 1886, but he really commented on the social airs of all upscale East Coast Americans. His brother William James taught at Harvard for many years, but he was too broad a thinker to be confined to a Boston outlook.

Did anyone realize there was a limit to how many horses that could exist in one city?

Some urban planners did, but the great majority of the populace believed that the horse, carriage, cart, and wagon would always be sufficient for their needs. The great change was underway by about 1885, when the bells and whistles of the electric street-cars began to compete with the pounding of iron hooves on the pavement. In the early period of electric street cars, there was plenty of room on the road for both transportation methods, and Boston saw as many horses as before (the bringing in of hay from the countryside was a business all to itself). But with each passing year, the street-cars carried more passengers, and a growing number of Bostonians either sold or gave away their horses.

How did Bostonians handle the big snowstorms of the late-nineteenth century?

The single biggest difference is that there was no need for hurry. Bostonians were quite aware of winter, and its dangers, but they brought out sleighs of all kinds, and the streets were generally passable even in the aftermath of a great storm. As the automobile became more important, there was a consequent rush to get the snow off the streets, and all sorts of new equipment were designed, and jobs were created, to bring about that state of affairs. The commentator of the year 1930 lamented the way modern times required such haste: "Witness the army of men who in 1930 spend their lives making such vehicles, repairing, tending, buying, selling insuring, and finding metals, varnishes and oils for them. Some men in 1930 say that the motor vehicle is not a gain on the whole but a loss."

Did the clothing of Bostonians change as the horse began to yield to the automobile?

Definitely. The Bostonians of 1880 had to be prepared for all sorts of emergencies, and when they departed work at 5 P.M., they anticipated ice and snow, cold and rain. The advent of the automobile meant that many Bostonians—or commuters from the suburbs—were able to make just one transit on the entire trip to and from work. As a result, the clothing became more lightweight.

Were there any areas of public life in which the late-nineteenth century was worse than what followed?

The one that strikes us most fully is the hazard that late-nineteenth-century Bostonians experienced from dangling wires. Electric lights but also telephone wires abounded, and there was, as yet, no zoning practice to keep these in check. As a result, many Bostonians did not get to enjoy a clear look at the skyline, and their looks upward were mostly in order to keep out of the way of danger. Several severe snowstorms toward the end of the nineteenth century persuaded public officials of the need for change, and most wires were placed underground.

What are some of the occupations that have since disappeared?

A great many occupations from that time—the late nineteenth century—have disappeared. On the streets, one met many hawkers and criers, men and women selling everything from bananas to coffee. On entering a middle-class home, one often was greeted by a servant. And the apartment houses and hotels were simply filled with personnel of whom only the butlers and maids remain today. This change did not happen with great speed, however, and the man or woman of 1890 sometimes did not notice the changes till they had fully taken place. In Boston, as in New York and Chicago, the great lament of the upper-class was that one could not find good help (servants) after about the year 1920. The reason is not hard to find: all sorts of new jobs in manufacturing allowed domestic servants to leave.

What were Sundays like in and around the year 1900?

Even in our time, Boston is quieter than the average American city on Sundays. But at the turn of the twentieth century, Boston seemed like a slow-motion imitation of itself. Sunday was the one day of the week when the horses did not come to town, and when the electric streetcars did not employ their loud whistles. The department stores were all closed, and very little business was conducted in Boston on the Sabbath. The contrast between Sunday morning and Saturday evening could hardly have been greater.

Did Bostonians drink a good deal?

Upper-class, middle, and working—they all seemed to drink. The municipal report of the year 1930 declares that Cambridge had previously been one long set of saloons.

> The double-hung half-doors which opened into these saloons, the crowds of men who frequented the room, the undulating cloud of tobacco smoke which floated near the ceilings, the vast mirrors decorated with patterns drawn in white on the glass itself, and the general combined fragrance of hops, casks, whiskey, spirits and beer have not been forgotten.

What did the policemen of this time look like?

They were not as heavily armed as our current-day police, but they tended to be formidable in appearance. The top hats were filled with medals, and the officer usually carried a night stick, rather than a gun. Boston hired its first female police (six of them) in April 1921, and they were, not surprisingly, called the "flapper squad."

What kinds of alarms did the police of that time respond to?

Then as now, domestic scenes were the number-one cause of trouble. Boston police tended not to enter private homes for anything less than direct circumstances, but these happened all the time. Though daily life in our time often suffers by comparison with the early twentieth century, such is not the case with domestic violence, which may well have been greater at that time.

359

What was so important about the Boston police strike of 1919?

The most important thing is that looting began almost immediately. Many Bostonians were shocked that this happened. In the aftermath of the strike, which led to the firing of the entire Boston police department, advocates of law and order won more elections than previously.

Did Boston see much change during the 1920s?

Boston was less affected by the 1920s than other major American cities. A strong conservative reaction set in immediately after the failed police strike, and Boston experienced less turmoil than many other U.S. cities. The really big changes waited till the end of World War II.

A photo showing President Calvin Coolidge reviewing militiamen during the 1919 police strike.

Why was the conclusion of the World War II such an important time in Boston's history?

Nine times out of ten, the changes were brought about by the return of young servicemen from overseas. These men, who were in their twenties and thirties, had weathered the Great Depression and then survived World War II. While they tended to be hardy, even tough, these young men were done with sacrifices: they wanted to see the world become a better place.

Suburban districts, shopping malls, and expansion of railways and commuter lines all came about as a result. The young men who returned from World War II tended to marry quickly, and to raise large families; as a result, there was a great need for new elementary, and then secondary schools. Boston was well positioned to meet many of the new needs. What it lacked was physical room, and a set of roads that could bring people in to the downtown area.

How many roads and highways were built in the three decades that followed World War II?

The Mass Turnpike was, of course, the best-known and most costly. Early advertisers for the Pike claimed that all the expenses would be met in twenty years, and that motorists would drive for free thereafter (as of this writing, this has never been the case). But even the Mass Turnpike proved inadequate to the need, and two concentric bands, or beltways were soon built. These were Route 495 (the outer belt) and Route 128 (the inner belt, closer to the metropolis).

How did the lives of Bostonians—and their suburban cousins—change as a result?

Almost everyone had to figure in the hours of their weekly commute. The total number of hours people worked actually increased, once one counted the hours spent on the roadways. Family life suffered as a result.

Was this seen right away?

No. The major highways were built between 1950 and 1965, and it was shortly thereafter that Bostonians noticed the changes in family life. Not only did fathers—and working mothers—spend more time on their daily commutes, but the children and teenagers showed a strong proclivity for escape: they used cars, streetcars, and subway lines to escape the confines of the home. Boston was not unusual—many other American cities experienced similar situations—but the rebellious streak Bostonians had once demonstrated in their resistance to Great Britain and King George's taxes seemed to rebound, and fall on the shoulders of the parents and taxpayers.

THE WEATHER

What was the hardest of times for modern Bostonians—meaning the coldest?

When the Boston Marathon was run in temperatures that exceeded 90 degrees, it seemed Boston and perhaps all of New England was in for a long period of warming. This was shown to be shockingly wrong, however, when Boston entered one of the coldest stretches of its long history, at the end of the 1970s and the beginning of the 1980s.

January 1981 witnessed the single lowest temperature ever recorded in Massachusetts, and that winter was followed by one equally severe in 1982. The winters of 1983 and 1984 were notable for record amounts of snowfall. For the average Bostonian, close to an oil-fired furnace or a wood stove, these hard winters were just one more example of how New England can be a difficult place to live. But for the thousands of homeless, the early 1980s were a time of real suffering.

How did Boston handle its homeless problem?

There was no single solution. Record numbers of Americans around the nation were homeless during the late 1980s. Remarkably, the trend halted, and then reversed itself in the mid-1990s. And at the same time, the climate did something that few expected. Heat now became the major problem.

How did Bostonians of the late twentieth century handle the increase in heat?

As long as life and limb are not endangered, Bostonians generally prefer extreme cold to extreme heat. Their houses are built to maximize the holding of heat. Sometime around 1995, the great concern over extreme winters yielded to one concerning the new heat of the summers, and this trend has continued.

GENERATION SHIFT

When did the baby boom take over in the Greater Boston area?

The baby boomers' parents were still alive and well in 1985, but this was the year when the youngsters began taking over major responsibility, sometimes replacing their parents as the big decision-makers. It's no coincidence that the overall appearance of Greater Boston began to change in the late 1980s. The baby boomers had definite ideas about what was elegant, fashionable, or merely okay, and they worked to produce more of the former.

How important did the automobile become in the last decade of the twentieth century?

Given all the other means of transportation—ranging from taxicabs to streetcars—one would think Boston would see a tail off in the enthusiasm for the automobile. The precise opposite occurred. Perhaps it was the influence of the baby boomers (then again it may have been the popularity of the sports utility vehicle), but Boston saw a major increase in the number of cars, and the number of miles driven. Heading to "The Cape" for the weekend was as popular as ever, but many Boston families now made longer treks, to the northern coast of Maine.

Did Boston experience a serious alarm in the wake of the 9-11 terrorist attacks?

Bostonians could hardly avoid looking at the situation. The four planes that were hijacked on September 11, 2001, all took off from Logan Airport. Bostonians experienced the same shock as the rest of the nation, but there was a special sense of vulnerability because of the city's high-profile status. It seemed entirely possible that the terrorists would strike at Boston next.

How did the overall pace of life in Boston change during the first decade of the twenty-first century?

Boston's pace had always been fast, but it became a bit faster. The incredible speed of the new communications, including email and cell phones, appealed to many Bostonians, who declared they lived in a new time, one in which the old rules could be suspended. This was especially true for the young millennials, those that came of age just as the new century dawned.

At the same time, however, Boston also became a place known for its fun. This had seldom been the case in the past. The longstanding image of the grim middle-aged male Bostonian, accompanied by his uncomplaining wife, was being replaced by a new, joyful young couple often of different races. Bostonians had fewer children than in the past, and lavished great affection on them.

Will Boston continue to be one of the cities that changes a great deal? Or will there be a conservative reaction?

At the time of this writing—in 2016—it seems quite likely that Boston will continue on its merry way, as the city where the young people come to attend college, and where many of them choose to remain. As *Boston* magazine expressed it in March 2016:

"The Good News Is Boston Has Never Been Better...The Bad News Is No One Can Afford It."

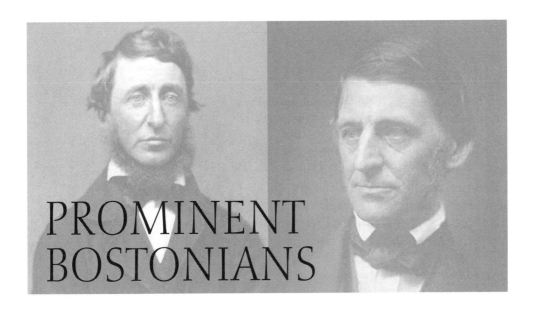

PROMINENT BOSTONIANS

Boston is perhaps best known for its famous families, but which name trumps all the others?

Beyond doubt, the name *Kennedy* comes at the very top of the list. Ever since John F. Kennedy (1917–1963) rose to the presidency in 1961, the name of Kennedy has conjured up images of sailboats on the Charles, speeches at Harvard University, and football games between Harvard and Yale. John F. Kennedy's untimely death in 1963 did nothing to detract from that image. If anything, his legacy becomes larger with each passing decade.

What was it that allowed voters—and TV watchers—to identify John Kennedy so strongly with Boston?

A lot of it has to do with the Boston accent. Kennedy spoke in a marvelous combination of downtown Bostonian and elegant Harvard Yard. The richness of his speech—made more melodious because of the occasional pause or halt—endeared him to millions. Too, although Kennedy came from great wealth (most of it collected by his father, Joseph P. Kennedy, Sr.) he was Boston Irish, which meant that he and his family had known struggles in various forms. When Kennedy famously declared to the press, "Life is not fair," people took him seriously. They believed that he knew of what he spoke.

Did any of the other family members manage to continue the Kennedy legacy?

John F. Kennedy's younger brother, Robert F. Kennedy (1925–1968), was the first to pick up the fallen standard. Because he moved to New York and ran for the U.S. Senate from that state, Robert Kennedy was never as clearly "Boston" as his elder brother had been. And when Robert was assassinated in June 1968, the family standard naturally passed to Edward ("Ted") Kennedy (1932–2009). He was the youngest of the four brothers. The eldest, Joseph P. Kennedy, Jr., had been killed in World War II.

Ted Kennedy was clearly the under-performer of the family, at least until he reached middle age. Neither as handsome as his brother John nor as eloquent as his brother Robert, Ted struggled in their shadow for many years. By the 1990s, however, Ted Kennedy had become as "Boston" as any person could possibly be. Gifted with a sonorous voice and a deep concern for his constituents, Kennedy served faithfully in the U.S. Senate for more than four decades. His fingerprints are all over the major pieces of liberal legislation that passed the U.S. Congress in the 1980s and 1990s. At the time of his death, Ted had clearly reached equality with his elder brothers, and many political observers declared that he was the most effective of the three.

(Left to right) John, Robert, and Ted Kennedy. Many of the Kennedys went into politics and had considerable influence at the state and national levels.

How important was Rose Kennedy to the family story?

Born in the North End of Boston in 1890, Rose Kennedy (1890–1995) lived to the remarkable age of one hundred and five. She was the matriarch of the Kennedy clan, the person who most clearly won the affection of the general public. A decade after her death, the City of Boston built the Rose Kennedy Greenway, which places green sections and a picnic-like atmosphere into major sections of the city.

If the Kennedys are the number-one family from Boston, then who comes in at number two?

Beyond doubt, the Adamses of Quincy are the second most famous family to be connected with Boston. The founding father of the clan was John Adams (1735–1826). Born in Quincy (then named Braintree), he became first a lawyer and then a member of the First and Second Continental Congresses. Adams was greatly respected by his colleagues but not much liked; he ruefully admitted that it was not in his nature to curry favor, either with colleagues or the voters. Adams rose to become the first vice president (1789–1797) and then the second president (1797–1801) of the nation. He would not have succeeded to this extent without his remarkable wife, Abigail Smith Adams (1744–1818).

They married when they were young, and they formed a wonderfully intimate bond that remained strong through all the separations caused by his political career. She had to run the family farm at Braintree and became as familiar as any pioneer woman with the demands of horses, cows, acres, and crops. They went to New York, Philadelphia, and finally to Washington, D.C., during the height of his political success, but their hearts were set on home. Once they returned to Braintree in 1801 they kept close to the family farm, which today is the Adams National Historical Park.

Who led the second generation of the Adams family?

John Quincy Adams (1767–1848) was the eldest son of John and Abigail. Tasked with high responsibility at an early age (he was his father's confidential secretary), John Quincy became an incredibly knowledgeable person, and when he won election to the presidency in 1824, it seemed no one could be better qualified. But, like a number of people who are well qualified, John Quincy Adams was not well suited to the job. Like his father, he found it impossible to reach out to the voters and curry their favor. As a result, he was thrown out of office and replaced by Andrew Jackson in the election of 1828.

John Quincy Adams refused to give up, however. He never ran again for president, but he ran and won election to the U.S. House of Representatives (he is the only former president to have served in Congress). In the House he became known as "Old Man Eloquent."

Was that it for the Adams clan?

By no means. Charles Francis Adams (1807–1886)—the son of John Quincy—served as American ambassador to England during the American Civil War. Charles Francis had a very tough task. President Lincoln made it plain that he, Adams, must warn the British against becoming involved in the Civil War, and he had to do so in ways so diplomatic that the British would not be offended. Adams steered a good path about ninety percent of the time, and he managed to keep Britain out of the war. His son, Henry Adams (1838–1918), wrote one of the most respected of all American autobiographies, but by that time the Adams family was less identified with the City of Boston—they belonged to the nation rather than to any particular city or state.

Is there any other Boston family that has provided so many civil servants and people of note?

The Lowells and the Cabots are near the top of the list. A famous old expression runs as follows: "So here's to old Boston, the town of the bean and the cod, where the Cabots talk only to the Lowells, and the Lowells only to God." Both families were in Boston from early Puritan times, and both rose to prominence during the industrial development of the early nineteenth century. The Lowells and Cabots both made fortunes in the textile industry, and they have remained faithful families of Boston—providing one generation of public servants after another.

Why does the name Eliot crop up in the record so many times?

The Eliots arrived in Massachusetts in the 1670s and have been prominent ever since. Samuel Atkins Eliot (1798–1862) was a popular mayor of Boston in the 1830s, and his son, Charles W. Eliot (1834–1926), was the longest-serving president of Harvard University (1869–1909). During his long tenure, Eliot reshaped Harvard and indirectly influenced the rest of the nation's institutions of higher learning. Eliot introduced the elective system under which young men—and later, women—could choose many of the courses they would take. Prior to this, the Harvard undergraduate program had been clearly laid out by the professors and deans with very little student choice involved.

Charles W. Eliot was famous for his work in higher education; his son Samuel A. Eliot II (1862–1950) became well known as a religious leader. Samuel A. Eliot was president of the Unitarian-Universalist organization and pastor of Arlington Street

Poet and dramatist T. S. Eliot was a Nobel Prize winner and one of the most famous literary figures to come from Boston.

Church for three decades. His son, Thomas Hopkinson Eliot (1907–1991) served as a U.S. congressman and helped to write the Social Security Act. And of course, the most famous of all the Eliots was the poet T. S. Eliot.

Why do we hear so little of Boston in the poetry of T. S. Eliot?

First and foremost, T. S. Eliot (1888–1965) felt drawn to universal themes, ones that cannot be confined to any one area. Winner of the 1948 Nobel Prize in Literature, Eliot was a Modernist poet and dramatist best known for the poem "The Love Song of J. Alfred Prufrock" (1915), the poetry collection *The Waste Land* (1922), and the play *Murder in the Cathedral* (1935). But he was an Eliot of Boston, and when he went to live in London he knew that he would enter a status in which he was never quite *English* enough for the British and never quite *American* enough for his fellow countrymen. It's worth noting, however, that Eliot drew much of his inspiration from the natural world and that early days of sailing and canoeing in the Boston area provided fodder for his poetry.

RUGGED INDIVIDUALS

Boston may be the land of tight-knit families, but New England is known for its rugged individuals. How many of these does Boston claim?

So many come from Boston that the list would extend beyond the confines of this book. At the very top of the list, however, would be Ralph Waldo Emerson (1803–1882). Born in Boston, he came from an old Puritan family and was intended for the ministry. He preached for a year or two and then dropped out to become an independent scholar (a dubious vocational choice). Emerson gave several outstanding speeches to large groups such as at the Harvard Commencement of 1838, but he became as well known for his essays, which seemed to pour out of him. Moving to Concord, where the second battle of the Revolutionary War had been fought, Emerson became one of the leaders of the Transcendental movement.

What marked Emerson from the start was the belief that nineteenth-century Bostonians—and Americans—needed to look to their own roots to develop poetry and philosophy. He disdained the approach that was so common at the time of looking to England or Europe for inspiration: there was plenty of inspiration to be found in America, he declared. Enough people agreed with him that Emerson became the prophet of American self-reliance in intellectual as well as physical matters. One of his closest friends was Henry David Thoreau, who sometimes lived at the Emerson home.

Why does Thoreau seem so rough and unkempt to us, even over the distance of two centuries?

Because that is how he appeared to his friends and neighbors at the time! Born in Concord, Henry David Thoreau (1817–1862) was a decade and a half behind his friend, Ralph Waldo Emerson, and not only in a chronological sense. Throughout his life, Thoreau envied the ease with which Emerson moved in higher circles and the doors that seemed

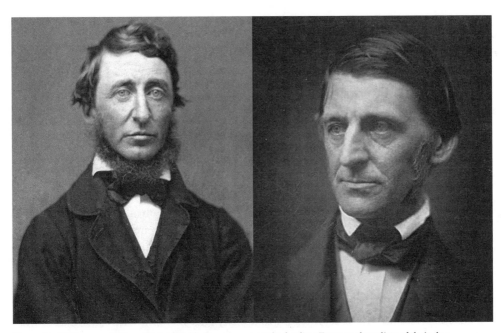

Henry David Thoreau (left) and Ralph Waldo Emerson were the leading Transcendentalists of their day.

369

to open so easily for him. Thoreau's mind was quite as good as Emerson's, but he lacked the smoothness, the intellectual agility that might have won him a substantial audience. Knowing that he was sometimes too rough and uncouth to make it in high society, Thoreau determined to follow another path, and his year spent living in a cabin in the woods by Walden Pond was the result. Much like Emerson, Thoreau believed in self-reliance, both for the individual and the nation.

Thoreau died young as a result of tuberculosis. Emerson gave the eulogy at his funeral. Between them, these two men did much to shape the beliefs and attitudes of upper-class Bostonians, and their words continue to influence college students everywhere.

If the Transcendentalists were so keen on self-reliance, why did they not do more for women?

Because they believed the women should do this for themselves. Self-reliance implies that one can shape one's own life and future better than any outside force or person. But the Transcendalists certainly were friendlier to women than almost any social or intellectual group of the time. The author Lydia Maria Child and the reformer and novelist Louisa May Alcott can attest to this. So can Julia Ward Howe, the woman who wrote the marching song "John Brown's Body." Perhaps the most famous of all the female Transcentalists, however, was Margaret Fuller (1810–1850). Born in Cambridge, she became one of the loudest and strongest voices of the Transcendental movement. She died at the age of forty, when the ship that was bringing her back from Europe wrecked off the Long Island coast.

Why were the Transcendentalists not more successful?

By its very nature, the Transcendentalist group was not intended for political, or even social, success. Men such as Emerson and Thoreau and women like Louisa May Alcott and Margaret Fuller sought neither fame nor wealth. Their intention was to show the rest of us how trivial and short-lived such pursuits are. It is not surprising, therefore, that they were not loved by their neighbors, many of whom were thoroughly embarked on the traditional path to success. What the Transcendentalists have given us is a body of literature and thought that has long outlived the people themselves.

Who was the leader of Boston society during the late nineteenth century?

Oliver Wendell Holmes, Sr. (1809–1894) held this position for nearly three decades. A physician, essayist, and man of letters, he was one the most popular of all Bostonians. Holmes' poetry often centered on Boston themes, such as when he wrote in favor of keeping the U.S.S. *Constitution* afloat. Holmes was, quite likely, the person who coined the expression "The Hub" to describe Greater Boston, a nickname that has stood the test of time.

Holmes, Sr., also left a major legacy to the city and the Commonwealth. Oliver Wendell Holmes Jr. (1841–1935) was not as convivial as his father, but he was just as distinguished. After serving in the Union cavalry during the Civil War, the younger Holmes entered law and rose to become an associate justice of the U.S. Supreme Court.

MEN AND WOMEN OF ACTION

Who is the best-loved figure from Boston history, the one Bostonians identify with the most?

Robert Gould Shaw (1837–1863), who was lieutenant colonel in the 54th Massachusetts Infantry Regiment, died leading this first all-black regiment in the battle at Fort Wagner, South Carolina in 1863. The magnificent sculpture that stands directly across Beacon Street from the Massachusetts State House depicts Colonel Shaw leading these brave men. His story and that of the regiment is told in the 1989 film *Glory*.

Who is the man or woman of action who is most misunderstood?

Clearly, this spot belongs to Malcolm X (1925–1965). Born Malcolm Little in Omaha, Nebraska, he knew serious oppression during his upbringing in the Midwest. Malcolm arrived in Boston—in Roxbury, to be precise—around 1940, and lived with relatives. His teenage years were not a good time in his life: they ended with his being incarcerated in the Boston Reformatory. But Malcolm remembered Boston as the first place where he had seen African Americans doing well. Perhaps they were not prosperous, but there was a quiet dignity to their lives.

Malcolm went on to become the number two leader of the Nation of Islam (the Honorable Elijah Muhammad was number one). During the early 1960s, many white Americans were frightened by the presence of the dynamic Malcolm X, who was frequently interviewed and who nearly always delivered vigorous, vehement answers to reporters' questions. Bostonians did not take Malcolm as "one of their own" for a long time, but the 1994 movie *Malcolm X* helped to bring about a better response on their part, and from the nation as a whole.

Who was the most beloved—yet misunderstood—woman of action?

Helen Keller (1880–1968) was not a native Bostonian. She grew up in rural Georgia and seemed doomed from the start to live a pathetic life as a deaf, dumb, and blind human being. She was rescued from this state by Anne Sullivan, who came from Massachusetts, and the student and her beloved teacher spent many years in and around Boston. People of education and good sense were nearly always impressed by Helen Keller, and many of them came to love her. For her part, she declared Boston the best of cities. This does not mean there was no conflict, however.

At the advent of World War I, Keller spoke out against the war. She was a pacifist in the best sense of the word, but her stance won her no love from the majority of Americans who felt betrayed by the girl-turned-woman whom they had previously taken into their hearts. Her popularity plummeted for more than a decade, and it was not until the mid-1930s that she was—once again—among the most beloved of Americans.

Who was Mary Baker Eddy, and why is her memory so revered?

Born in New Hampshire, Mary Baker Eddy (1821–1910) experienced poor health from an early age. Her first husband died young, and her second marriage ended in divorce. Life seemed to have failed her in any number of ways when in 1866, she was suddenly restored to health after experiencing a bad fall. She was reading from the Book of Matthew (9:1–8) at the time of her spontaneous healing, and she soon became convinced both of Christ's goodness and His capacity to heal. For the rest of her long life, Eddy preached a new gospel, one of self-reliance and dependence on God for all sorts of healings and miracles. As a result, her followers came to reject modern science and medicine, declaring that it was best to approach God directly for healing.

Eddy's Science and Health was first published in 1875 and was revised many times afterwards. Her followers became known as Christian Scientists, and the First Church of Christ, Scientist was built in Boston. Today it is one of the most recognizable landmarks in the city, and one can obtain a magnificent view of it from the Prudential Center Skywalk.

Who is the most recognizable "man of action" in Boston history?

It is a tie between Samuel Adams (1722–1803) and Paul Revere (1734–1818). The two knew each other well, and Adams frequently commissioned Revere to carry the dispatch and messages of the Committee of Safety to distant locations. Adams, who was by most reports a rather chilly, even frosty person, is honored with a statue right in front of Faneuil Hall. The Paul Revere statue, which displays him on horseback, is in the North End.

Of course, Bostonians tend to overlook some of the less pleasant facts. Paul Revere was—by most accounts—everyone's favorite person in town, but he got into really hot water in 1779, when as second in command of the failed Penobscot Bay expedition he was court martialed. Revere was let off without punishment, but this serves as yet another cautionary tale about the powerful and famous.

This famous portrait of Paul Revere shows him as an accomplished silversmith.

THE ARTISTS

What is the first name that comes up when one mentions art and Boston?

Almost certainly it is John Singleton Copley (1738–1815). Born and raised in Boston, Copley came into fortunate circumstances that almost ensured he would be a Loyalist when the Revolution commenced. In the decade that preceded the Revolution, Copley painted dozens of Bostonians, most of them from the town's upper class. Copley had great skill with the brush, but one wonders sometimes if he did not make some of his subjects even prettier or more handsome than was really the case. If the upper-class Bostonians were as good looking and well preserved as he shows, then it must have been a great place to live at the time. Most of these Copley portraits are held at the Museum of Fine Arts.

When the Revolution began, Copley left home and went to London. Not only did he continue to paint, but some of his real masterpieces came after the move to England. One of the best known is "Watson and the Shark." To the American observer, though, Copley's finest work seems to have been accomplished while he was in Boston. Copley Square in the very center of Boston is named in his honor.

How did a European-born painter become so identified with Boston?

John Singer Sargent (1856–1925) was born in Florence, Italy, to American parents. Much of his work was accomplished while living in London, but when he first came to the United States in 1876, he became a citizen. Sargent soon made Boston his new home, and he labored for *twenty-six years* on a set of murals for the Boston Public Library. He also painted murals for Harvard's Widener Library and for the Museum of Fine Arts. There are those who claim that Sargent never became an American—that he remained a European throughout life. If he were alive, he would surely reject this argument.

How did Francis Parkman (1823–1893) write so eloquently of areas he had never seen?

This remains one of the great questions, but the answer—surely—is that he possessed a great imagination. Born and bred in Boston, Parkman went on the Oregon Trail in youth, and turned out his first book on that subject. Travel later became impossible for him, as he slowly went blind. But Parkman forged ahead, penning masterpieces such as *Montcalm and Wolfe*.

Who was Phillis Wheatley?

Born in Senegal, she came to Boston as a child of eight or nine and was immediately sold into slavery. Her owners, the Wheatley family, named her for the ship on which she came. The Wheatleys were an unusually caring family, especially where slaves were concerned. They taught Phillis to read and write, and she became known as a prodigy, the

373

first known black poetess in America. One wishes that the story of the rest of her life was happier. Her masters died during the Revolution, and she—now a free woman—had an unhappy marriage to another African American. She continued to write fine poetry, including a poem in honor of General George Washington. She died in Boston in 1784 and was buried in an unmarked grave. Her memory is best preserved by a remarkable statue on the Mall of Commonwealth Avenue.

What Bostonian become the authority on the conquest of Mexico and Peru?

It seems that a Mexican or a Spaniard should have accomplished the task, but in those early years of history writing (done before the study of history became a profession), it was reclusive Bostonians such as William H. Prescott (1796–1859) who wrote many classics about Mexico and Peru.

How did Edgar Allan Poe become associated with Boston?

Many of us know that the author Edgar Allan Poe (1809–1949), famous for his stories of mystery, horror, and the macabre, was born in Boston, even though his formative years were spent in Virginia. He also attended the U.S. Military Academy at West Point (however briefly). One has to be a real Bostonian to know, however, that Poe spent some of his most creative years in Boston.

One does not normally associate Kahlil Gibran with Boston. Did he live there?

Only for three years. But upper-class Bostonians took to Gibran, and to his *The Prophet,* in a way that has seldom been equaled. Born in Lebanon in 1883, Gibran first came to Boston at the age of twelve. Though he bounced from there back to Lebanon, and then to London and finally Manhattan, Gibran always found his most receptive audience among Bostonians. Perhaps it was because there were so many upper-class Bostonians interested in matters of religion and faith, yet disenchanted with the answers they received from traditional churches. When *The Prophet* was published in 1923—with Gibran supplying the illustrations as well as the writing—people knew that a new era had dawned. Bostonians tend to look inward much of the time, but when they embrace someone or something from the outside, they do so in a big way.

Bostonian Edgar Allan Poe was famous for spooky poems such as "The Raven" and tales such as "The Fall of the House of Usher" and "The Pit and the Pendulum."

374

How did Leonard Nimoy ever become so associated with Boston?

Leonard Nimoy (1931–2015) is best known for playing Spock on the science fiction television series *Star Trek*. Nimoy came from Boston's West End, and always claimed he was happy to be a product of Boston. Ever since *Star Trek* first aired, there have been MIT students who openly identified with Nimoy and Spock, saying that they feel the tension between the rational and the mystical. As *Boston* magazine expressed it, "Most Bostonians are more Kirk than Spock," quick to action and slow to deliberation.

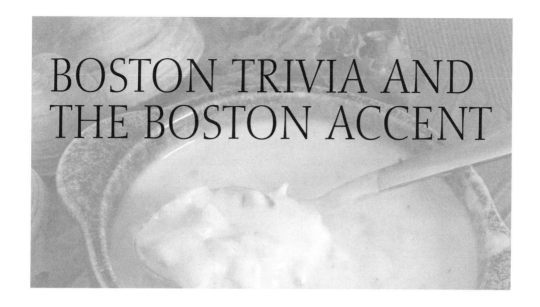

BOSTON TRIVIA AND THE BOSTON ACCENT

Where does the Boston accent come from?

People have asked this ever since John F. Kennedy appeared on the national scene, during the 1950s. Kennedys accent provoked all sorts of commentary because his flat, almost nasal delivery contrasted so strongly with his good looks and patrician background.

Bostonians had—until Kennedy's time—never really questioned their accent. It was so prevalent, from downtown Boston to Cape Cod, and from the North Shore to the coast of Maine that it seemed perfectly normal to them. But Kennedy's elevation to the presidency, plus the rather sudden appearance of television, made the accent more noticeable. Scholars have since spent much time on the question, and they generally concur that the Boston accent comes from southeastern England, also known as East Anglia. Precisely when it came remains in question, however. Did the seventeenth-century Puritans speak in tones such as those we hear in popular movies of our time? Or did the Boston accent come later?

Where does one hear the strictest pronunciation of the Boston accent?

One hears it most distinctly in the working-class neighborhoods of Greater Boston. Revere, Dorchester, and Hyde Park are full of people exhibiting a strict Boston accent, while the more affluent towns of Allston, Brighton, and Cambridge witness a drop-off in the accent. If the current trend continues, the Boston accent may disappear in the next two generations.

What is the signature sound of the Boston accent?

For decades, Bostonians have poked fun at themselves by declaring that you "caa-n-t pahk your cah in Havaad Yaard." The *r* sound generally gets dropped, but there are exceptions, as when the *r* is followed by a vowel sound.

377

When did the Boston accent first appear on TV and in the movies?

The first generation of movie-goers made their desires plain: the Midwestern accent, preferably from Ohio, was preferred above all others. As a result, most of the great movie stars of the 1930s and 1940s spoke an uninflected Midwestern accent (this accent continues to be favored by airline passengers, and most airline pilots learn to speak it).

The great exception to the rule was James Cagney (1889–1986). Born in Manhattan, Cagney learned his hard, sometimes harsh tones from his Irish father. Once he appeared in the movies, Cagney became an indelible presence, the tough-talking fellow who sometimes joined the gangsters and sometimes fought them.

COLLOQUIALISMS

How did Boston ever get to have so many odd turns of phrase and speech?

In part this is because Boston and its people have been around so much longer than is the case with other important American cities. Bostonians have had nearly four centuries to develop the colloquial expressions for which they now are (in)famous. But there is a second part to the answer: Bostonians also maintain their expressions simply because they want to. They do not wish to be just like New Yorkers, Philadelphians, and other big-city people.

What are some of the best-known of Boston's many colloquialisms?

Let's start with "across the river." In a city like New York, this would not make sense because there are so many rivers involved, but in Boston these words always mean "the other side of the Charles River." Bostonians often employ this expression in a derogatory manner, meaning that what happens on the other side of the river—in Cambridge—is not very important.

How and when did Boston become known as the "Athens of America"?

Boston and Philadelphia both wanted this title, but the city on the Charles eventually won out. The reason for this is that a small group of highly educated and highly ambitious Bostonians—most of whom were members of the newly formed Unitarian Church—did their best to promote Boston as the center of learning and the arts. The thing they most dreaded was that Boston might one day be called the "Sparta of America," meaning that it would be associated with militarism. This small group succeeded by the time of the Civil War: Boston was seen as number one wherever liberal politics and social progressivism were concerned.

What is the shortest and simplest of all Boston colloquialisms?

This is a tie between the "Bs" and the "T." The first refers to the Boston Bruins and the second refers to the Massachusetts Bay Transportation Authority.

To millions of Bostonians and their country cousins, the "T" is the institution they love to hate. It is responsible for virtually all the buses, trains, and streetcars that run through the metro area. To outsiders such as casual tourists, the "T" is often seen as a quaint, even charming experience; to the regular Bostonian, it is a source of continual vexation. Not only do the routes and times change frequently, but the managers of the "T" appear oblivious to criticism, even the constructive kind. As a result, Bostonians generally loathe the "T" and speak in scalding terms when it becomes a subject of conversation. On a lighter note, Bostonians also enjoy singing a song (sung by the Kingston Trio) that celebrates the haphazard side of life.

> Well, did he ever return?
> No he never returned
> And his fate is still unlearned
> He may ride forever
> 'Neath the streets of Boston
> He's the man who never returned.

What is the "Pike?"

There are hundreds of turnpikes on America's East Coast and perhaps millions of miles of turnpike, but there is one and only one "Pike." That is the Massachusetts Turnpike, which is beloved by some and loathed by others.

Previous to the creation of the Mass Turnpike in the 1950s, transportation in eastern Massachusetts was a confused jumble of cars, streetcars, buses, and trains. There are those who say that nothing has improved over the last half-century, but this is because they did not witness the traffic jams of the 1940s and 1950s. Once the Pike was laid down, people on the east side of Boston could reach the west side in a matter of minutes (just so long as they traveled at the right time of day). Previous to this, one could easily have spent an hour—even an hour and a half—going from Chinatown to Newton. Bostonians tend to criticize the high toll rates on the Mass Pike, but they have little idea of how much more difficult their lives would be without it. The people of central and western Massachusetts, by contrast, are well aware of how much better the Pike makes their lives; they can scoot into Boston early in the morning and be home by midafternoon (again, just so long as the traffic pattern conforms).

What is meant by the "breakdown lane"?

People in other parts of the country call this the highway shoulder; Bostonians—with their rich sense of humor—call it the breakdown lane. The not-so-funny part is that no one wants to use the so-called "breakdown lane" in Greater Boston; other automobiles are coming with such speed that they may well crash into the person who has pulled over.

What do Bostonians mean by "cabbage night"?

Boston has a long tradition of street fights and scuffles between opposing groups. One of the most famous was the longstanding rivalry between the gangs of the Old North End and the Old South End. It's quite possible that cabbage night—which refers to the throwing of cabbage, eggs, and other edibles in the street on the night before Halloween—comes from some of those old rivalries.

Does anyone know who first used the expression "chowderhead"?

No. The origins of this one remain shrouded in mystery. There's no doubt what it means, however. A chowderhead is someone who is lost in his New England clam chowder and does not look up to see the wider world—a stupid person.

One used to hear the expression "Combat Zone" all the time. What happened to that?

In the 1960s and 1970s, the area around Park Street just south of the Common was the dirtiest—and some would say most exciting—part of town. Peep shows and prostitutes competed for attention. Tourists, especially those who came by bus, were sometimes appalled. The area earned its name from the large number of men in uniform—soldiers and sailors alike. The Combat Zone was largely cleaned up in the late 1980s, but memories of it—the good times and the sordid conditions alike—exert a powerful memory.

Everyone knows that Bostonians like to escape to "The Cape." But what is meant by "down the Cape"?

Until about the 1940s, Cape Cod was a distant area for most Bostonians. When they

A person who is really enjoying his or her clam chowder to the point of not noticing anything else going on is a "chowderhead."

> ### How long does it take to make it from downtown Boston to Hyannis, which is typically considered the most attractive part of Cape Cod?
>
> If one leaves early enough and beats the traffic, it can be accomplished in just under two hours. If one leaves Boston at the *wrong* time of day (any time after 2 P.M.) and gets snarled in traffic, it could take up to five hours.

wanted sunshine and seacoast, they went to neighboring Nantasket, which is just eight miles away, or perhaps to Revere Beach. The advent of the automobile changed the lives of many Bostonians, especially those who wanted to get away for the weekend. Somewhere between 1945 and 1965, the expression "down the Cape" came to mean either going to or being at Cape Cod.

What does "lace curtain Irish" mean?

It's not used as much as in the past, but during the 1930s and 1940s it referred to a large group of Irishmen who made it from the shanty-like dwellings of the North End (at that time) to better living quarters in Dorchester and Boston's South End.

Is Boston where the expression "five and ten store" began?

It's hard to say because the expression traveled far and wide in the early twentieth century. The "Five and Ten" meant a local, neighborhood store, where most of the items sold for a nickel or a dime. It's difficult to find prices like that anywhere in our time.

What is mean by the "Fairy Ferry"?

By this, Bostonians mean the ferry that runs from Boston Harbor to Provincetown. The latter became known as a haven for gays as early as the 1940s.

What is meant by "Lynn, Lynn, the city of sin"?

Lynn is a city in its own right that is about twelve miles northeast of Boston. There was a time when Lynn was a hard-working and rather successful place. It is where Lydia Pinkham designed and marketed her many herbal remedies. Lynn fell on hard

A label for one of Lydia Pinkham's once-popular herbal remedies.

381

times after World War II, however, and Bostonians often skipped out of town for a lover's meeting in "the city of sin."

What do Bostonians mean by "Man's Greatest Hospital"?

Bostonians know how great Mass General Hospital is, and they know that people travel thousands of miles to receive treatment there. But they get tired of hearing about it. "Man's Greatest Hospital" is a derogatory remark, directed more at the people who come from far away than at the hospital itself.

Sometimes one hears the word, or expression, "Meffa." What on Earth does that mean?

Bostonians have long looked down on the people of neighboring Medford, and Medfordites have no great love for Boston. The accent in Medford is, if anything, stronger than that of downtown Boston, and "Meffa" has come to stand for Medford.

What is "The Green Monster," or just "The Monster" or "Monstah"?

This refers to the thirty-seven-foot, left-field wall of Fenway Park. It's hard to say just how many home runs have been lifted over the Monstah, or how many late, ninth-inning rallies have been squelched when what could have been a double ricocheted off the Monster and was thrown in very quickly. What we can say is that the Red Sox fans around "The Monstah" are the loudest ones in all of Fenway Park.

Speaking of Fenway, how much do the famous Fenway Franks cost?

Fenway Franks—or hot dogs—used to sell for as little as seventy-five cents apiece. At the time of this writing in 2016, they are more in the area of six dollars. Fans continue to purchase them, even while declaring that the Red Sox management is out to make its living on the backs of the working class.

Who invented the expression "the packie"?

Like so many of these great colloquialisms, the person who first coined it is lost in history. Virtually all Bostonians know that "the packie" means the liquor store, however.

Do most Bostonians call them the "Pats," "The Patriots," or the "New England Patriots"?

It really depends on the social context. It's quite possible that the same Bostonian on the same day might employ all three expressions, depending on whether he was at home in his local neighborhood, or in a highbrow setting.

What does "pissa" mean?

That's one of the simplest of all to answer. "Pissa" means good, and "Wicked Pissa" means fantastic.

What is meant by "The Pru"?

Ever since the Prudential Building went up in the mid-1960s, it has been the outstanding landmark of downtown Boston. Bostonians orient where they are relative to two such landmarks: the Prudential Building and the CITGO sign.

When did "Red Sox Nation" become part of the conversation?

It was never used until the Red Sox became real contenders, which means 2003. That was an extremely painful year because the Sox bobbled things one more time. But 2003 was the last year of humiliation. Since then the Sox have won three World Series titles. And it was sometime in 2003–2004 that people began using "Red Sox Nation" to refer to real tried-and-true Red Sox fans, wherever they may live.

What is a "ripper"?

It's a big party, what college students often call a "kegger."

What is a "skid"?

A "skid" may be a person who is just down on his or her luck, but it often means someone who has slid, or skidded, so far down the social ladder that he is no longer acceptable.

What is meant by "the Square"?

Despite all the great squares of downtown Boston, including Copley, everyone knows that "the Square" means Harvard Square on the other side of the river.

What does "The Teddy," or "The Ted," mean?

This means the Ted Williams Tunnel, which carries the traveler from the Mass Pike to Logan Airport in record time. Williams was known for the speed of his bat, and the tunnel has greatly improved the lives of travelers to and from the Boston area.

What does "The Town" and "The Townie" refer to?

Nine times out of ten, "The Town" means Charlestown and "The Townie" means a resident who lives there.

Why do Bostonians sometimes call Sommerville "Slummerville"?

Bostonians tend not to be nice where neighboring cities and towns are concerned. They think of themselves as number one, and a lot of the time they are correct. Slummerville refers to the fact that housing in that town used to be low-cost. More recently, though, prices in Sommerville have risen, as they have all over the Boston area.

What do Bostonians mean by a "triple decker"?

Though it sounds like a sandwich, the "triple decker" actually refers to the kind of housing that was built in the late nineteenth century and that now serves at least three families on different floors. "Triple deckers" come in various shapes and sizes, but they tend either to be fantastic (or pissa) or really terrible.

What does it mean to make a "U-ie"?

This is one Boston expression that has spread to much of the rest of the nation. To make a "U-ie" means to make a U-turn, and there are many places in Boston where this action is illegal.

Does anyone really doubt what "whateva" means?

Here's another Boston colloquialism that has spread to the rest of the nation. "Whatever" was around by the late 1980s, but it was TV sitcoms such as *Friends* and *Seinfeld* that really made it known all over.

What do Bostonians mean by "The Zakim"?

They mean the Leonard P. Zakim Bunker Hill Bridge, the ultramodern bridge that was part of the work of the Big Dig. The Zakim has replaced Longfellow Bridge as the best known of all bridges of the Boston area.

To what are Bostonians referring when they say "ZooMass"?

They mean the University of Massachusetts, and though there are several campuses, Bostonians refer to the one at Amherst that is ninety miles west of the city. Hundreds of thousands of hard-working, young Bostonians have gone to "ZooMass" over the decades, and they often see it as one of the best parts of their lives, especially because of the many beer parties.

How many college students reside in Boston?

Somewhere between 100,000 and 200,000 college students live in the city. When one adds all the colleges, universities, and vocational schools, and then makes allowance for those who stay at home and study online, the student population comes to about one-eighth that of Boston and Cambridge combined. Unlike many college cities, Boston does not witness a major drop off in population during the summer months. A majority of the young people who study in Boston during the academic year remain during the summer months. Many of them work the stands of Fenway Park, while others serve whiskey and beer in any number of bars, with Kenmore Square being home to the largest number of these.

TRIVIA

What cities and towns compose the "Greater Boston" region?

First are the twenty-two neighborhoods that make up Boston itself (these have been discussed in a previous chapter). Then there are outlying towns that are definitely outside Boston's jurisdiction, but which are close enough that the residents feel a strong affinity with Boston. These are Needham, Dedham, and Milton to the south, and Watertown, Somerville, and Everett to the north. Newton is officially part of Boston, but it points to the suburbs and bedroom communities such as Natick and Framingham.

How important is Route 128 to the people of Boston?

Many Bostonians—residents of the city itself—don't use Route 128 that much. Their suburban cousins use it all the time, though. Route 128 has become the unofficial boundary line between Greater Boston and the bedroom communities. It also acts as a launchpad for those who scoot away for the weekend, either to Maine or the Cape.

Who designed Boston's "Emerald Necklace"?

This was accomplished by Frederick Law Olmsted (1822–1903), America's premier, nineteenth-century landscape architect. Born in Hartford, Connecticut, Olmsted traveled a great deal before settling permanently in Boston in 1878. Previous to this, he served as the landscape architect for New York City's Central Park. Once in Boston, Olmsted became famous for his desire to create parks, which would serve as "lungs" for Greater Boston. He realized that Boston did not have the space for a great "central" park like the one in Manhattan; he therefore designed the Emerald Necklace, which was intended to ring the center part of Boston with a series of small parks that acted like oases. To a large extent he succeeded, and the air quality of Boston is notably better than in other East Coast cities.

How significant has the Rose Kennedy Greenway been?

As the Big Dig neared completion in 2005, Boston city elders decided to perpetuate the memory of Rose Fitzgerald Kennedy, the wife of Joseph Patrick Kennedy, Sr., and the mother of John F., Robert F., and Ted. The Rose Kennedy Greenway picks up where the Emerald Necklace left off, bringing fresh air and green spaces to parts of Boston that were previously dark and dank. The Greenway has been a spectacular success on the east side of the city, and in the streets that approach the Old North End. Motorists sometimes drive by with looks of envy on their faces as they see Bostonians at lunch hour soaking up the sun.

What is the most intriguing—and eccentric—of Boston's many statues?

Almost every Boston street has a major statue, and some have more than one. The statue that attracts the most comments is that of Edgar Allan Poe, which is near the intersection of Boylston Street and Charles Street South. Poe's hair is unkempt and he seems in a great hurry—perhaps to catch the winds of inspiration. A raven precedes him.

Who was Boston's longest-serving mayor?

Though his many years in City Hall were broken up by sudden vacancies, James Michael Curley (1874–1958) surely holds the all-time record for occupancy. He first won election as Mayor of Boston in 1913 and served from 1914 to 1918. The state legislature passed a law preventing the mayor of Boston from succeeding himself, so Curley was out of office for four years. He swept back to victory in 1921, and served from 1922 to 1926. The state law again prevented him from running, but he came back to win yet again in 1929 (serving 1930 to 1934), and won a final term in 1945 (1946 to 1950). At stages along the way, he also served as governor of Massachusetts (1935–1937) and as a member of the U.S. House of Representatives (1911–1913; 1913–1914; 1943–1947). That he spent more time in City Hall than any other man is beyond dispute, but it does not completely delineate Curley's remarkable career. No other person bridged the gap between the last days of the Yankee plutocrats and the Irish politicians, and none did more to define the typical "Irish pol."

What do the colored lights on top of the old Hancock building say about the weather?

The old John Hancock Building—not to be confused with the elegant skyscraper that was built in the 1970s—has a row of colored lights atop; few Bostonians realize that the lights have a function.

- Steady blue lights mean … clear view
- Flashing blue lights mean … clouds due or changes due
- Steady red lights mean … rain ahead
- Flashing red lights mean … snow
- Flashing red lights during the spring and summer mean that the Red Sox game has been called off due to weather (something that seldom happens)

What do Ben Franklin, Sam Adams, James Taylor, and Taylor Schilling have in common?

On the face of it, it seems that they share little if anything in common. Ben Franklin was a humanist who sought to elevate himself and to make the world a better

The new John Hancock Building.

place at the same time. Sam Adams was a humorless drudge who toiled for decades in pursuit of American liberty. James Taylor was one of the most gifted folk songwriters American has yet produced. And Taylor Schilling is a well-known actress. What they share is quite simple: they all were born in Boston!

Are "tonics" and "whoopee pies" available at most "spas"?

The answer to this question has more to do with linguistics than practicalities. Bostonians have long called almost any drink other than water or hard alcohol a "tonic": this applies to soft drinks as well as cider. Whoppie pies are a New England delicacy that have yet to catch on with the rest of the nation. And spas are neighborhood shops that sell groceries, sandwiches, and other prepared foods. So the basic answer is yes.

Appendix:
Mayors of Boston

Name	Political Party	Years in Office
John Phillips	Federalist	1822–1823
Josiah P. Quincy	Federalist	1823–1829
Harrison Gray Otis	Federalist	1829–1832
Charles B. Wells	N/R	1832–1834
Theodore Lyman, Jr.	Democrat	1834–1836
Samuel T. Armstrong	Whig	1836–1837
Samuel Atkins Eliot	Whig	1837–1840
Jonathan Chapman	Whig	1840–1843
Martin Brimmer	Whig	1843–1845
William Parker	Whig	1845–1847
Thomas Aspinwall Davis (died in office)	Native American Party	1845
Benson Leavitt (acting mayor)	Whig	1845
Josiah Quincy Jr.	Whig	1845–1849
John P. Bigelow	Whig	1849–1852
Benjamin Seaver	Whig	1852–1854
Jerome V.C. Smith	Native American Party	1854–1856
Alexander H. Rice	Republican	1856–1858
Frederick W. Lincoln Jr.	Republican	1858–1861
Joseph Wightman	Democrat	1861–1863
Frederick W. Lincoln Jr.	Republican	1863–1867
Otis Norcross	Republican	1867–1868
Nathaniel B. Shurtleff	Democrat	1868–1871
William Gaston	Democrat	1871–1873
Henry L Pierce (resigned)	Nonpartisan	1873
Leonard Cutter (acting mayor)	Democrat	1873–1874
Samuel C. Cobb	Nonpartisan	1874–1877
Frederick O. Prince	Democrat	1877–1878
Henry L. Pierce	Republican	1878–1879
Frederick O. Prince	Democrat	1879–1882
Samuel A. Green	Republican	1882–1883
Albert Palmer	Democrat	1883–1884
Augustus P. Martin	Republican	1884–1885
Hugh O'Brien	Democrat	1885–1889

Name	Political Party	Years in Office
Thomas N. Hart	Republican	1889–1890
Nathan Matthews Jr.	Democrat	1891–1894
Edwin Upton Curtis	Republican	1895
Josiah Quincy	Democrat	1896–1899
Thomas N. Hart	Republican	1900–1902
Patrick Collins	Democrat	1902–1905
David A. Whelton	Democrat	1905–1906
John F. Fitzgerald	Democrat	1906–1908
George A. Hibbard	Republican	1908–1910
John F. Fitzgerald	Democrat	1910–1914
James Michael Curley	Democrat	1914–1918
Andrew M. Peters	Democrat	1918–1922
James Michael Curley	Democrat	1922–1926
Malcolm Nichols	Republican	1926–1930
James Michael Curley	Democrat	1930–1934
Frederick Mansfield	Democrat	1934–1938
Maurice J. Tobin	Democrat	1938–1945
John E. Kerrigan (acting mayor)	Democrat	1945–1946
James Michael Curley	Democrat	1946–1950
John B. Hynes (acting mayor)	Democrat	1947
John B. Hynes	Democrat	1950–1960
John F. Collins	Democrat	1960–1968
Kevin H. White	Democrat	1968–1984
Raymond L. Flynn	Democrat	1984–1993
Thomas H. Menino	Democrat	1993–2014
Martin J. Walsh	Democrat	2014–

Further Reading

Alan, Carter. *Radio Free Boston: The Rise and Fall of WBCN*. Boston: Northeastern University Press, 2013.

Albion, Robert G., and others. *New England and the Sea*. Mystic, CT: Mystic Seaport Museum, 2004.

Bahne, Charles. *Chronicles of Old Boston: Exploring New England's Historic Capital*. New York: Museyon, 2012.

Beagle, Jonathan. *Boston: A Visual History*. Watertown, MA: Imagine Publishing, 2013.

Benton. J. H. *The Story of the Old Boston Town House, 1658–1711*. Boston: privately printed, 1908.

Botticelli, Jim. *Dirty Old Boston: Four Decades of a City in Transition*. Boston: Union Park Press, 2014.

Bourne, Russell. *Cradle of Violence: How Boston's Waterfront Mobs Ignited the American Revolution*. Hoboken, NJ: John Wiley & Sons, 2006.

Cannell, Michael. *I. M. Pei: Mandarin of Modernism*. New York: Carol Southern Books, 1995.

Connelly, Michael. *26.2 Miles to Boston: A Journey into the Heart of the Boston Marathon*. Guilford, CT: Lyons Press, 2014.

Crompton, Samuel Willard. *The Boston Tea Party: Colonists Protest the British Government*. New York: Chelsea House, 2011.

Curtis. John Gould. *History of the Town of Brookline, Massachusetts*. Boston: Houghton Mifflin Company, 1933.

Derderian, Tom. *Boston Marathon: The History of the World's Premier Running Event*. Champaign, IL: Human Kinetics Publishing, 1994.

———. *The Boston Marathon: A Celebration of America's Greatest Race*. Chicago: Triumph Books, 2014.

Dickerson, Oliver Morton, editor. *Boston under Military Rule*. Westport, CT: Greenwood Press, 1971.

Drake, Samuel Adams, with Walter K. Watkins. *Old Boston Taverns and Tavern Clubs*. Boston: W.A. Butterfield, 1917.

Fifty Years of Boston: A Memorial Volume. Compiled by the Subcommittee on Memorial History. Boston, 1932.

Glennon, Sean. *Tom Brady vs. The NFL: The Case for Football's Greatest Quarterback.* Chicago: Triumph Books, 2012.

The Glorious Ninety-two Members of the House of Representatives. Boston: Joint Committee for the Convention of the Senate and House of Representatives, 1949.

Grange, Michael. *Basketball's Greatest Stars.* New York: Firefly Books, 2012.

Halpert, Steven, and Brenda Halpert, editors. *Brahmins & BullyBoys: G. Frank Radway's Boston Album.* Boston: Houghton Mifflin, 1973.

Harvard University. Quinquennial Catalogue of the Officers and Graduates, 1636–1920. Cambridge: Harvard University Press, 1920.

Holley, Michael. *Patriot Reign: Bill Bellichick, the Coaches, and the Players Who Built a Champion.* New York: Harper, 2004.

Howe, M. A. DeWolfe. *Boston: The Place and the People.* New York: The Macmillan Company, 1903.

Johnson, H. Earle. *Symphony Hall, Boston.* Boston: Little, Brown and Company, 1950.

Kirker, Harold, and James Kirker. *Bulfinch's Boston, 1787–1817.* New York: Oxford University Press, 1964.

Lewis, Frederick. *Young at Heart: The Story of Johnny Kelley, Boston's Marathon Man.* Waco, TX: WRS Publishing, 1992.

Lodge, Henry Cabot. *Historic Towns: Boston.* London, UK: Longman's Green, 1891.

MacCambridge, Michael. *America's Game: The Epic Story of How Pro Football Captured a Nation.* New York: Random House, 2004.

Masur, Louis P. *The Soiling of Old Glory: The Story of a Photograph That Shocked America.* New York: Bloomsbury Press, 2008.

Nason, Elias. *A Gazetteer of the State of Massachusetts.* Boston: B.B. Russell, 1874.

Newman, William A., and Wilfred E. Holton. *Boston's Back Bay: The Story of America's Greatest Nineteenth-Century Landfill Project.* Boston: Northeastern University Press, 2006.

O'Connor, Thomas H. *Civil War Boston: Home Front & Battlefield.* Boston: Northeastern University Press, 1997.

———. *South Boston: My Home Town.* Boston: Northeastern University Press, 1994.

Philbrick, Nathaniel. *Bunker Hill: A City, a Siege, a Revolution.* New York: Viking, 2013.

Rodgers, Bill, and Matthew Shepatin. *Marathon Man: My 26.2 Mile Journey from Unknown Grad Student to the Top of the Running World.* New York: Thomas Dunne Books, 2013.

Rossiter, William S., editor. *Days and Ways in Old Boston.* Boston: R.H. Stearns, 1915.

Schultz, Nancy Lusignan. *Fire & Roses: The Burning of the Charlestown Convent, 1834.* New York: The Free Press, 2000.

Shurtleff, Nathaniel B. *A Topographical and Historical Description of Boston.* Boston: Rockwell & Churchill, 1891.

Smith, Harmon. *My Friend, My Friend: The Story of Thoreau's Relationship with Emerson.* Amherst: University of Massachusetts Press, 1999.

Snow, Edgar Rowe. *The Islands of Boston Harbor*. New York: Dodd, Mead & Company, 1936, 1971.

Stracher, Cameron. *Kings of the Road: How Frank Shorter, Bill Rodgers, and Alberto Salazar Made Running Go Boom*. Boston: Houghton Mifflin, 2013.

Vanderwarker, Peter. *The Big Dig: Reshaping an American City*. Boston: Little, Brown and Company, 2001.

Vrabel, Jim. *A People's History of the New Boston*. Amherst: University of Massachusetts Press, 2014.

Whitehill, Walter Muir. *Boston & Cambridge: Portrait of Two Cities*. Barre, MA: Barre Publishers, 1972.

Wiseman, Carter. *I.M. Pei: A Profile in American Architecture*. New York: Abrams, 1990.

Index

Note: (ill.) indicates photos and illustrations.

B

X–Z